Joanna Baillie

A Literary Life

Portrait of Joanna Baillie by John James Masquerier (1812)
Special Collections, University of Glasgow

Joanna Baillie

A Literary Life

Judith Bailey Slagle

Madison · Teaneck
Fairleigh Dickinson University Press
London: Associated University Presses

© 2002 by Rosemont Publishing & Printing Corp.

All rights reserved. Authorization to photocopy items for internal or personal use, or the internal or personal use of specific clients, is granted by the copyright owner, provided that a base fee of $10.00, plus eight cents per page, per copy is paid directly to the Copyright Clearance Center, 222 Rosewood Drive, Danvers, Massachusetts 01923. [0–8386–3949–6/02 $10.00 + 8¢ pp, pc.]

Associated University Presses
440 Forsgate Drive
Cranbury, NJ 08512

Associated University Presses
16 Barter Street
London WC1A 2AH, England

Associated University Presses
P.O. Box 338, Port Credit
Mississauga, Ontario
Canada L5G 4L8

The paper used in this publication meets the requirements of the American National Standard for Permanence of Paper for Printed Library Materials Z39.48–1984.

Library of Congress Cataloging-in-Publication Data

Slagle, Judith Bailey
    Joanna Baillie, a literary life / Judith Bailey Slagle.
       p. cm.
    Includes bibliographical references and index.
    ISBN 0-8386-3949-6 (alk. paper)
    1. Baillie, Joanna, 1762-1851. 2. Dramatists, Scottish—19th century—Biography. 3. Women and literature—Scotland—History—19th century. 4. Scotland—Intellectual life—19th century. I. Title.

PR4056.S58 2002
822'.7—dc21
[B]
                                                  2001054478

PRINTED IN THE UNITED STATES OF AMERICA

for Don, Paula, and the NEH Fellows

Contents

Preface		9
Acknowledgments		13
List of Abbreviations		17
Introduction		19
Chronology		25
1.	"My fanciful untaught mind": Ghosts and the Growing Imagination (1762–1790)	34
2.	"Like a burnt child": Theatre Theory and the Price of Fame (1791–1805)	70
3.	"Beyond mere words": Baillie and Scott (1806–1832)	125
4.	"Not a semblance of display": A Circle of Friends (1808–1830s)	176
5.	"The stamp of her strong mind": Critical Reading and Religious Philosophy (1831–1850)	231
6.	"The majesty of a genius": Epilogue for a Poet (1851)	288
Bibliography		300
Index		315

Preface

In March 1994, having applied for a National Endowment for the Humanities summer seminar for college teachers, I received a gracious telephone call from seminar director Professor Paula Backscheider, advising that my proposal for the London-based seminars on writing biography had been accepted. The proposal, admittedly something prepared rather hastily from a small project on Joanna Baillie I had completed for Professor Nancy Goslee's graduate course at The University of Tennessee, was to complete research for and write *The Life of Joanna Baillie*. My ignorance at the time is now obvious, and Dr. Backscheider has since reminded me of my asking, "Do you think there's any Baillie information in London?" It was probably all she could do to retain composure, because she had inadvertently uncovered some of the Baillie manuscripts that would eventually change, or at least delay for some years, my plan for a biography.

Beginning at the National Registry of Archives just off Chancery Lane and working my way through dozens of repositories (whose many Baillie holdings were not registered at the time), my research in England and Scotland began to uncover hundreds of unpublished letters from Baillie to family members, literary figures, scientists, religious leaders, artists, and friends in England, Scotland, and the United States. These letters documented problems with publishers, solicited other writers for poems for collections, described encounters with William Wordsworth and diverse literary figures, outlined a long relationship with Sir Walter Scott, Mary Berry, Lady Byron, and others, and placed an active literary woman in the historical and social setting of early to mid-nineteenth-century Britain. My former plan to write a biography became, instead, a project to collect the letters and to annotate and explain what was necessary to make them useful to eighteenth- and nineteenth-century scholars of British, Scottish, and American studies and of women's studies. I returned to England in summer 1995 through an American Philosophical Society grant to collect the letters archived in English repositories and followed with trips to the Houghton Library, the Harry Ransom Humanities Research Center, and the Huntington Library for letters there. Finally, I collected the Scotland letters in 1996 through a summer research grant from Middle Tennessee State University and an honorary research fellowship at The University of Edinburgh Institute for Advanced Studies in the Humanities. Having published *The Collected Letters of Joanna Baillie* in 1999 and having worked for several years on the collected material at home, I returned to Scotland and England in summer 2000 to complete biographical research through a major research grant from East Tennessee State University's Research Development Committee.

Unfortunately, early biographical accounts of Joanna Baillie have often been inexact and largely undocumented by evidence. The only work representing a full biography emerged in 1923 as a part of the *Yale Studies in English* series, but author Margaret Carhart did not have access to the majority of Baillie's correspondence; and, as a result, her work contains conjectures and inaccuracies about Baillie's personal life and motivations. Because of their own speculative nature, I have avoided using many of the secondary sources cited by Carhart as well. For example, almost all early biographical sources report that the Baillie women moved to Hampstead in 1791 after Dr. Matthew Baillie married Sophia Denman and then moved to Bolton House in 1806 where they remained the rest of their lives; an impressive plaque on the front of Bolton House even attests to the fact. Unfortunately, when editing the letters, I took those sources, many of them historical sources on Hampstead in particular, to be accurate and repeated some of their data. However, in checking *Rate Books* (tax records), census reports, and other documents in summer 2000, I found both statements regarding their moves to be incorrect. Since publication of the *Letters*, I have found other types of errors in some accepted secondary sources.

Despite some inaccuracies and oversights, however, Margaret Carhart's contribution is significant. She did not have access to most of the types of sources that we have today, and she is sometimes ambivalent about her praise of Baillie's genius. Furthermore, almost all early biographical sources approach Baillie as an "uninteresting" woman at best, minimizing her work as a poet and playwright and forgetting that she lived to be almost ninety, a fact that accounts for her being somewhat less active in the last two decades of her life than in her earlier years![1] Short works such as Donald Carswell's *Sir Walter: A Four-Part Study in Biography (Scott,*

---

1. Margaret Carhart writes, for example, that "The years between 1800 and 1804 offer little of biographical interest" (*The Life and Work of Joanna Baillie, Yale Studies in English* [New Haven: Yale University Press, 1923], 18). Instead, this was probably one of Baillie's most prolific periods.

Hogg, Lockhart, Joanna Baillie) from Murray in 1930 often take a condescending view of Baillie as an "old-maidish" writer mostly distinguished by her friendship with Scott and of her poetry as "artless and virginal."[2] In the past decade, however, some very fine critical analyses of Baillie's theories, drama, and poetry have emerged, and I have acknowledged these in the "Introduction"; however, short biographical accounts have remained an extension of early works. This *Literary Life* presents evidence that will change the misconceptions about Baillie as a "sheltered," unexciting individual and invite readers to see her as a strong, creative, and ambitious woman whose productivity was terminated only by her death in 1851.

The two volumes entitled *The Collected Letters of Joanna Baillie* (Fairleigh Dickinson University Press, 1999) certainly represent the vast majority of Baillie's correspondence (more than 800 letters) and, along with other archival research and critical readings of her works, form the basis for this *Literary Life*. I have quoted a great deal from these letters and also from biographical accounts of her correspondents included in the volumes. No method is perfect, however, and letters often give, as Backscheider argues in *Reflections on Biography*, a somewhat "fleeting mood." But the fact that they show, according to biographer John Garraty, a person "in one form of interaction" with contemporaries and, according to Backscheider, offer "insights into personality," though "not an unfiltered, clear window to it," makes them essential for this *Life*.[3]

I begin this biography with the Chronology listing family births, marriages, and deaths and add Baillie's publication dates and the performance dates for her plays. After the Introduction's statement of purpose and theoretical stance, I provide in chapter 1 an account of Baillie's childhood and education based on archival research and on her own autobiographical papers, and the ensuing chapters move toward her death in 1851. While I have attempted to manage the biographical material and critical comments in a simple chronological manner, I have found the years of Baillie's relationship with Scott too unwieldy to be included in her interaction with other writers and friends. Therefore, I have devoted chapter 3 almost solely to Baillie and Scott, following that chapter with accounts of her

---

2. Donald Carswell, *Sir Walter: A Four-Part Study in Biography (Scott, Hogg, Lockhart, Joanna Baillie)* (London: Murray, 1930), 271.

3. Paula R. Backscheider, *Reflections on Biography* (Oxford and New York: Oxford University Press, 1999), 74–5.

other relationships that paralleled most of those same years. As a result, I hope that chapter 4 does not read simply like a "Who's Who" of nineteenth-century *literati* and hope that readers will not find this method disruptive to the continuum of her life; one chapter covering these years and including the Scott relationship with other friendships would have been unmanageable. People, literary works, historical events, etc., are identified on their first occurrence in this text, but the footnote is not repeated if they appear again later in the text.

Acknowledgments

I am grateful to many people for their support of this long research project which began with collecting the letters of Joanna Baillie, especially to my family and friends. I thank Dr. Nancy Goslee, The University of Tennessee, for initially sparking my interest in Joanna Baillie. I thank the National Endowment for the Humanities (1994 summer seminar award), the American Philosophical Society (1995 summer research grant), and Middle Tennessee State University (1996 summer research grant) for funding, and the University of Edinburgh Institute for Advanced Studies in the Humanities for providing an honorary research fellowship (1996 summer). I especially thank East Tennessee State University for research and travel grants in 2000, which made completion of the biography possible; and I thank ETSU graduate research assistant Staci Lewis for painstaking proofreading and instructor Kim Crowder-Vaughn for creative advice. I am especially grateful to Auburn University doctoral candidate Patsy Fowler for suggestions and for copyediting and to Catherine Burroughs for her support in every way. Finally, I thank Dr. Paula Backscheider, Stevens Eminent Scholar at Auburn University, for reading, for direction, and for sharing her knowledge of British repositories from the onset; without her neither the letters nor this biography would have evolved.

I owe a great debt to all of the archivists and librarians who allowed me to work in their repositories or to publish holdings with permission as follows. Without their assistance and archived material, this biography could not have been written.

    Bodleian Library, University of Oxford
    Boston Public Library
    British Library
    British Museum
    Brotherton Collection, Leeds University Library
    Cambridge University Library
    Camden Local Studies and Archives Centre
    Courtney Library, Royal Institution of Cornwall
    Dartmouth College, Baker Library
    Edinburgh University Library
    Fitzwilliam Museum, University of Cambridge
    Folger Shakespeare Library
    Hamilton Central Library

Harrowby Mss Trust
Hornby Library, Liverpool City Libraries
Houghton Library, Harvard University
Hunter House Museum
Huntington Library
Keele University Library
Lilly Library, Indiana University
London Public Record Office
Mitchell Library, Glasgow City Libraries
National Library of Scotland
New York Public Library, Berg and Pforzheimer Collections
Pierpont Morgan Library
National Archives of Scotland, General Register House
Harry Ransom Humanities Research Center, University of Texas
Robinson Library, University of Newcastle upon Tyne
Royal Academy of Art
Royal College of Surgeons of Edinburgh
Royal College of Surgeons of England
Royal College of Physicians and Surgeons of Glasgow
Royal Society of London
John Rylands Research Institute, University of Manchester
Trinity College Cambridge, Master and Fellows
University of Birmingham
University College London
University of Glasgow
University of Nottingham, Hallward Library
University of Reading
Victoria and Albert Museum
Wellcome Institute for the History of Medicine
Dr. Williams's Library
Wisbech & Fenland Museum
Wordsworth Trust, Dove Cottage

In addition, I thank the Royal Commission on Historical Manuscripts, the Corporation of London Records Office, Guildhall Library, the Greater London Record Office and History Library, the National Maritime Museum, and the University of London Library for allowing me access to their records and services. And, especially, I am most grateful to The University of Tennessee Hodges Library and to the English department faculty, the latter for both moral and monetary support.

Finally, I am indebted to scholars who have researched the Baillies and/or the Hunters in the last few decades, most of whose published works or works in progress I have consulted for this biography: Susan Bennett, Jennifer Breen, William Brewer, Ken Bugajski, Catherine Burroughs, Julie Carlson, Jeffrey Cox, Franco Crainz, Thomas Crochunis, Ellen Donkin, Maureen Dowd, Peter Duthie, Beth Friedman-Romell, Michael Gamer, Deirdre Gilbert, Amanda Gilroy, Andrea Henderson, Laurie Hughes, Greg Kucich, Chester Lambertson, Mary McKerrow, Dorothy McMillan, Anne Mellor, Victoria Meyers, Aloma Noble, Janice Patton, Marjean Purinton, Donald Reiman, Marlon Ross, Barbara Schnorrenberg, Adrienne Scullion, Richard Sher, Janet Todd, Daniel Watkins, Guy Wallace White, Jonathan Wordsworth, Mary Yudin, and P. M. Zall.[1]

---

1. See complete bibliographical information in "Bibliography." There is such a profusion of Baillie scholarship appearing at this time that I may have missed some of the most recent, for which I apologize.

Abbreviations

Literary Sources

BMGC	*British Museum General Catalogue of Printed Books to 1955*
DAB	*Dictionary of American Biography*
DLB	*Dictionary of Literary Biography*
DNB	*Dictionary of National Biography*
DPW	*The Dramatic and Poetical Works of Joanna Baillie* (1851)
NUC	*National Union Catalogue Pre-1956 Imprints*
OCEL	*Oxford Companion to English Literature*
OED	*Oxford English Dictionary*
SND	*Scottish National Dictionary*

Archives

BL	British Library
CLS	Camden Local Studies and Archives Centre
EU	Edinburgh University
HL	Huntington Library
HRH	Harry Ransom Humanities Research Center
HU	Harvard University, Houghton Library
ML	Mitchell Library
NLS	National Library of Scotland
NYPL	New York Public Library
OU	Oxford University, Bodleian Library
RA	Royal Academy of Art
RCPSG	Royal College of Physicians and Surgeons of Glasgow
RCS	Royal College of Surgeons of England
RS	Royal Society
UCL	University College London
UG	University of Glasgow
UN	University of Nottingham
WI	Wellcome Institute for the History of Medicine

Introduction

"The most important playwright in nineteenth-century Scotland," argues Adrienne Scullion in *A History of Scottish Women's Writing*, "is Joanna Baillie."[1] Scottish playwright and theatre theorist Joanna Baillie (1762–1851) was a vibrant woman born into a patriarchal world; her life spanned the second half of the eighteenth century and the first half of the nineteenth. In addition to her twenty-seven plays, eight metrical legends, and more than a hundred songs and poems, her legacy lies in hundreds of eloquent letters from which historians and literary scholars can formulate a sense of the intellectual society emerging with early Romanticism. Hers was a time of social, political, and intellectual change, prompted not only by two major revolutions, but also by major shifts in literary style and focus of the imagination on the sublime.[2] Joanna Baillie somehow resolved her nationalism and her conservatism with her feminism; she was a participant in her era, commenting on the salient issues of her time. To conclude, as some writers have, that her life was uneventful and her later years pitiable is both uninformed and critically naive, for even Baillie's late letters reveal a tenacious and ambitious woman, one receiving visits from friends and family, publishing *Ahalya Baee* in 1849, and editing her complete works nearly to the time of her death in 1851 at the age of eighty-eight.[3] What is pitiable, however, is Baillie's lack of genuine acceptance in a male-dominated literary society which, while it may have accepted her as an accomplished "gentlewoman," marginalized her critical intelligence and afforded her visibility mostly through her relationships with famous men, from her uncles and brother to Sir Walter Scott and others. I present Joanna Baillie as the intelligent, creative, critical artist that she was in her own right.

---

1. Adrienne Scullion, "Some Women of the Nineteenth-century Scottish Theatre: Joanna Baillie, Frances Wright and Helen MacGregor," *A History of Scottish Women's Writing*, ed. Douglas Gifford and Dorothy McMillan (Edinburgh: Edinburgh University Press, 1997), 160.

2. Jeffrey N. Cox believes Baillie is central to the Gothic tradition "because her plays offer a self-conscious examination of some of the fundamental conventions of the Gothic and of their implications for the construction of the feminine." See *Seven Gothic Dramas, 1789–1825* (Athens: Ohio University Press, 1992), 51.

3. For whatever reason, Margaret Carhart states that Baillie's closing years were "pathetic" (66).

Virginia Woolf says that writing a biography should be a craft, fiction an art. Certainly, one of the most important things discussed in Paula Backscheider's 1994 NEH seminar on "Biography and the Use of Biographical Evidence" was that fiction has no place in a scholarly biography. Yet a biography must still entertain and engage its reader; and in the case of Joanna Baillie, whose long life presents "dry periods" for which there is little or no biographical evidence, the biographer must sometimes try to read what is *not* written, especially with Baillie's correspondence. Before her paradoxical overnight, though anonymous, success with the appearance of volume one of *A Series of Plays: in which it is attempted to delineate the stronger passions of the mind—each passion being the subject of a tragedy and a comedy* (published by Cadell and Davies in 1798), few kept up with the goings-on of Joanna Baillie, who had only published anonymous *Poems* in 1790. Soon after 1798, however, friends, family, and authors began to retain Baillie's letters. As a result, there is more material in Baillie's correspondence than I could possibly condense into a biography, especially with the addition of any critical examination of her works. I have included, however, whether in summaries or in quoted material, what I know about Baillie, for she is one of the most fascinating women of the late eighteenth and early nineteenth centuries.

In *All Sides of the Subject*, Dale Spender suggests that "we need biographies to learn about the collective/individual past of women," but about *which* women is the question.[4] Whether we examine the biographical evidence about famous women, neglected women, or "lost" women, we should certainly question the accepted accounts that may have been published earlier. But "it is partly the absence of recorded history that sends women now to women past for the detailed documentation of their daily lives."[5] What Baillie's massive correspondence does is document clearly her daily life and work; what many earlier biographical accounts have done is *speculate* about how she worked and thought. It is amazing that Baillie's own brief autobiographical accounts contained herein have remained unpublished until the *Collected Letters*; but, as Donna Stanton argues in *The Female Autograph*, it should "surely come as no surprise that beyond their tacit agreement to exclude women's texts, critics disagreed about the specific nature and substance of

---

4. Qtd. in *All Sides of the Subject*, ed. Teresa Iles (New York: Teachers College Press, 1992), viii.

5. Spender, ix.

autobiography."⁶ Is Baillie's autobiography a creative interpretation bordering on fiction or simply a retrospective "narrative in prose"? I hope to demonstrate that her letters and autobiographical papers are more directly the latter. For that reason, I have chosen to let Baillie often speak for herself, and I provide many quotes from her letters in doing so. This method may be irksome to some seasoned readers of biography, but I have far too much respect for Baillie to ignore what *she* says to us.

In her recent *Reflections on Biography*, Paula Backscheider, acknowledging great biographers like Richard Ellmann, Virginia Woolf, and many others, contends that biography "is read so avidly and seriously because readers recognize that ways of understanding and relating to the world and human experience in the world are the subject." In addition,

> The best biographers know that they are inventing through their selection and arrangement of materials; they are establishing cause-effect and other relationships, and they are determining what was most formative and important for someone else, someone they do not know.⁷

Having been a part of Dr. Backscheider's NEH seminar, I hope that I learned first hand the art of finding a voice, of arranging materials, of establishing cause-effect relationships, and of treating my biographical subject fairly and objectively. But while this work is based on biographical evidence, "objective evidence" on how Baillie worked and on the choices she made, I must not fail to note my own subjectivity. Further, it follows from the fact that this work is decidedly feminist in its approach that my interpretation of missing years and of some of Baillie's works must be somewhat subjective. But, as Elizabeth Young-Bruehl explains in *Subject to Biography*, a certain amount of empathy between the biographer and her subject is a necessity:

> It is a kind of homing instinct for the territory of the biographical subject's emotional and intellectual formation and, in general, of her formative experiences. It is a mimetic movement, unpremeditated, but based upon the biographer's

---

6. *The Female Autograph*, ed. Donna C. Stanton (Chicago: University of Chicago Press, 1987), 7.
7. Backscheider, 17–18.

reflective habits of a lifetime, which tracks into the subject's ways of thinking and talking about herself.[8]

Criticism of any sort is an active, assertive reading that in itself creates meaning. As a female biographer researching a female writer, I cannot approach my subject in the same way a male critic might, because, to paraphrase from Simone de Beauvoir's *The Second Sex* (1953), possible sex-linked models are based on the self-other dichotomy. To the female critic applying this theory, female is "self" and male "other." My reading of the "truth" about Baillie's life and work, therefore, must necessarily be influenced by my own interpretation of her actions in a masculine world, but I also believe that she saw herself as the "other" in such a world. My approach acknowledges that women's lives *were* different from men's lives and that even Baillie realized that in a patriarchal and hierarchical world women were viewed as subordinate to men, not only in the home, but also, and maybe especially, in the professional world. Because Baillie was not a wife or mother, this biography deals little with domesticity and focuses instead on creative work and on relationships with people who were important in her life.

Joanna Baillie was an imaginative, strong, determined female from her early years on. She played outdoors with rural parish children, listened to ghost stories, and read whatever interested her. Probably, except for formal education, her parents did not raise their two daughters much differently from their son Matthew, who later became a famous physician. Like her mother, Dorothea Hunter, Joanna Baillie grew up with intelligent, powerful men. Most likely, she, encouraged especially by her brother, saw herself as their equal and feared very little in life. Only after her move to London, and after the revelation that she was the author of *A Series of Plays*, did Baillie come to recognize that she would, in fact, be treated differently because of her sex. It undoubtedly made her somewhat bitter and may have resulted in fewer creations from her pen later in her life, but it is doubtful that she ever believed she *was* inferior because of her sex.

In *Closet Stages: Joanna Baillie and the Theater Theory of British Romantic Women Writers*, Catherine B. Burroughs analyzes the

---

8. Elizabeth Young-Bruehl, *Subject to Biography: Psychoanalysis, Feminism, and Writing Women's Lives* (Cambridge: Harvard University Press, 1998), 17.

cause of Baillie's being considered only a minor playwright after her death and of her subsequent omission from the canon:

> four years after Baillie's death, one can see emerging an interpretation of her life and work that: (1) emphasizes her failure as a dramatist; (2) portrays her theory and playwrighting as tedious; and (3) tropes her as masculine for seeking fame in theater. Sarah Josepha Hale's 1855 sketch of Baillic offers a good example of how this process began. First, Hale describes her not as a literary artist in her own right but as the "sister of the celebrated Dr. Baillie", her famous anatomist brother. Even more detrimentally, she diminishes Baillie's achievement by wondering "whether in selecting the drama as her path of literature, [Baillie] judged wisely."[9]

Further, Burroughs explains, Hale had suggested shortly after Baillie's death that the playwright might have more appropriately chosen to be an essayist or novelist rather than plunge into such a "masculine" genre. Even Elizabeth Inchbald cited Baillie's *De Monfort* in particular as unconvincing, the product of a reader and not a spectator. Thus was the stage set for the Victorians to consider Baillie "unfeminine" and implausible and to destroy her estimation in their era. Notwithstanding, later in the period, writes Burroughs, Catherine Hamilton "asserted that 'while some women authors were graceful and amusing and fanciful, Joanna Baillie had a condensed strength and a grasp of her subject such as few men have'." In addition, in 1922 "Alice Meynell resurrected the playwright only to damn her work as dull and erudite."[10] And Margaret Carhart, Baillie's early biographer, was only tentative about her praise of Baillie. One of the most insulting accounts, however, comes from C. Robert Rudolf's Hunterian Society address on 3 May 1965 entitled "Newly-Found Additions to the Hunter-Baillie MSS," to which I can only do justice by quoting:

> It must not be thought that Joanna Baillie's preoccupation with the drama was her sole interest in life. She was very far from being a blue-stocking or the native equivalent of the

---

9. Catherine B. Burroughs, *Closet Stages: Joanna Baillie and the Theater Theory of British Romantic Women Writers* (Philadelphia: University of Pennsylvania Press, 1997), 99.

10. Ibid., 100.

salonists across the channel. Both the sisters were highly domesticated and the recipe of Mrs. Joanna Baillie's pudding, taken from a popular cookery book belonging to Mrs. E. Stewart which we thought was not inappropriate for our sweet this evening, reflects her reputation in the culinary art. [Recipe is also printed therein.][11]

In addition to serving Baillie's pudding, the Society also displayed examples of her "skilled needlework" for the attendees, *not* her drama or poetry.

Fortunately, recent scholarship is re-shaping these supercilious images of Joanna Baillie; unfortunately, however, Laetitia Barbauld predicted the playwright's immediate future when she speculated that Baillie "was an excellent woman who was raised to an unchallenged eminence in the lettered circles of her day" but was "in danger of being undervalued in other generations."[12]

---

11. C. Robert Rudolf, Hunterian Society, 139th Session 1964–65, "Annual General Meeting Address" (London: Metropolis Press, 1965), 21.

12. Grace A. Ellis, *A Memoir of Mrs. Anna Laetitia Barbauld, with Many of Her Letters* (Boston: James R. Osgood, 1874), 231.

Chronology

The following chronological table extends from the birth of Joanna Baillie's parents (1721-22) to the death of her nephew William Hunter Baillie (1894) and includes birth, death, and marriage dates along with Baillie's publication dates (in bold), drama performances, and recorded first meetings with significant writers and friends.[1] The many songs that Baillie wrote for George Thomson are not cited individually below (see letters to Thomson in *The Collected Letters of Joanna Baillie* for these).

(Key: JB = Joanna Baillie; b = birth; d = death; m = marriage; p = publication)

1721	26 January	Dorothea Hunter, JB's mother, b
1722	5 August	James Baillie, JB's father, b
1757	7 December	James Baillie m Dorothea Hunter
1759		William [James] Baillie, JB's brother, b
1760		William [James] Baillie, d
	24 September	Agnes Baillie, JB's sister, b
1761	2 September	Rev. James Baillie becomes Minister at Bothwell, Scotland
	27 October	Matthew Baillie, JB's brother, b
1762	11 September	Joanna Baillie b; twin sister dies
1766	23 October	Rev. James Baillie becomes Minister at Hamilton, Scotland
1771	9 July	Margaret and Sophia Denman b
1772		JB and Agnes sent to boarding school in Glasgow
1775	19 December	Rev. James Baillie becomes Prof. of Divinity, Glasgow University
1778	28 April	Rev. Prof. James Baillie d

---

1. In addition to public birth and death records, I have used Franco Crainz's *The Life and Works of Matthew Baillie, MD, FRS, L&E, FRCP, etc (1761-1823)* (Santa Palomba, Italy: PelitiAssociati, 1995) as a consistent source, though Crainz provides much more detail for events in the life of Matthew (publications, great grand children, etc.), which I exclude here. I have recorded first meetings with significant writers when Baillie records them, but most often I do not have specific dates with which to identify these. Also see Ken A. Bugajski's "Joanna Baillie: An Annotated Bibliography," *Romanticism on the Net* 12 (Nov. 1998).

1779	9	April	Matthew Baillie matriculates Balliol College, Oxford
1783	15	March	William Hunter, JB's uncle, d
1784			JB, Agnes, and their mother move to London to live with Matthew Baillie
1787			Robert Milligan, Matthew Baillie's son-in-law, b
1789	3	November	Margaret Denman m Richard Croft
1790			Anonymous *Poems: Wherein It is Attempted to Describe Certain Views of Nature and of Rustic Manners, etc.*, p in London by Johnson
1790–91			JB spends a year in Scotland
1791	5	May	Sophia Denman m Matthew Baillie
1791–?			JB, Agnes, and their mother move to several locations in the country, finally settling in Colchester
1792	26	September	James Baillie, Matthew Baillie's first child, b
1793	11	January	James Baillie d
			1st ed. of Matthew Baillie's *The Morbid Anatomy* p
	16	October	John Hunter, JB's uncle, d
1794	12	February	Elizabeth Margaret Baillie, Matthew Baillie's daughter and JB's niece, b
1797	14	September	William Hunter Baillie, Matthew Baillie's son and JB's nephew, b
1798			Vol. 1 of *A Series of Plays: in which it is attempted to delineate the stronger passions of the mind—each passion being the subject of a tragedy and a comedy* p anonymously in London by Cadell and Davies (incl. *Count Basil, The Tryal, De Monfort*)
1799			2d ed. of Vol. 1 of *A Series of Plays, etc.*, p in London by Cadell and Davies
			First record in St. John parish *Rate Books* of JB, Agnes, and Dorothea living in Hampstead at Nag's Head Side

Chronology 27

1798–1800	JB meets Mrs. Siddons and John Kemble
1800	3d ed. of Vol. 1 of *A Series of Plays, etc.*, p in London by Cadell and Davies
April–May	*De Monfort* performed at Drury Lane Theatre, London (8 performances)[2]
13 April	*De Monfort* performed at the Park Theatre, New York
November	"Epilogue to the Theatrical Representation at Strawberry Hill" p (no imprint) 1801
1802	Vol. 2 of *A Series of Plays: in which it is attempted to delineate the stronger passions, etc.*, p by Cadell and Davies (incl. *The Election, Ethwald,* pts. 1 and 2, *The Second Marriage*) (2 editions)
	4th ed. of Vol. 1 of *A Series of Plays, etc.*, p in London by Cadell and Davies
1804	*Miscellaneous Plays* p by Longman, Hurst, Rees, and Orme (incl. *Rayner, The Country Inn, Constantine Paleologus*)
	JB begins to write lyrics for Thomson's Welsh airs
1805	2d ed. of *Miscellaneous Plays* p in London by Longman, Hurst, Rees, and Orme (adding *The Family Legend*)
1806	*Die Leidenschaften* (*A Series of Plays*) p in Amsterdam and Leipzig (again in 1807)
	JB introduced to Walter Scott by Sotheby

---

2. The performances of Baillie's plays listed here come from notes in the Hamilton Central Library in Scotland and from the appendix to Aloma E. Noble's "Joanna Baillie as a Dramatic Artist" (Ph.D. diss., University of Iowa, 1983), 188–93.

		5th ed. of Vol. 1 of *A Series of Plays*, etc., p in London by Longman, Hurst, Rees, and Orme
		3d ed. of Vol. 2 of *A Series of Plays*, etc., p in London by Longman, Hurst, Rees, and Orme
1807	30 September	Dorothea Baillie, JB's mother, d
1808		*Ethwald, ein Trauerspiel in fünf Acten* p in Amsterdam
		Henrietta Duff, Matthew Baillie's daughter-in-law, b
		JB meets Wordsworth
		De Monfort p in London by Longman Hurst, Rees, Orme, and Brown
	7 November	*Constantine Paleologus* performed at the Theatre Royal, Liverpool
		Constantine Paleologus performed as *Constantine and Valeria* at the Surrey Theatre, London
1809	November	*De Monfort* performed at the Park Theatre, New York (3 performances)
		De Monfort p in New York by Longworth
1810		*Plays* p in New York by Longworth
		The Family Legend p in Edinburgh (2 editions) by Ballantyne; in London by Longman, Hurst, Rees, Orme, and Brown; and in New York by Longworth
	January	*The Family Legend* performed at the Theatre Royal, Edinburgh (14 performances)
	20 February	*De Monfort* performed at the Theatre Royal, Edinburgh
	March	*De Monfort* performed the Theatre Royal, Edinburgh
	27 October	Matthew Baillie appointed Physician Extraordinary to George III
	12 November	*De Monfort* performed at the Baltimore Theatre, Baltimore
1810–13		JB meets Margaret Holford
1811		*Basil* p in Philadelphia by Carey and Lea (again in 1823)

	The Election p in Philadelphia by Carey and Lea
	The Tryal p in Philadelphia by Carey and Lea
8 February	*De Monfort* performed at the Chestnut St. Theatre, Philadelphia
March	*The Family Legend* performed at the Theatre Royal, Newcastle, and at Bath
	The Family Legend performed at the Theatre Royal, Edinburgh
1812	Vol. 3 of *A Series of Plays: in which it is attempted to delineate the stronger passions*, etc., p in London by Longman, Hurst, Rees, and Orme (incl. *Orra, The Dream, The Siege, The Beacon*)
	The Beacon p in New York by Longworth
	The Dream p in New York by Longworth
	Orra p in New York by Longworth
	The Siege p in New York by Longworth
	JB meets Anne Isabella Milbanke (later Lady Byron)
	JB sits for Masquerier (portrait hangs in University of Glasgow Special Collections)
1813	JB meets Maria Edgeworth
	The Family Legend performed at the Theatre Royal, Newcastle
1813–15	JB meets Lord Byron
1815 29 May	*The Family Legend* performed at Drury Lane
	The Beacon p in London by Strahan and Preston
1816 22 and 27 March	*The Family Legend* performed at the Chestnut St. Theatre, Philadelphia
7 June	*The Family Legend* performed at the Baltimore Theatre
11 July	Elizabeth Margaret Baillie m Robert Milligan

22 July	Matthew Baillie appointed Physician in Ordinary to Princess Charlotte Augusta (d. November 1817)
1817 June–July	*The Election* performed as a musical drama at the English Opera House (Lyceum), London (11 performances)
4 July	Sophia Milligan b to Elizabeth and Robert Milligan
1818–20	JB meets John Gibson Lockhart
1820	*Constantine Paleologus* performed at the Theatre Royal, Edinburgh
	De Monfort performed at the Theatre Royal, Edinburgh
	De Monfort performed at the Park St. Theatre, New York
	JB and Agnes move to Holly Bush Hill (indicated in parish *Rate Books* as Windmill Hill)
1821	*Metrical Legends of Exalted Characters* p in London by Longman, Hurst, Rees, Orme, and Brown (2 editions in 1821)
	New edition of *A Series of Plays* (3 vols.) p in London by Longman, Hurst, Rees, Orme, and Brown
November–December	*De Monfort* performed at Drury Lane (4 performances)
1822 14 January	*De Monfort* performed at the Walnut St. Theatre, Philadelphia
19 June	*De Monfort* performed at Bath
July	*De Monfort* performed at the Theatre Royal, Birmingham (4 performances)
1823	*A Collection of Poems, Chiefly Manuscript, and from Living Authors* p by Longman
1823 23 September	Matthew Baillie, JB's only brother, d
1825 30 June	*Constantine Paleologus* performed at the Theatre Royal, Dublin (several performances)
1826	"A Lesson Intended for the Use of the Hampstead School" p in Camden

		Town by Miller

                         The Martyr p in London by Longman, Hurst, Rees, Orme, Brown, and Green

        4 December   *De Monfort* performed at the Park St. Theatre, New York

1828   *The Bride* p in London by Colburn and in Philadelphia by Neal and by Diggens

1830   *Un Mariage du grand monde. Tradiut de l'anglais de Miss Baillie* [or rather the Hon. Caroline Lucy, Lady Scholl], *par Madame***traducteur d'Elisa Rivers*, etc., p in Paris

1831   *A View of the General Tenour of the New Testament Regarding the Nature and Dignity of Jesus Christ* p in London by Longman, Rees, Orme, Brown, and Green

1832   *The Complete Poetical Works of Joanna Baillie* p in Philadelphia by Carey and Lea–1st American ed.

                          2d ed. of *A Collection of Poems, Chiefly Manuscript, and from Living Authors* p in London

                          "Lines on the Death of Sir Walter Scott" p

1835 23 June   William Hunter Baillie m Henrietta Duff

1836   *Dramas* p (3 vols.) in London by Longman, Hurst, Rees, Orme, and Brown

                          "Epistles to Literati," No. 9, p in *Fraser's Magazine*

        25 February   *The Separation* performed at Covent Garden

        19 March   *Henriquez* performed at Drury Lane

        18 April   Sophia Joanna Baillie b to William and Henrietta Baillie

1837 7 July   Matthew John Baillie b to William and Henrietta Baillie

1838 12 November   William Hunter Baillie, Jr., b to William

		and Henrietta Baillie
		2d ed. of *A View of the General Tenour of the New Testament Regarding the Nature and Dignity of Jesus Christ* p in London by Taylor
1840		*Fugitive Verses* p in London by Moxon
		JB elected honorary member of the Historical Society of Michigan
1841	21 February	John Baron Baillie b to William and Henrietta Baillie
1842		2d ed. of *Fugitive Verses* p in London by Moxon
1843	26 May	Helen Mary Henrietta Baillie b to William and Henrietta Baillie
1845	5 August	Sophia Denman Baillie, JB's sister-in-law, d
1846	23 April	Agnes Elizabeth Baillie b to William and Henrietta Baillie
1847	24 September	Margaret Denman Croft, Sophia Baillie's twin sister, d
1849		*Ahalya Baee: A Poem* p in London by Spottiswoods and Shaw
1850	27 February	Robert Denman Baillie b to William and Henrietta Baillie
1851		1st and 2d ed. of *The Dramatic and Poetical Works of Joanna Baillie* p in London by Longman, Brown, Green, and Longmans–last publication JB oversees
1851	23 February	Joanna Baillie d
1853	25 August	Henrietta Clara Marion Baillie b to William and Heniretta Baillie
		3d ed. of *The Dramatic and Poetical Works of Joanna Baillie* p in London by Longman, Brown, Green, and Longmans
1857	3 February	Henrietta Duff Baillie, William Baillie's wife, d
1861	27 April	Agnes Baillie, JB's only sister, d
1864		3d ed. of *Fugitive Verses* p in London by Moxon
1875	21 December	Robert Milligan, Matthew Baillie's son-

Chronology

		in-law, d
1876	25 June	Elizabeth Margaret Baillie Milligan, Matthew's daughter and JB's niece, d
1882		Sophia Milligan, Baillie's niece, d
1894	24 December	William Hunter Baillie, JB's nephew, d

1

🐑 "My fanciful untaught mind": Ghosts and the Growing Imagination (1762–1790)

"Scotland, or North Britain, struggles with many natural disadvantages," wrote Sir John Sinclair in 1784; "the climate is cold, the sky seldom serene, the weather variable, the soil unfruitful, the mountains bleak, barren, rocky, often covered with snows, and the appearance of the country in many places very forbidding to strangers."[1] Into this physical landscape was born Scottish writer Joanna Baillie. Fortunately, the mental landscape, while still variable, was not so barren; and only a few years after the last Jacobite uprising of 1745, intellectuals in Scotland found themselves among enlightened literati such as David Hume, John Millar, Adam Ferguson, Hugh Blair, William Robertson, William Cullen, Robert Burns, James Macpherson, and Adam Smith and among meritorious Calvinist clergy such as John Erskine of the Popular party in the kirk. Many of these intellectuals were located in Glasgow, Lanark, Stirling, and Renfrew. Young evangelicals were also emerging on the clerical scene.[2] Certainly, the majority of those who formed the Scottish Enlightenment were university professors, ministers of the kirk, and lawyers. Meanwhile, creative writers were becoming sensitive to the influence of European Romanticism, and the most important legislation of the century concerning publishing was about to emerge in the Copyright Act of 1774.

It was this disparate society into which poet and playwright Joanna Baillie was born in 1762, the circumstances setting the stage for her own somewhat conflicting passion for secular literature and religious doctrine. Her life contains other similar conflicts: supporting women writers through her association with famous literary men, admiring Lord Byron's poetry and ultimately despising the man, remaining a close friend to many famous men but rejecting them as intimate partners, and seeking detachment from but

---

1. Qtd. in Alexander Broadie, ed., *The Scottish Enlightenment: An Anthology* (Edinburgh: Canongate, 1997), 373.
2. See Ned C. Landsman, "Presbyterians and Provincial Society: The Evangelical Enlightenment in the West of Scotland, 1740–1775," in *Sociability and Society In Eighteenth–Century Scotland*, ed. John Dwyer and Richard B. Sher (Edinburgh: Mercat Press, 1993), 194–95, and Broadie noted above.

remaining disappointed at the reception of her work. Raised among intelligent, famous men, Baillie, a feminist in innumerable ways, chose to reject the path of wife and mother in the late eighteenth century and, instead, to compete with the writers of her time. In some ways she was successful; in others she was just another casualty of gender bias. Nevertheless, hers is the story of an intelligent woman writer finding a voice, forming a critical stance, and influencing both male and female writers across continents, from Sir Walter Scott and Maria Edgeworth to Catharine Maria Sedgwick and Edgar Allan Poe, who in 1835 labeled her "the first literary lady in England."[3]

In 1757 Joanna Baillie's father, the Reverend James Baillie (1722–1778), married Dorothea Hunter (1721–1806), sister of the famous Hunter physicians of Glasgow and London.[4] Their first child, William [James] Baillie, died as an infant in 1760.[5] Their second child, Agnes Baillie (1760–1861), became the lifelong companion of her more famous younger sister. The only surviving son, Matthew Baillie (1761–1823), became a celebrated London physician. The last children born to Dorothea and James were Joanna Baillie (1762–1851) and her twin sister, who died a few

---

3. See Poe's comment in "Critical Notices," from *Southern Literary Messenger* (August 1835): 714–16. My thanks to Prof. John Morefield for finding this. In addition, Virginia Woolf wrote in 1929 that "it scarcely seems necessary to consider again the influence of the tragedies of Joanna Baillie upon the poetry of Edgar Allan Poe" (from Woolf's *A Room of One's Own*, qtd. in Catherine Burroughs, "Out of the Pale of Social Kindred Cast," in *Romantic Women Writers: Voices and Countervoices*, ed. Paula R. Feldman and Theresa M. Kelley [Hanover and London: University Press of New England, 1995], 223).

4. In addition to invaluable information in the Hunterian Museum at the University of Glasgow (William Hunter) and the Hunterian Museum at the Royal College of Surgeons (John Hunter), important Hunter/Baillie biographies include the following: Jessie Dobson, *John Hunter* (Edinburgh and London: Livingstone, 1969); J. Kobler, *The Reluctant Surgeon: A Biography of John Hunter* (New York: Doubleday, 1960); G. R. Mather, *Two Great Scotsmen, The Brothers William and John Hunter* (Glasgow: James Maclehose & Sons, 1894); G. C. Peachey, *A Memoir of William and John Hunter* (Plymouth: William Brendon & Son, 1924). Throughout this biography, I quote from Joanna Baillie's letters, now published in *The Collected Letters of Joanna Baillie*, ed. Judith Bailey Slagle, 2 vols. (Madison: Fairleigh Dickinson University Press, 1999). Quotes are identified herein as *Letters* and also by library manuscript notation.

5. There is some confusion about whether this first child was called William or James. Cranz, Matthew Baillie's latest biographer, lists him as James, but Hunter House Museum records him as William.

hours after their premature delivery on 11 September 1762.[6] Baillie's parents had just moved on 2 September 1762 to the manse of Bothwell in Lanarkshire, Scotland, the Rev. Baillie having left his position in the parish of Shotts for an improved position there. In a memoir dated 22 February 1838 to her nephew William Hunter Baillie (1797–1894),[7] Joanna answered some of his questions about the Baillie descent as it was partially traced by her friend John Richardson:[8]

> General Baillie seems to point out our descent as being from his family and probably by a Brother of Principal Baillie.[9] Your best way will be to get the life of Principal Baillie which is published at the beginning of his letters, a work still extant, for he was much connected with public affairs in his days, and see what account is given there of his Father's family. Mr Richardson has ascertained that the first School

---

6. Although this is commonly recorded genealogical information, I have verified dates, etc., through the genealogical data bank maintained by the Church of Jesus Christ of Latter-Day Saints in their London Public Record Office location during summer 1994 and through the Hunter House Museum in East Kilbride. There is no record of Joanna Baillie's twin sister having been named.

7. William Hunter Baillie (1797–1894) the only son of Matthew and Sophia Baillie, graduated from Oxford, married Henrietta Duff in 1835, lived many years in Hampstead, moved to Richmond and later back to Upper Harley Street in Joanna's last years. William and Henrietta were the parents of eight children: Sophia Joanna (1836–82), Matthew John (1837–66), William Hunter (1838–95), John Baron (1841–68), Helen Mary Henrietta (1843–1929), Agnes Elizabeth (1846–1925), Robert Denman (1850–70), and Henrietta Clara Marion (1853–78).

8. John Richardson (1780–1864), parliamentary solicitor who for thirty years discharged the duties of crown agent for Scotland, was reputed to be the most learned peerage lawyer of his time. He had literary tastes and in 1821 introduced George Crabbe to Thomas Campbell in Joanna Baillie's house. He regularly corresponded with Walter Scott and attended his deathbed. Richardson married Elizabeth Hill, a close friend of Thomas Campbell, in 1811 and had several children (*DNB*, XVI:1118–19). Richardson submitted "Song–Her features speak the warmest heart" for Baillie's 1823 *Collection* and, in a very personal letter dated 18 January 1842, assures Baillie that "It is, as it has long been, a great pride and gratification to me to have enjoyed your friendship; & few circumstances of my life have afforded me more real pleasure" (NLS 3990, f.41).

9. Robert Baillie, D.D., Principal (President) of Glasgow College (1599–1662), was one of the most learned of the early Scottish divines and much connected with public affairs. He is identified as Baillie of Jerviston/Jerviswood (*DNB* I:892-94).

master of our name in the Parish of Chrighton [Crichton] was called Andrew Baillie, and if there be a Brother Principal Baillie mention'd as bearing the name of Andrew, he is more than probably the man who fled to Holland and on his return became Schoolmaster of Chrighton. Your Grand Father's only Brother was named Andrew. I can think of nothing else to be done and this will not make the descent a certain thing, but, with other corroborating circumstances, pretty near it.—Our ancestor fled to Holland no doubt on account of his religion and of having been connected with Baillie of Jerviswood,[10] and it is possible that his opinions might not agree in many points with those of his Brother and the Principal & he have [sic] little intercourse with one another which may account for my Father never mentioning, as far as I know, any thing of his family or their consanguinity to Principal Baillie.—As to making out a genealogy for your little Matthew, you need give yourself little concern, for he will be very well off with the immediate descent that undoubtedly belongs to him, though it would make but a poor figure in a Welch Pedigree. His Father a Gloucester Sh^r Squire, Lord of the Manor of Duntisbourn; his Grand father an eminent Court Physician and his Great Grand father a distinguished Scotch Clergyman & Professor of Divinity in the University of Glasgow. Surely this is very respectable, and more than this, though you could trace his direct line to Baliol king of Scotland[11] would do him little good.[12]

This genealogy is difficult to verify beyond a doubt, and, obviously, Baillie was unclear about it herself. In a work from the University of Glasgow's Special Collections entitled *Lives of the Baillies*, the Baillie line is traced to the Baliols from Bailleul in the province of French Flanders, and the family reportedly came to

---

10. Like her ancestor, Baillie would also brave religious controversy in her later years with the publication of *A View of the General Tenour of the New Testament Regarding the Nature and Dignity of Jesus Christ* (1831).

11. There is some confusion about the pedigree of the Baliol family, but at least two were kings of Scotland, namely, John de Baliol (d. 1315) and his son Edward Baliol (d. 1363). Another, John de Baliol (d. 1269), was founder of Balliol College, Oxford (*DNB* I:981-90).

12. See complete letter MS 5613/60 from the Wellcome Institute for the History of Medicine in *Letters*, "To Family."

England with William the Conqueror. The Baillies then split into several different locations, Jerviswood being one of them as the home of George and Robert Baillie.[13] Nevertheless, Joanna Baillie's parents could both claim respectable backgrounds. Her father, the Rev. James Baillie, was born at Crichton, Lothian, on 5 August 1722, the first child of Matthew Baillie, a schoolmaster, and Ann Kirkwood Baillie. According to both John Richardson and Joanna Baillie, James Baillie had one brother named Andrew (b. 1735), who died unmarried, and three sisters: Jean (b. 1724), Margaret (b. 1728) and Anna (b. 1731). No one seems to have recorded the lives of the brother and three sisters.[14]

In a brief biography of Joanna's brother Dr. Matthew Baillie, based on the physician's own medical and autobiographical papers, Dr. Franco Crainz reports that Joanna's father James Baillie was educated at the Musselburgh Grammar School and, finally, at the University of Edinburgh. He was licensed by the Presbytery of Dalkeith on 27 April 1749 and presented by the Duke of Hamilton as Minister of Shotts and ordained on 7 November 1754. James was then transferred to Bothwell in September 1762 and promoted to Hamilton as Second Charge in October 1766. He received his Doctor of Divinity from Glasgow University in 1772, where he was appointed Professor of Divinity in November 1775, remaining there until his death on 28 April 1778.[15] This same information is recorded in Coutt's *History of the University of Glasgow* and in Reid's *Divinity Professors in the University of Glasgow*, with a further note that James Baillie's "rapid promotion was due to the powerful Hamilton influence, as well as to his connection with the famous brothers, John and William Hunter, whose sister Dorothy he had married." In addition, Reid credits Joanna Baillie with securing her father's place in history and cites her "To James B. Baillie, An Infant" as a glimpse into his character:

---

13. This is not to say that John Richardson and William Baillie were incorrect, just that I have been unable to verify the descent. Some of this original Baillie family, however, did eventually locate around Hamilton, originally Jerviswood, and Lanark. See James William Baillie's *Lives of the Baillies* (Edinburgh: Edmonston and Douglas, 1872). Also see WI MS 5613/13-14, documents from the seventeenth and early eighteenth centuries which name these early Baillies. WI MS 5613/16 is John Richardson's 1838 account of the family.

14. See WI MS 5613/19, "Pedigree."

15. Crainz, 7–8.

> Thou wearst his name, who in his stinted span
> Of human life, a generous useful man,
> Did well the pastor's honour'd task perform.
> The toilsome way, the winter's beating storm,
> Ne'er kept him from the peasant's distant cot
> Where want or suffering were the inmate's lot,
> Who look'd for comfort in his friendly face,
> As by the sick-bed's side he took his place.
> A peace-maker in each divided home
> To him all strife-perplexed folk would come.
> In after years, how earnestly he strove
> In sacred lore his students to improve!
> As they met round the academic chair
> Each felt a zealous friend adress'd him there.
> He was thy grandsire's sire, who in his day,
> That, many years gone by, hath pass'd away,
> On human gratitude had many claims; —
> Be thou as good a man, my little James![16]

Joanna Baillie was only fifteen when her father died; she wrote fondly of him but never revealed a very personal relationship, though her brother Matthew reported that their father was

> a man of the most respectable character, of excellent understanding, of polish'd and dignified manners, and of a highly cultivated mind—In the course of a few years He was successively the Minister of Shot[t]s, of Bothwell, of Hamilton, and was ultimately the Professor of Divinity in the University of Glasgow—He was an excellent Preacher both when He compos'd his Sermons, and in Ex tempore speaking, and was so generally liked and esteemed that his House was very much frequented, more especially by the younger Clergy, who were glad to have his Countenance and his advice.[17]

---

16. H. M. B. Reid, *The Divinity Professors in the University of Glasgow*, 2 vols. (Glasgow: Maclehose, Jackson and Company, 1923), 266–67. Also recorded in the *Fasti*. These lines are from Baillie's poem "To James B. Baillie, An Infant," in *The Dramatic and Poetical Works of Joanna Baillie* (London: Longman, Brown, Green and Longmans, 1851), 821, and must be in honor of Matthew and Sophia Baillie's first son James Baillie (1792–93) who died an infant.

17. Qtd. in Crainz, 7.

Writer Lucy Aikin,[18] Joanna's close friend, elucidated that Agnes Baillie remembered the Rev. James Baillie as an excellent parent and related the story that once when Joanna was bitten by a dog thought to be rabid, he sucked the wound at the hazard of his own life. In contrast, it is also Aikin who reported that James Baillie never kissed his daughter Joanna and that she yearned for more affection as a child,[19] though Baillie never reveals such disappointment in her autobiographical papers or correspondence. Unfortunately, there is little personal information about James Baillie that is not anecdotal and as such should be repeated with caution, but one such story in the Hunterian Society minutes reveals that while he was at Shotts there was a serious outbreak of small pox. Realizing that unsanitary conditions in the parish were probably partly to blame, James Baillie attended medical classes at the University of Glasgow and began to serve the ailing community both as doctor and clergyman. When it was time for him to leave his post as minister, his successor was allegedly so protested that the military police had to be called in to break up a street riot.[20]

Nevertheless, a Presbyterian minister in late eighteenth-century Glasgow would have proved a strict taskmaster even in the midst of increasing liberalism. But the Rev. James Baillie, as his daughter illustrated, was not caught up in the evangelical fervor of the times. She wrote to friend Margaret Holford Hodson[21] in 1836 that

---

18. Lucy Aikin (1781–1864), daughter of Martha and physician John Aikin and niece of Anna Laetitia Aikin Barbauld, was a translator and a writer, an early fictional work being *Lorimer, a Tale* (1814). Her earlier *Epistles on Women* (1810) was followed by historical works and *The Life of Joseph Addison* (1843), written during her residence in Hampstead. She and Joanna became close friends, and her "Recollections of Joanna Baillie" provides an enticing look both at Baillie and at their circle of friends. She was also a friend of Channing. See *Memoirs, Miscellanies and Letters of the late Lucy Aikin*, ed. Philip Hemery Le Breton (London: Longman, Green, Longman, Roberts, and Green, 1864).

19. Le Breton, 8.

20. Rudolf, 8–9.

21. Margaret Holford Hodson (1778–1852) was the daughter of Allen Holford and writer Margaret Wrench Holford and became the wife of Rev. Septimus Hodson in 1826. Margaret Holford published *Wallace, or the Fight of Falkirk* (1809), *Poems* (1811), *Margaret of Anjou* (1816), *Warbeck of Wolfstein* (1820), and other works. She probably met Baillie between 1810 and 1813 and was a close friend of Robert Southey (see *DNB*, IX:968 and *The Feminist Companion to Literature in English*). See volume 2 of my *Collected Letters* for complete letters to Hodson.

> I have been pretty well and busy looking over a great mass of Ms sermons of my Father's, written some fifty years ago; an employment interesting to me but very fatiguing for my eyes from the very minute hand in which they are written. He preached good works strenuously in opposition to the then recent doctrines of Whitfield [sic] & his followers the Evangelicals of those days,[22] and was more popular amongst the higher than the lower orders of his parishioners, who only loved him for his active benevolence and the good he did amongst them, sparing himself as a parish pastor upon no occasion. His Ms Lectures, while he filled the divinity chair in Glasgow I have not yet looked over, but hope to do it ere long.[23]

The Rev. Baillie's sermons were apparently never published, and very few of his letters survive; because he was in the position at Glasgow for only three years, there is also very little biographical information available through the university. It has been noted that Baillie was a Moderate on the strength that in 1768 he supported a minister named Alexander Ferguson in a theology dispute, and Baillie later defeated a well-connected Moderate named William Wight for the chair. The University of Glasgow was not generally a place where Moderates advanced, so James Baillie must have had the right political and social connections, probably the result of his family link to the famous Hunters.[24] In a letter from Hamilton dated 25 October 1775, James Baillie wrote to John Hunter about the upcoming election for the Chair of Divinity, for which he believed he had some but not unanimous support, and cited three of his friends who had prior commitments to his opposition, Dr. Wight. In the same letter he stated that if offered the position and "having had time to deliberate a little longer, & consulting with Mrs Baillie," they

---

22. George Whitefield (1714–70), well-known evangelist and leader of Calvinistic Methodists, published several volumes of journals and religious tracts during his life. A collected edition of his works was edited and published in 1771 by John Gillie, D.D. (*DNB*, XXI:85-92).

23. CLS Ms 69; *Letters*, 661.

24. Professor Sher, New Jersey Institute of Technology, pointed out for me a letter from David Hume to William Strahan dated 13 November 1775 in which Hume writes, "I am afraid, however, that all Efforts in favour of Dr Wight will be in Vain. It seems, Dr Hunter supports a Friend of his; and nothing can be refused him by the University" (J. Y. T. Greig, ed., *The Letters of David Hume*, 2 vols. [Oxford: Clarendon, 1932], 2:305).

would decide whether or not the change was expedient.[25] The fact that a man in Baillie's position in 1775 would care that the move be both merited by him and amenable to his wife sheds a positive light on his character, for he certainly could have moved without unanimous support from the university or without Dorothea's approval. On 23 November 1775, John Hunter responded to the Rev. Baillie's speculation that the appointment, after it was offered, was due to family connections:

> I thank you for your very kind and obliging Letter. I also congratulate you upon your preferment. Altho' you modestly say it was upon your family's account that you received it, yet it is what you should not have refused upon your own. There is hardly any character so low, or so high, but what will receive dignity from Title, and when it is given as a reward for merit, it gives the graces to it.[26]

Additionally, in a letter as early as 15 February 1763, James Stuart Mackenzie (brother of Lord Bute, then prime minister) wrote Mure of Caldwell that he intended Baillie for a Glasgow post, calling him one of the "worthiest fellows."[27] If James Baillie was, in fact, a Moderate, his appointment at Glasgow probably surprised some because the movement known as "Moderatism" was not considered the result of growing enlightenment; rather, in some ways, it was considered a revolt against strict church procedure. Somehow this all seems to fit the profile of the James Baillie who raised his children to play on the heath with his parishioners and who worked with community small pox victims. It also follows that Joanna would in her adult years turn to a religion based on practical morality and ethical concerns—Unitarianism—stressing the goodness of humanity and respect for human achievements. Her father may not have been the rigid unaffectionate disciplinarian that Aikin characterized.

---

25. This letter is probably to John Hunter, but there are also a few letters in the collection from James Baillie to William Hunter about financial affairs Baillie was handling for him in Scotland. The letter above only begins "Dear Sir"; whether the recipient is John or William is not clear. See RCS HB.i.4.

26. Qtd. in Dobson, 134–35. Hunter (along with "Anny") also fondly gives his best wishes to his sister "Dolly" and his nephew and nieces, hoping "to see the young man in London soon."

27. See NLS Mure of Caldwell Papers, 1:171. Again, I thank Richard Sher for this reference.

Before this appointment to the University of Glasgow and while he was performing his duties as Minister of Shotts, James Baillie had met and married Dorothea Hunter on 7 December 1757. Joanna's brother Matthew wrote that their mother "was a woman of excellent Sense, of a mild Temper, with the manners, and very much the appearance of a Lady."[28] Dorothea Hunter had been born on 26 January 1721 in a rough-hewn stone house in Long Calderwood,[29] about a mile from the old village of Kilbride, to John Hunter, a farmer and grain merchant, and Agnes Paul Hunter, the daughter of the Treasurer of the City of Glasgow. Her birth came after that of her siblings John (1708–22), Elizabeth (1710–11), Andrew (1711–14), Janet (1713–49), James (1715–45), Agnes (1716–41), and William (1718–83). Isobel followed Dorothea in 1725 (d. 1742), and when John, the first-born, died at age fourteen on 27 February 1722, the parents named their last child John as well—he would later become the surgeon John Hunter (1728–1793). Elizabeth and Andrew died as young children, and this farm couple, with their remaining children and seventy-five acres, did well to see that those children were educated or apprenticed when the time came.[30]

Unfortunately, the only Hunter children about whom anything is written are William, Dorothea, and John; but except for William and John, all of Dorothea's other siblings were dead before the Baillie children were born. Some of Dorothea's history is traceable through what we know about her famous children, Matthew and Joanna, but it is difficult to find more than just factual information or to get a sense of her personality aside from what her own children wrote about her. Her older brother William was always an eager scholar and was originally sent to the University of Glasgow at the age of thirteen to study for the ministry, but he soon turned his interest to medicine and studied with Dr. William Cullen in Hamilton. While William was in medical school, his younger brother John was at home, much preferring nature to books. By the time William had received his M.D. from the University of Glasgow in 1750, John, a practical thinker who had originally trained as a

---

28. Qtd. in Crainz, 9.
29. This house is now Hunter House Museum. It is difficult to determine after renovations what the house would have looked like in the mid-eighteenth century, but by today's standards, it is not small; the stone structure would have been also enhanced by outbuildings.
30. Dobson, 3–4.

carpenter, had come to London to work with him.[31] While Scotland was clearly the seat of medical training, London afforded more opportunities for acclaim in the field, and both Hunter brothers had amassed a fortune there by the end of their lives. So close to the final Jacobite rebellion of 1745, however, the London political climate at the brothers' mid-century move granted limited tolerance to Scots; consequently William, in particular, probably found it necessary to dress like the Londoners and to alter his accent as much as possible in order to be accepted into the medical and social scene. He was clearly successful. By the time John, who cared far less about social acceptance, was entering the medical profession there, a great deal of the Scots stigma was removed, though one is reminded of Dr. Samuel Johnson's occasional aversion toward Scots in the later eighteenth century.

Before William Hunter opened his own offices in London, he had worked with Dr. William Smellie, leaving him in the autumn of 1741 to become an assistant to Dr. James Douglas, a physician who was then developing techniques that would later lead William Hunter into the field of modern gynecology. Hunter was a tutor to Douglas's youngest son, who was then studying medicine, and he reportedly became engaged to Douglas's daughter Martha Jane (1716–44). While William Hunter was away in Paris attending Antoine Ferrein's anatomy lectures in 1744, however, Martha Jane Douglas died. William never married, nor did he pay tribute to Dr. Douglas in his published works.[32]

John Hunter, Sr. had died of tuberculosis in 1741, so after the death of their mother in 1751, John Hunter left his course of spring lectures in 1752 to return to Scotland for Dorothea, bringing her to London to live with him and William, who was by then in private practice. Recalling this period in her life some thirty years later, Dorothea Hunter Baillie said that John was to her "a very affectionate Brother, cheerful, open, pleasant, and of a familiar and

---

31. For the information in this paragraph, I thank Hunter House Museum at East Kilbride, Helen Collins, and assistants Janice McAuslan, Gerard Smith, and Joanne McCartney. Not only is there valuable information there on the Hunter physicians, but there is also a very personal ambiance in this museum which helps one understand the brilliant minds with which Joanna Baillie would have been associated.

32. The information in this paragraph comes from Edwin Clarke, M.D., F.R.C.P., ed., "James Douglas of the Pouch," *Medical History: A Quarterly Journal Devoted to the History of Medicine and Related Sciences* 18 (1974): 162–71 and 379-402.

domestic disposition." John had had great difficulty with reading in his early school years,[33] much like Joanna Baillie later indicated she had, and he may have been somewhat intimidated by the brilliance of his older brother William. In her later years, Joanna wrote to Dr. Andrews Norton[34] that although she never met William he was said to have been very jovial:

> I have heard my Brother say that he [William] told a humorous story better than any man he ever knew, and it was thought by his friends that had he been differently circumstanced in the world, he might have been at the very head of the profession as a Comedian. I never saw him which I regret. My Uncle John Hunter I knew well and loved him very heartily, (for that was the kind of love that belonged to him) not tenderly.[35]

This anecdote is particularly fascinating since William has been described historically as a strict academician; but he must certainly have been entertaining, for his lecture audiences ranged from medical students to established non-medical men such as economist Adam Smith. Dr. William Hunter, ultimately known as the father of modern gynecology, was just reaching acclaim in the medical field as a male midwife and lecturer when Dorothea moved to London in the spring of 1752. And John, under William's tutelage, was writing essays on his first experiments and preparing specimens for demonstrations at William's lectures.[36]

Both Hunter House Museum and one of John Hunter's several biographers record that a few years later, in the spring of 1756, William Hunter moved his office to 42 Jermyn Street, just off St. James Square, possibly because living in such close proximity to the dissecting room with the constant traffic and bustle was distasteful to Dorothea Hunter and because the new residence would be in a much more desirable part of London. John, a surgeon's pupil at St. George's Hospital, eventually moved into the Jermyn Street house

---

33. Dobson, 28.
34. Dr. Andrews Norton (1786–1853) was a literary and biblical scholar and Harvard divinity professor, who carried on a long correspondence with Baillie and was instrumental in promoting interest in her works in America. See *Letters*, vol. 2.
35. HU MS Eng 944 (8); *Letters*, 923.
36. Dobson, 28–29.

when William's home at Great Windmill Street was ready in 1768.[37] Presentations at Hunter House Museum clearly establish John as an adept and practical hands-on scientist, and it was he who dealt with the grave robbers who supplied the cadavers for the brothers' studies in anatomy. But, anxious to be on his own, in 1760 John Hunter made a definitive career move—he joined the army as a staff surgeon. It was the Seven Years War, and John began to make discoveries in healing gunshot wounds and to study the working of the blood. It was probably these experiments with circulation that lead to the Hunter brothers' division on William's publishing *The Anatomy of the Human Gravid Uterus* in 1774, for John felt that William had used his research on circulation in the mother and fetus without giving him credit. William died nine years later with the brothers still distant toward each other, but it is possible that because of its sensational nature this argument has been exaggerated by the Hunters' biographers; Joanna Baillie never mentions it.[38] In addition, as the older brother and as John's first medical tutor, William would probably have considered that any work the two shared was largely his for publication.

In 1756 Dorothea Hunter continued to keep house for her brother William in the new residence at Jermyn Street. But she would not dwell there long, for late in the year 1757 she became engaged to marry the Rev. James Baillie of Hamilton, near East Kilbride. The marriage took place at St. James's, Piccadilly, on 7 December 1757 in the presence of John Hunter and John Benefold, Jr.[39] She was almost thirty-six years old when she married James Baillie and in the next five years gave birth to five children, three of whom survived: Agnes, Matthew, and Joanna. Lucy Aikin speculates that the children were raised in a strict household, for she attributes Baillie's reticence at the publication of the first volume of *A Series of Plays* to a cultured "repression of all emotions, even the gentlest . . .

---

37. In 1766 William Hunter built a house on Great Windmill Street at the cost of over £6,000 and moved there in 1768; the architect was Robert Mylne. Matthew Baillie would later inherit this residence (Dobson, 123; Crainz, 20).

38. I thank Elizabeth Allen, Hunterian Curator, Royal College of Surgeons, for sharing her knowledge of the Hunters and for discussing this "controversy" with me at length.

39. Dobson, 36. The marriage settlement is preserved at the Royal College of Surgeons, an interesting document which mentions the will and the marriage settlement of Dorothea's father.

indeed the constant lesson of her Presbyterian home."[40] It is difficult to believe, however, that Dorothea Hunter, so much a part of the lives of her gregarious brothers, would have forced such reticence on her children. And the Rev. Baillie, as pointed out earlier, seems to have been an unconventional minister. We do know from Joanna's memoir, however, that Dorothea was wary of encouraging her daughter's flair for acting,[41] for life in the theater still bore a certain stigma for a proper lady.

During the 1830s both Baillie's nephew William Baillie and her friend Mary Berry were encouraging Baillie, already in her seventies, to provide them with a memoir, along with information about her ancestors. In such an autobiographical manuscript (1831) written at Berry's request,[42] Joanna related her earliest memories of childhood:

> The farthest back thing that I can remember is sitting with my Sister on the steps of the s[t]air in Bothwell Manse, repeating after her as loud as I could roar the letters of the Alphabet while she held in her hand a paper on which was marked in large letters the A B C &c. I was then about 3 years old, and this was, I suppose the very beginning of my education. . . . not being able to read but in a very imperfect manner at the age of eight or nine. . . . My Mother took pains to teach me and I was sent to day-school at Hamilton where my Father was then settled as Clergyman, but even the sight of a book was hateful to me. . . . I was an active stirring child, quick in apprehending & learning any thing else, my parents the more provoked at my uncommon dulness in learning this most useful of all acquirements. However I ought not to say <u>provoked</u> for they had more patience with me than I deserved.[43]

In her "Memoirs Written to please my Nephew William Baillie," Joanna further elaborated,

---

40. Le Breton, 8.
41. WI MS 5613/68/1-6, quoted later in this chapter.
42. Writer Mary Berry (1763–1852) was a long-time friend of Baillie and one of the first to praise her *A Series of Plays: in which it is attempted to delineate the stronger passions,* etc. Berry asked Baillie to provide the prologue to her *Fashionable Friends,* produced in 1800 at Drury Lane. Berry was probably just beginning to write notes on her own early life at this time, which she finished in 1848–49.
43. RCS manuscript HB.ii.56c; *Letters,* 3.

My first faint recollections are of Bothwell where I was born and passed the first four years of my life. They are chiefly out of door recollections—running in the garden and looking at the flowers and seeing pigeons flying in the air or gathered on the round roof of a pigeon house that belonged to the manse and above all an occasional walk to the Clyde with my Sister, when our Nurse-maid put us both into the water to be <u>douket</u>[44] and dance & splash about as we pleased. It is curious enough that remembering these little circumstances pretty vividly, almost every thing that passed within doors are almost entirely lost; and that the important change of going to a new residence—Hamilton is in my mind a blanc altogether. My being sent to the reading-school I dont remember, but well do I remember sitting there on a weary bench day after day working on letters & stories which I did not understand and had no desire to know—the worst or one of the worst scholars in the School. My only bright time was when playing out of doors with other Children—playing at make-believe grown people or Gentlemen & Ladies, generally in some open cart or wagon that served us for a house. It is such a common pastime with Children that it would scarcely be worth while to mention it only that I was so particularly fond of it and my Sister who could read and amused herself with books never entered into it at all. But there was one occupation which we both joined in with equal avidity—listening to Ghost stories told us by the sexton of parish who, frequently came to the house of a winter evening and sat by the Kitchen fire. We always, I dont know how, contrived to escape from the parlor when we heard that <u>John Leipen</u>, so he was called, was in the house. His stories excited us much, and as the house we lived in was said to be haunted by the ghost of a man who had in former years hanged himself in the Garret, we became so frighten'd that we durst not go up stairs alone even in broad day light.[45]

---

44. douk or douke: to dive or dip forcibly under water (*Dictionary of the Older Scottish Language*).

45. This comes from the WI MS 5613/68/1–6 which has no address but a note from William Baillie as follows: "This version must not be published or allowed to be read out of the family, May 25, 1860." There does not appear to me any reason for William Baillie's secrecy, for the

Clearly fond of the open air, Baillie also confirmed to Berry that ghost stories had a great deal to do with arousing the sisters' imaginations and making them fear the dark as children: "My Father & Mother were never aware of the state of our minds in this respect," she explains, "for we durst not acknowledge it lest we should be obliged to be alone & in the dark to get the better of our timidity."[46]

Joanna's companion, Agnes, though she seems somewhat overshadowed by her sister, had, according to brother Matthew, "a quick ready Understanding, with a good deal of various knowle[d]ge, so as to be much beyond the common level of Women in these respects";[47] and, certainly, Joanna's many references to what Agnes read and did outside the home prove that her sister was equal to her in discriminating literary tastes and interests—but not in ambition. There are many anecdotes, however, about Agnes's acute sense of humor. Through Joanna and in her own right, Agnes met famous writers and thinkers in and about London and was apparently a closer friend to the famous painter Sir Thomas Lawrence than Joanna was. Her letters, though scattered meagerly throughout collections of Joanna's, along with Joanna's own accounts, reveal Agnes's interest in travel, history, and classical as well as contemporary literature. The fact that Baillie mentions her in almost every one of her hundreds of letters is a testament to their affection. Matthew Baillie later summarized, "The Characters of both [Agnes and Joanna] are most highly respectable, and their Society has been more courted than in proportion to their situation in the world."[48]

Joanna Baillie also recalled in her brief autobiography one of her first "play-fellows," the only daughter (unidentified) of a nearby farmer, whose house she often visited on winter days; it was in this house that the two girls engaged in make believe and spent many pleasant hours together. Both Joanna and Agnes Baillie were obviously well liked by neighbors and others who knew the family, and Joanna reported that "when visitors from a distance" came to her father's house and asked that the sisters be allowed to accompany them to local sites and gardens, "it was also a delightful

---

brief and incomplete memoirs, clearly written in Joanna's hand, only reinforce her powers of imagination even in childhood; in honor of his request, however, I only summarize and provide some excerpts from the manuscript.

46. RSC HB.ii.56c; *Letters*, 4.
47. Crainz, 10.
48. Ibid.

thing," the pictures in nearby palaces stimulating their imaginations. These visits, along with excursions into the old forest, wrote Baillie,

> did my fanciful untaught mind much good. . . . but into the Town itself I never looked to go except in a Fair-day when the streets were crowded with country people & Lads & Lasses, dressed in their holiday gear . . . where the sound of fiddles & dancing gave notice of the merry-making within, to say nothing of the booths with all their tempting treasure and the people & children looking wistfully at them . . . . Yet the Fair itself was almost eclypsed by the amusement received by standing at the entry of our house to see the Fair-folk, as we called them, returning home in the evening, jesting & laughing & roaring & glorious as Tam o' Shanter. Every different humour was then to be traced amoung the motley groups.[49]

In documenting her early flair for spectacle and performance, Baillie also revealed her lack of arrogance. According to Lucy Aikin, Joanna's father, then situated in a rural parish, allowed his children to run about with those of his "humble parishioners, barefoot like the rest." In addition, Aikin knew of Baillie later to "prevail upon prejudiced English parents to allow their children to partake in so *healthful* an indulgence."[50]

Joanna and Agnes went away to Miss Macdonald's Boarding School in Glasgow in 1772, where, when Joanna was about ten years old, she finally developed an interest in books, learning to read before she began school there in order to avoid embarrassment. But Joanna Baillie was restless and found that even though she could read she had no real pleasure in books and only read them because it was a shameful thing for "Young Ladies" not to.[51] But her enthusiasm for pranks had not abated. In the memoir for her nephew, she related an incident that happened one night after the girls' evening prayers. As they were going to bed, one of them saw an open canister of sugar and decided it would be fun for each of them to take a little upstairs to the common bedroom. Sugar being very dear, Miss Macdonald shortly appeared in the girls' bedroom, angrily holding the empty canister. Because all the girls were involved, none

---

49. WI MS 5613/68/1–6; *Letters*, 5.
50. Le Breton, 9.
51. RCS HB.ii.56c.

would confess; however, Joanna admitted that because Miss Macdonald thought her innocent, she felt particularly guilty and wanted to confess to the crime. Her companions convinced her that if she confessed to be a part of it, then the mistress would ask whose idea it was, so Joanna kept quiet to save the rest. Baillie later wrote to her nephew,

> This opened my thoughts to the working of a strong passion, and traces of it will be found in the Character of Edward in The Tragedy of Ethwald, who could not bear, after his first battle from which he had fled, to have the honour of preeminent valour imputed to him, though he was truly the cause of the victory.[52]

Again, a childhood incident was to influence Baillie's focus on human nature. Aikin records that as a schoolgirl Joanna often "was the ringleader in all pranks and frolics, and used to entertain her companions with an endless string of stories of her own invention," and she was "addicted to clambering on the roof of the house, to act over her scenes alone and in secret."[53] Joanna's interest in reading changed, however, when shortly before her venture to boarding school she stumbled on some broken bottles, cut her ankle and was required by the doctor to lie upon the sofa for some weeks:

> Agnes, like a kind Sister came to me with books in her hand and coaxed me to try reading some story . . . in this way Oceans [Ossian's] Poems[54] became the first book I ever read of my own good will without being obliged to do it. . . . I then read of my own accord various poetical works & afterwards prose, though I had not pleasure enough in the occupation

---

52. WI MS 5613/68/1–6.
53. Le Breton, 9. In her autobiography for Berry, Baillie also writes that when the other girls told stories and it was her turn, she was often obliged to "invent one upon the spot" (RCS HB.ii.56c).
54. In his introduction to the recent edition of Baillie's *Poems, 1790* (Oxford and New York: Woodstock, 1994), Jonathan Wordsworth notes that, growing up in Glasgow, Baillie "would have known Blair's primitivist *Dissertation on Ossian* (1765) and *Lectures on rhetoric and belles letters* (1783)." And of course she knew Burns, "who made the link between ancient poetry of the heart . . . and its modern rural equivalent." Also see Fiona Stafford's "Blair's Ossian, Romanticism and the teaching of Literature," *The Scottish Invention of English Literature*, ed. Robert Crawford (Cambridge: Cambridge University Press, 1998), 68–88.

> to sit at it long at a time. What first induced me to read history was the pleasure of reading by my Brother, sitting by his side & doing as he did, my love for him was beyond all the affection I felt for any body else. . . . When the summer was ended, he went to College and I was put to a boarding school at Glasgow. This great change of scene and mingling with so many new companions, quickened my mind & opened my ideas & notions in many respects.[55]

To her surprise, at boarding school Joanna found herself as proficient a reader as the other young girls; this somewhat resolved her insecurity, but her spelling was still imperfect. "This defect has made me all my life an uneasy bad writer of letters," she later wrote in her memoir for Berry, and at the same time she cited her difficulties in setting verses to memory. Her real interest was in play and in using her imagination, which later translated into a love of drama:

> When we lived at Long Calderwood we were fortunate in having Professor Millar & his family for our near Neighbours during the summer.[56] He was very fond of Theatrical amusements, and when Mrs Siddons in the beginning of her glory came to Glasgow,[57] he left the country with Mrs Millar

---

55. WI MS 5613/68/1-6; *Letters*, 5. Matthew Baillie matriculated Glasgow University in 1774 (Crainz, 173).

56. Anne Millar, a childhood friend of Joanna and Agnes, was the daughter of John Millar, a professor at the University of Glasgow and colleague of Joanna's father James. John Millar had three sons and six daughters; one daughter married Professor James Mylne and one, probably Helen, married Dr. John Thomson (*DNB*, XIII:401-403). I have not identified the Miss Graham mentioned in this memoir.

57. Sarah Siddons (1755-1831), actress and eldest child of Sarah and Roger Kemble, received much attention as a young beauty. As a young girl, she was sent to be lady's maid to Mrs. Greatheed, where she often recited Shakespeare before aristocratic company. Her parents reluctantly consented to her marriage to actor William Siddons in 1773. Hearing of her talent shortly thereafter, Garrick sent one of his men to see her in *The Fair Penitent* and hired her at £5/week for Drury Lane, where she became the foremost tragic actress of the day. A friend of Baillie and the Milbankes, Siddons achieved celebrity under Garrick's management, giving her farewell performance as Lady Macbeth at Covent Garden in 1812 but continuing to give private readings. Siddons played the role of Jane in Baillie's *De Monfort* in 1800 (*DNB*, VIII:195-202; many biographies are accessible).

> & all his children who were old enough to enjoy it, and lived in his College residence all the time she acted there, having a box secured for them every night. How I longed to have been of their party need not be said. . . . I dont know how long it was after this that in the dining room at Long Calderwood with Miss Graham & Anne Millar, then staying in the house, I attempted to act that scene in Measure for Measure where Isabella pleads with Angelo for the life of her Brother. . . . Our two maid servants were summoned from the kitchen and they with my Mother & Sister made the audience. First when we began, they all laughed without restraint at our strange appearance but, as I proceeded in my part, they became grave and ended by sheding [sic] tears, and this was a great triumph for me. Every one praised me but my Mother who, very wisely did not like to give me any kind of encouragement. At another time too I acted Hamlet in the Ghost scene with great commendation.[58]

This penchant for performance would later reveal itself in Baillie's capacity for writing drama and in her personal life as well.

Unfortunately, Baillie never had any formal training in theater, knowledge that would have certainly enhanced her dramatic writing later on; and the sisters' formal education varied greatly from their brother Matthew's. While Matthew attended the Latin School at Hamilton before he was seven years old and remained there six years to prepare for the University of Glasgow, where he went through the full system of classical and philosophical education, Agnes and Joanna were afforded no such training. Eighteenth-century boarding schools in general, explains Mary Borer in *Willingly to School*, offered little to stimulate a young girl's mind, teaching reading—but not Latin or Greek—dancing, needlework, drawing and cooking: "The curriculum was nearly always the same. It was the conditions which varied—from the spartan and squalid to the comfortable and even luxurious."[59] Unfortunately, there is no detailed information available on Miss Macdonald's boarding school in particular; and few subjects in the history of Scotland remain so ill understood, explains William Ferguson, as the state of schools there in the eighteenth century. Since the burgh and grammar schools claimed

---

58. WI MS 5613/68/1–6 to William Baillie.
59. Mary Cathcart Borer, *Willingly to School: A History of Women's Education* (London: Lutterworth Press, 1975), 184.

very few prominent Enlightenment leaders, most of the information gathered in the past has related to parish schools.[60] However, Miss Macdonald's school certainly produced an enlightened leader in Joanna Baillie. Schools were becoming more secular at this time, especially in Glasgow; so the little formal training Baillie received, her later curiosity to read extraordinary works, and her active imagination were enough to activate her genius. By the time Baillie was in her teens, she was writing "a few things of no value" which were "carefully concealed" and at the same time developing an interest in drama and attempting, without success according to her, to read *Paradise Lost*.[61]

Only three years after James Baillie's appointment as professor of divinity at the University of Glasgow in December 1775, he died in Glasgow on 28 April 1778. Being left with only a small inheritance, the prudent Dorothea Hunter Baillie and her three children were now supported by the generosity of her brother Dr. William Hunter, who provided them the family home at Long Calderwood in Scotland. Matthew Baillie had received a fellowship in Balliol College, Oxford,[62] so he left the family home for England and soon became a lecturer in anatomy at William Hunter's medical school in Great Windmill Street, London. John Hunter, too, was by then a prominent surgeon, later credited for making surgery a science rather than a trade.[63] But the two brothers were already somewhat at odds. Joanna knew only her uncle John, since William was dead when she moved to London around 1784 where both he and John had been since before her birth. Shortly before the move to London, Dorothea Baillie wrote to her son Matthew that "You[r] sisters and I have not been one night from home this winter" and noted that she

---

60. William Ferguson, *Scotland 1689 to Present*, 4 vols. (Edinburgh: Oliver and Boyd, 1968), 198.

61. RCS HB.ii.56c.

62. Matthew Baillie's degrees are as follows: BA, January 1783; MA, June 1786; BM, July 1786; MF, 1789 (Crainz, 25).

63. By the end of the seventeenth century, some surgeons were supplementing their craft apprenticeship with formal education in medical schools, but by the early nineteenth century virtually all were doctors of surgery, and the field had become established as one of the great subdivisions of medicine. The Barber Surgeons of Edinburgh eventually became the Royal College of Surgeons of Edinburgh, from its earliest origins an examining body (I. F. MacLaren, "Meeting of the West Midlands Surgical Society, 26 April 1987: Quality Control in Surgical Training," *Journal of the Royal College of Surgeons, Edinburgh* 33 [1988]: 98–102).

had written to her brother about his intentions of coming to Scotland. Clearly, these were financially difficult times for Dorothea and her two daughters, because a subsequent letter from Long Calderwood to Matthew stated that "as the Professors widows lose half a year of the annuity" she would draw little from that during the year and would not be able to send him money for his school debts until after summer.[64] By 1784 Dorothea Hunter Baillie, now with two teenaged daughters at home, would have to rely on her brothers to rescue her to London for a second time.

In London Joanna Baillie maintained a close relationship with John Hunter and his wife, the poet Anne Home Hunter, as well as with their daughter Agnes, later Lady Campbell. Anne Home, daughter of surgeon Robert Boyne Home, had met John Hunter while he was a pupil at Westminster School and married him in July 1771 after a seven-year courtship. In 1783 they moved from Jermyn Street to Leicester Square.[65] John Hunter probably had some sway on Joanna's concern for animals,[66] for in addition to his work on the human anatomy, he was a member of the first Board of Directors of the Royal Humane Society in 1774. He also helped found the Royal Veterinary College in 1781, in addition to keeping an assembly of large animals at his country home at Earl's Court. Students and other visitors were reportedly at John and Anne Hunter's home around the clock, and it is said that John worked a twenty-four hour day. Since Joanna Baillie visited there often, she was a part of that energetic and diverse environment. And she later confessed that it was her aunt Anne Home Hunter who was her genuine inspiration, for Anne had written several beautiful and popular songs and began to read to Joanna "every new composition as it came from her pen." It was this first literary influence that Joanna Baillie acknowledged:

> To write as she did was far beyond any attempt of mine, but it turned my thoughts to poetical composition. . . . One dark morning of a dull winter day, standing on the hearth in Windmill Street and looking at the mean dirty houses on the opposite side of the street, the contrast of my situation from the winter scenes of my own country came powerfully to my

---

64. RCS HB.ii.19–20.
65. Dobson, 133, 235.
66. In 1826 Baillie published a pamphlet entitled "A Lesson Intended for the Use of the Hampstead School" on the abuse of animals.

mind. . . . and with little further deliberation I forthwith set myself to write the "Winter day" in blank verse.[67]

After Dr. William Hunter's death in 1783, Joanna, Agnes, and their mother Dorothea had moved to London to be with and keep house for Matthew Baillie. William Hunter had left Dr. Baillie his practice, about £5,000 in money, and Long Calderwood, the small estate in Scotland; however, Matthew gave the Scotland property to William Hunter's brother John in 1784 since he believed that it should rightfully be the younger brother's.[68] In addition, William left Joanna and Agnes £2,000, no small sum in the late eighteenth century.[69] Before Matthew's marriage and at her initial move to London in 1784, Joanna Baillie, then twenty-two, must have begun to write seriously. However, in an account of her earliest literary inspiration, she revealed to Mary Berry,

> My Father had a man-servant who was very vain & particular about his dress though at the same time very uncouth. . . . My first verses were composed in ridicule of him and sung by myself & others to a ballad tune to his great mortification & annoyance. . . . he came privately to me, beseeching me not to sing it, and promising in return to give me a ride behind him every time he took my Father's horse to be watered. I consented: he kept his promise; and this was the first reward I received for what might be termed literary labours. . . . my Brother came one day from the Grammar school, some what disturbed by the Master's having enjoined him & some of his boys of his class to compose a few couplets on the seasons,—My Father saying to him, 'tut man! Jack (the name I then went by) could do that.['] I was set to it forthwith and composed a few common-place lines upon the

---

67. WI MS 5613/68/1-6; *Letters*, 9.
68. Crainz, 20-23; Dobson, 134-36. In addition, Dr. Hunter left Dr. Baillie his house and premises in Great Windmill Street at the end of thirty years from his death, along with the use of the museum for thirty years; the museum collection would ultimately become the property of his alma mater, Glasgow University. The estate in Scotland became the property of Matthew's son William in 1838, when John Hunter's last surviving child died. (John Hunter's children included, Agnes Margaretta Hunter Campbell [1776-1838], James Hunter [1774-75], John Banks Hunter [1772-1838], and Mary Anne Hunter [1773-76].)
69. George Eyre-Todd, *History of Glasgow*, 3 vols. (Glasgow: Jackson, Wylie and Company, 1934), 3:391-92.

subject, the copy of which has happily been long since lost. . . . However my Mother very sensibly knocked that on the head, by saying to me when I had completed my tenth year, "Remember you are no longer a child and must give up making verses."[70]

After her mother suggested that young ladies of ten and more should "give up making verses," "I followed her advice," Baillie wrote, "and thought no more at that time & long after, of writing verse." During her teenage years, however, Baillie began to read plays; "a love for the Drama took hold of me," she confirmed, "and I began to borrow Play books and to read them with great avidity. . . . The only Dramatic books which my Father's library afforded—a copy of Shakespear [sic] with no pictures in it was sadly overlooked & neglected." Joanna related in her brief autobiography for William Baillie that, after her father's election to the Divinity Chair in Glasgow, a gentleman of the town often stayed at the house of her friend Miss Graham and had in his possession a copy of *Bell's Theatre*, with engravings of actors and actresses in stage costumes.[71] This work, certainly more intriguing for a young girl than the unillustrated Shakespeare edition, enhanced her interest in tragedy and comedy. But, Baillie explained, "nothing in a dramatic form ever charmed me so much as Milton's *Comus* which I read (I forget exactly when) a year or two before we left Scotland."[72] She would have been about twenty years old when she read this early closet drama.

---

70. RCS HB.ii.56c; *Letters*, 7.

71. See *Bell's Edition of Shakespeare's Plays, As they are now performed at the Theatres Royal in London* (London: John Bell, 1774). Each play is prefaced by a picture of actors in full costume from a specific scene of the play that follows.

72. WI MS 5613/68/1-6; *Letters*, 8. She confirms to Berry that when she was about 15,
>having heard a great deal about Milton I thought I must read Paradise Lost, but after going through the two first books, I could not proceed; it was beyond the level of my mind at that time. But when I was about 3 years older I fortunately met with Comus, and read it with so much delight that I took courage and began again to try Paradise; then indeed I did perceive the grandeur, sublimity & beauty of the Poem, and read through it with great admiration & interest, though the many learned allusions & the Theology did often make it heavy, and I could not help wishing that the great Poet had been a less learned man. (RCS HB.ii.56c; *Letters*, 8)

In 1791 Dr. Matthew Baillie married Sophia Denman (1771–1845), daughter of Thomas Denman and Elizabeth Brodie;[73] and Joanna and Agnes then moved to the country with their mother.[74] She later related to her nephew that after the publication of her *Poems* in 1790 she spent a year in Scotland, and

> On my return to London my Brother was married to your Mother, an event which we have all our life long had good cause to bless. We went to reside in the Country, changing our place of abode two or three times till we settled at length in Colchester. Our previous home to that was dull enough where there was little or no society and dulness & leisure set me again to create a fanciful world of my own, and the idea of writing Dramas on the stronger passions of the heart, took possession of me strongly.[75]

While seclusion and boredom were engendering Baillie's focus on dramatic passions, her visits to the home of her new-found friend and sister-in-law Sophia were anticipated and frequent. In a note written many years after Sophia's marriage to Matthew (14

---

73. Sophia Denman Baillie (1771–1845), daughter of Dr. Thomas Denman (1733–1815) and Elizabeth Brodie Denman (1746–1833), and sister of Lord chief-justice Thomas Denman (1779–1854) and Margaret Denman Croft (1771–1838), married Joanna's only brother Dr. Matthew Baillie on 5 May 1791; Sophia and Matthew's two children were William Hunter Baillie (1797–1894) and Elizabeth Margaret Baillie Milligan (1794–1876). Another son, James Baillie, was born in 1792 but died an infant (Crainz genealogy table).

74. Discrepancies appear in addresses recorded earlier for Agnes and Joanna after their move from Dr. Baillie's in 1791, and certainly biographers who have stated that Baillie moved to Hampstead immediately after his marriage are incorrect. (Regrettably, relying on these sources for my *Collected Letters*, I also wrongly reported the move to Hampstead in 1791.) A newspaper account, proofread by nephew William Baillie on Joanna's death, correctly states that Joanna, Agnes, and their mother moved to Colchester in 1791, where "they passed some years" (WI MS 5615/37). To add to the misconceptions, Guildhall Pamphlet FO 3155 reports that after their mother's death in 1806 they settled at Bolton House, Windmill Hill, Hampstead, where they remained the rest of their lives. (The historical plaque on the house attests to this.) Letters 11 and 12 to Margaret Holford, however, prove this to be inaccurate: "But it seems to be a season of change–with us, for Agnes & I also are about to quit the house in which we spent 21 years, and my Brother has at last been released from his long attendance at Windsor" (#11, 12 February 1820).

75. WI MS 5613/68/1–6.

November 1844), Baillie assured her of "all the enjoyment" she had relished "so quietly & comfortably" in her society: "Always kind & considerate & affectionate to us! much cause we have to bless God that our lots have been so connected for many years."[76] In his own autobiographical papers, Dr. Matthew Baillie gave the following account of his wife Sophia:

> In the Year 1791 I married Sophia the youngest of the Twin Daughters of Dr Denman,[77] and I have been most fortunate in my Choice___ She has one of the clearest understandings that I have ever known, which has been much cultivated by various reading, a very sweet Tempter, and great sensibility of Heart___ I have now lived with Her for 26 years, and there has never an unkind word pass'[d between us, and indeed I do not know a Fault which She has___ She well deserves this Record, and I give it, with every feeling of Affection and Gratitude___ From this marriage there have been three Children, the eldest James named after my Father, who died when He was a few months old, Elizabeth Margaret, and William Hunter Baillie, who promise by their good principles, and the cultivation of their minds to be a great comfort to both their Parents throughout the remaining part of their lives___ [78]

Sophia Denman had come from a medical family as well, so the life into which she entered with Matthew was familiar. Anecdotes in the Wellcome papers indicate that twins Sophia and Margaret Denman were almost opposites in personality, Sophia being the more serious and dutiful daughter. In fact, every mention of her by Joanna and Matthew confirms her tenderness and devotion to her family. Because Matthew now had a wife to manage his household, Joanna, Agnes, and their mother Dorothea clearly needed a place of their own. But there seems to have been nothing awkward in the necessity of a new location in 1791, for Baillie always considered

---

76. ML 218c; *Letters*, 77.
77. Dr. Thomas Denman (1733–1815), a physician and son of an apothecary, began practicing as a physician at Winchester in 1764. Denman married Elizabeth Brodie (d. 1833) and they had a son, Thomas, and twin daughters; Sophia married Matthew Baillie, and Margaret married Dr. Richard Croft (1762–1818), one of the physicians present when Princess Charlotte gave birth to a still-born child (*DNB*, V:808).
78. Qtd. in Crainz, 28.

Sophia her closest female friend, constantly employed her as a reviewer for new creations, and took seriously her criticism and encouragement. The new location would eventually be Colchester and, near the end of the decade, Hampstead. In 1842 Joanna's nephew William Baillie, ever researching his lineage, wrote his mother Sophia for help in determining the family's earlier addresses. A fragment from her reply of 28 August 1842 concerning his aunt Joanna follows:

> With respect to your Aunt Joanna's places of residence, I can tell you where she lived, but I am sorry to say that I can at present give you no accurate information concerning dates. . . . Upon her Brother's marriage [1791], till then they lived in Windmill Street, her Mother, her Sister & herself went to live at Sunbury, where I think they lived about two years, & then they removed to Hythe, near Sandgate in Kent. I believe they did not remain there quite so long, & then they were recommended by some Friends to go to Maldon in Essex, [letter ends here][79]

Just before the move from her brother's home in London, Joanna Baillie's first published volume had appeared anonymously in 1790. It was called POEMS; *wherein it is attempted to describe* CERTAIN VIEWS OF NATURE *and of* RUSTIC MANNERS; *and also, to point out, in some instances, the different influence which the same circumstances produce on different character* (London: Printed for J. Johnson, St. Paul's Church-Yard) and apparently did not meet with much critical success, though the poems from the volume were later included in her successful *Fugitive Verses* (1840). The collection was composed after at least two failed attempts at drama and after Baillie had finished *Rayner*. In her memoir to William, she explained,

> When it [*Rayner*] was completed I became busy in preparing my miscellaneous verses for the press and afterwards set out to make a visit to my friends in Scotland, where I stayed nearly a year, and there, they, being ignorant of my poetical

---

79. WI MS 5615/104. Sunbury is in Surrey, Sandgate in Kent, and Maldon in Essex as Sophia records. It is exasperating that the last leaf of the letter is missing for confirmation, but it appears that these are the "two or three" places in the country Baillie recalls before their move to Colchester. Thus the sisters could not have possibly have been living in Hampstead as early as 1791.

pretentions, I almost forgot them myself. On my return to London my Brother was married to your Mother, an event which we have all our lives long had good cause to bless.[80]

Away from the country she loved so, Baillie must have found writing a necessary catharsis while she lived in the crowded, dark streets of London. *Poems* was the product of those early days of exile. With its concrete title alone, explains editor Jonathan Wordsworth, the reader is being "told how to read and what to look for—by an author who doesn't even put her name to the book."[81] William Wordsworth and Samuel Taylor Coleridge would follow with a similar explanation for their second edition of *Lyrical Ballads* in 1800. In her last year, editing *The Dramatic and Poetical Works of Joanna Baillie*, Baillie acknowledged the little volume in the preface to the section titled *Fugitive Verses* after the 1840 publication of the same title:

> The early poems that stand first in the arrangement of this book, I now mention last. They are taken from a small volume, published by me anonymously many years ago, but not noticed by the public, or circulated in any considerable degree. Indeed, in the course of after years it became almost forgotten by myself, and the feelings of my mind in a good measure coincided with the neglect it had met with. A review, of those days, had spoken of it encouragingly, and the chief commendation bestowed was, that it contained true unsophisticated representations of nature. This cheered me at the time, and then gradually faded from my thoughts.[82]

---

80. WI MS 5613/68/1–6.
81. Jonathan Wordsworth, "Introduction."
82. See preface to *Fugitive Verses* (London: Moxon, 1840); and *The Dramatic and Poetical Works of Joanna Baillie*, 771. All quotations herein from Baillie's works come from this complete *Dramatic and Poetical Works*, abbreviated afterwards as *DPW*. The original book of *Poems* from 1790 includes the following:
A Winter Day
A Summer Day
Night Scenes of Other Times
"A Reverie"
"A Disappointment"
"A Lamentation"
An Address to the Muses
"A Melancholy Lover's Farewell to His Mistress"

First in the section of *Poems* is *A Winter's Day*, the composition born of the disparity between the dreary city of London and the poet's native Scotland in winter and beginning,

> The cock, warm roosting 'mid his feather'd mates,
> Now Lifts his beak and snuffs the morning air,
> Stretches his neck and claps his heavy wings,
> Gives three hoarse crows, and glad his task is done,
> Low chuckling turns himself upon the roost,
> Then nestles down again into his place.[83]

This poem, explains Jonathan Wordsworth, has its roots in Robert Burns's *Cotter's Saturday night*.[84] Similar images from the pen of Baillie's contemporary William Wordsworth would not follow until 1798, and in this first poem about transitions in the seasons, Baillie acknowledges in nature's sublimity its destructive capabilities which limit both mankind and beast. She does not, however, annoy her reader unnecessarily with her stated purpose; instead, as Jonathan Wordsworth points out, she provides a brief introduction followed by poems complete with natural images and no artificiality. She even manages to offer a series of four lovers, with four different temperaments (melancholy, cheer, pride, and sound-heartedness) mid-way through the volume. While these lovers exhibit passions similar to those which later become a focus of her own plays, the

---

"A Cheerful Tempered Lover's Farewell to His Mistress"
"A Proud Lover's Farewell to His Mistress"
"A Poet, or, Sound-Hearted Lover's Farewell to His Mistress"
"The Storm-Beat Maid"
"Thunder"
"Wind"
An Address to the Night: A Fearful Mind, A Discontented Mind, A Sorrowful Mind, A Joyful Mind
"To Fear"
A Story of Other Times (In Imitation of the Poems of Ossian)
"A Mother to Her Waking Infant"
"A Child to His Sick Grandfather"
"The Horse and His Rider"

83. *DPW*, 772.
84. Jonathan Wordsworth, "Introduction."

poems must have also influenced other poets. For, as Jonathan Wordsworth explains, "It is clear that Baillie's thinking in the Introductory Address was known to Coleridge and Wordsworth as they worked on *Lyrical ballads*, and influenced the wording of the Advertisement," though in 1790 the trend toward "naturalness and simplicity" was less visible than it would be in 1798. Further, he asserts,

> That Wordsworth did borrow from Baillie, we know. Two to three months before the *Prelude* "spots of time" were composed, he had based *There was a boy* on a speech in *De Monfort*. Could he perhaps in 1789-9 have had access to *Poems 1790* as well as the *Series of plays*? It is a curious thought that if he did, he might well not have known that the volumes were by the same writer. Baillie's anonymity was carefully preserved.[85]

In addition to her nature poems, Baillie's first small volume also contains lovers' laments from varying perspectives, poems about families, and *A Story of Other Times* as an imitation of Ossian, whose poems she had read as a child. All in all, her poetical language is simple, her images clear, and her meter usually regular; additionally, poems like "A Disappointment" and "A Lamentation" reveal Baillie's aim at sensibility checked by reality.

Around the late 1790s or shortly before, Baillie met, probably through her aunt Anne Home Hunter, writers Samuel Rogers, Laetitia Barbauld, William Sotheby and others.[86] Samuel Rogers

---

85. Jonathan Wordsworth, "Introduction." Wordsworth certainly could have read Baillie's works, but by her own account, she does not meet the poet personally until 1808.

86. Samuel Rogers (1763-1855) was a banker and well-known art collector who became a highly successful poet in his lifetime. Between 1822-28 he published a collection of verse tales entitled *Italy*.

Anna Laetitia Barbauld (1743-1825) was the only daughter of classicist and nonconformist minister John Aikin and became one of the teachers at the new Dissenting academy in Warrington. In 1774 she married Rochemont Barbauld, also a Nonconformist cleric, who took over a congregation in Palgrave, Suffolk, where Laetitia took charge of a school for young boys. The Barbaulds traveled in Europe for a while and settled

wrote in his journal that Joanna Baillie was "a very pretty woman with a broad Scotch accent" and much admired.[87] Rogers, a banker, had found writing to be his intellectual outlet and in 1781 published several short essays in *The Gentleman's Magazine*. After trying his hand at opera, he found his niche as a poet with his anonymous publication of *An Ode to Superstition, with some other Poems* in 1786; in 1792 Rogers published his best-known work, *The Pleasures of Memory*. In 1802 Samuel's younger brother Henry relieved him of the management of the bank and freed him to follow his literary and societal interests; Rogers remained a central figure in the literary scene of the time. Baillie and Rogers became very close friends, and her letters to him are warm and informal. Significantly, on Baillie's death on 23 February 1851, her nephew William notified Samuel Rogers first.

At this same time Baillie's friend and writer Lucy Aikin revealed that "the first thing which drew upon Joanna the admiring notice of Hampstead society was the devoted assiduity of her attention to her mother, then blind as well as aged, whom she attended day and night."[88] Certainly, Baillie was becoming a part of the London intellectual circle before her first volume of plays appeared in 1798, but she wrote that when her *Poems* appeared in 1790 she knew very

---

in Hampstead where Mr. Barbauld ministered to a congregation and Laetitia took pupils. Mr. Barbauld was never very stable and died insane in 1808. In 1782–86 Laetitia, in conjunction with her brother, wrote *Evenings at Home* for her son and in 1804 edited *The Correspondence of Samuel Richardson* in six volumes and *The British Novelists*, in 50 volumes, in 1810, along with *The Female Speaker* (1811), selections of the best British prose and poetry long used in the education of girls (Janet Todd, ed., *British Women Writers*, [New York: Continuum, 1989], 37–40; *DNB* I:1064-66). Barbauld contributed "On the King's Illness" and "On Returning a Plant after the Bloom was over" to Baillie's *A Collection of Poems, Chiefly Manuscript* in 1823.

William Sotheby (1757–1833) was a prodigious poet, playwright, and translator and the consummate man of letters in the Romantic Era. Though Byron disliked him, satirizing him as Mr. Botherby in *Beppo* (1818), Sotheby provided a societal focal point for many of the brightest literary minds of his time. Baillie, Scott, Wordsworth, Coleridge, and Southey were his friends (*DLB*, XCIII:160–170).

87. Carhart, 13. Carhart argues that Rogers and other literary men and women met Baillie in connection with Mrs. John Hunter in the 1790s. It is to Rogers that Joanna's nephew William sends the first poignant word of her death on 23 February 1851.

88. See Guildhall Library Pamphlet FO 2218, "Joanna Baillie and her Circle, 1790–1850" (London: Camden History Society, 1973). Dorothea Hunter Baillie died on 30 September 1806, not 1808 as Carhart states.

few famous writers and had been touched primarily by the rhymes of Robert Burns:[89]

> When these poems were written, the author was young in years, and still younger in literary knowledge. Of all our eminent poets of modern times, not one was then known. Mr. Hayley and Miss Seward,[90] and a few other cultivated poetical writers, were the poets spoken of in literary circles. Burns, read and appreciated as he deserved by his own countrymen, was known to few readers south of the Tweed, where I then resided. A poet (if I dare so style myself) of a simpler and more homely character, was either, among such contemporaries, placed in a favourable or unfavourable

---

89. Robert Burns (1759-96) was born to tenant farmers and came to know firsthand the ballads, legends, and songs of the Scottish peasantry. An apt pupil, Burns read everything he could, his favorite writers being Sterne, Mackenzie, and Macpherson. Heavy farm labor in his early years instigated the rheumatic heart disease which eventually killed him, but in his short life he contributed some of the most significant Scottish poetry, including, *Poems Chiefly in the Scottish Dialect* (1786), *Tam O'Shanter* (1791), and *Poems* (2 vols., 1793). Using the language of common people, Burns anticipated Wordsworth by nearly 15 years (see Thomas Crawford's *Burns: A Study of the Poems and Songs* [Stanford: Stanford University Press, 1960]). Baillie clearly reveres Burns and mentions him in several letters.

90. Poet William Hayley (1745-1820) entered Trinity Hall, Cambridge, in 1763 where he first published *Ode on the Birth of the Prince of Wales* in the *Cambridge Collection* and reprinted it in *The Gentleman's Magazine*. Taking a degree in 1767, he toured Scotland and produced several poems, his most successful *The Triumphs of Temper*, which ran through 12-14 editions, and his *Triumphs of Music* were ridiculed by Byron in *English Bards and Scotch Reviewers*. Hayley wrote several biographical works, but one of his most reprinted works was his *Essay on Old Maids* (3 vols., 1785). A friend of Cowper and Southey, the latter once said that "Everything about that man is good except his poetry," but his verse was popularly successful; and on the death of Warton, he was offered and declined the laureateship (*DNB*, IX:295-96).

Anna Seward (1747-1809), known as the "Swan of Lichfield," developed literary tastes early. She published a well-received novel entitled *Louisa: a poetical novel* in 1782, which won Hayley's admiration, and various poems afterwards, encouraged by her friend Erasmus Darwin. In 1802 Seward wrote to Scott commending his volumes of *Minstrelsy of the Scottish Border*, and he later included one of her own Scottish ballads ("Rich auld Willie's Farewell") in a section of his *Border Minstrelsy*. When she died in 1809, Seward bequeathed her literary works to Scott who edited and published them in 3 volumes in 1810 (*DNB*, XVIII:1218-20).

> position, as the taste and fashion of the day might direct; and I have, perhaps, no great reason to regret that my vanity was not stirred up at that time to more active exertions.[91]

However, stirred to more active exertions she would soon become, having already composed *Basil* and *De Monfort* in her early twenties. Thus her first attempt at writing plays obviously came before her publication of *Poems* in 1790 when she was twenty-eight and certainly before her move to Hampstead. Encouragement from her brother Matthew was all she needed to reinforce her confidence, for she was devoted to him and respected his criticism, even though his own *Morbid Anatomy* in progress was a medical text rather than a creative one.[92] The move to London and Joanna's ability to see "Mrs Siddons and other good Actors in Theatres" increased her love for drama, and one day, Joanna explained,

> seeing a quantity of white paper lying on the floor which from a circumstance needless to mention had been left there . . . it came into my head that one might write something upon it . . . that the <u>something</u> might be a play. The play was written or rather composed while my fingers were employed in sprigging muslin for an apron and afterwards transferred to the paper, and though my Brother did not much like such a bent given to my mind, he bestowed upon it so much hearty & manly praise, that my favorite propensity was fixed for ever. I was just two & twenty when we first came to London and this took place I believe the following summer about 9 months afterwards.[93]

Further, she had been impressed early as a young girl with theatrical performances in Glasgow and illustrated their imprint on her imagination,

---

91. *DPW*, 772.

92. Dr. Matthew Baillie's famous *The Morbid Anatomy of some of the most important Parts of the Human Body* was first published in 1793 with the atlas following in 1799–1803. Unlike Morgagni's classical treatise on the same topic (1761), Baillie's book on pathological anatomy was less influential because it was entirely descriptive and advanced no concepts. Nevertheless, there were eight British editions, three American, two French, and one each German, Italian, and Russian (Clarke, 379–402).

93. RCS HB.ii.56c; *Letters*, 8.

> I now beheld a lighted up Theatre with fine painted scenes and gay dressed Gentlemen & Ladies acting a story on the stage, like busy agitated people in their own dwellings and my attention was riveted with delight. It very naturally touched upon my old passion for make-believe, and took possession of me entirely. The play was a singing sentimental comedy not very interesting in itself but the after-piece was one of Foott's Farces. . . . I with my young companions went home with our heads full of it; each repeating all the scraps from it she could possibly remember.[94]

This early influence provided Baillie with the imagination she would need when she moved from her native home to the commotion of London. She demonstrated in her memoir to William Baillie that it was a great transition from her unreserved country home in Scotland to those dark, restrictive streets, and the move did little to awaken her imagination. She kept her curiosity alive to see places she had read of and had seen in pictures. And from the British Museum Joanna began to read the dramatic works of French poets Corneille, Racine, Voltaire, and Molière, later adding the plays of Beaumont and Fletcher and older English dramatists.[95] "However," she elucidates, "I did not find much in our old plays to interest me . . . I proceeded in my work, following simply my own notions of real nature, I began to feel imaginary scenes & Theatrical representation."[96] Baillie says that when she was about twenty-seven, however, she occupied her mind at a very singular task:

> I heard a friend of ours, a mathematician, talking one day about squaring the circle as a discovery which had been often attempted but never found out . . . I very simply set my wits to find it out. . . . "But surely" thought I "it will be found in Euclid," so I borrowed from my friend Miss Fordyce, now Lady Bentham,[97] an old copy of Euclid. . . . I

---

94. WI MS 5613/68/1–6; *Letters*, 8.

95. Baillie says that she read from the British Library, but it would have actually been the British Museum; the British Library did not come into existence until 1973 (see British Library website http://www.bl.uk).

96. In this long memoir, Baillie goes on to explain briefly how she came to be inspired for plays she later wrote, most of it quoted herein (WI MS 5613/68/1–6).

97. Lady Bentham, Mary Sophia Fordyce (d 1858), married Sir Samuel Bentham (1757–1831) in 1796 but survived him many years. Sir

> went through it by myself as well as I could, though in no very plodding way, being only intent on this one purpose. . . . But my disappointment & mortification may easily be guessed, when on arriving at the apendix [sic] of the book, in a small collection of particular discoveries. . . I found my own discovery . . . proved in a different manner. "So I have mistaken what is meant by squaring the circle" said I very bitterly to myself, and thus ended my mathematical pursuits. I had by this time written Basil & De Monfort and very soon consoled myself for such a wild goose chace.[98]

"Wild goose chase" or not, this admission reveals Baillie's constant curiosity and willingness to try her hand at different employments, the result of which would prove to be her attraction to all types of writing. Also suggested in this early contest with mathematics is Baillie's methodical mind. Had she been afforded the same education as her brother, she might have proved an equally competent scientist; but without the training for science, mathematics, or medicine, she turned her talents to experimentation with words.

While biographical evidence is somewhat sketchy regarding these early years in the creative development of Joanna Baillie, her own brief autobiographical notes and the comments of contemporaries provide some background for her evolution as a writer. Hers was a creative family, from medical geniuses to renowned writers. Her aunt Anne Hunter published poetry, her sister-in-law Sophia wrote poetry privately, her niece Elizabeth drew beautiful sketches, and even her nephew William tried his hand at poetry.[99] Some of William's children were also writers. That Baillie held a clear vision of what she wanted to become is evident from her early twenties on, long before she was involved in the intellectual life of Hampstead. Many of the events of her childhood in Scotland induced a creative

---

Samuel was a naval architect, engineer, and inventor of mechanical contrivances. He was knighted and later died in 1831, a year before the death of his brother Jeremy Bentham (*DNB*, II:281–84). Children Baillie mentions in her letters include Sarah (180–64) and Mary Sophia (1797–1865).

98. RCS HB.ii.56c; *Letters*, 10. This would have taken place around 1789 while Baillie was still at her brother's house in London.

99. Examples of all these can be found in the Hunter/Baillie papers at both the Royal College of Surgeons and at the Wellcome Institute for the History of Medicine in London.

imagination. But her professional success would not begin until the anonymous publication of *A Series of Plays: in which it is attempted to delineate the stronger passions of the mind, each passion being the subject of a tragedy and a comedy* (1798), as she became a part of London's evolving Romantic spirit.

2

"Like a burnt child": Theatre Theory and The Price of Fame (1791–1805)

According to the sentimental philosophy of Scottish writer Francis Hutcheson,[1] "men and women are not only naturally benevolent but also sociable beings who love nothing better than to convey their discoveries to one another and to create harmony through shared judgements and ideals."[2] Works of imagination by writers who understood the human heart were considered appropriate to aid this developmental process as the Enlightenment constructed a society in which human nature was investigated from philosophical, linguistic, historical, and aesthetic perspectives. As audiences and literary tastes were changing in the late eighteenth century, Joanna Baillie was holding to Hutcheson's creation of harmony through shared judgments. And while she did not yield to the commodification of literature also taking place, she did, in a sense, use a shrewd marketing technique by introducing something just as fresh as the acclaimed *Lyrical Ballads*. Furthering the philosophies of fellow Scots John Locke, David Hume, Adam Smith, and others,[3] Baillie's first important volume of plays focused on

---

1. Philosopher Francis Hutcheson (1694–1746), born into an "ancient and respectable" family from Ayrshire, studied philosophy, classics, literature, and theology for six years at Glasgow and published *Four Essays* anonymously in 1725 and 1728. His *Thoughts on Laughter* (attacking Hobbes) and his *Observations on* [Mandeville's] *Fable of the Bees* were contributed to *Hibernicus's Letters* in 1725–27. One of the first exponents of a decided utilitarianism, Hutcheson was elected to the chair of moral philosophy at Glasgow in 1729, where he spent the remainder of his life. He taught Adam Smith, corresponded with David Hume, and had a great influence on the Scottish philosophers of the "common-sense" school (*DNB*, X:333–34).

2. Qtd. in John Dwyer's "Introduction—A 'Peculiar Blessing': Social Converse in Scotland from Hutcheson to Burns," in *Sociability and Society In Eighteenth-Century Scotland*, ed. John Dwyer and Richard B. Sher (Edinburgh: Mercat Press, 1993), 1, 3.

3. See "Of Modes of Pleasure and Pain" in Locke's *Essay Concerning Human Understanding* (1690); Book 2, Part 2, of Hume's *Treatise of Human Nature* (1739–40); and "Of Sympathy" in Part 1, Section 2, of Smith's *Theory of Moral Sentiments* (1759). These essays are reprinted in Peter Duthie's recent edition of Baillie's *Plays on the Passions* (Ontario: Broadview, 2001).

man's passions—a comedy and a tragedy for each—with those elemental instincts that prompted Shakespeare's characters to action over two hundred years before. Baillie was by her own accounts a performer as a child, and it was natural that she should later become employed in the writing of plays. She had been intrigued by human behavior as a young woman and wrote to Mary Berry that

> Traits of human nature whether in Books or in real life have always had most power in arresting my attention & keeping place in my recollection. This has often made me a watcher of children at play or under any excitement, and a frequenter in early life of the habitations of labouring & country people which happily for me I had many opportunities of doing. I might forget the dialogue in which it was displayed and could not therefore make a truthful anecdote of it, but the trait itself remained perhaps for ever.[4]

She also explained to her nephew William Baillie that having "worked in the dark" for many years, she always let her brother Matthew read what she had written, knowing that he would point out any falsities and affectations; with her permission, Matthew had sent *Basil* to writer Archibald Alison, who gave it "high commendation."[5] This, added to her early propensity for performance and her later friendship with Berry, encouraged her career as a dramatist:

> You will find in a paper now in the possession of Miss Berry that a very homely sordid & whimsical circumstance was my first immediate inducement to write a play. However, as I proceeded in my work, as if I had fallen into an occupation that suited me, all my former imaginary scenes & Theatrical representations returned upon me and a Tragedy was

---

4. RCS HB.ii.56c.
5. WI MS 5613/68/1-6. Archibald Alison (1757-1839) was a writer on "taste" and became minister of the Episcopal chapel, Cowgate, Edinburgh, in 1800, where he remained the rest of his life. Sir Francis Jeffrey gave an admiring exposition of Alison's theories in the *Edinburgh Review* for May 1811. His sermons were much admired, and two volumes published in 1814-15 went through several editions. Alison was married to Dorothea Gregory, daughter of Dr. John Gregory, author of *A Father's Legacy to his Daughters* (*DNB*, I:286-87).

finished at odd times as I could find leisure which had, I believe, some good passages in it, but only deserves to be mentioned as the first step in a path that has led to some degree of distinction. The plot is an American story entirely of my own invention, or rather I should say the scene is laid in America. It has never been published and I hope never will; I have only preserved it as a curiosity.—Rayner, preceded by a first part, was the next I attempted; the first part in the form of a serious comedy I afterwards burnt.[6]

As a result of this early psychological study, Baillie's experimental plan for *A Series of Plays: in which it is attempted to delineate the stronger passions of the mind, each passion being the subject of a tragedy and a comedy* focused less on plot than on human nature which, she hoped, would better enable readers to understand human motivation—or the human heart, as Hutcheson would have said. She explains in her "Introductory Discourse" that

> If man is an object of so much attention to man, engaged in the ordinary occurrences of life, how much more does he excite his curiosity and interest when placed in extraordinary situations of difficulty and distress? . . . To see a human being bearing himself up under such circumstances, or struggling with the terrible apprehensions which such a situation impresses, must be the powerful incentive, that makes us press forward to behold what we shrink from, and wait with trembling expectation for what we dread.[7]

Baillie's intimate scenes with impassioned characters resonate with her awareness of social and psychological behavior, perhaps a result of her early interaction with men of medicine and philosophy.[8] Moreover, Baillie argues for gender equality in roles of the heart and declares that

> I believe there is no man that ever lived, who has behaved in a certain manner on a certain occasion, who has not had

---

6. This is probably a reference to Baillie's "lost play" *Arnold: An American Story*. WI MS 5613/68/1–6 to William Baillie.
7. *DPW*, 2.
8. Dr. William Hunter had been interested in neural links to emotion and Dr. Matthew Baillie in human behavior and the social process.

amongst women some corresponding spirit, who, on the like occasion, and every way similarly circumstanced, would have behaved in the like manner. With some degree of softening and refinement, each class of tragic heroes I have mentioned has its corresponding one amongst the heroines.[9]

Baillie believed, too, in the strength and passion of women, and she herself exemplified the very refinement she discusses, apparently confining her own passions to pen and paper.

In presenting her theater theory, Baillie justifies her systematic outline of the passions in the plays to follow in this and the next two volumes. Her well-defined plan is a virtual scientific experiment which reflects the influence of the scientific community in which she had grown up. Further, Baillie's "Discourse" is "preeminently a theoretical argument for the primacy of drama among literary genres. And in these plays, Andrea Henderson further explains, "The fascination with goods and with external signs of rank yields to the healthy, natural interest in human states of mind. An angry man 'naturally' commands the hushed attention usually reserved for a person of rank with a gaudy equipage."[10] For Baillie's experiment in human behavior to triumph with her audience, of course, there had to be an identification with the characters, a shared moral code, and an ability to see life as performance. Baillie never believed that she achieved this necessary union with the public, especially once her identity was revealed. She later confessed to her nephew William Baillie the sexism that she encountered on finally admitting authorship:

> The first vol of Plays lay for some months at the Booksellers, who had refused to publish them at his own risk and cared very little about its success, without being called for or noticed, notwithstanding a review of them full of the highest & most liberal praise, published in the first Review for reputation in those days, the writer of it being equally ignorant of the Author. . . . None of those literary persons, as far as I know, took any notice of it but Miss Berry, who saw much company at her house and spoke in the highest terms of it to every body. To her zeal in the cause I have always felt

---

9. *DPW*, 9n.
10. Andrea Henderson, "Passion and Fashion in Joanna Baillie's 'Introductory Discourse'." *PMLA* March (1997): 198–213.

> myself to be a debtor. Thus, after a time, it got into circulation, became a subject of conversation in the upper circles, and John Kemble through the medium of my book sellers, asked leave to bring out De Monfort at Drury lane. . . . Thus envigorated, without being intoxicated, I began to write Ethwald . . . so passed away the earlier & brightest part of my career, till the feeble success of de Monfort on the stage, and the discovery of the hitherto conceald [sic] Dramatist being not a man of letters but a private Gentlewoman of no mark or likelihood, turned the tide of publing [public] favour, and then influential critics and Reviewers from all quarters North & South, attacked the intention of the work as delineating in each of the Dramas only one passion, and therefore quite unnatural & absurd. . . . the inferences drawn from their <u>own</u> remarks was all that they deigned to lay before their Readers.[11]

Thus was feminist passion set against masculinist control. By 29 April 1800 a theatrical magazine entitled *The Dramatic Censor; or, Weekly Theatrical Report. Comprising, in the Form of a Journal, A Complete History of the Stage* (No. 18) had reported the author of *De Monfort*, formerly attributed to Anne Home Hunter, to Ann Radcliffe and/or to others, to be "Miss Bailey" [sic].[12] For better or worse, London began to take notice of this new playwright.

One such deliberate observer of Baillie's unfolding career was Hester Thrale Piozzi, who wrote the following letter to Penelope Pennington in May of that year:

> Here's much to do with *Hate* and more with *Love* as Juliet says in Shakespear[e]. A propos to Hatred I am delighted that we know the Author of De Monfort: She must be a fine Creature and will excite no small share of the Hatred She describes.—I *felt* it was a Woman's Writing, No Man makes Female Characters *respectable*—no Man of the present Day I

---

11. WI MS 5613/68/1-6; *Letters*, 11–12. One such attack came from the *Edinburgh Review*'s Francis Jeffery. See William D. Brewer's "Joanna Baillie and Lord Byron," *KSJ* 44 (1995): 165–181; and Ellen Donkin's "Joanna Baillie vs. the Termites Bellicosus," in *Getting Into the Act: Women Playwrights in London, 1776–1829* (London and New York: Routledge, 1994) for details on Byron's help with reviving *De Monfort* and suppositions about Baillie's failure on the stage.

12. RCS HB.ix.27; *Letters*, 89–90.

mean, they only make them lovely; We must except Doctor Moore.[13]

A month later Piozzi followed up with Pennington:

> Miss Bayley [sic], a Lady who lives with Mrs. John Hunter, and is related to her; has at length modestly owned herself Author of a Drama that every one would have been most happy to have written: but Mr. Chappelow (no bad Mirror of the fashionable World,) says People think it too *Solemn*:—they *are not amused. I* say they are like old Polonius, See Hamlet's Character of *him* as a *Critic.*"[14]

Piozzi's prophecy about Baillie's acceptance was astute, for the dramatist would later face the rejection of theater managers and the poison pen of critics. In her *Commonplace Book*, Piozzi later lamented, "What a goose Joanna must have been to reveal her sex and name! Spite and malice have pursued her ever since. . . . She is a Zebra devoured by African Ants—the Termites Bellicosus."[15] Unfortunately, writes Ellen Donkin, Piozzi failed to name the termites. Many years after Baillie's first meeting with Walter Scott in 1806, in a letter to him (1826) regarding her friend Fanny Head's translation of Klopstock's *Messiah*, she herself would disclose that a woman writer's gravest mistake was in revealing her identity:

> She [Miss Head] would fain have kept her name & sex unknown, if her friends would have allowed it, and they were not very wise friends who thwarted her on this point. I speak feelingly on this subject like a burnt child. John <u>any-body</u> would have stood higher with the critics than Joanna Baillie. I too was unwisely thwarted on this point.[16]

---

13. Edward A. Bloom and Lillian D. Bloom, eds., *The Piozzi Letters: Correspondence of Hester Lynch Piozzi, 1784–1821*, 3 vols. (Newark: University of Delaware Press, 1991), 3:192.
14. Bloom and Bloom, 3:198. See *Hamlet*, 2.2. Kemble created an elaborate set for *De Monfort* with representations of a fourteenth-century church; but the incidents were "gloomy, and dark, and deadly," which may have hurt its success. I have not verified that Baillie was ever living with her aunt Anne Hunter, though she was often at her home.
15. Qtd. in Donkin, 165.
16. See NLS letter 3903 ff.131–33 to Scott (13 October 1826); *Letters*, 438–39.

Baillie must have learned from her eighteenth-century female predecessors, for her hypothesis that anonymity, even by the nineteenth century, was the best path for a woman writer was perceptive rather than paranoid. As Catherine Burroughs argues in *Closet Stages*, "British female playwrights were still being regarded as 'culprits' during the late eighteenth and early nineteenth centuries," causing "some of them, in their play prefaces, dedications, and advertisements, to portray themselves as 'anxious' and 'trembling' before the prospect of public representation." At the same time, "many prefaced their plays with language that alluded to—if not directly addressed—the difficulties women encountered when they chose to offer their work up to public scrutiny."[17] In deliberate rather than timid language, Baillie does just that, explaining in her "Discourse" that

> It is natural for a writer, who is about to submit his works to the Public, to feel a strong inclination, by some Preliminary Address, to conciliate the favour of his reader, and dispose him, if possible, to peruse them with a favourable eye. I am well aware, however, that his endeavours are generally fruitless: in his situation our hearts revolt from all appearance of confidence, and we consider his diffidence as hypocrisy. Our own word is frequently taken for what we say of ourselves, but very rarely for what we say of our works.[18]

But writers like Elizabeth Carter and those in her circle were especially eager to read female writers;[19] and, as Jacqueline Pearson states in *Women's Reading in Britain, 1750-1835*, Carter "felt a kind

---

17. Burroughs, *Closet*, 74.
18. *DPW*, 1.
19. Poet, translator, and miscellaneous writer, Elizabeth Carter (1717–1806) was born in Kent to a mother of some means who later lost her fortune in the South Sea stocks and died when Elizabeth was about ten. Her father, a Latin, Greek, and Hebrew scholar, took over her education, and she later learned various modern languages along with those her father taught her. She was interested in astronomy, history, geography, and later became an accomplished musician. Dr. Johnson once said that she "could make a pudding as well as translate Epictetus from the Greek." She began writing verse as a teenager and published *Poems upon particular Occasions* in 1738. She is best known for *All the Works of Epictetus* (~1752) in multiple editions (*DNB*, III:1103–5).

of triumph' when she discovered the author of the admired *Plays on the Passions* was a woman, Joanna Baillie."[20]

However unpopular Baillie might have thought she was before or after the emergence of volume one of *A Series of Plays*, including *Count Basil*, *The Trial*, and *De Monfort* and published anonymously in London in 1798, intellectuals sought her company. Her life was not sheltered as early critics have suggested.[21] Baillie's long-time friend Lucy Aikin remembered her, excepting Mrs. Barbauld, as making "by far the deepest impression" on her when they eventually met:

> I was a young girl when I first met her at Mrs. Barbauld's, to whom she had become known through her residence at Hampstead, her attendance on Mr. B.'s ministry, and her connection with the Denman family. Her genius had shrouded itself under so thick a veil of silent reserve, that its existence seems scarcely to have been even suspected beyond the domestic circle, when the 'Plays on the Passions' burst on the world. The dedication to Dr. Baillie gave a hint in what quarter the author was to be sought; but the person chiefly suspected was the accomplished widow of his uncle John Hunter. Of Joanna no one dreamt, on the occasion.[22]

Why would no one have dreamt of Joanna's being the author of those first plays? She had already published *Poems* in 1790 and had clearly been working on the plays included in these first volumes for several years before she moved to Hampstead in the later 1790s.[23] In her "Introductory Discourse" to *A Series of Plays*, Baillie offers an

---

20. Jacqueline Pearson, *Women's Reading in Britain, 1750–1835: A Dangerous Recreation* (Cambridge: Cambridge University Press, 1999), 141.
21. Such is suggested both in Carhart's biography and P. M. Zall's "The Cool World of Samuel Taylor Coleridge: The Question of Joanna Baillie," *The Wordsworth Circle* 13:1 (1982): 17–20.
22. Le Breton, 7.
23. Baillie, by her own account, moved to the country and then to Colchester with her mother and sister after Dr. Baillie married Sophia Denman in 1791 (WI 5613/68/1-6). The Baillies do not appear in the *Rate Books* (tax records) for Hampstead until early 1799, then listed in the general area of Nag's Head Side (taking in the area of Red Lion Hill). She moves from that address to Holly Bush Hill (probably Bolton House) in 1820 but does *not* live in Bolton House, as reported by historians, for over fifty years.

apology in case she has inadvertently borrowed from another author, for while writing these first plays, she had been,

> situated where I have no library to consult; my reading through the whole of my life has been of a loose, scattered, unmethodical kind, with no determined direction, and I have not been blessed by nature with the advantages of a retentive or accurate memory.[24]

The act of borrowing from previous literary works, of course, had been prevalent from the Renaissance through the eighteenth century. Even yet, explains Laura Rosenthal, "dramatic writing raises particular ambiguities of intertextuality and originality":

> As a commercial genre, theater had since the Renaissance been under some pressure to offer something that the audience had not seen the previous week; still, retelling familiar stories had also been customary and rarely understood as plagiarism.[25]

If Baillie repeated themes from other dramatic works, some were the themes of Shakespeare not original to him, for even he had been accused of copying "from the feminized genre of romance" and certainly from historical chronicles.[26] Baillie, who had grown up reading dramas, could not have avoided their influence on her thought, so her "anxiety of influence" was not without foundation.

"Male geniuses of the Romantic period," argues Rosenthal, "appropriated the feminine position of extreme subjecthood, tendency toward madness, and excessive creativity; the emotional capacity expected of women could potentially signify genius in men."[27] So though she was sometimes subtly imposing, Baillie's unobtrusive nature contributed to her apparent lack of notice in 1798, and as a woman she was not considered to be the genius behind *A Series of Plays*. Laetitia Barbauld confirmed that, even after the publication of and praise given volume one, Baillie "came to Mr. Barbauld's meeting all the while with as innocent a face as if she

---

24. *DPW*, 17.
25. Laura J. Rosenthal, *Playwrights and Plagiarists in Early Modern England: Gender, Authorship, Literary Property* (Ithaca and London: Cornell University Press), 7.
26. Ibid., 36.
27. Ibid., 19.

had never written a line."[28] That she was small, attractive and genteel with a broad Scots accent is documented by her acquaintances and in newspaper accounts such as the one below, written when Baillie was around fifty:

> There is something exceedingly striking in the appearance of Joanna Baillie. Though she is no longer young, and her features have lost the glow and freshness of youth, the rays of beauty still linger about her countenance, and over its expression the tyrant has had no power. Her face is decidedly tragic, not altogether unlike that of Mrs. Siddons—and capable of pourtraying the strongest and deepest emotion. Her air is lofty and reserved; and if there be a dash of hauteur in her manner, amounting, at times, almost to sternness, there is, on the other hand, something delightfully winning in the tone of her deep fine voice. Her eye—I hesitated long before I could decide its hue, and, after all, I am not quite certain whether it be dark blue or hazel—has a most melancholy expression; though time has not quenched its fire, or bent, in the slightest, her erect but attenuated form.[29]

This account of Baillie's "tragic" face is very telling, for she clearly had to feel passion in order to write about it; if tragedy showed in her face, it was because her inner passions were only revealed through her characters, but her poise was fixed. One has only to look at Masquerier's portrait of Baillie in Special Collections at the University of Glasgow to see how splendid she could look, draped in her scarlet shawl. Aikin often observed particularly Baillie's "Scottishness," which she never "Anglicised":

> Whether she and her sister actually took pains to keep up their native dialect, I know not, but it is certain that on their revisiting Glasgow twenty or thirty years after they had first quitted it, their friends were surprised to find them speaking with a broader accent than themselves, by whom the English

---

28. Qtd. from a letter to Mrs. Kenrick in *A Memoir of Mrs. Anna Laetitia Barbauld, with Many of Her Letters* (Ellis, 232).
29. This is an excerpt from the newspaper reprint of *The Living and the Dead*, this copy owned by Dr. Williams's Library in London and reprinted on Joanna's death. She was about fifty years of age when the interview took place. See obituaries in chapter 6.

> pronunciation had long been anxiously cultivated as a genteel accomplishment.[30]

Because the sisters spent so much time in each other's company, it was unlikely they would have ever lost their accents without great effort; and Baillie, fiercely proud of her heritage, was not inclined to work at becoming "English."

Scottish as Joanna Baillie remained, Aikin explained that Baillie was an innate gentlewoman with a genuine dignity, "capable of repelling arrogance, and striking unworthiness with blank awe." Moreover, her intelligence, passion, and sense of humor were ever present, especially in her correspondence. But because she was a woman, albeit intelligent and well bred, and because she was not over confident or pretentious, no one seemed to think of her as an author in 1798. Aikin continued,

> She and her sister—I well remember the scene—arrived on a morning call at Mrs. Barbauld's; my aunt immediately introduced the topic of the anonymous tragedies, and gave utterance to her admiration with that generous delight in the manifestation of kindred genius, which distinguished her. But not even the sudden delight of such praise, so given, could seduce our Scottish damsel into self-betrayal. The faithful sister rushed forward, as we afterwards recollected, to bear the brunt, while the unsuspected author lay snug in the asylum of her taciturnity.[31]

Somewhat reticent in business affairs as well, Baillie allowed her brother Dr. Matthew Baillie to handle some of the details of her early publishing, evident in his 1799 letter to publishers Cadell and Davies:

> Dr Baillie presents his compliments to Mess[rs] Cadell & Davies—The Author of the Series of Plays does not mean to give away any copies of the second Edition, and therefore it will be unnecessary to send her any—If any Person should occur to whom she may think it right to send a copy, she

---

30. Qtd. in Le Breton, 9–10.
31. Ibid., 8. This is also quoted in similar words in Ellis's *A Memoir of Mrs. Anna Laetitia Barbauld*, 230–32.

presumes that Messrs Cadell & Davies will readily permit her to have one, free of expence——
Gt Windmill Street³²

The playwright would later conduct her own business affairs, but at times she still sought the professional advice of friends like Walter Scott and Samuel Rogers.

As a result of Matthew Baillie's negotiations suggested above, the leaf from an account book at the Royal College of Surgeons of England shows that Cadell and Davies printed a combined total of 1,250 copies of the 1798 first edition and the 1799 second edition of *A Series of Plays*. Deducting Baillie's own gift copies, advertising and other expenses, profits amounted to £70 by February 1800 to be divided between publisher and author—a meager sum for such a work.³³ As she became more and more prolific, of course, Baillie did deal with publishers herself, working out the details of contracts, demanding her share of author's copies, and often donating profits to charity. But she seemed always to have found the "business" of publishing distasteful, even though her publisher Thomas Longman was a neighbor and friend.³⁴ And she eventually learned to dislike reviewers even more than publishers. Many reviews of her anonymous first volume were positive, however, as illustrated in a long and detailed essay in the *Critical Review* of September 1798:

> This title impressed us with no favourable prepossession; we were inclined to smile at a plan so methodical and so arduous. The preface, however, gave us a better opinion of

---

32. Written at the bottom of the leaf in another hand is the following note: "Ans^d the 22^d that C. & D. would with Pleasure furnish the Author with as many Copies for Presents as she would do them the Favour to accept" (UG Ms Gen 542/21; *Letters*, 89).

33. RSC HB.ix.1. Volume one also appeared in 3 more editions: 1800, 1802 and 1806 (5 editions in all).

34. Thomas Norton Longman (1771–1842) also published such authors as Wordsworth, Coleridge, and Sir Walter Scott, carrying on the publishing tradition of Thomas Longman (1699–1755), who founded the firm which still exists today. After the collapse of Archibald Constable in 1826, the firm became the sole proprietors of the *Edinburgh Review*, of which they had previously owned one half; but by this time the firm had become Longman, Hurst, Rees, Orme, Brown, & Green. Thomas Longman died at Hampstead on 29 August 1842 (*OCEL*, 585). (See OU Lovelace/Byron Collection 93, ff.229–230, letter to Mary Montgomery dated 9 September 1842).

the author, whose good sense and modesty it strongly exhibits; we perused the volume with attention and delight; and it is with sincere pleasure that we announce this commencement of a work which, we trust, will not only be honourable to the writer, but to the literature of our country.[35]

Having discussed each of the three plays, the reviewer concludes that the plays "form only a small part of the projected plan; but they are sufficient to prove that the design is excellent, and that the author is equal to the task of properly executing it." In turn, the reviewer suggests that the writer study the versification of Shakespeare and others from his period so that "*He* may soon versify with their facility," for "*he* has already avoided the faults of our modern theatrical authors" (my emphasis). Ironically, Baillie's plays were clearly *good* enough to be considered by many the work of a man.

It is difficult to determine whether or not Baillie thought she could overcome her lack of practical stage experience as she wrote her plays. It is clear, however, that she wrote these dramas to be acted and desired more to arouse spectators than to enthuse readers, for she states consistently in her letters that these were to be "acting plays." Baillie advocated the airing of her psychological dramas on a small, intimate stage, but that should not be confused with the "closet." Because she mixes prose and blank verse in the style of Shakespeare, her plays may not have been considered contemporary enough for the London theater managers, even though Shakespeare was by now *the* acknowledged national poet. However, as Michael Booth explains, the early 1800s also "announced to the new century a new direction in theatre," as melodrama, spectacle, and gothic darkness "marked a strong romanticism."[36] In light of this modern trend, Baillie also introduced gothic and Romantic themes, provided strong roles for heroines, and represented the private traumas of real people. In fact, Baillie was at her best when at her most experimental. Perhaps theater managers

---

35. "*A Series of Plays*, etc." *The Critical Review; or Annals of Literature* 24 (1798): 13–22. There is a similar manuscript in the RCS (HB.ix.4) written for the *Monthly Review*, September 1798.

36. Michael R. Booth, "Nineteenth-Century Theatre," in *The Oxford Illustrated History of the Theatre*, ed. John Russell Brown (Oxford and New York: Oxford University Press, 2001), 299–300.

as well as theater goers were not ready for such private interiority which exposed human passions and their consequent diseases.³⁷

Volume one of *A Series of Plays* begins with Baillie's first play on the passion of love, *Count Basil: A Tragedy*, set in Mantua and its environs in the sixteenth century, "*when* CHARLES *the Fifth defeated* FRANCIS *the First, at the battle of* Pavia."³⁸ Baillie credited the moralistic plays of French dramatist Louis-Sebastien Mercier³⁹ for some inspiration and explained to her nephew that

> Perhaps having read, so long before, Mercier's Plays, a copy of which Professor Millar had kindly brought me from Paris, had something to do with rousing my natural propensity, but I can scarcely venture to say so. The good sense & feeling of his Pieces, free from the exaggerations that had so often offended me in other Dramatic works, pleased me very much. I then with some envigourating hope that it would not be in vain, began that arduous task which has been so much praised & censured during a long course of years. In writing Basil I took great pains with particular passages, composing them often several times over. . . . De Monfort was written more rapidly and with more interruption from visitors.⁴⁰

One of several plays Baillie wrote about the military, *Basil* presents a character who, when removed from the arena of battle,

---

37. See Mary Yudin's discussion of such "interiority" in "Joanna Baillie's Introductory Discourse as a Precursor to Wordsworth's Preface to Lyrical Ballads," *Compar(a)ison: An International Journal of Comparative Literature* 1 (1994): 101–12.

38. *DPW*, 18.

39. Louis-Sebastien Mercier (1740–1814) was a French dramatist and exponent of the *drame bourgeois* popularized by Diderot. His plays, in which he gives elaborate directions for scenery, were more popular outside France than in because of their unimpeachable morality and declamatory style. His works include *La Brouette du Vinaigrier* (1784), and he earlier adapted Lillo's *The London Merchant* as *Jenneval* (1768), allowing the hero to escape punishment by a last minute conversion (Phyllis Hartnoll, ed., *The Oxford Companion to the Theatre*, 4th ed. [Oxford: Oxford University Press, 1983], 542).

40. WI MS 5613/68/1–6.

finds it difficult to perform as something other than a soldier. Furthermore, argues Catherine Burroughs, "the male bonding of military culture in *Basil* casts the performance of 'the feminine' as an impediment to warrior might."[41] Basil can react to comrade soldiers in the public sphere but finds it difficult to "perform" in Victoria's domestic sphere, though he loves her passionately. The self-absorbed Victoria, however, is simply her father's unsuspecting decoy for keeping Basil in Mantua, and the audience become sort of co-conspirators eavesdropping on the scheme. The two processions which begin the play separate the male and female characters from the onset—while Basil and his soldiers march toward battle, Victoria leads a group of women to the shrine of St. Francis. In this play about love, pride, and consequent discord, its subplot driven by deception in Mantua's court, the protagonist, unable to resolve the conflict between his passion for Victoria and his duty to his soldiers, dallies too long in her court while the troops of his comrade Pescara defeat the French without his aid. While Victoria admits that she has "fool'd a noble heart," Basil, unable to live with his disgrace, ultimately fires a pistol into his head and speaks final words to his friend Rosinberg:

> I feel my weakness now, I own my pride.
> Give me thy hand, my time is near the close;
> Do this for me: thou knowst my love, Victoria—[42]

One wants to add Horatio's "Now cracks a noble heart"[43] to this mournful scene for which both Victoria and Basil are responsible—Victoria for her selfishness and masquerade and Basil for his inability to reconcile duty with passion.[44] While Rosinberg, as Burroughs argues, reveals his misogyny and his personal investment, he implies that love for a woman weakens a military leader.[45] Rosinberg's insinuation that women "weaken" men in general recalls Francis Bacon's "Of Marriage and Single Life" (1612),

---

41. Burroughs, *Closet*, 131–32.
42. *DPW*, 46.
43. Horatio on Hamlet's death in William Shakespeare's *Hamlet*, in *The Riverside Shakespeare*, ed. G. Blakemore Evans (Boston: Houghton Mifflin, 1974), 5.2.358.
44. See Deirdre Gilbert's important work entitled "Joanna Baillie, Passionate Anatomist: From Masquerade to Gothic" (Ph.D. diss., University of Denver, forthcoming 2002).
45 Burroughs, *Closet*, 134.

as Basil proves his theory that married men, or men in love in this case, are unlikely to be heroes. Basil cannot reconcile his military and personal arenas; but Victoria suffers too, declaring on Basil's death that "Cold as his grave shall be my earthly bed."[46] Baillie, however, salvages women's reason in the character of Countess Albini, who tries to guide Victoria rather than criticize her. In general, Baillie's principal female characters are practical, yet they have emotional depth and are often skeptical of marriage; and they often suffer "defeat" in some personal arena.

Baillie has little to say about *Basil* in her letters, writing only to Margaret Holford in 1826 that she is flattered by Arch Deacon Wrangham's reading *Basil* so often and wanting to meet her. And she has only a note in the third edition of the play which addresses her composition and editing:

> My first idea when I wrote this play was to represent Basil as having seen Victoria for the first time in the procession, that I might show more perfectly the passion from its first beginning, and also its sudden power over the mind; but I was induced, from the criticism of one whose judgment I very much respect, to alter it, and represent him as having formerly seen and loved her. The first Review that took notice of this work objected to Basil's having seen her before as a defect; and, as we are all easily determined to follow our own opinion, I have upon after-consideration, given the play in this edition [third], as far as this is concerned, exactly in its original state.[47]

This note on her revision process reveals Baillie's early anxiety about her writing and her concern that other critical opinions might be more sound than her own; however, by her own account she had written both *Basil* and *De Monfort* before she was twenty-seven, and she always sought out friendly critics. Although she does not identify the initial reader who proposed the change alluded to above, since the revision would have taken place before 1798 when she wanted to remain anonymous, it was probably her brother Matthew, her sister-in-law Sophia, her sister Agnes, or even their aunt Anne Hunter. When Baillie was almost seventy, she praised especially her

---

46. *DPW*, 48.
47. Ibid., 22.

sister's enthusiasm for her work in "Lines To Agnes Baillie On Her Birthday":[48]

> 'Twas thou who woo'dst me first to look
> Upon the page of printed book,
> That thing by me abhorr'd, and with address
> Didst win me from my thoughtless idleness,
> When all too old become with bootless haste
> In fitful sports the precious time to waste.
> Thy love of tale and story was the stroke
> At which my dormant fancy first awoke,
> And ghosts and witches in my busy brain
> Arose in sombre show, a motley train.
> This new-found path attempting, proud was I,
> Lurking approval on thy face to spy,
> Or hear thee say, as grew thy roused attention,
> "What! is this story all thine own invention?"

Although Baillie continued to seek critical insight from other readers, her confidence grew with experience, and she was in later years less inclined to edit her work because of them.

Many critics have implied that Baillie's lack of "real" theater experience may have diminished the performance potential of her plays. However, her use of spectacle in plays like *Basil*, *The Trial*, *De Monfort*, *The Family Legend*, *Romiero*, *Henriquez*, and many others, along with her specific and often detailed stage directions and notes, demonstrate just the opposite. While she may not have been trained as an actor, she knew people in the theater, attended performances of plays, and read drama all of her life. As the later performance success of her *Family Legend* proves, consistent support from theater managers and directors may have made her professional life a very different story.

Following the tragedy *Basil* as a bit of comic relief is Baillie's second play on love, *The Trial: A Comedy* (*Tryal* in the first edition) set in Bath "*and in* MR. WITHRINGTON's *house in the environs of* Bath."[49] Burroughs explains that the "theater of the closet, though not exclusive to women, was particularly friendly to women's creative endeavors, and it is this theatrical context that Joanna

---

48. Excerpt from "Lines To Agnes Baillie On Her Birthday" in "Miscellaneous Poems" of *Fugitive Verses* (*DPW*, 811).
49. *DPW*, 49.

Baillie's earliest comedy, *The Tryal* (1798), explores," along with her other plays, "contributing to the eighteenth-century trend to focus on domestic space in order to celebrate women's cultural worth."[50] In the eighteenth century, however, the "closet" was defined as an individual's private space; and used in the context of nineteenth-century theater, it becomes a confining, or conceivably nebulous, term. Baillie explained that her plays dealt with passions that men and women might only reveal in their closets, their private spaces; but she did not mean to confine her dramatization of those passions to the private space. Instead, she aimed to reveal them on the public stage in order to exhibit what diseases might erupt from passions gone awry.

In *The Trial*, in order to assert some degree of control over her domestic life, heiress Agnes Withrington devises a plot through which to reveal the motives of several men who want to marry her. Here characters "act out acting"; in the end their performance is successful. Through a series of masquerades, the heroine, a playful, independent young woman, finally gets Harwood—devoted, sensitive and clearly the man for her. Agnes's patriarchal and somewhat cynical Uncle Withrington is in on her plot, but he exemplifies the very type of man that a "modern" woman should not marry. As Deirdre Gilbert explains in her forthcoming dissertation, this play also exemplifies Baillie's penchant for spectacle; and her choice of Bath as the setting, with its ever changing population, welcomes the intrigue and deception that will ensue.[51] Agnes's masquerade as a young woman of no fortune shows her determination to find a man who loves her for what she is. Keeping her identity a secret—or "masked" as Gilbert points out—makes Agnes much like Baillie on the anonymous publication of her first volume of *A Series of Plays*, and many have speculated that the author's "unmasking" was her undoing.

Baillie does not discuss *The Trial* in her letters, but her contention that "Our desire to know what men are in the closet as well as in the field, by the blazing hearth and at the social board as well as in the council and the throne" emphasizes in the "Discourse" exactly what Agnes wants to discover.[52] Agnes argues to her uncle,

---

50. Burroughs, *Closet*, 144–43.
51. In her seminal work, Gilbert also compares this play to Hannah Cowley's *The Belle's Stratagem* (produced often after 1780), a play Baillie was very likely to have read and seen.
52. *DPW*, 5.

"For if I am to marry at all, I am resolved to have a respectable man, and a man who is attached to me; and to find out such an one in my present situation is impossible."[53] In this comedy, while Agnes does get her man in the end, the serious note is that she is now placed between two patriarchal figures—her uncle and her future husband. Baillie's affinity for comedy, even with its serious moments, however, reveals something further about the playwright's unconventional nature. Comedy requires a certain amount of "unladylike" scheming, aggression, disruption, and exhibition, traits prevalent but "masked," as Gilbert explains, in Baillie's personality. Following this comedy based on trust and truth, however, is a more serious and more famous drama.

Volume one of *A Series of Plays* closes with probably Baillie's most enduring play, *De Monfort: A Tragedy*, set in "*a town in Germany.*"[54] This play on hatred and revenge was just suited to the impassioned acting styles of Kemble and Siddons and,[55] along with Baillie's *Family Legend*, was the most performed of her plays.[56] In a review of the 29 April 1800 performance at Drury Lane, *The Dramatic Censor* reported as follows:

---

53. Ibid., 49.
54. Ibid., 76.
55. John Philip Kemble (1757–1823), one of England's most famous actors, began playing parts in his father's company in early childhood. His sister, Sarah Kemble Siddons, first recommended him to the Chamberlain's company as Theodosius in Lee's tragedy in 1776, with dozens of parts to follow. Kemble was a scholar, a man of breeding and a fine actor with a larger range of characters in which he excelled than any English tragedian. He wrote prologues for charitable institutions in York and Leeds, where he appeared for the first time in *Hamlet*-he is said to have written out the part over forty times. He managed the Edinburgh Theater for a while in 1781, and his first appearance in London was at Drury Lane as Hamlet in 1783. He remained at Drury Lane for nineteen years, presenting over 120 characters himself; on 29 April 1800, Kemble played De Monfort in Baillie's play. In 1802 he acquired a share of Covent Garden, but in 1808 when the house burned, taking twenty lives, Kemble and other investors were nearly ruined for lack of insurance. A loan of £10,000 from Lord Percy helped him reopen the new Covent Garden. Portraits of John Kemble abound, several of which are by Sir Thomas Lawrence, notably Kemble as Cato, as Hamlet, and as Rolla (*DNB*, X:1260–66). See note 57 on Sarah Siddons in chapter 1.
56. *De Monfort* was first performed in 1800 at Drury Lane. Later performances of this and *The Family Legend* are listed in the "Chronology" and are also addressed in the following two chapters.

> The literary reader scarcely need to be informed that the *printed* Tragedy, on which Mr. Kemble has employed his practical skill in scenic representation, is one of a series of Plays, illustrative of the passions, published without the name of the author, but tacitly acknowledged to be the production of a female writer, and generally attributed to the pen of Mrs. Hunter, the widow of the late celebrated anatomist. This report has recently been contradicted, and the Play in question is now referred to Miss Bailey [sic], sister to the physician of that name. . . . Hence it appears, that to appreciate the merits of the new Tragedy, as a dramatic composition . . . it is essentially necessary to compare the Play, as now *acted* (with Mr Kemble's alterations) at Drury-Lane, with the original, as *written* by Miss Bailey.[57]

By the next evening, 30 April 1800, the scene "which ushered in the fourth act" had been cut, and the critic for the *Dramatic Censor* argued that the play was still too long, suggesting that the part of Conrad be omitted entirely.[58] From the first evening's performance to a crowded house, the audience declined substantially by 9 May 1800, when the critic ultimately declared that the fault was in Baillie's text rather than in direction and performance.

It is doubtful that Kemble would have tampered with the play of a living established male dramatist as he did with Baillie's, but he was clearly the master actor in Sheridan's company and felt no compunction at editing her play. In 1800 Sheridan's Drury Lane Theatre, which would be rebuilt after a great fire in 1809, boasted a large-scale stage and ample audience seating formed on a semicircular plan. The theater contained a pit, eight boxes on each side of the pit, two rows of boxes above them, and two galleries which commanded a full view of the entire stage. On each side of the galleries were two more rows of boxes, and the proscenium was fitted up with boxes but lacked any stage door or the usual large

---

57. From *The Dramatic Censor; or, Weekly Theatrical Report. Comprising, in the Form of a Journal, A Complete History of the Stage* (No. 18) owned by the Royal College of Surgeons of England (HB.ix.27). I know of no extant copy of Kembel's edited version.

58. See Duthie's Appendix E, 455. Duthie also includes a substantial list of contemporary reviews.

columns.[59] Sheridan's company, rich in talent from the days of David Garrick, included two of the greatest actors in England. John Kemble was considered no less than majestic in most of his roles, with his husky voice and clear articulation; and his face and form were reportedly a painter's ideal. His sister Sarah Kemble Siddons was equally energetic, graceful and self-possessed. She was totally comfortable on stage, vocalizing rhymed couplets as naturally as prose. The relationship between Baillie and Siddons, however, developed very slowly, for as late as 1819 Baillie wrote to Sophia Scott Lockhart:

> I dont dislike the elder M[rs] Siddon[s] in her way, I ought rather to say I am beginning to like her; and I flatter myself that she is beginning to like me, for she has invited me very kindly to see her which I have done, and I am this very day employed in sewing some tatting (do you know what tatting is?) upon a handkerchief which she made me a present of very lately, the work of her own Queenly fingers, and it is the most beautiful tatting I ever saw.[60]

Later Baillie would write her poem "To Mrs. Siddons," beginning,

> Gifted of heaven! who hast, in days gone by,
> Moved every heart, delighted every eye;
> While age and youth, of high and low degree,
> In sympathy were join'd, beholding thee,
> As in the Drama's ever changing scene,
> Thou heldst thy splendid state, our tragic queen!
> No barriers there thy fair domains confined,
> Thy sovereign sway was o'er the human mind;
> And, in the triumph of that witching hour,
> Thy lofty bearing well became thy power.[61]

In addition to her stage presence, biographers of Siddons have noted that whereas most actresses of the period were indifferent to their stage dress, Siddons was indifferent about very little, especially in performance of gender. She generally shunned male parts which

---

59. See A. M. Nagler, *A Source Book in Theatrical History* (New York: Dover, 1952), 408–11.
60. NLS 1551 f.229–30; *Letters*, 821.
61. "To Mrs. Siddons," *DPW*, 829.

required cross-dressing, but she did play Hamlet frequently and successfully; and the power of her acting was sometimes considered "masculine" in roles of either gender. Masculine attire, however, was not without complication for Siddons, and she often refused the "usual breeches costume in favor of more modest apparel."[62] Furthermore, her stage dress for female roles always combined originality and beauty, and Siddons's stage presence as Jane De Monfort reportedly met Kemble's role both in intensity and sublimity.

However *De Monfort* may have been altered by Kemble and Siddons, from its opening act there is mystery surrounding De Monfort—why he has left his sister Jane, why his personality has changed, and why he is perpetually gloomy. He is a haunted hero, pre-Byronic with his festering soul. His hatred for Rezenvelt completely clouds his reason after he sees Rezenvelt take the hand of his sister Jane De Monfort:

> Hell's direst torment seize the infernal villain!
> Detested of my soul! I will have vengeance!
> I'll crush thy swelling pride—I'll still thy vaunting—
> I'll do a deed of blood![63]

This Gothic play contains "Radcliffean" elements and an over-romanticized implication that the protagonist dies of grief after he murders Rezenvelt.[64] The tragic ending with Freberg's Fortinbras-like speech reminds one of *Hamlet*; but unlike a Shakespeare play, *De Monfort* shifts from event to passion. Jeffrey Cox and Catherine Burroughs point out that even though the play is titled *De Monfort* the title should not "compel readers to focus solely on the way in which the dramaturgy moves the male sibling of the De Monfort family through the culture of the play"; for Jane De Monfort "also wrests from De Monfort's murder of Rezenvelt an interpretation that

---

62. See discussion of Mrs. Siddons in Laura J. Rosenthal's "The Sublime, the Beautiful, 'The Siddons'," in *The Clothes That Wear Us: Essays on Dressing and Transgressing in Eighteenth-Century Culture*, ed. Jessica Munns and Penny Richards (Newark: University of Delaware Press, 1999), 56–79.

63. *DPW*, 94.

64. However, Aloma Noble argues that because "over 135 Gothic plays, of which ten are by Joanna Baillie, were written and produced in England between 1768 and 1810" the success of *De Monfort* was almost certain (131).

maintains the illusion of his heroic stature" and continues to distinguish him from more common criminals. Additionally, Jane is the "epitome of perfect womanhood by the standards of late-eighteenth-century middle-class London society, the character . . . written to be performed in the world of the play with a carefully controlled gesture and speech."[65] It is difficult to imagine that Sarah Siddons's performance as Jane in 1800 was overshadowed by Kemble's because it was not her style to be a subordinate on the stage. Nevertheless, what makes Jane De Monfort engaging is that her quiet strength is the antithesis of her brother's frenzy, of his "homoerotically charged hatred," as Burroughs contends. A few years later, after having no success in getting *De Monfort* reenacted in London, Baillie wrote to Scott, "I never was better pleased than upon hearing that De Monfort was acted at a country fair, in a great waggon along side of the wild beasts"[66]—that reception far more pleasing to Baillie than what was ultimately afforded at Drury Lane. Moreover, this country representation attests to the play's reception as part of the popular culture.

After *De Monfort*'s initial success with Mrs. Siddons in April 1800, the actress reportedly visited Baillie and asked her to write more plays with strong female parts like Jane De Monfort's,[67] for Jane is arguably the real protagonist in this drama. In *Getting Into the Act*, Ellen Donkin suggests that Baillie then began *Constantine Paleologus* in response to Siddons, who also assured her of support from her brother John Kemble. Baillie reportedly wrote to Kemble in October of 1801 that the play was ready for his perusal but that it still needed revision, and she suggested he not present it to manager Richard Brinsley Sheridan if he felt it was not ready. Baillie went on to write her friend Anne Millar in December about her strategy and about the surprising response from Kemble:

> Last spring in reading Gibbon's history of the Siege of Constantinople by Mahomet the 2^d I was very much pleased with the character of Constantine the last of the Greecian [sic] or Roman Emperors, and the noble stand that he made with his generous band of volunteers against the power of the Turks. The subject I found haunted my mind and I

---

65. Burroughs, *Closet*, 119.
66. NLS 3879 ff.266–69 (dated 28 November 1810); *Letters*, 275.
67. This is reported in Carhart (119), but I have found no other evidence.

determined to write upon it. This being the case, I thought I had better offer it to Drury lane; and therefore before I began to write I sent a letter to Mrs Siddons, telling her what I had in my thoughts, and wishing that a place might be kept for bringing out my play the following spring, if the Proprietors of the Theatre should approve of it. I received from her a flattering letter, encouraging me to proceed, and assuring me of the friendly dispositions of herself & Mr Kemble. Shortly after this I was informed by my friend Miss Berry that Mr Kemble was very eager in the business wishing, me to begin immediately, and expressing himself very warmly. Not many days after this I met Mr Kemble at Miss Berry's, the only time in my life that I have ever met him, and still he express'd a desire that I should begin to write immediately. So encouraged I began to write my Play, which took me seven weeks of writing the first rough copy, and layd it by me till the end of harvest; when I wrote to Mr K., telling him what I had done, and saying, I should be glad to have as long time allowed me as possible before I should put the piece into his hands: he wrote to me in answer, expressing himself very much pleased at what I had inform'd him of, and fix'd the beginning of december for sending it to him, and accordingly by that time I copied it out fair & sent it to him. Along with the manuscript I sent him a letter saying that I was not at all sanguine in regard to the play, nor anxious to have it brought out . . . that if he & Mrs Siddons did not like the parts I had written for them, not to present it to the Proprietors at all, and if this should be the case, I gave him my word it should not discourage me from attempting to do something better for them another time. . . . After all this, Mr Kemble, about a week ago, returned my manuscript with a short stiff letter; entering into no particulars of any kind, but just saying, he doubted of the success of the piece, and taking no notice at all of the last part of my letter. I was very much disposed before hand to think that my play would not be accepted of, but I must confess to you that I had not the least idea of the business ending in this manner, and that I have been hurt by it. That Kemble should not like my Play is not at all surprising, but that he should signify his opinion in this manner, after all that has passed between us, is to me perfectly unaccountable. It is so much so that I dont venture even to form any conjectures in regard to it. I have for a long time heard from so many different quarters that Mr Sheridan (for you guess very right) is unfriendly to me, that I cant help giving credit to it, but in the present case it does not appear that he has had any thing to do with it. . . . There is just one thing of which I am assured, that my connexion with Drury Lane Theatre is for ever at an end.[68]

Kemble's response to Baillie is inexplicable and must have been a result of the gender politics frequently practiced by Sheridan. Furthermore, while Kemble may have simply not liked the script, explains Donkin, his rejection seems to be a "categorical rejection, rather than a rejection of a specific play." Kemble did what he was told by Sheridan in the matter of play selection, evidenced, says Donkin, in Frances Burney's bad experience with *Edwy and Elgiva*. Sheridan could have rejected Baillie for other reasons, but he shared Baillie's proto-liberal Whig sympathies and had held various ministerial offices as a proponent of Whig leader Charles James Fox.[69] Furthermore, because *De Monfort* was a successful first attempt, Baillie should have received more support from London theaters than she did. But in her "Introductory Discourse" she had been critical of contemporary comedy, and Sheridan, certainly the foremost contemporary English playwright of the time, was probably offended. The fact that the play opened with the author still unidentified, with Baillie's identity revealed on the second night of performance, may explain why that play was not vetoed in the first place. In addition, the box receipts dropped from £308 on opening night to £273, £239, and £166 on subsequent nights.[70] Looking forward to the difficulty Byron would have in getting Baillie revived at Drury Lane in 1815, however, one has to suspect that Sheridan undermined her efforts at representation and/or that once theatergoers realized this was an unknown playwright, and a woman at that, they were not inclined to support her.

In his "Introduction" to the recent edition of Baillie's *Poems* (1790), editor Jonathan Wordsworth also speculates on why her

---

68. See Baillie's 25 December 1801 letter to friend Anne Millar, NLS 9236 ff.3–7 and *Letters*, 1105, for an account of this; I have not found the original correspondence with Kemble that is identified by Donkin.

69. After losing his seat in the House of Commons, Sheridan could be arrested for debt and was actually imprisoned for brief periods. He died in 1816.

70. Donkin, 164–69.

plays might not have achieved the fame they could have at another time:

> Baillie, like the Wordsworth of *Lyrical ballads*, is funny, sad, tender, affectionate, capable of many moods of "passion genuine and true to nature." As a playwright she achieved a very high reputation among her contemporaries. Looking back, though, it seems a pity that such a good writer should have turned to drama in a period when no one quite pulled it off. She had it in her to be a poet of real stature.[71]

But unlike Wordsworth, argues William Brewer, the "Introductory Discourse" to Baillie's plays avoided a "masculinist focus on the introspective process of an individual poet" and attempted to connect with rather than isolate the poet from the mind of her audience.[72] While Jonathan Wordsworth implies that Baillie might have been "safer" with poetry, a less public form of writing, than with drama, the reality is that no Romantic playwrights were thriving in the theater, Wordsworth and Coleridge included. Baillie's plays often exhibit a rhetoric of pathos much like Wordsworth's in *The Borderers*, a blank-verse play which explored the darkest aspects of the human psyche and was also written in the style of Shakespeare just as many of Baillie's plays. But it, too, met with little success.

Nevertheless, volume two, now bearing the author's name, followed volume one in 1802 and contained *The Election*, *Ethwald* (Parts 1 and 2), and *The Second Marriage*.[73] Volume two, argues Deirdre Gilbert, moves from Baillie's former emphasis on masquerade to much darker issues. At the time of the second volume's appearance, a reviewer for the *British Critic* wrote that "Miss J. Baillie, even if her pen were now to be inactive, which is not likely, would be always celebrated among the brightest luminaries of the present period."[74] Furthermore, a later *Imperial Review* of March 1804 admitted, condescendingly, that Baillie was in fact under scrutiny because of her gender, while he praised her "native

---

71. Jonathan Wordsworth, "Introduction."
72. See William D. Brewer's "The Prefaces of Joanna Baillie and William Wordsworth," *Friend: Comment on Romanticism* 1.2-3 (1991-92): 34-47.
73. Many of the plays contained in the three-volume work were also published as single edition copies both in England and America.
74. Qtd. in Henderson, 198.

strength, which, without the usual aids, could soar to so lofty an elevation":

> The sex of the author is a consideration which must enhance our estimate of the measure and the force of her genius. A female writer has many impediments to surmount before she can rise to a given height in literature. These should be allowed to bespeak for her an equal share of encouraging partiality with an author of the other sex, whose circumstances had precluded him from the benefit of early instruction. . . . these advantages a female must fabricate for herself.[75]

And the *Critical Review* again applauded her effort, but this time the reviewer seemed to discern an impending gloom:

> The first volume of this work appeared with an unpromising title—for all plays are designed to delineate some passion; it came anonymously into the world; and the author was not even suspected. But these circumstances were all favourable to a work of such great and original merit; the reader was pleased; and the more so, because he had not been taught to expect pleasure; and anonymous writers, like the dead, are praised more willingly, than those who, by displaying their own powers, offend the inferiority of their contemporaries. This volume, we fear, will be taken up, by the generality of readers, rather with an expectation than a disposition to be pleased.[76]

The reviewer concludes, however, even after revealing the faults of the volume, that

> Miss Baillie's dramatic powers are of the highest order. With the miserable stage-writers of the day, it would be insult to compare her; nor is it much commendation to rank her above

---

75. Qtd. in Duthie, 439–40.
76. "*A Series of Plays*, etc.," *The Critical Review* 37 (1803): 200–12. See also Marjean Purinton's "The Sexual Politics of *The Election*: French Feminism and the Scottish Playwright Joanna Baillie," *Intertexts* 2.2 (1998): 119–30.

Young, and Rowe, and Southerne. . . . She has a near approach to Shak[e]speare.

With the second volume's dedication to her brother Matthew, Baillie added a new "Preface" and thanked her readers for their kind reception of volume one, explaining that she was "perfectly sensible, that from the length of these tragedies, and, perhaps, some other defects, they are not altogether adapted to the stage," with the exception of both parts of *Ethwald*, which might indeed be turned into an "acting play."[77] Even as Baillie apologizes for her plays' defects for performance, through *The Election*'s Charles Baltimore she hints at her own commitment to live performance as he tells Isabella that no story read can ever compare to a story "told by a pair of moving lips." Baillie's disappointment at getting her plays on stage is apparent in dozens of her letters, and while many early critics have analyzed her as retiring and private, she was instead strong-willed, ambitious, and public during her most prolific period. If in later years she became less so, it was a result of her being disappointed so many times by theater managers, audiences, and critics.

The Election: A Comedy, In Five Acts, is based on hatred and a companion to the tragedy *De Monfort*. The main characters struggle with issues of class distinction and prejudice during an election for parliamentary representation for the borough of Westown. A declared Whig herself and always interested in politics, Baillie gives form to a Tory candidate in Baltimore, an aristocrat whose fortune has fallen into decay and who hates the ostentatious Freeman, a Whiggish candidate and wealthy middle-class merchant. Neither candidate is particularly admirable as Baillie outlines both their faults, but Baltimore is the less tolerant of the two. The resolution in Act 5 is somewhat problematic when the two men settle their differences only because they discover they are half-brothers who have shared the same father. Baltimore does not overcome his disdain for the middle class; he just welcomes Freeman into his home because he is now, through consanguinity, worthy of Baltimore's own class. *The Election* does, however, have some comic moments, one of which comes when Isabella Baltimore and Charlotte Freeman discuss women's letter writing:

> *Charl.* Do you know I have often thought of writing to you, but then I don't know what to say. It is strange now! I

---

77. *DPW*, 104–5.

> know ladies, who love one another, write such long letters to one another every day, and yet I don't know what to say.
>
> *Mrs. B.* And I have known, my dear Charlotte, ladies who did not love one another do just the same thing.
>
> *Charl.* Have you, indeed? La, that is wonderful! But don't you very often write long letters to the friends you love most?
>
> *Mrs. B.* Indeed I don't write very often, nor very long letters to any body; and yet I have some friends whom I very dearly love.[78]

An adept and copious letter writer herself, Baillie's own occasional comments to correspondents that she hates to write letters is likewise amusing. Another letter writer, Hester Thrale Piozzi, continued to keep abreast of Baillie's new publications and apprised the Rev. Robert Gray in March 1802 of *The Election*:

> Has it been in your way to look at a Miss Baillie's *Dramas* written, not for the stage, but for purpose of tracing the progress of the passions? Her *Tragedy* on *Hatred* was deservedly admired three years ago—and called De Monfort. She now has published a *Comedy* on *Hatred* very striking indeed, and possessing, in my mind, wonderful merit.[79]

Baillie does not discuss *The Election* at length in her correspondence, but in a letter dated 30 June 1817, she wrote to a friend (probably Anne Millar) about a later, rather curious musical adaptation of this play:

> Since I wrote you last we have had our stated visit from our Devon Friend Mrs Elliott, who only left us last week; and we have been more occupied & gayer than usual.[80] One thing that occupied & interested us was my comedy of the Election. It has been converted into an Opera by Mr Arnold the propriator [sic] of the Lycuem Theatre—or English Opera house and has been tolerably well received & very well

---

78. Ibid., 119.
79. Bloom and Bloom, 3:347.
80. Anne Elliott, a long-time friend of Baillie, was a frequent visitor to Baillie's home, as she was to Elliott's home in Devon.

acted.⁸¹ This new Theatre, however, is struggling with many difficulties, above all the terrible misfortune of not being reckoned <u>genteel</u>, and M͟r Arnold has not had such good houses as he & his actors deserved either when the Election or any other piece was represented. My good Friend M͟r͟s Wilmot (the Lady whom you must have heard of—who is well known for her many talents) in her great kindness has made a great effort to wipe of[f] this stigma from the English Opera, with what success remains to be shewn.⁸² She got the Duke of Wellington to bespeak the Election & a favorite after piece last Thursday and sit in the stage box which drew a full audience;⁸³ and John Bull had clapping & roaring & staring at the great man to his hearts content. I sat in a private box opposite to the Duke and was rather more amused than pleased with his manner of receiving it which was I thought both awkward & ungracious. After all the uproar of his entry was over, another uproar took place from a mad or drunken man who came into one of the side boxes, accusing the Duke aloud of the murder of two Soldiers, for which he demanded justice, and continued vociferating till he was carried out of the box neck & heels. All this noise consoled me a little for the disgrace that was thrown upon my poor play by the Duke not entering the house till it was over; for had he come in earlier, the audience could not & would not have listened to

---

81. Dramatist and theater manager Samuel James Arnold (1774–1852) had several plays represented at Drury Lane and in 1809 obtained a license to open the Lyceum in the Strand as an English opera house, remodeled and enlarged by architect Samuel Beazley in 1816 (*DNB*, I:584–85). *The Election* had appeared in volume 2 of *A Series of Plays: in which it is attempted to delineate the stronger passions*, etc. See letter of 9 August 1817 to Mary Berry, in which Baillie also discusses *The Election* being brought out as an opera.

82. Lady Dacre, Barbarina Brand [Wilmot] (1768–1854), was a poet, dramatist, translator, and sculptor. The third daughter of Admiral Sir Chaloner Ogle, Bart., and Hester, she married Valentine Henry Wilmot in 1789, an officer in the Guards. After Wilmot's death she married Thomas Brand, 20th baron Dacre, in 1819. Her published works include the erotic gothic *Libertine* (1807) and later *Pedarias* (1811), *Ina* (produced at Drury Lane in 1815), *Translations from the Italian* (1836) (*DNB*, II:1120). Lady Dacre contributed "Stanzas suggested by a Canzone of Petrarch" to Baillie's 1823 *Collection of Poems*. Lord Dacre was appointed arbitrator for Lady Byron on the death of her mother in 1822.

83. Arthur Wellesley, 1st Duke of Wellington, was a national hero because of his defeat of Napoleon. The closing of this letter is missing.

> it so attentively as they did. I think I may say altogether that it acts well and does not flay in any part. Miss Kelly who does the part of Charlotte acts admirably, and Bartl[e]y who is a very good comedian with H. Johnson did Freeman & Baltimore. It is stuffed full of songs written by Mr Arnold and this <u>must be</u>, else it would not be deemed an opera and would not therefore be allowed to be acted in that house.[84]

Baillie related the same account to Mary Berry a few weeks later. Such an adaptation authenticates Baillie's early popular appeal; but, characteristically, her comments reveal an appetite for success tempered with a keen sense of humor in the face of a boisterous London theater audience. In another letter to Berry bearing no date or postmark, she also asked for her friend's evaluation of a manuscript which at first glance appears to be *Ethwald*,[85] but the character types she mentions are instead closer to those in *The Election*. This letter also reveals Baillie's constant process of writing, revising, and collaborating and must have been written early in her career, some time before the emergence of volume two of *A Series of Plays*:

> You will see by what I send you inclosed, that I am willing to lose no time in setting you to some employment, tho' it may not perhaps be an employment so favourable for the peace of mind you pine after as could be wish'd. . . . You will look over the story I have given you, which I think might be turn'd into both an amusing & interesting piece, for I mean both Mrs B.—& the Baron to be characters, tho' in some degree perverted by bad example & unlucky circumstances in their youth, and therefore still returning when necessity calls for it the artifice & readiness in resource of people train'd in the adventurous world, still natively good and at the time of the play opens heartily greaved [sic] for the errors of their early life. If you think it can be made such a thing as you would like to write upon let me know what alterations you would wish to have made upon it, for I dont flatter my self that it

---

84. NLS 9236 ff.84–5; *Letters*, 1126–27.
85. The untitled manuscript Baillie mentions is not with her letters in the WI, but there is one included in the Berry letters in the RCS Library: HB.ix.69a–c, a story of M^{rs} B, catalogued as part of the manuscript of Baillie's *Ethwald*.

will just at first be all that you could wish, and I shall alter it
& re-alter it twenty times over till I get it to suit you. But if
you should not fancy it at all, tell me so frankly and then I
will try to rake something else out of my noddle that will do
better; only in this case you will be so good as to give me an
idea of what kind of a story you would like. As to devisions
[sic] of scenes and sketching of character, we shall say
nothing of that at present: it will be time enough to talk of it
when the story or outline of the plot is fix'd upon.[86]

In a more serious vein, *Ethwald* followed *The Election*.

Ethwald: A Tragedy, In Five Acts, Part First, is set in "England, *in the kingdom of Mercia, and the time near the end of the Heptarchy.*"[87] Here, along with the two remaining plays in the volume, Baillie focuses on ambition, a passion, she argues, far less transient than the others and requiring exposure in more than one situation:

Ambition alone acquires strength from gratification, and after
having gained one object, still sees another rise before it to
which it as eagerly pushes on; and the dominion which it
usurps over the mind is capable of enduring from youth to
extreme age. To give a full view, therefore, of this passion, it
was necessary to show the subject of it in many different
situations, and passing through a considerable course of
events.[88]

Ethwald not only incites a war in order to emerge a hero, but in a *Macbeth*-like scene, he also solicits the aid of three mystics to show him the future. The specter he is shown wears a crown and gives Ethwald the impetus he needs to control the future and move from soldier to king. In the process of "aspiring to be great," Ethwald's passions prove "hostile to public good," as he leaves particularly the women characters unable to survive in his patriarchal wasteland. The play ends as the protagonist questions his motives for conquest.[89]

---

86. WI MS 5616/69; *Letters*, 175.
87. *DPW*, 134. See Baillie's account of her inspiration for *Ethwald* in chapter 1.
88. Ibid., 105.
89. Ibid., 150, 162.

Ethwald: A Tragedy, In Five Acts, Part Second, opens on an unrepentant King Ethwald and ultimately proves that a leader's ambition and thirst for glory in battle destroys his citizens. Catherine Burroughs explains that *Part Second* culminates in "a lengthy scene that forecasts Bertolt Brecht's *Mother Courage*, as women, babies, the sick, and the elderly flee the horrors of a war created by Ethwald's rage for glory," depicting a battle field strewn with the slain.[90] Like Macbeth, Ethwald loses his life in Act 5 to enemies of a noble thane, Ethelbert. Concerned that the large cast of *Ethwald, Part Second*, might not be able to sustain the "expression of strong passion,"[91] Baillie altered the play in 1815 and wrote to Scott in October:

> I have been busy of late putting my house—that is to say my chest of papers in order, not expecting to die the sooner for having done so, but being better prepared (in this respect at least) for that event if it should please God to bring it suddenly upon me. I have altered Rayner so as to make it an acting play if <u>any</u> manager of <u>any</u> Theatre should hereafter wish to produce it; and I have done or think I have done the same good turn for the 2^d part of Ethwald. Oh how I wish you were my next door neighbour that I might run in to you with my papers in my hand![92]

In December of that same year, she reiterated her revisions to Scott and made clear that she wanted *Ethwald* to be an "acting play" and was willing to alter this play on ambition accordingly. Baillie, as unassuming as she may have appeared to friends, knew first hand about ambition and desired her literary efforts not only to be appreciated for the moment, but to endure. It was the reason for her continued disappointment at critical reception and the reason for compiling a last complete edition in 1851 for her heirs.

Following *Ethwald*, *The Second Marriage: A Comedy, In Five Acts*, is set in "SEABRIGHT's *house in the country, not far from* London, *and a small country inn near it.*"[93] Through enduring themes about intolerance and ambition, Baillie introduces a second wife unaccepted in a family that has just lost a mother. In *The Second*

---

90. Burroughs, *Closet*, 130–31.
91. Qtd. in Burroughs, *Closet*, 112.
92. NLS 3886 ff.188–90; *Letters*, 341.
93. *DPW*, 198.

Marriage, argues Burroughs, "Baillie confronts anxious responses to class struggle and social mobility" by showing how the family's persecution of a second wife "expresses an ideology of domestic insularity." Further, the comedy makes one question why Lady Sarah "must be banished at play's end, when she has actually shown herself a virtuous wife" and has simply supported her husband's ambitions in doing so.[94] Yet this ambiguous comedy speaks clearly about the inequitable mistrust of women and about a family's narrow-mindedness.

This ends volume two of *A Series of Plays*. And, argues Deirdre Gilbert, whereas volume one may present us with three types of womanhood that are, though potent, somewhat cliche—the coquette, the schemer, and the good sister—volume two presents a far darker picture of women displaced, reshaped, and virtually destroyed by the patriarchy.

In an introduction to his 1977 reprint of *A Series of Plays*, Donald Reiman concludes that there are three qualities which make Baillie's dramatic and poetic work especially impressive. First, the blank verse in her early plays is possibly the best dramatic blank verse of the Romantic period—simple and natural. Second, her use of language allows human psychology to shine through and proves that the same motives that lead lesser people to the petty actions of ordinary life also form the fabric of heroism and tragedy. Finally, her theme of universal passions is her strongest, possibly hindered by Scott's later intervention and urging that she turn her attention to historical poems. In addition, argues Reiman, if Baillie's work had been written on a false psychological or moral theory, as Hazlitt seemed later to imply in his lecture "On the Living Poets," she could never have had the impact she had on her contemporaries; even Hazlitt himself preferred her *De Monfort* to Coleridge's *Remorse*, a play about the growth of evil in a formerly good man.[95] Furthermore, says Reiman, Byron later suggested that he used Baillie's example of a unified action to focus attention on the moral and psychological situation, the important dramatic action taking place within the

---

94. Burroughs, *Closet*, 163.
95. See Rosemary Ashton's analysis of *Remorse* in *The Life of Samuel Taylor Coleridge* (Oxford: Blackwell, 1996), 102-3. *Remorse* had a successful stage run in 1813 during one of the darker periods of Coleridge's life. (My thanks to Dr. Michael Neth for this note.)

mind of the protagonist.[96] But, apparently, neither Baillie nor her publishers were pleased with sales of volume two. She responded assertively about this to Cadell and Davies in December 1803 as follows:

> The information you have given me in regard to the 2$^{\underline{d}}$ vol: of the "Series of Plays" is certainly not pleasant to me, yet I thank you for it sincerely. It is very proper that I should know how things really are, especially when the <u>really confined</u>, but <u>apparently general</u> circulation of the work are so considerably at varience [sic], and may therefore be supposed so materially to deceive me. However, as I have flatter'd myself and do still flatter myself that the sale of it, tho' of late it may have greatly diminish'd, will be of a permanent nature, I am not so uneasy about it as on your account I should otherwise be. The first vol: you allow to have been a very successful work, yet it was 2 years, if I rightly recollect, before the second edition was sold, and the half of the profits of both first & second edition amounted only to 38 pounds. When I put into your hands the copy right of the 2d vol:, I believed that I put you in possession of that from which you would continue to derive some profit during the course even of a long life, as well as the advantages of the first sale, and you must pardon me for thinking so still. The lesson I ought to learn from the decrease of its late sale is, not to fatigue the Public by making too many demands upon its attention. People are accustomed to read one new Play at a time and have done with it: to have a whole volume of them put into their hands at once, which they must read one after another, because they are new and because they have been at the trouble of either buying or borrowing them, is, perhaps, rather unreasonable. The Series of Plays must for many reasons be published in this manner, but to publish unconnected Plays so, is probably not very wise.[97]

---

96. Donald H. Reiman, ed., Introduction to *A Series of Plays: in which it is attempted to delineate the stronger passions of the mind*, 3 vols. (New York and London: Garland, 1977).

97. NLS Acc 9026; *Letters*, 1109–10. In this letter Baillie also asks for the copyright.

As in many of her other letters, Baillie displays here her keen sense of business and marketing, along with her desire to control her personal and professional province.

Notwithstanding her disappointment in the sale of her first two volumes, Baillie continued in a tremendous flourish of creativity during this period. Next came *Miscellaneous Plays* in 1804 from Longman. Including *Rayner, The Country Inn, Constantine Paleologus*, and, added to the second edition of 1805, *The Family Legend*, this volume, as Baillie states in the "Preface" to the second edition, digresses from her *Series of Plays* devoted to human passions and presents dramas less strenuous to individual actors, an intelligent marketing plan:

> I have long since proposed to myself not to confine my pen entirely to one task, but to write from time to time, as inclination might lead me or circumstances suggest, an unconnected or (may I so call it?) a free, independent play, that might have a chance of pleasing upon a stage, circumstanced as stages generally are, with no particular advantages. I have wished to leave behind me in the world a few plays, some of which might have a chance of continuing to be acted even in our canvass theatres and barns; and of preserving to my name some remembrance with those who are lovers of that species of amusement which I have above every other enjoyed.[98]

This reiterates Baillie's ambition, her desire for accomplishment and her willingness to experiment in order to create plays more accessible to contemporary actors. While these *Miscellaneous Plays* were supposedly more suitable for representation on the stage, Baillie still imparts in the "Preface" her lack of success in this arena and begins with her defense of *Rayner*. She was well aware that "having succeeded in one species of writing" gave her "no sure grounds to presume" that the public would be receptive to something new.[99]

Rayner: A Tragedy, In Five Acts, is set in "Germany, *near the frontiers of* Poland *and* Silesia."[100] Of the hero Baillie writes that she has attempted

---

98. *DPW*, 387.
99. Ibid.
100. Ibid., 391.

> to exhibit a young man of an easy, amiable temper, with delicacy of sentiment and a well principled mind, tempted, in the extremity of distress, to join with unworthy men in the proposed commission of a detestable deed; and afterwards, under one of the severest trials that human fortitude can be called upon to endure, bearing himself up, not with the proud and lofty firmness of a hero, but with the struggles of a man, who, conscious of the weakness of nature with him, feels diffident of himself to the last, and modestly aims at no more than what, being a soldier and the son of a brave father, he considers as respectable and becoming.[101]

She further explains in her "Preface" that *Rayner* was written years ago when she was not very old, and, though not an apology for its "defects," that may account for its lack of verisimilitude. As do many of Baillie's other plays, this tragedy lends itself to Marxist interpretation, as its antagonist Count Zaterloo and his lawless band prey on the wealthy simply *because* they are wealthy. Included in this hierarchical cast is a courtesan and a spiteful "Negro" named Ohio, attached to the prison. Anne Mellor sees this as one of many Romantic plays exhibiting "global consciousness or tolerance of ethnic and racial diversity," but Baillie's representation of Ohio is somewhat ambiguous, especially in light of her usual stance as human and animal rights activist.[102] Nevertheless, monk Mardonio declares that the protagonist, Rayner, once tempted to join Zaterloo's gang and wrongfully accused of murder, is gallant in the end:

> When urged by strong temptation to the brink
> Of guilt and ruin, stands the virtuous mind
> With scarce a step between; all pitying heaven,
> Severe in mercy, chast'ning in its love,
> Ofttimes, in dark and awful visitation,
> Doth interpose and leads the wand'rer back
> To the straight path, to be for ever after

---

101. Ibid., 388.
102. Anne K. Mellor, *Mothers of the Nation: Women's Political Writing in England* (Bloomington and Indianapolis: University of Indiana Press, 2000), 145. See Baillie's poems "School Rhymes for Negro Children" and "Devotional Song for a Negro Child" and her animal rights pamphlet "A Lesson Intended for the Use of the Hampstead School" (1826).

> A firm, undaunted, onward-bearing traveller,
> Strong in humility, who swerves no more.[103]

Rayner's love, Elizabeth, is distraught at his death sentence but shows little strength or psychological depth in most of her scenes. Baillie, however, achieves Shakespearean closure as she has Elizabeth fall into Rayner's arms when he is released in the final act, and the crowd gathers eagerly around them in a kind of protective circle.

As stated earlier, Baillie mentions alterations to *Rayner* several times in her letters. In October 1815 she notified Scott that she had altered *Rayner* to make it a better "acting play if any manager of any Theatre should hereafter wish to produce it";[104] but, sadly, that was not to be. She also wrote to Dr. Andrews Norton about her editing, though she was not specific about the changes, and sent him a copy in 1830.[105] Maybe it is because *Rayner* was one of the first plays Baillie wrote that she showed a special fondness for it, for she was happy about the reception Sir John and Lady Herschel gave the play even as late as 1850.[106]

Following *Rayner*, *The Country Inn: A Comedy, In Five Acts*, is set in "*A country inn, on one of the cross-roads leading from the north of England to London.*" According to the author, those accustomed to "quick turns of thought, pointed expression," and "witty repartee" would find "but few attractions" in this comedy.[107] In the character Miss Martin, Baillie provides the audience with another strong, independent female voice, a woman who wants simply to marry on

---

103. *DPW*, 419.
104. NLS 3886 ff.188–90; *Letters*, 341.
105. Dr. Andrews Norton (1786–1853) was a literary and Biblical scholar and Harvard divinity professor, who carried on a long correspondence with Baillie and was instrumental in promoting interest in her works in America.
106. Sir John and Lady Herschel were friends of Baillie, though it is unclear when or where they first met her; it is probable they met through her brother Dr. Matthew Baillie. Sir John Herschel must have admired her work, for his journal entry for 1 January 1837 states that he has just "Read Miss Baillie's Martyr" (*Herschel at the Cape: Diaries and Correspondence of Sir John Herschel, 1834–1838*, ed. David S. Evans, et al. [Austin: University of Texas Press, 1969], 273). It appears from some of the other letters in the Royal Society collection, however, that Herschel might have had a more familiar relationship with Agnes (see *Dictionary of Scientific Biography*, ed. Charles Coulston Gillispie [New York: Charles Scribner's Sons, 1972], VI:323–28).
107. *DPW*, 389.

her own terms; but in "To The Reader" for her second edition of *Miscellaneous Plays* (1805), Baillie herself hopes that *The Country Inn* will be taken for the light comedy that it is:

> Of the Comedy that follows [*Rayner*] I shall say but little. To those who are chiefly accustomed, in works of this kind, to admire quick turns of thought, pointed expression, witty repartee, and the ludicrous display of the transient passing follies and fashions of the world, this play will have but few attractions. The representation of a few characters . . . who are connected together in a very simple plot . . . my readers will not, I flatter myself, find fault with me for having made it a kind of division or stepping-stone between the two Tragedies.[108]

Nevertheless, though the dialogue is in fact witty, the play does not trivialize its theme—the necessity for women to marry on their own terms. Unfortunately, *The Country Inn*, as Baillie was well aware, was not well liked, nor was it performed in her lifetime.

The first edition of *Miscellaneous Plays* ends with *Constantine Paleologus; or, The Last Of The Ceasars: A Tragedy, In Five Acts*, the scene "Constantinople, *and in the camp of* MAHOMET, *near the city*."[109] This tragedy, Baillie had hoped, "would be brought out upon our largest theatre, enriched as it then was by two actors whose noble appearance and strong powers of expression seemed to me peculiarly suited to its two principal characters."[110] Based on Gibbon's account of the siege of Constantinople by the Turks, the drama turns to military characters and their seafaring lives. This play, critic Allardyce Nicoll reluctantly admits, shows that Baillie "possessed more of the theatre sense" than "the majority of her poetic companions."[111] In her preface, Baillie explains that her meaning has been sometimes misunderstood in Act 1, for it was never intended for the reader to think that the emperor yields to his wife's fears and sends his friends into danger. Baillie wrote about early problems in getting the play staged to her friend Anne Millar in

---

108. Ibid., 389.
109. Ibid., 446.
110. Ibid., 389–90. The principal actors were most likely Edmund Kean and John Kemble at Drury Lane. Baillie justifies her use of pomp and show in this tragedy because it was intended for a large theater.
111. Allardyce Nicoll, *A History of Early Nineteenth-Century Drama*, 2 vols. (Cambridge: Cambridge University Press, 1930), 1:159.

December 1801 and revealed her disappointment at its treatment at Drury Lane after the short success of *De Monfort*:

> ——You are very kind, my dear Anne, to be so anxiously concerned about my Theatrical matters, and I will, in return for your kindness, tell you every thing about them that I know myself; which may perhaps amuse you a little, if this letter should come to your hands in a dull winter day, as it probably will, when news of every kind are particularly acceptable. In the first place, the Play which I have prepared for the Stage, and which you have been watching for, you need give yourself no further concern about, for it is not to be brought upon the stage at all.[112]

While *Constantine Paleologus* was represented in Liverpool in 1808, in London (as *Constantine and Valeria*) in 1817, in Edinburgh in 1820, and in Dublin in 1825, it was never particularly successful on stage. In "Staging the state: Joanna Baillie's 'Constantine Paleologus'," Beth Friedman-Romell argues that this play, Baillie's most explicitly historical tragedy, actually departs from Gibbon's historical account of the fall of a Greek emperor "by staging the conflicted relationship between domesticity and the state," as the male protagonist endeavors to choose between love and honor. According to Friedman-Romell, the play raises certain questions in the minds of a British audience living through the Napoleonic wars: "What is the individual's responsibility to the state, and vice versa? What kinds of leaders do we need? What sort of government best serves the public? Are we citizens, subjects, or slaves?"[113] Like Basil, Constantine is conflicted in his desires for the feminine, for hearth and home, and for the masculine, for the military and fellowship with his men. But Baillie's original disposition was for a play recognizing the masculine, for she states in her "To the Reader" that

> So much was I pleased with those generous ties—may I be permitted to make use of a Scripture phrase, and say, those "cords of a man?" binding together the noble Paleologus and

---

112. NLS 9236 ff.3–7; *Letters*, 1105–7.
113. "Staging the state: Joanna Baillie's 'Constantine Paleologus'," in *Woman and Playwriting in Nineteenth-Century Britain*, ed. Tracy C. Davis and Ellen Donkin (Cambridge: Cambridge University Press, 1999), 151–73. Friedman-Romell's essay also includes detailed accounts of the four performances of *Constantine*.

his brave imperial band, that, had I followed my own inclination, delineating those would have been the principal object of the piece. But convinced that something more was requisite to interest a common audience, and give sufficient variety to the scenes, I introduced the character of Valeria, and brought forward the domestic qualities of Constantine as well as those of the unfortunate prince and beloved leader.[114]

Friedman-Romell argues that critics and managers were uncomfortable with Constantine's domesticity and with the homoerotic undertones in various scenes of the play and even with images of Christianity and Islam. By the time they had edited the play for production, it probably had little to do with Baillie's original design, and she was again surmounted by the patriarchy.

There were several positive critical reviews of *Miscellaneous Plays* in general, but as ever Francis Jeffrey was at the forefront with his criticism in the *Edinburgh Review*. He points out that the author did, in fact, stray from the original plan to which he so much objected but that "in spite of this little deviation, she has no sort of intention to relinquish it." Thus he suspected that her original plan must have also influenced this composition, and so he moves on to chastise her for not heeding him after all. After a detailed analysis of each play, Jeffrey draws the following conclusion:

> Upon the whole, however, we are afraid that this volume will by no means add to Miss Baillie's reputation. A pretty large proportion of it is unequivocally bad, and those parts which might have appeared excellent in an unknown writer, make but an indifferent figure when contrasted with her own previous productions. . . . We earnestly exhort Miss Baillie to write no more comedies; to keep her assay tragedies in her portfolio; and not to give any new ones to the world, till she has submitted them to the revision of some experienced and impartial friend.[115]

It was common for writers to read each others' manuscripts, and Baillie had sought critical readers from outside long before Jeffrey's chastisement; but it is little wonder that she later sent almost

---

114. *DPW*, 390.
115. "Miss Baillie's *Miscellaneous Plays*," *The Edinburgh Review* 5 (1804–5): 405–21.

everything she wrote to literary friends for their suggestions. Their very interference, however, may have made her work less than it could have been had she trusted more in her own genius.

A second edition of *Miscellaneous Plays* released in 1805 ends with *The Family Legend: A Tragedy, In Five Acts*, dedicated to Walter Scott who would be instrumental in its success and performance history. This play, set "*in the* Island of Mull, *and the opposite coast,* &c., *and afterwards in* ARGYLL's *castle*,[116] contains its own preface; but because its fame came a few years later with Scott's support, it is discussed in the following chapter on the Baillie-Scott relationship. For the faults of this entire collection, however, Baillie apologizes in her "To The Reader" of the second edition:

> I must also mention, that each of the plays contained in this volume has been, at one time or other, offered for representation to one or other of our winter theatres, and been rejected. This my reader will readily believe is not done in the spirit of vanity; and I beg of him also to believe, that neither is it at all done in that of complaint. I merely mention it, because otherwise it must have appeared absurd to introduce from the press what has been expressly written to come before the public in a different manner, without making any attempt to present it in its own peculiar mode. I must, in this case, have either appeared pusillanimously timid in shrinking from that open trial to which my contemporaries submit, or sullenly and ungraciously fastidious.
>
> The chief thing to be regretted in this failure of my attempts is, that having no opportunity of seeing any of my pieces exhibited, many faults respecting stage effect and general impression will to me remain undiscovered, and those I may hereafter write be of course unimproved.[117]

Baillie's apology was certainly justified, for how was she ever to understand the subtleties of performance without the benefit of a mentoring producer and director?

---

116. *DPW*, 481.
117. Ibid., 388.

At the same time Baillie was finishing *Miscellaneous Plays*, she was beginning a long correspondence in 1804 with music publisher/historian George Thomson and contributing literally dozens of lyrics for his Scottish, Welsh, and Irish song collections (in all, eleven volumes, culminated by a royal octavo edition of six volumes in 1822), which appeared over two decades.[118] Since there were no introductory or concluding symphonies to the airs he collected, Thomson determined to supply them himself, calling on Pleyel, Kozeluch, Haydn, Beethoven, Weber, Hummel and Bishop to provide the accompaniments; it was Bishop who suggested he set Burns's "Jolly Beggers" to music. Because Thomson found some of the original words to the old airs objectionable, he solicited the talents of Robert Burns, Walter Scott, James Hogg, Thomas Moore, Lord Byron, Thomas Campbell, and Joanna Baillie for revisions. In addition to his collections of airs, he edited the poems of Mrs. Anne Grant of Laggan in 1802. Baillie was a natural choice for his collection, and Thomson's biographer, J. Cuthbert Hadden, explains that if Thomson had taken her word for her inability to write songs, she would not have enriched his collection so extensively.[119] Although Baillie argued repeatedly that she had no talent for song writing, she repeatedly produced exactly what he wanted.

It was in February 1804 that Baillie finally affirmed, "to the Friend of Burns and my own countryman, it is impossible to refuse, in such a work as you are engaged in, any little assistance that I am able to give."[120] Her aunt Anne Hunter was also involved in supplying lyrics for Thomson, but Baillie must have found it difficult to meet his demands for new lines while she was in the midst of

---

118. George Thomson (1757–1851), son of schoolmaster Robert Thomson and Anne Stirling Thomson, was a collector of Scottish music and one of the directors of the first Edinburgh music festival in 1815. He played the violin and took an active role in Edinburgh's St. Celia concerts of his day. Hearing Tenducci's rendering of Scottish songs at these concerts, he conceived the idea of collecting songs for the national arts, ultimately issuing three folio collections: the Scottish in six volumes (1793–1841), the Welsh in three volumes (1809–14), and the Irish in two volumes (1814–16). A royal octavo edition in six volumes made up from all these appeared in 1822. Thomson's only daughter Georgina married George Hogarth, and their daughter Catherine Hogarth later became the wife of Charles Dickens (J. Cuthbert Hadden, *George Thomson, The Friend of Burns: His Life & Correspondence* [London: John C. Nimmo, 1898]; *DNB*, XIX:722).

119. Hadden, 226.

120. BL Add. Ms. 35,263 f. 217; *Letters*, 93.

finishing *Miscellaneous Plays* and working on the third volume of a *Series of Plays*. As a result, she was sometimes curt with him about his imposed deadlines, and her letters reveal both her authorial integrity and her refusal to bend her creativity to suit his meter. When in April 1804 Thomson asked her to alter "The Maid of Llanwellyn," Baillie responded, "As for the last stanza which you think inferior to the rest, I must e'en in the sturdy spirit of an author say that I think it is rather the best of them all tho' I am willing enough to admit there is not one of them very good."[121] While she did work with him diligently on revisions, she most often retained her authority as author and justified the closely chosen words for her " 'Song Written for a Welsh Air, Called 'The New Year's Gift' " and "The Black Cock" in February 1805:

> I intended those verses as an address from a husband and not from a Lover; and when I make him say "Last year of earth's treasures I gave thee my part," it is as much to say, "I endowed thee with all my worldly goods" which will, I should think, in this country at least, where similar words are used in the marriage ceremony, be perfectly understood; and as the music is Welch & not Scotch, I think if you please, it had better remain as it is. The next thing is the "crimson moon" in the heath-cock.[122] I meant this to express the kind of arched spot of deep red that is over each of the eyes of this bird; but as I never really saw the bird but once a long time ago, and take my account at him from a book, it may probably not be sufficiently discriptive. If you are not acquainted with the heath-cock yourself, you had better refer the matter, if you think it is worth while to be at so much trouble, to some of your friends who are acquainted with him. If the present expression is not approved of, you may change it into "Thy crimson moon'd and azure eye" or "Thy crimson-arched azure eye" best if it is admissible.[123]

---

121. BL Add. Ms. 35,363 f. 227; *Letters*, 98. See this letter and following ones in *The Collected Letters* for the entire editing process for this poem.

122. See "The Black Cock" (*DPW*, 831).

123. BL Add. Ms. 35,263 f.257; *Letters*, 104. The line remains, "Thy crimson moon and azure eye" in *DPW*.

This reluctance to revise without good reason attests both to Baillie's confidence as a professional woman and to her tenacity as a writer.

At the same time Baillie humbly asked that if Thomson put her name to any of the songs it be simply "Joanna Baillie," without the formality of title, for she was unceasingly dignified without being pompous. Many of the songs appearing later in Baillie's *Dramatic and Poetical Works* (1851) were first written for Thomson's collection and included "The Maid of Llanwellyn," "The Black Cock, Written for a Welsh Air, Called 'The Note of the Black Cock'," "Song Written for a Welsh Air, Called 'The New Year's Gift'," "Song, Written for a Welsh Air, Called 'The Pursuit of Love'," "A Song, Written for an Irish Melody," "Song, 'Woo'd and Married and A'," "Hooly and Fairly. (Founded on an Old Scotch Song.)," and others. Correspondence and work with Thomson continued into the next decade of Baillie's life and extended sporadically into the 1840s; and though she accepted copies of the volumes from him as payment for her collaboration, she was adamant that he not send her money or gifts for her contributions.

Meanwhile, in this flurry of composing both lyrics and dramas, Joanna was also taking care of her invalid mother, Dorothea Hunter Baillie, who had been widowed in 1778. Just as Dorothea had nursed her own mother until her death in 1751, the two Baillie sisters nursed their mother through many years of illness and through her eventual blindness. The constant care probably diminished Joanna's creativity, as she wrote to George Thomson in November of 1804:

> You were so obliging as to allow me to take my leisure in providing words for the music you sent me, yet I should not quite so far have taken advantage of it if family distress, on account of my Mother's illness, who is now recovering very slowly from an alarming complaint, had not made me unfit to attend to any thing of the kind. I now send you two songs of my own writing & two written by a friend which fills up your demand; and if nothing better suited to the music should happen to fall in your way, I hope they will be useful to you.[124]

---

124. BL Add. Ms. 35,263 f.247; *Letters*, 102.

In a subsequent letter from February 1805, she thanked Thomson for asking about Dorothea and explained that she had been "in the same state she has been in for some months, entirely confined to her bed, but free from pain."[125] Similar remarks about Dorothea's health appear in other correspondence to friends and acquaintances, but a letter written on 25 December 1805 to Joanna's friend Mary Berry revealed most poignantly the sisters' mental struggle with their mother's illness:

> A merry Christmas to you, and many good things beside! I think with satisfaction that few if any of my friends will spend this day in so lonely & melancholly a way as I and my poor Sister shall, and it pleases me to think so. Give my kindest wishes to your Sister & to Mr Berry: I hope you are well & comfortable whether you are at your own fire side or that of a friend.[126]

Dorothea Hunter Baillie died in Hampstead at home with Joanna and Agnes on 30 September 1806, almost eighty-six years old; and while Joanna and Agnes felt the loss deeply, they must have been somewhat relieved at the end of this suffering. Outside the parish church of St. John in Hampstead, built in the year 1745, a worn slab today bears the inscription:

TO THE MEMORY OF

MRS. DOROTHEA BAILLIE

WIDOW OF THE REV^D JAMES BAILLIE, D.D.,

PROFESSOR OF DIVINITY

UNIVERSITY OF GLASGOW

WHO DIED IN THIS PARISH SEPTEMBER 30, 1806

IN THE 86TH YEAR OF HER AGE.[127]

---

125. BL Add. Ms. 35,263 f.257; *Letters*, 105.
126. WI MS 5616/64; *Letters*, 156.
127. Dr. Matthew Baillie paid for their mother's funeral and monument at £144 (Crainz, 144). The inscription above is from the Camden Historical Society Gravestone Survey by G. G. Harris, September 1978. Inscriptions for Joanna and Agnes followed.

Daughters Joanna and Agnes would follow their mother to this same site many years later.

The two sisters were now alone in the house near Red Lion Inn in Hampstead, and while Baillie was realistic about the plight of a single woman in nineteenth-century Britain, she chose to remain unmarried. Why is a mystery, though one could speculate that she knew marriage would mean a loss of independence. There is no evidence even of an early love affair, though one might speculate about romantic friendships. It is quite likely that, given her association with medical men, Baillie understood too well the mental and physical dangers of domesticity and childbearing. She was clear on the subject, however, when in 1806 her friend Mary Berry was pursued by a certain "Gentleman of Yorkshire." Baillie advised,

> You wish for employment, and you wish to be useful in the world: as the Wife of a man of fortune you will have this much more in your power than you are ever likely to have by remaining single. . . . This is enough in the mean time to set you thinking upon it seriously which is all I want.—Now in what I am saying to you I am most disinterested, for every single woman, who is to remain so, has great pride in seeing such a woman as you of her Sister hood, and cannot possibly see you quitting the ranks but with considerable regret.[128]

She had met Mary Berry (1763–1852), born in Kirkbridge, Yorkshire, to Elizabeth Seton and merchant Robert Berry, probably some time in the late 1790s and wrote the "Prologue" and "Epilogue" for Berry's *Fashionable Friends* around 1800. Certainly, by the late 1790s Baillie respected Berry as a friend and fellow writer because, as Berry related to her friend Mrs. Cholmeley in March of 1799, she had sent her an anonymous package containing volume one of her *Series of Plays* almost a year before:

> Do you remember my speaking to you in high terms of a series of plays upon the passions of the human mind, which had been sent to me last winter by the author? I talked to everybody else in the same terms of them at the time, anxiously enquiring for the author; but nobody knew them,

---

128. See WI MS 5616/64 to Mary Berry, dated 25 December 1805; *Letters*, 156–57.

nobody cared for them, nobody would listen to me; and at last I unwillingly held my tongue, for fear it should be supposed that I thought highly of them only because they had been sent to me. This winter the first question upon everybody's lips is "Have you read the series of plays?" Everybody talks in the raptures (I always thought they deserved) of the tragedies and of the introduction as of a new an admirable piece of criticism. . . . But whoever the author is, they still persist in preserving a strict incognito, for which I honour their honest pride, which scorns to be indebted to *any* name for the success of such a work, and, with the patient sense of real merit, has quietly waited a whole twelvemonth for the impression it has at last made on the obdurate public.[129]

It is very likely that Berry did not discover the identity of the author any sooner than others did. Later collaborating with Berry on *Fashionable Friends*, Baillie contributed the prologue and described it as "a plain simple Prologue of no pretensions, but such I hope as you will not dislike; if you do, throw it aside, and I shall not be at all offended. Whatever I have done in the way of poetry I am sure I have lied well for you, and that is all the merit I can claim."[130]

Mary Berry and her sister Agnes had been raised by their grandmother in Yorkshire and were largely self educated but extremely well read. Much like Joanna and Agnes Baillie, the two sisters remained together for more than eighty years. Berry never married but was to declare near the end of her life that a courtship with Gerald O'Hara in 1796 had been her happiest time. Rumor had it that sculptor Anne Damer was also pursuing Berry by the end of the decade.[131] Horace Walpole met the Berry sisters in 1788 when he

---

129. Lady Theresa Lewis, ed., *Extracts of the Journals and Correspondence of Miss Berry from the Year 1783 to 1852*, 3 vols. (London: Longmans, Green, and Co., 1865), 2:88.

130. Ibid., 2:117n.

131. Anne Seymour Damer (1749–1828) was the only child of Field-Marshall Henry Seymour Conway and his wife Lady Caroline Campbell, daughter of the 4th duke of Argyll and widow of Lord Aylesbury. She was a favorite of Horace Walpole and adored by her father. She studied anatomy under Cruikshank and took lessons from Ceracchi. In 1767 she married John Damer, heir to his father Lord Milton's fortune. She was a staunch Whig, met Josephine and Napoleon, and presented the latter with a bust of Fox; he presented her with a diamond snuffbox with his portrait (now in the British Museum). In 1800 she produced Mary Berry's *Fashionable*

was over seventy and was so fond of them that he called them his "wives," dedicating several works to them and prevailing upon them in 1791 to take a house he called "Little Strawberry Hill." Walpole's letters record his distress at the sisters' travels to the continent and Paris in 1791 in the midst of the French Revolution, and in 1797 he provided each one the interest from £4,000, ultimately relieving them of any financial strain. Although she traveled extensively, Mary Berry spent more time in London than in Twickenham, writing plays, historical works such as *A Comparative View of Social Life in England and France* (1828–31), and attracting visitors which included Baillie, Anne Damer, Catharine Fanshawe, Harriet Martineau, Lord Byron, Francis Jeffrey, Samuel Rogers, William Sotheby, Thomas Malthus, Charles Dickens, and Fanny Kemble. Madame de Staël, one of the most brilliant women of her time, is said to have declared Baillie the cleverest woman in England.[132]

Baillie's letters to Berry are both caring and humorous, and in November 1804 she wrote to her friend:

> Tales of Wonder, at least such as I write, unless they be meant at the same time (as one of our reviewers said) for tales of plunder, are good for nothing else but amusing ones friends of a winter evening in the country by the fireside, and so I very willingly send you my two <u>things</u> to get as much amusement out of as you can. This will depend very much upon yourselves. If you read them pretty late at night by a good fire & all the house still, they may do pretty well, but if

---

Friends at Drury Lane to ill reviews (*DNB*, V:450–51). Mrs. Damer was known for her masculine attire; her friendships with women, especially with Mary Berry, were the subject of much gossip. See Randolph Trumbach, "London's Sapphists: From Three Sexes to Four Genders in the Making of Modern Culture," in *Body Guards*, ed. Julia Epstein and Kristina Straub (New York and London: Routledge, 1991), 131-32; and Emma Donoghue, *Passions Between Women* (New York: Harper Collins, 1995), 145-47.

132. For general information see *The Feminist Companion to Literature in English: Women Writers from the Middle Ages to the Present*, ed. Virginia Blain, Patricia Clements, and Isobel Grundy (London: B. T. Batsford, 1990), 88; and Paul Schlueter and June Schlueter, *An Encyclopedia of British Women Writers* (New York: Garland, 1988), 36–38. See also Lewis Melville, *The Berry Papers: Being the Correspondence Hitherto Unpublished of Mary and Agnes Berry (1763–1852)* (London: John Lane, 1914); and Tess Lewis, "Madame de Staël: The Inveterate Idealist," *The Hudson Review* LIV:3 (2001): 416-416-26.

> you read them in day light with servants' feet clattering up & down stairs and Busy barking, they will be good for nothing. I have sent them to Town this morning to be left at Mrs Damer's upper Brook St: till call'd for, and you may return them to me again when it is convenient, only dont lose them. I would have mention'd them in my last letter, as you had said you should like to see them, but I completely forgot it.[133]

Baillie often allowed Berry and Anne Seymour Damer to read her works in progress, and she thanked them both in a letter postmarked 1806 for their comments on *The Family Legend*:

> Mrs Damer tells me in her note which came to my hand yesterday that there are some corrections you have to make on the last acts of my Family Legend, and I should be glad to know what they are as soon as may be. I hope you have noted them down or at least have them so in your head that you can note them down & send them to me in the course of this week, as I am busy writing out the new copy which is to be sent off without loss of time to its destination. They [sic] two last acts I sent to Mrs D. without having even looked over them after they were written, and Mrs Baillie told me there were many inaccuracies which she had found out and should mark on the Margin before the manuscript was return'd; and I suppose this has been done, as I see a good many pencil marks upon it; but besides Mrs Damer's corrections & hers, I should like to have yours too, if you can find time enough to bestow upon me[.][134]

It would, of course, be too much to hope that these editorial comments and marked manuscript copies were extant; at least I have not found them. Plainly, though, Baillie trusted Berry as a critical reader, and though their correspondence is sparse, the letters that survive provide important evidence of Baillie's editorial process and of their friendship and the way in which these literary women worked together to ensure each other's success.

Joanna Baillie was not only comfortable with the critical estimation of other women writers, but she solicited criticism from literary men as well. Another early Hampstead companion was

---

133. RSC HB.ix.15; *Letters*, 154.
134. WI MS 5616/65; *Letters*, 158–59.

author and translator William Sotheby, born in London on 9 November 1757 to Elizabeth Sloan, daughter of William Sloan, esq., and William Sotheby, colonel in the Coldstream guards. When William's father died in 1766, his guardians were Charles Philip Yorke, fourth earl of Hardwicke, and his maternal uncle Hans Sloane; William later succeeded to the estate of Sewardstone, Epping Forest. Educated at Harrow, at seventeen he purchased a commission as ensign in the dragoons and proceeded to study at the military academy of Angers. He was then stationed in Edinburgh, where he met Walter Scott for the first time. In July 1780 he married heiress Mary Isted, which enabled him to retire from the army and settle at his residence of Bevis Mount to take up a literary life. The couple had five sons and two daughters, three of whom died.[135]

Sotheby devoted himself to studying the classics, and his own first publication was a volume in the Romantic tradition entitled *Poems* (1790; reissued in 1794), derived primarily from a walking tour he and his brother Thomas had made through Wales. In 1791 Sotheby moved to London where he occupied Fair Mead Lodge and acted as a master-keeper of the adjoining Epping Forest. He soon became a prominent figure in London literary society and joined the Dilettante Society in 1792 and the Society of Antiquaries and the Royal Society in 1794. As early as 1799 he was corresponding with Mary Berry, sending her poems to review such as his *Battle of the Nile*. He entertained literary figures regularly and took Walter Scott to Hampstead to meet Baillie in 1806, and in 1807 Sotheby and Sir George Beaumont encouraged Coleridge to publish *The Friend*.[136]

William Sotheby gained a sound reputation as a translator by publishing Wieland's German poem *Oberon* (a second edition illustrated by Fuseli in 1805), the later basis for a masque in five acts; further, his verse translation of Virgil's *Georgics* (1800) was applauded even by the severe Edinburgh critic Francis Jeffrey.[137]

---

135. General biographical information comes from the *DNB*, XVIII:673–76.

136. See Donald H. Reiman's introduction to William Sotheby's *Saul and Constance de Castille. Romantic Context: Poetry* (New York and London: Garland, 1978), vi. Reiman states that Sotheby often lent books to Coleridge and in 1804 gave him £100 against Wordsworth's promissory note. In 1803, while on their way to France to meet Annette Vallon and Caroline, William and Dorothy Wordsworth were guests at Sotheby's London home (Reiman, vi).

137. Reiman writes that because there were so many translations of Virgil and so many literary figures who read the original in Latin, Sotheby's greatest effort had little impact; however, his translation of

Although Sotheby began as a poet, he had a strong affinity for drama, his tragedy *Bertram and Matilda* being acted privately by him and his friends in 1790. He published several other five-act historical tragedies in blank verse, including *The Cambrian Hero, or Llewelyn the Great* (no date), *The Siege of Cuzco* (1800), *Julian and Agnes, or the Monks of the Great St. Bernard* (1801), *Orestes* (1802), and *Ellen, or the Confession* (1816). Three previously unpublished tragedies, *Ivan*, *The Death of Darnley*, and *Zamorin and Zama*, appeared as part of his 1814 collection entitled *Five Tragedies*. There is convincing evidence in some of their letters, however, that Baillie supplied Sotheby with the plots for some of his plays. Apparently, only one of his tragedies was ever staged professionally, *Julian and Agnes* being acted at Drury Lane in April 1800 by Mrs. Siddons and Kemble. Sotheby was painted by Sir Thomas Lawrence and was both revered and criticized as a writer. On 30 December 1833 Wordsworth wrote to Samuel Rogers about his genuine grief at the death of Sotheby, Coleridge referred to him always as a "Brother Poet," and Byron declared that Sotheby had only "imitated everybody, and occasionally surpassed his models."[138] Sotheby's wife Mary died shortly after him on 14 October 1834.

Joanna Baillie and William Sotheby were friends, neighbors, and literary collaborators, and his "To Joanna Baillie" is one of many poetical tributes to her from distinguished men and women of letters. Baillie's correspondence with Sotheby from 1804 into the late 1830s verifies that they read, criticized, and praised each other's work, in addition to keeping up closely with each other's domestic lives. Their families visited regularly, and Sotheby clearly sought Baillie's critical eye; but he wished her own expertise aimed at poetry rather than drama, for he felt it was there where she excelled. On 12 December 1804, the publication year of *Miscellaneous Plays*, she replied to his criticism as follows:

> —But why do you say, out upon me for my inflexibility in persevering to attempt acting Plays? A play certainly is more perfect for being fitted for the stage as well as the closet, and why should not I aim with all my strength to make my things as perfect as possible, however short I may fall of the mark?

Wieland's German, claims Professor Werner William Beyer, had a strong influence on Keats, Coleridge, Wordsworth, Southey, and others (x).

138. *DNB*, XVIII:676. Baillie's "Lines on the Death of William Sotheby" affirmed their friendship.

> Dont be afraid that I shall injure them as reading plays on this account. It is endeavouring to suit pieces to the temporary circumstances of particular theatres, and not to the stage in general that injure them in this way. One who never expects as long as she lives to see a play of her own acted, and who never intends to offer a play to any of our Theatres under their present management, is not very likely to do her works much harm by keeping the stage in her eye. Dont you therefore find fault with me, or encrease the number of those who are for quietly setting me aside as a closet writer. I will still go on, having my drums & my trumpets, & my striking situations, & my side scenes & my back scenes, & all the rest of it in my mind, whilst I write, notwithstanding all that you can say to the contrary.[139]

Baillie's refusal to give up playwriting attests both to her determination and to her courage. Subsequently, she called on Sotheby's expertise as a translator a few days later:

> I have got a favour to ask of you; and tho' you have given me some hopes of seeing you soon, in this bad weather (when indeed I should almost be sorry to see you), I will not trust to that, but prefer my request in this way which is not so good as face to face yet I trust will do. I have a friend in Scotland who is studying German with great eagerness, and wishes much to translate some light amusing german novel, which she (for it is a Lady) might afterwards if she has a mind dispose of to a Bookseller. I have already spoken to my Bookseller about it: what I want you to do for us is to take in to consideration all the german novels of this discription that have not yet been translated into English, particularly those that are lately publish'd and chuse out one for us that you think will not greatly fatigue the Translator and at the same time be likely to have some little success with the public. About two volumes is as long, I think, as it ought to be. Pray have the goodness to give this a thought![140]

---

139. RSC HB.ix.20; *Letters*, 179–80.
140. RSC HB.ix.8; *Letters*, 181.

Here again, Baillie continued to support the endeavors of women writers and scholars, even though she often had to solicit the aid of men in their behalf.

In following years Baillie supplied Sotheby with a feasible plot entitled "An Old Story," read and offered editorial suggestions for his poem *Constance de Castille* (1810), an imitation of Scott's *Lady of the Lake*, and criticized his *Ivan* (1814). In addition, she solicited his input for a "little book of psalmody" and his poems for her 1823 *A Collection of Poems, Chiefly Manuscript, and from Living Authors*. He clearly trusted her as a critic, and the two remained close friends until his death in 1834.

For Baillie, a steady source of pleasure came not only from these friends, writers, and frequent visitors to Hampstead, but also from her immediate family. Joanna's brother Dr. Matthew Baillie was now a prominent London physician and would soon be appointed one of the court physicians to George III; in addition, his patients included such notables as Edward Gibbon, Lord Byron, William Pitt the younger, Walter Scott, Richard Brinsley Sheridan, and Cardinal Consalvi, Pope Pius VII's Secretary of State.[141] He and his wife Sophia Denman Baillie were the parents of three children, of whom only one, James Baillie (1792–1793), did not survive them. Their daughter Elizabeth Margaret Baillie (1794–1876) and son William Hunter Baillie (1797–1894) are frequent topics of Baillie's letters, and they appear a very constant family. Baillie's niece Elizabeth Margaret was from the beginning a favorite of Joanna and Agnes and was fond of both music and poetry. It is also clear that nephew William doted on Joanna and Agnes, especially, in their later years.[142] Before she married Capt. Robert Milligan, Elizabeth Margaret was a companion of Sir Walter Scott's oldest daughter Sophia (later Mrs. John Lockhart) whenever Sophia accompanied him to London; and William, who studied law at Oxford, eventually became a landowner, gentleman farmer, and father of eight children.[143]

In addition to being included in Dr. Matthew Baillie's family activities, receiving calls and visiting friends of her own, Baillie loved the spectacle of the theater. She wrote eagerly to William Sotheby

---

141. Crainz, 59–66.

142. Elizabeth Margaret Baillie Milligan (1794–1876), the only daughter of Matthew and Sophia Denman Baillie, married Capt. Robert Milligan (1781–1875) on 11 July 1816, and the couple, with their only daughter Sophia (1817–1882), lived at Ryde on the Isle of Wight for most of Joanna's life.

143. See chapter 1, note 7.

about Mrs. Wilmot's play coming out at Drury Lane (probably *Ina*) in 1815 and hoped he would help secure opening-night box seats for her and a large party.[144] Moreover, she was disappointed when her sister-in-law Sophia and niece Elizabeth saw Scott's *Lady of the Lake* at the Royal Circus without her. She was also always excited to hear about performances of her plays at fairs and in the outdoors. Throughout their lives, she and her sister attended art exhibits as a friend of painter Sir Thomas Lawrence, celebrations for new monarchs, and festivals of every description.

It is disappointing that almost no early letters survive, especially before 1800, in Joanna Baillie's hand (at least this research has not uncovered any) to provide better insight into her young adult life and into her early years as a writer. But from 1804 to her death in 1851, her letters, autobiographical papers, and literary works provide a record of her activities, friends, and passions. Subsequent years would bring both the exhilaration of seeing a few of her plays performed and the exasperation of unfulfilled promises from Drury Lane and Covent Garden. The price of fame was high for Baillie—it certainly resulted in professional frustrations and disappointments; more personally, it may have also cost her sexual and emotional satisfaction. In the short period of time from the emergence of *Poems* in 1790 to the emergence of volume two of *A Series of Plays* in 1802, however, Joanna Baillie produced dozens of poems, song lyrics, and no less than eleven five-act plays—all this, *significantly*, before she had even met Scott, Wordsworth, Byron, and other great writers of the era.

---

144. RSC HB.ix.16; *Letters*, 198.

3

 "Beyond mere words": Baillie and Scott
(1806–1832)

> When she, the bold Enchantress, came
> With fearless hand and heart on flame!
> From the pale willow snatch'd the treasure,
> And swept it with a kindred measure,
> Till Avon's swans, while rung the grove
> With Monfort's hate and Basil's love,
> Awakening at the inspired strain,
> Deem'd their own Shakespeare liv'd again.

So writes Sir Walter Scott in his introduction to the Third Canto of *Marmion* (1808) in honor of his friend and colleague Joanna Baillie.[1] Certainly, Baillie's close collaborative relationship with Scott, to whom she was introduced in 1806 by writer and friend William Sotheby, touched her life and work in various ways, just as it did his. Their exchange of criticism and gifts, along with the casual tone in which the two corresponded, imparts an intimacy neither shared with other correspondents. It is unfortunate that this biography cannot possibly reproduce all of Scott's letters to Baillie, for they intensify the story of their relationship. As Paula Backscheider argues, "Giant matrixes of how important events are described to different correspondents need to be constructed" when one uses letters as a source of biographical evidence;[2] and, reading Grierson's edition of Scott's correspondence can certainly enhance the Baillie letters quoted herein.

Scott began his literary career with the anonymous publication of *The Chase* and *William and Helen* in 1796, translated from German. Falling in love with Williamina Belsches, he proposed marriage at this time, but she refused. On Christmas Eve 1797, however, he married Margaret Charlotte Carpenter, the daughter of a French royalist refugee. They soon moved to Lasswade, about six

---

1. This inscription also appears on a monument erected in Baillie's honor by James Donald in the 1890s at St. Bride's Church, Bothwell; its beautiful mosaic panels were hand made in Venice and are intact today. Inside the church is a lovely, small portrait of a young Joanna Baillie.

2. Backscheider, 65.

miles from Edinburgh, where he was appointed Sheriff of Selkirkshire in 1799, and in 1802 the couple moved to 39 Castle Street, a home they later maintained while they also owned Abbotsford. Biographer John Sutherland credits Charlotte's love of novels and theater for influencing Scott and argues that "Before she was brought down by child-bearing and chronic illness Charlotte effervesced Scott's life and social habits in ways that a younger Scottish wife bred to respectable Edinburgh ways might not have done."[3] Their oldest daughter Charlotte Sophia (later Mrs. John Lockhart) was born in 1799 (d. 1837); their son Walter was born in 1801 (d. 1847); Anne followed in 1803 (d. 1833); and their last son Charles was born in 1805 (d. 1841).

Between 1801 and 1808, Scott was writing profusely, producing *Minstrelsy of the Scottish Border* (1802), *The Lay of the Last Minstrel* (1805), *Ballads and Lyrical Pieces* (1806), *The Works of Dryden*, and *Marmion* (1808), and entering into the secret business partnership with publisher James Ballantyne that would eventually lead to the financial ruin of all involved. In 1809 he promoted the founding of the Tory *Quarterly Review* and in 1812 moved to a cottage at Abbotsford on the Tweed, with plans to build a castle and revive the ways of a feudal laird. On the brink of financial disaster in 1813, Scott was rescued by publisher Archibald Constable who had read the opening chapters of *Waverley* begun earlier. But even with the acclaim which ensued, Scott was convinced that he was eclipsed by Byron as the poet of the age and declined the offer of poet laureate, recommending Robert Southey for the position. When "Scott gave up verse for prose and sat down to finish *Waverley* in 1814," writes editor Russell Noyes, "he had already proved himself a master of dramatic narrative, scenic painting, and the delineation of a wide variety of characters and situations."[4] By 1819 he had reached the height of his popularity as a novelist, admired both by his fellow countrymen and a universal audience. The first major writer to unite great historical events with the lives of ordinary people, Scott focused on the virtues of morality and self-sacrifice and was so popular that almost every writer of his time aspired to produce at least one work in this historical form. In 1820 he was made a baronet, but following the great commercial crash of 1825, partly

---

3. John Sutherland, *The Life of Walter Scott* (Oxford: Blackwell, 1995), 69.

4. Russell Noyes, ed., Introduction to Scott in *English Romantic Poetry and Prose* (New York: Oxford University Press, 1956), 517.

because of his own borrowing and partly through the mismanagement of his publishing partner James Ballantyne, Scott found himself involved with Ballantyne and Constable in a financial disaster, personally responsible for approximately £130,000. In an effort to save Abbotsford for his family, he tried desperately to clear this enormous debt by writing; and while successful, the stressful effort probably shortened his life. His wife died the following year (1826), and in 1830 Scott suffered a stroke of apoplexy. In failing health, he died 21 September 1832 at Abbotsford and was buried at Dryburgh Abbey. Baillie herself solicited contributions for his monument. Commissioned later in August 1846, Edinburgh's Scott memorial, designed by George Kemp with a statue designed by Sir John Steele, is a testament to his popularity and influence.[5]

When Baillie met Walter Scott in 1806 at William Sotheby's home, she was already reaching the pinnacle of her career, just as Scott was approaching his. After her publication of *Poems*, two volumes of *A Series of Plays*, and *Miscellaneous Plays* in multiple editions, along with lyrics for music collector George Thomson, Baillie was now revising *The Family Legend*.[6] She had just finished reading *The Lay of the Last Minstrel*, and her first impression of Scott was that he did not possess the "elegance and refinement of feature" that she had imagined; but she later related to John Lockhart that had she "fixed upon that face among a thousand," she would have measured in it Scott's benevolence, shrewdness, and ability to aid her "in any strait."[7] By the time she was writing to Scott in 1808, she had already established an alliance with him and his family, arranging dinner plans around the Scotts' stay in London and around all their visits to Mrs. Siddons and others. The first two thousand copies of Scott's *Marmion* had appeared in February 1808, with six thousand sold by the following May, and

---

5. For brevity's sake this general information on Scott comes from sources which include the *DNB*, XVII:1018–43, and Noyes, 514–20. More specific information, however, comes from the following biographical sources: Edgar Johnson, *Sir Walter Scott: The Great Unknown*, 2 vols. (New York: Macmillan, 1970); John Gibson Lockhart, *Memoirs of the Life of Sir Walter Scott,* 5 vols. (Boston and New York: Houghton Mifflin, 1901); and John Sutherland, *The Life of Walter Scott* noted above. In addition, *The Letters of Sir Walter Scott*, ed. H. J. C. Grierson, 12 vols. (London: Constable, 1932–37) are invaluable because they provide his letters to Joanna Baillie and some excerpts from her own responses.

6. See 1806 letters to Mary Berry, WI MS 5616/65, 66 and 67; *Letters*, 158–61.

7. Qtd. in Lockhart, I:478–9.

Baillie addressed her "unabaiting delight" at his "exquisite description of inanimate objects, and characteristic sketches of human beings" therein. Her own imagination fired, she vowed to go back to Hampstead and "try, both for your credit & my own, to do something better than I have yet done."[8] Theirs had been an instant mutual admiration, and in only two years Baillie and Scott had progressed from acquaintances to confidants.

Agnes and Joanna Baillie traveled to Glasgow, to the Scottish Highlands, and on to Scott's home in Edinburgh in the spring of 1808, after which Scott declared to Charles Kirkpatrick Sharpe that "Miss Baillie is the only *writing* lady with whose manners in society I have been very much delighted. But she is simplicity itself, and most of them whom I have seen were the very cream of affectation."[9] The bond was formed; Scott was both artistically and politically influential and supported Baillie's talents as well as those of writers she recommended to him. In addition, he was always quick to handle tedious problems for her with no thought of personal gain. When Baillie wrote to Scott in the spring of 1808 and asked that he request publisher Archibald Constable to allow the poet John Struthers twenty-five to thirty copies of his forthcoming book for his own dispersion, Scott handled the negotiations within two weeks.[10] Scott

---

8. NLS 3876 ff.48–49; *Letters*, 233. Notably, critic Francis Jeffrey had reported *Marmion*'s success would be "less than brilliant" (Johnson, 281).

9. Qtd. in Johnson, 286.

10. NLS 3877 ff.5–7, 39–40, 59–60; *Letters*, 236–38. Archibald Constable (1774–1827), Scottish publisher, set up his own shop on the north side of High Street, Edinburgh, in 1795 after several years of apprenticeship. His tendency to take risks and accept varied publications enabled him to transform the business of publishing. In 1802 the start of the *Edinburgh Review* saw his connection with Walter Scott, and he had a share with Messrs. Longman & Co. in the publication of *Lay of the Last Minstrel* (1805). In 1814 the first chapters of *Waverley* were shown to Constable, who detected the author and arranged to publish it by dividing the profits with Scott. On the advice of James Ballantyne, Scott afterwards sometimes deserted Constable for other publishers, but they remained friends. On the failure in 1826 of Hurst, Robinson, & Co., the London agents for Constable & Co., the latter firm became insolvent along with James Ballantyne & Co., consuming the investments of Scott along with theirs (*DNB*, IV:957–58).

John Struthers (1776–1853), Scottish poet, was born in Lanarkshire while Baillie's family were residents of Long Calderwood, and they read to him and played with him while he was a child. Struthers became a shoemaker in Glasgow but, reading widely and writing considerably, began to earn some literary reputation. He gave up his trade to become an

trusted Baillie's abilities as well; and she assisted him during her stay in Edinburgh by reading at his request the manuscript of his Gothic melodrama, *The House of Aspen*, a work that her plays had put him "entirely out of conceit with."[11] In it she found similarities to her own tragedy entitled *The Separation*, in which a wife discovers the guilt of her husband through the death-bed confession of a servant, and she implored Scott not to think she had borrowed the idea from him when he read her play in a future publication. Praising specific scenes and characters in *Aspen*, Baillie candidly suggested that his future plays might improve with a better dramatic plan which allowed his "delightful imagination more liberally to enrich the work."[12]

When Joanna and Agnes left Edinburgh in late May, Baillie, at the Scotts's request, wrote immediately to Charlotte Scott on their safe arrival in London and thanked her for the "friendly attentions" they had received while on their visit. Since the house Joanna and Agnes lived in near Red Lion Hill was in a state of remodeling, with "Blacksmiths & housepainters" creating great confusion, the sisters were staying at their brother's house on Grosvenor Street.[13] Matthew and Sophia Baillie's daughter Elizabeth Margaret and son William were now young teenagers, and Joanna had been testing some of Thomson's tunes and her lyrics through her niece's playing and singing. Dr. Baillie had not yet been appointed physician to George III, but his practice at this time was garnering an ample income of over £9,000 per year, and he sometimes helped his sisters with major household expenses. After the remodeling, the sisters arranged a trip to the Lake District in the fall of 1808; there they met Wordsworth and Southey. When she wrote to Scott in October, she detailed that meeting, discussed reading Southey's *The Chronicle of the Cid*, and also asked for Scott's support of James Grahame, who

---

editor for two different publishing firms, finally becoming librarian of Stirling's public library in Glasgow. His most popular publication was *The Poor Man's Sabbath* (1804), which went into four editions, followed by *The Peasant's Death* (1806), *The Winter Day* (1811), and *Poems, Moral and Religious* (1814) (*DNB*, XIX:63).

11. Qtd. in Johnson, 186.

12. NLS 3877 ff.3–4; *Letters*, 234–35. See more detailed discussion of *The Separation* in chapter 5.

13. Baillie gives simple directions to her house in a letter to Margaret Holford Hodson, March 1813: "Our house is the 2d on the left hand as you enter the Village near the Red Lion Inn" (CLS 2; *Letters*, 540). The area is listed in the Hampstead *Rate Books* as Nag's Head Side. See note 83 following for more detail.

was then seeking a church position.[14] Early in 1809 Scott told Baillie that his great ambition was "to get up some of your dramas and shew the people what plays ought to be,"[15] and they began serious collaboration on a performance of her *Family Legend*. Scott had given the play to Henry Siddons by September 1809. Siddons, the eldest son of dramatic actress Sarah Siddons, had married Harriet Murray, also an actress, and the couple had moved to Edinburgh to manage the Edinburgh Theatre. Usually suffering from monetary losses, the theater would finally reach a turning point with its popular production in February 1819 of Scott's *Rob Roy*. Meanwhile, Siddons replied to Scott that he was returning the play "with some few curtailments and very slight alterations" and believed it could be well dramatized, though if Baillie intended to make a profit, "the London Theatres must be her mark."[16] All too aware of the political nature of the London stage, however, Baillie and her colleague determined to present the play in Edinburgh:

> I need scarcely tell you—indeed I cannot tell you how sensibly I feel the friendly interest you take in the success of my Play. Your zeal in getting so immediately the drawing of a highland Lady's dress from Mrs Maclean and the tartans of the two clans, is like the happy eagerness of a school-boy

---

14. NLS 3877 ff.158-61; *Letters*, 239-43. James Grahame (1765-1811) was a Scottish poet born in Glasgow. He studied for the church and was admitted to the Society of Writers to the Signet in 1791. In 1809 he was ordained by the Bishop of Norwich and appointed curate of Shipton Moyne, Gloucestershire, but left to attend to family matters in 1810. He was an unsuccessful candidate for St. George's Chapel, Edinburgh, but was later appointed sub-curate of St. Margaret's, Durham, transferring to Sedgefield in the same diocese. His poems were admired by Scott and attacked by Byron; works include *The Sabbath* (1804), *Birds of Scotland* (1806), *British Georgics* (1808), and *Poems on the Abolition of the Slave Trade* (1810) (*DNB*, VIII:366).

15. Qtd. in Sutherland, 134.

16. See RCS HB.ix.52 from Siddons to Scott. In a long published letter dated 19 October 1805 from Joanna to Dr. Matthew Baillie, she had politely rejected Sir John Sinclair's (1754-1835) advice on writing tragedies adapted for stage effect (he offered her *On the Fall of Darius* to consider). She did, however, accept Sinclair's suggestion to write a play for charitable reasons and produced *The Family Legend* in Edinburgh to such end. This letter to Matthew may be extant because Matthew forwarded it to Sinclair with his own attached note (dated 20 November 1805), but Sinclair probably retained it for his own collection of miscellaneous letters. I have not located the original.

who works with his whole heart & soul to get up his holyday Drama. . . . I thank you then for Lady Louisa Stuart's note as well as your own,[17] and shall take an early opportunity of looking over the Play in reference to what she says of the character of Sir Hubert. . . . You asked leave to show the play to your Friend Mr W. Erskin which I granted willingly,[18] as I shall be glad to have the benefit of his remarks upon it; and there is another Gentleman to whom I wish to have it shewn, both from the opinion I have of his taste, and because I feel that I owe him this attention, viz. Mr Mackenzie the Man of Feeling.[19]

Clearly, Baillie respected and solicited Scott's criticism. That does not imply, however, that she was uncertain of her abilities, only that she trusted his experience, his expertise, and that of his own literary colleagues.

The Family Legend: A Tragedy, In Five Acts, Baillie's Highland play which had appeared at the end of the second edition of *Miscellaneous Plays* in 1805, was dedicated to Sir Walter Scott. Scott wrote the "Prologue," and his friend Henry Mackenzie supplied the "Epilogue" for the 1810 Edinburgh stage production. In her "Preface" to the tragedy, Baillie explains that the plot was given to her in 1805 by Anne Damer as a legend handed down to her from her maternal grandmother, and Damer believed it might be well

---

17. Lady Louisa Stuart was daughter of Lord Vere Bertie and wife of Sir Charles Stuart (1753–1801) (*DNB*, XIX:74).

18. William Erskine, Lord Kinneder (1769–1822), became an intimate friend of Scott when the two young men began to study German together in the 1790s. It was Erskine who negotiated for Scott's translation of Burger's ballad "Lenore" in 1796, helping launch Scott's literary career; and Scott dedicated the Third Canto of *Marmion* to Erskine in 1808. Erskine became sheriff deputy of Orkney in 1809, and in 1814 Scott accompanied him and other friends on a voyage to the Orkney Islands. Lockhart credits Erskine with the critical estimate of the Waverley novels. In 1822 Erskine was promoted to the bench as Lord Kinneder but died shortly afterward under the stress of having been unjustly accused of "improper liaisons" (*DNB*, VI:864–65, and Johnson).

19. Henry Mackenzie (1745–1831), miscellaneous writer and novelist, was born in Edinburgh. His first sentimental novel entitled *The Man of Feeling* (1771), influenced by Sterne, appeared anonymously and was mistakenly attributed for a while to a Mr. Eccles, a clergyman of Bath. One of the earliest members of the Royal Society of Edinburgh, Mackenzie was a friend of Hume, Home, Davy, and Scott (*DNB*, XII:594–96).

suited to the stage.[20] Adrienne Scullion contends that this play, then, "is a story about a woman passed down through generations of women and finally made public through the pen of another woman."[21] But Baillie gave the credit for its ultimate success to Scott:

> I cannot take leave of my reader without begging leave to offer my warmest acknowledgments to my friend Mr. Scott, at whose desire, cheered with much friendly encouragement, I offered the Family Legend to the Edinburgh Theatre, and who has done more for its service than I could have done had I been upon the spot myself.[22]

Also thanking Henry Mackenzie, William Erskine, and Mr. and Mrs. Henry Siddons for the production, Baillie seemed genuinely proud of the acceptance of her play. But she was not totally preoccupied with the production of *Legend*, for in October 1809 she apologized to Scott for failing to answer two of his letters, having "been wandering to & fro upon the face of the earth for these 3 months past."[23] Part of the "wandering" was in Devonshire, the home of her friend Anne Elliott;[24] when she returned, her thoughts turned back to the play. At the onset of their collaboration, Scott had assured Baillie that the play would probably run nine nights and that she might expect it to earn no less than £300–400; the new theater in Leith Walk was elegantly fitted and just sufficiently large enough for the play—well suited for Baillie who considered large theaters "a bane and pest to the Drama."[25] Henry Mackenzie wrote to Baillie in December 1809 that he had finished the epilogue but requested, "Tell me candidly in Answer to this, if you approve this Epilogue & think it will answer the purpose," because his interest in her play was "beyond mere words."[26] Paradoxically, while this play probably suffered the most

---

20. Carhart argues that *Legend*'s theme, however, had also been the focus of Thomas Holcroft's *The Lady of the Rocks* acted earlier at Drury Lane (24).
21. Scullion, 167.
22. *DPW*, 481.
23. NLS 3878 ff.180–84; *Letters*, 245.
24. Anne Elliott of Honiton, Devonshire, also visited Baillie often when she was seeing relatives at Fenchurch Street in London, and Baillie often traveled to Devon to see Elliott. See further discussion of Elliott in chapter 4.
25. Qtd. in Johnson, 323.
26. RCS HB.ix.50.

tampering, it also received the most care and attention in production than did any of her other plays. If her other dramas had benefited from the expertise of those more adept at staging than she was, they may well have proved just as successful.

Charlotte Scott brought thirty friends to the premier, but even Walter must have been surprised when *The Family Legend* opened at the Edinburgh Theatre on 29 January 1810 to a packed house and scored such a tremendous success for three weeks that it was immediately followed by a revival of *De Monfort* on February 20 and yet another run of the play in March, producing, Scott said, a "deep and powerful effect" on the Edinburgh audience.[27] Concurrently, *De Monfort* was running in American theaters as well. But *The Family Legend* was certainly Baillie's most popular play in Scotland, and Scullion attributes *Legend*'s success to its "heroically Ossianic tone" which coincided with the patriotic mood of Edinburgh at the time. It is a play about deceit, revenge and retribution, lost loves, innocence at risk, concealed identity, and espionage, culminating in a bloody duel. More theoretically, Scullion argues, "The principle of patriarchy, authority and social order are the key thematic concerns of *The Family Legend*—principles which have allowed Helen to be sold as a pawn in a male plot." The play is

> certainly revealing of the morality imposed upon women in the late eighteenth and early nineteenth centuries that the traditionally romantic "happy" ending is curtailed. . . . there is no tableau of united lovers, no anticipation of wedding celebrations . . . merely a declamatory prayer from Argyll.

In addition, argues Scullion, Baillie's "clear interest in the actual and metaphoric function of the family as a point of social and economic organisation contributes to the central debates of the Romantic identity."[28] However, while this drama, like most of Baillie's plays, probes the psychology of relationships, its success in Scotland was probably the result of its ethnicity. *Legend* also ran in Newcastle the same year and in Bath the following year.

While Scott consulted with Baillie throughout the Edinburgh production of *Legend*, it did not appear without editing. In June 1809, while he was working on authentic Highland costumes, Scott, having also given the play to Lady Louisa Stuart to read, asked

---

27. Johnson, 223–24. See also Scott's letters (ed. Grierson).
28. Scullion, 163–64.

Baillie's permission to alter some of the characterizations. Baillie, grateful but somewhat reluctant to make major revisions, conceded to look over the play in reference to what Lady Stuart had said of the character of Sir Hubert:

> If I have made him appear insensible to the wrongs of his Mistress, it is very faulty indeed, and must be rectified. Perhaps, however, if this is attended to, that through out the play the Clans men & not Maclean himself are represented in wishing to get rid of Helen, that she in telling her story would naturally throw the whole blame upon them, and that Sir Hubert had not like John of Lorne any previous dislike or prejudice against him, it will not appear so very objectionable. In regard to his going away and leaving his friends to fight it out with their enemies themselves, the enemy were to come to the Castle as peaceable visitors, few in number, therefore staying to assist them would have been a post of no danger and altogether useless. But do not think I am defending myself from an unwillingness to alter what I have written. If the character of Sir Hubert makes any thing of the same impression on yourself when you shall have the goodness to read it a second time that it has done upon her Ladyship, it is not right, and must be set to rights; tho' we must avoid having two people vehemently loud upon the stage about the same thing.[29]

While Baillie defended her character to a point, this kind of collaboration and revision was not uncommon but was, instead, the very nature of theater production. By October 1809 Baillie seemed convinced that Scott's suggestions were valid and responded that she agreed with the changes and planned to set about the alterations immediately:

> tho' I shall have difficulty in doing it, from having no copy of the play by me to refer to, except the original rough copy, so blotted, & interlined, & different in many parts from the other, that I question whether I shall be able to unravel it. When I put the play into your hands, I thought I had another copy of it which Mrs Baillie was kind enough to write out for me; but drawers, & trunks, & even band-boxes have

---

29. NLS 3878 ff.78–9; *Letters*, 243–44.

> been searched in vain; it is no where to be found; I believe the Brownies or Fairies have taken it. What regards the Lover's character, that he may have no blot, as you say, on his scutcheon, I will contrive to alter myself, and I shall also try to shorten the Cavern Scene; but as for altering names & all the other improvements, I must beg that you, or Mr W. Erskin[e], (of whose approbation I am always very proud,) or any of your friends who may be willing to undertake the task, will have the goodness to make them for me. I shall be well pleased with all you may do or appoint to be done in this way, and shall thank you with all my heart.[30]

Most of these *early* changes were nonsubstantive, and Baillie was grateful for Scott's help. Meanwhile, he was investing all the time he could spare from his own writing to make *Legend* work on stage. It was truly a mutual production effort.

Scott and Mackenzie attended all rehearsals, and later alterations were significant; even Henry Siddons demanded drastic cuts to bring the play within normal performance time. Some of these, Scott felt, "resembled less the work of a pruning knife than of a tomahawk"; but when the play was performed, he admitted that the cuts "had the effect of tearing ornaments from a balloon. The piece was less elegant. . . but it rose more lightly."[31] Baillie was cheered by the play's eventual success, but in her letter of thanks to Scott on 4 February 1810, she revealed her apprehensions and anticipated his own on the play's opening:

> You have indeed sent me a loud & hearty cheer from my native land, and I feel it at my heart sensibly & dearly. The applause of the most brilliant London Theatre I could not so feel, and I receive it as a gift from that great hand which has bestowed upon me many blessings for which I must endeavour to be as thankful as I can. And now, before I proceed one line further, what shall I say to you, my brave & burly champion, who have taken the field so zealously in my behalf, and thro' many difficulties gained for me this proud day? I have nothing to say but a great deal to think, and it will be matter of grateful & pleasant reflection to me as long as I live. . . . And so you sat shaking last monday night lest

---

30. NLS 3878 FF.180–84; *Letters*, 245–46.
31. Qtd. in Johnson, 323.

any awkward blunder should bring disgrace upon us (for I will say us) and I sat by the fireside here with the most composed assurance that Mrs Siddons, according to my usual cross luck was still confined with her eyes, and that the play would be put off for some time, not withstanding you told me monday was the day. Once or twice during the evening it came across me that my Legend might at that moment be in representation at Edin^r, but my Sister began reading Froisard [sic]³² and it went out of my head. This would not have been the case with me ten years ago when De Monfort was acted; but so many disappointments & cross fortunes have visited me since that time, that I have become now, as to hope, like a very aged person. Well; if hope with me has grown old, a sensibility to honourable notice & the partial kindness of kin & country has not, and I trust never will.³³

Baillie was wise to be apprehensive, for her dealings with Drury Lane, Sheridan, and his celebrities had taught her nothing if not wariness. The burden of the female pen had clearly taken its toll on the playwright.

Profits from *The Family Legend*, featuring Scott's friend the actor Daniel Terry as Argyle,³⁴ were substantial; but from the onset Baillie had designated a significant portion for charity, the benefactor a somewhat unappreciative Mr. Henderson who was taking care of seven sisters and two brothers and who was to receive the copyright for two editions.³⁵ This type of generosity was not uncommon for

---

32. This is probably the annotated edition of the Old English *Froissart*, edited by Henry Weber, that Scott suggested Murray publish as a reprint project around 1809 (Johnson, 307–8).

33. NLS 3879 ff.13–14; *Letters*, 250–51.

34. Daniel Terry (1780?–1829), actor and playwright born at Bath and respected in London and Edinburgh alike, idolized Scott and imitated him in manner and style. Terry, who performed dozens of roles opposite such greats as Mrs. Siddons and Kean, on 12 March 1816 produced a musical adaptation of Scott's *Guy Mannering*. Terry's second wife Elizabeth Nasmyth was known for her taste in design and reportedly aided in decorating Abbotsford. After Terry's death she married lexicographer Charles Richardson (*DNB*, XIX:563–66).

35. Baillie writes to Scott on 27 October 1810:
> Just before we left Hampstead, I received a letter from Mr Balantine [sic] inclosing a draft for, I believe, £70 as the copy money for the Family Legend. I told him in answer, as perhaps he

Baillie, for she believed in Christian charity and was prosperous enough to practice it—she would later designate profits of more than £2,000 from *A Collection of Poems* for her childhood friend Mrs. James Stirling—and she was not afraid to call in favors to help support various causes. For *Legend*, however, Baillie's reward came in a more personal form from Scott in November 1810 after his Highland visit to Staffa as the guest of Laird Ranald Macdonald. Traveling northwest above Glasgow to the seacoast resort of Oban, Scott took a boat over to the desolate but sublime Isle of Mull. The journey to Oban itself would have been no small feat by coach or horseback in 1810, for even today the travel by train through the barren rocky terrain is slow. Once there, the Scotts passed close to the Lady's Rock in the Sound of Mull, the rock mentioned in Baillie's *Family Legend*. Rowing across the sea to Iona, Scott and his wife encountered children on the beach who offered some green stones for sale, each said to have the virtue of granting a wish. Charlotte Scott bought a few for a necklace, and Walter bought several which he later had set into a brooch for Baillie. Receiving the gift in November, she responded as follows:

> Your harp of the north is a most beautiful & elegant harp, not to mention the other virtues it possesses; and as soon as this mourning [morning] is over, I'll buy me a new gown to put respect upon it, and ware [sic] it in the stomacher of the same very gallantly. Many thanks to you for the kindly gift! and I will fancy I may thank Mrs Scott also for the very elegant taste of the thing; no impeachment to your skill in these matters neither. The green stones of St: Columbus do indeed possess the virtues ascribed to them; for I have already put it to the proof by wishing a wish over the smallest of them viz a fine day for a Friend of ours who left us this morning for Scotland to travel in, and behold a beautiful sunny morning after many days of gloom & rain. I am reserving the largest stone to wish my Brother back from

---

has told you, that he must write to Mr Henderson upon the subject, for that I meant only to receive what you & he agreed on as right for two Editions, leaving Mr H. to make the best bargain for himself that he could for what remained of the entire copy right. This Mr H. is a strange man; I dont know what to make of him: I find he never called on either yourself or Mr Balantine last spring when he passed thro' Edin^r.–But I have teased your good nature upon this subject too often.– (NLS 3879 ff.236–39; *Letters*, 273)

Windsor to the comforts of his own fireside; and if that succeed also, I shall take my next largest stone to wish you up from Edin^r in the course of the winter or spring, with as much business to do as will make it perfectly prudent in you to indulge it. You must come & see how well I shall look with my broach & my new gown; were there no other thing for you to do but this, it were cause sufficient.[36]

This was a sentimental, intimate gift from Scott, and Baillie felt his devotion acutely. Meanwhile, she also apprised Scott of her plans to see the upcoming dramatization of *Lady of the Lake* and of her excitement on hearing that *De Monfort* had been acted at a county fair, which clearly spoke of the play's popular appeal. Scott had sent *Lady of the Lake* to her in the summer of 1810, and on June 10 he replied to her that

> I am gratified by your appreciation of the Lady of the Lake for were I to be asked who in Great Britain I should most wish to please by my poetical attempts I would certainly name the person whose works had afforded me the highest degree of interest & pleasure & in this respect I know not any one who comes within a bowshot of you.[37]

Her sister-in-law and niece had just seen *Lady of the Lake* at the Royal Circus, and Baillie was interested in every detail. Engaged in production details and revisions for her own *Family Legend*, she was at this time particularly absorbed in the idea of performance.

In addition to this professional success, Baillie seemed content also in her personal life during this time. Her brother Matthew and his wife Sophia were traveling in Scotland in 1809 but were sorry they could not turn their journey toward Scott's Ashestiel. Mathew, Sophia, and Scott were in her thoughts; but at the same time she and Agnes, always outdoors women at heart, had been

> scrambling amongst the marble rocks of Torquay & coasting along the beautiful well wooded shores of Devon, and pacing thru' the solemn wiles of Exeter Cathedral by moonlight, with one candle carried before us which cast up its partial light upon the lofty pillars & arched roof, producing such striking

---

36. NLS 3879 ff.266–69; *Letters*, 274.
37. NLS 852, ff.9.

& various effects, as made the Devon Dames who were with us call out with one accord "are we not near the grave of Michael Scott?"[38]

This visit to her friend Anne Elliott in Devon was one of many such country visits there which always seemed to raise Baillie's spirits, and now in her late forties Baillie exhibited the same exuberance she had shown as a schoolgirl in Scotland. Soon back at home, she resumed her visiting and receiving visits from neighbors as usual, including Scott's "poetical" friend Edward Coxe (who would later contribute "On Reading Marmion" and another poem to Baillie's 1823 *A Collection of Poems*), William Sotheby, Mary Berry, Samuel Rogers, and others. She was also anxious about her brother's safe return from Scotland and looked forward to his account of their homeland, for he and Sophia were always her primary concern.

In 1810, amid a thriving practice, Dr. Matthew Baillie had been commanded by George III to attend on his youngest daughter Princess Amelia, but she died after a long illness on 2 November 1810 at the age of twenty-eight. Dr. Baillie attended on other members of the royal family as well and by the end of the year was appointed Physician Extraordinary to the king himself; he remained at Windsor for a total of 276 days between 1811 and 1812 during what Joanna called his "Thraldom." She saw Matthew only seldom during this appointment, and for a while even his wife Sophia could only meet him once a week at Cranford Bridge, between Windsor and London, for an hour of his company. Matthew, with concurrence of the other physicians in attendance on George III, kept a journal during this obviously stressful stay at Windsor. But Joanna made it clear that everyone felt great sympathy for the king and desired him well. Her anecdotes about the royal family in her letters to Scott during this time showed nothing less than sympathy and respect for both her brother and his patient. In January 1812, for example, she mourned that

> He [Dr. Baillie] still goes there every friday evening and remains till monday morning, and he might as well stay at

---

38. *Lay of the Last Minstrel* presents a scene in which William of Deloraine wanders through darkness of night to Melrose Abbey and the tomb of the wizard Michael Scott. Walter Scott claimed a debt to Coleridge's *Christabel* for elements of this poem (Johnson, 338). See NLS 3878 ff.180–84; *Letters*, 248.

home for any good he does or pretends to do. The poor King, I understand, is in very good bodily health, and as likely to live as if he were in every respect well. The Physicians will not now be released till the regency bill is up.[39]

Even though the reign of George III effectively ended in February 1811 when the Prince Regent took his oath of office, the "good old king," as Baillie sometimes called him, would not die until 1820. Dr. Baillie's attendance on the royal family kept her in touch with palace affairs for almost two decades and involved her in both the political and social arena of London—including the gossip. When in May of 1810 George III's bachelor son Prince Ernest (1771-1851) was found wounded in his apartment along with his dead valet, whose throat had been cut, Baillie supposed that Scott was, like everyone in London, busy discussing the "horrible story": "we are still engaged with it, tho' it is almost a week since it happen'd, and the more we think of it the more horrible & wonderful it seems."[40] In addition, she ended with a note about Chevalier Charles d'Éon de Beaumont (1728-1810), a writer and captain of dragoons who had been baptized as a boy; but congenital questions about his sex led to a public dedication at age three to the Virgin Mary under the feminine name Charlotte Geneviève Louise Augusta Timothea, and until the age of seven, d'Éon was dressed as a girl. He served France as a secret agent for many years in the guise of both male and female, but when he died in May 1810, it was finally revealed that he was, in fact, a man.[41] In the midst of such excitements, Baillie returned to her work.

After the success of her 1810 Edinburgh production of *The Family Legend*, Baillie commenced volume three of *A Series of Plays* and *Metrical Legends*. Encouraged by the stage success of *The Family Legend*, she revealed to Scott that she hoped her tragedy on fear, *The Dream*, would be well suited to the stage, though she would not offer it to the London managers she believed too proud to ask for any of her plays. Though Baillie wrote in November 1810 that "My great desire is that my plays should in this country become common acting plays," she knew that they were supposed by London theater

---

39. NLS 3882 ff.7-11; *Letters*, 294.
40. NLS 3879 ff.126-28; *Letters*, 267. Public opinion was that Sellis, the valet, had been murdered by the prince, though never confirmed by a jury (see Stanley Ayling's *George the Third* [New York: Knopf, 1972], 376).
41. NLS 3879 ff.126-28; *Letters*, 268. See Gary Kates, *Monsieur d'Eon is a Woman* (Baltimore: Johns Hopkins University Press, 2001).

management to be "only fit for the closet."⁴² The success of *Legend*'s representation in Edinburgh in 1811 had to have made her ill luck at Drury Lane after the 1800 presentation of *De Monfort* especially poignant, and Ellen Donkin attributes her lack of success there to animosity from manager Richard Brindley Sheridan, as did Baillie.⁴³ But she continued to work, visit friends, and attend the theater. On 7 February 1811 she wrote a long critique to Scott on the London performance of *Lady of the Lake*: "The day before yesterday, my Sister & I went with a large party to see the first representation of the Knight of Snowdoun at Covent Garden Theatre"; the play was well received and the theater was filled with "well dressed Gentleman-like men."⁴⁴ By July she was reading his *Vision of Don Roderick*, whose profits Scott dedicated to the Portuguese war sufferers, and she promised him her third volume of plays by December in time for Christmas. Scott responded in August 1811 that

> Were it possible for me to hasten the treat I expect by such a composition with [from?] you, I would promise to read the volume at the silence of noonday, upon the top of Minchmuir, or Windlestrawlaw. The hour is allowed, by those skilful in demonology, to be as full of witching as midnight itself; and I assure you, I have felt really oppressed with a sort of fearful loneliness, when looking around the naked and towering ridges of desolate barrenness. . . . It is in such a scene that the unknown author of a fine, but unequal poem, called Albania, places the remarkable superstition which consists in hearing the noise of a chase. . . . I have often repeated his verses with some sensations of awe in such a place, and I am sure yours would effect their purpose as completely.⁴⁵

Even with Scott's encouragement, some successful performances, and public acceptance of her as a writer, Baillie had now conceded

---

42. NLS 3879 ff.266–69; *Letters*, 277.
43. Donkin, 168. See more detailed explanation in chapter 4.
44. NLS 3880 ff.25–29; *Letters*, 278–79. Fitz-James, who called himself "the Knight of Snowdon," appears in Scott's *The Lady of the Lake*. Dramatic versions were presented in Edinburgh, Dublin and London between September 1810 and February 1811 (H. Philip Bolton, *Scott Dramatized* [London: Mansell, 1992], 14).
45. NLS 1750, f.109.

that her plays were confined to the *literati* and that she would simply lay them aside for her heirs:

> I have the mortification to find that, as they are not acted in the London Theatres, they are considered as not adapted to representation. . . . My scheme therefore is to go on writing, but to reserve all the rest of my plays in manuscript to be produced by my heirs upon the Theatre when we shall have, (as doubtless some time or other shall have) Theatres better fitted & better disposed to receive them.[46]

Baillie did not, of course, stop writing plays for publication, for volume three of *A Series of Plays* and *Dramas* would follow; but she now seemed resigned to her fate as a dramatist more read than performed, having been totally discouraged by the patriarchy of the London theater. Contemporaries such as Hannah Cowley, Elizabeth Inchbald, and Sophia Lee had reaped some success, however; and, as Catherine Burroughs suggests, the distinction of the closet stage piece was not necessarily detrimental to all early women dramatists:

> Rather than comparing the closet unfavorably with the formal theaters, a number of women who wrote about London playhouses theorized an approach to theater practice that allows, indeed encourages, an appreciation of the theatricality of both kinds of arenas. . . . a flexibility and imagination that may in part be tied to women's experience of performing femininity on social "stages" and to their understanding of how a cleavage between public and private realms obtruded upon their lives.[47]

It was still difficult, however, for any playwright to achieve success in the limited number of patent and royal theaters in Britain. Nevertheless, Baillie did not deal particularly well with her banishment, for having grown up among intelligent, respectful men in her family, who were supportive of rather than intimidated by her, she was not prepared for the scorn she faced with her debut in London. Baillie's self esteem clearly suffered, but she was tenacious

---

46. NLS 3880 ff.172–76; *Letters*, 283. Baillie did not, of course, leave forthcoming plays in manuscript but compiled *The Dramatic and Poetical Works of Joanna Baillie* in 1851.

47. Burroughs, *Closet*, 11.

about her craft and simply determined to reject the current commodification of literature for a more private sphere. Scott's promotion and the success of *The Family Legend* may have made her failure in the London theaters more intense, but she was grateful for his sincere support at a time when he was the most famous writer in the western world.

During 1811 and 1812 Baillie continued to correspond with Scott about writers such as Thomas Campbell, William Sotheby, Lord Byron, George Crabbe, and others; about politics and Napoleon; and about her brother's continued attendance at Windsor. In addition, she had been in the process of netting a money purse for Scott:

> Every body here enquires at me about a new Poem which you are writing, for which you are to receive 3000 guineas[48] (money enough this to fill the purse I am to net for you) and I in return, to pressure some little consequence consistent with the truth, say that I am only in your confidence in regard to your building & your Farming & the planting of your woods.[49]

Sending the finished purse in March, she was also still keeping up with Scott's ongoing construction of Abbotsford on Tweed, and he wrote to her that

> I have got a beautiful design for my cottage from Stark of Glasgow, a young man of exquisite taste. . . . I do not intend to proceed upon this great adventure for a while as yet. . . . While I was watching my infant or rather my embryo oaks you have been wandering under the shade of those celebrated by Pope and Denham, or in a still earlier age by James and Chaucer. How often have you visited the site of Herne's oak and called up the imaginary train of personages who fill the stage around it in representation? And was I obliged to your kindness or that of George Ellis for a bag of acorns from Windsor Forest which reached me lately?[50]

---

48. Scott was working on *The Bridal of Triermain* and *Rokeby* simultaneously, both appearing in 1813, and Baillie does not identify which work she means.
49. NLS 3882 ff.7–11; *Letters*, 291–96.
50. NLS 1750 f.118.

Baillie was completing volume three of *A Series of Plays* while Scott was working on *The Bridal of Triermain* and *Rokeby* (1813), and their letters always turned to these creative pursuits. Meanwhile, she was sitting for her "Highland" portrait by artist John James Masquerier and on its completion wrote humorously to Scott in May 1812 that it made her look melancholy and somewhat peevish, with a long body and short limbs, quite in reverse of her natural proportions.[51] She was also working on *Henriquez*, helping Sotheby with his own writing (assuring him that she would read it with the severity of a "Northern Critic"),[52] proofreading her third volume, and, homesick for Scotland, lamenting in August of 1811 that she and Agnes would gladly trade the beautiful forests at Windsor for the old bare sides of Ben Lomond.

Volume three of *A Series of Plays: in which it is attempted to delineate the stronger passions of the mind, each passion being the subject of a tragedy and a comedy* appeared in 1812 and included *Orra, The Dream, The Siege,* and *The Beacon*. Receiving an early copy in December 1811, Scott responded to Baillie:

> The whole character of Orra is exquisitely supported as well as imagined and the language distinguished by a rich variety of fancy which I know no instance of excepting Shakespeare. . . . I think the Dream extremely powerful indeed but I am rather glad we did not hazard the representation for the reasons mentioned in my last. . . . The latter half of the volume I have not perused with the same attention, though I have devoured both the comedy and the Beacon in a hasty manner.[53]

But the real "Northern Critic" was not to be as kind as Scott. Shortly before Scottish reviewer Francis Jeffrey attacked Baillie's third volume in 1812, he had noted in 1811, after the success of her *Family Legend*, that "Southey, and Wordsworth, and Coleridge, and

---

51. John James Masquerier (1778–1855) was the son of French parents and student of the Royal Academy, joining the studio of John Hoffner around 1796 and painting his friends as well as the famous. He retired to Brighton a wealthy man in 1823 (*DNB*, XIII:1–2). Masquerier's portrait of Joanna Baillie hangs in Special Collections at the University of Glasgow. See NLS 3882 ff.169–72; *Letters*, 306.

52. RCS HB.ix.42; *Letters*, 187–88. The humorous reference was, of course, to Jeffrey.

53. Grierson, 3:36.

Miss Baillie have all of them copied the manner of our old poets; and, along with this indication of good taste, have given great proofs of original genius."[54] But his review of Volume Three was brutal, and Baillie never forgot it. In February 1812 the *Edinburgh Review* printed his remarks:

> It is now, we think, something more than nine years since we first ventured to express our opinion of Miss Baillie's earlier productions; and to raise our warning voice against those narrow and peculiar views of dramatic excellence, by which, it appeared to us, that she had imprudently increased the difficulties of a very difficult undertaking. Notwithstanding this admonition, Miss Baillie has gone on (as we expected) in her own way; and has become (as we expected) both less popular, and less deserving of popularity, in every successive publication. . . . Miss Baillie, we think, has set the example of plays as poor in incident and character, and as sluggish in their pace, as any that languish on the Continental stage, without their grandeur, their elegance, or their interest; and, at the same time, as low and as irregular in their diction as our own early tragedies,—and certainly without their spirit, grace, or animation.[55]

While Jeffrey's "as we expected" condemns Baillie for her unfeminine independence, his criticism that her plays are "poor in incident and character" is not unlike the criticism he levels on more successful playwrights of the time. He moves on to give Baillie *some* praise but focuses on non-threatening traits like her pleasing lyrical verse and her intelligent morality. Chastised again for not adhering to the critic's own recommendations, Baillie had by now determined to write no more plays for publication. The reviewer's ignorant and unfair lash was to damage yet another writer's career.

---

54. Qtd. in James A. Greig, *Francis Jeffrey of The Edinburgh Review* (Edinburgh: Oliver and Boyd, 1948), 194. There were literally dozens of reviews on Baillie's publications; while I cite or quote from a few in this biography, there could certainly be a separate study done to focus on them alone.

55. "*A Series of Plays, etc.*" *The Edinburgh Review* 19 (1811–12): 261–90.

Volume three of *A Series of Plays* begins with *Orra: A Tragedy, In Five Acts*, set in "Switzerland, *in the canton of* Basle, *and afterwards on the borders of the Black Forest in* Suabia"[56] around the end of the fourteenth century. Having read the play before its publication, Scott wrote Baillie that "I have a great quarrel with this beautiful drama [*Orra*] for you must know you have utterly destroyed a song of mine precisely in the turn of your outlaws ditty and sung by persons in somewhat the same position."[57] The first of three plays dedicated to fear in this volume, *Orra* combines feminism and psychological terror—the result is the heroine's madness. Orra, in love with Theobald, is the ward of Hughobert, who exiles her to an allegedly haunted castle because she has refused to marry his son Glottenbal. In her own defense, Orra laments that because fate has made her a woman she must consign herself and her property, regrettably, into the hands of some proud man: "Take all, I pray, / And do me in return the grace and favour / To be my master."[58] Because she refuses Hughobert's son, she is sent away to be intimidated into the match. What manifestation she actually sees at the witching hour is not clear, but she never recovers from her psychological terror, and the final act ends with Theobald's failed attempt to restore her sanity. Orra's comment in Act 2 that "there is a joy in fear" sets the stage for her susceptibility to the stories of apparitions. While she is clearly the victim of a forced marriage scam, her overly excitable nature fails to make her a totally sympathetic character for readers today, though Scott thought the play was likely to have "a good effect on the stage."[59] As with many of Baillie's plays, *Orra* focuses on the emotional trepidation of marriage and reinforces her consistent message that gender equality seldom exists in such a contract.

Following *Orra* is *The Dream: A Tragedy, In Prose, In Three Acts*, set in "*the monastery of St. Maurice in* Switzerland; *a castle near it*"[60] about the middle of the fourteenth century. Once again, fear is the focus, with jealousy and revenge also providing impetus for the

---

56. *DPW*, 235.
57. Grierson, 3:35. I have not identified Scott's song, but he was at the time working on *The Bridal of Triermain* and *Rokeby* (1813), both of which contain songs.
58. *DPW*, 240 (2.1).
59. NLS 3882 ff.99–103 (her reply to Scott dated 4 March 1812); *Letters*, 297.
60. *DPW*, 260.

climax. Imperial General Osterloo's fear is a result of guilt, and his crime is eventually revealed through a dream appearing to two monks. When a long-buried corpse is discovered, Osterloo confesses to murdering this man, who turns out to be Montera, the brother of the Prior conducting the investigation. The Prior's conflict of interest brings Osterloo to the executioner, but just as he is about to be rescued by the imperial ambassador, Osterloo dies—the axe at his neck—of fear. Baillie introduces a strong female character in Leonora, who reiterates the playwright's common theme of being "hurried" into an "unequal marriage" and who finally attempts the remorseful Osterloo's rescue. *The Dream* is more suspenseful than its companion *Orra*, and Baillie thought it well suited to the stage; but Scott did not think it should be brought out in Edinburgh because of the difficulty in acting Osterloo's character, and Baillie had no intention of offering it to the London theaters. When Lord Byron became an advocate for her plays a few years later, however, *The Dream* was one he considered for the London stage—but that production was not to be.[61]

After *The Dream*, Baillie relieves the tragic tension with *The Siege: A Comedy, In Five Acts*, set in "*a castle on the French confines of Germany.*"[62] She began this comedy on fear at least as early as 1810, for she mentions it to Scott in November of that year. In her "To The Reader," Baillie explains that the hero of a comedy on fear may appear humiliating rather than amusing, but her hero is "represented as timid indeed, and endeavouring to conceal it by a boastful affectation of gallantry and courage."[63] Count Valdemere, however, is not actually a hero in this play, because he has wronged the young Nina who is in love with him, and he is successfully pursuing Livia, the object of Antonio's affection. These misguided love affairs are eventually redirected by Walter Baurchel and his friend Dartz, whose plot proves that Valdemere is really a coward. Their lies about an approaching enemy siege upon the castle produce the desired effect on Valdemere; but the final act introduces a real siege in which Baurchel, Dartz, and their actor-soldiers actually have to defend the castle, though the situation proves more comic than dangerous. Along with Baillie's humorous remarks on poets and poetry (Walter's brother the Baron is a poet), there is a

---

61. *The Dream* is mentioned in several NLS letters to Scott; see *Letters*, 291–94 and 343 in particular.

62. *DPW*, 277.

63. Ibid., 230.

comment by Baron Baurchel which is very ironical. In the face of the siege, the women servants clamor and wring their hands. Losing his patience, the Baron reprimands them and sends them to their chores, but Livia admonishes him for being intolerant of their fear. His response is severe: "They think it necessary to raise an outcry, because they are women, and it is expected from them. I have been long enough duped in this way: I have no patience with it now."[64] This play allows Baillie, in her usual fashion, to emphasize the frailties of both sexes and to hope for their improvement.

As a finale to *A Series of Plays*, Baillie presents something in a different strain, *The Beacon: A Serious Musical Drama, In Two Acts*, set in "*a small island of the Mediterranean*"[65] during the middle of the fourteenth century. In this short drama on hope, the saint-like perseverance of Aurora, who shuns the advances of Ulrick, lord of the island, finally results in a reunion with her lost love Ermingard. Her nightly beacon draws Ermingard to her shore, and, in a scene fraught with sexual tension, she learns that he took holy orders when he believed her to have become Ulrick's mistress during his absence. Aurora vows passionately to convey herself to a convent close to Ermingard's monastery so that "The same winds / That do o'nights through your still cloisters sigh, / Our quiet cells visiting with mournful harmony, / Shall lull my pillow too." The lovers are eventually saved by the Pope's Legate, who explains that because Ermingard took his holy orders as the result of false reports of Aurora's love for Ulrick, Ermingard will be allowed to "doff with honour this thy sacred mantle, / And in its stead a bridegroom's robe assume."[66] Baillie does not mention *The Beacon* specifically in her letters and may have felt it was less powerful than the other three plays in this volume, because in her "To The Reader" she confesses that this passion is not so "powerfully interesting as those that are more turbulent" and might be in danger of becoming "tiresome, if long dwelt upon."[67] Even though *The Beacon* is a short drama, it seems well suited for the stage and its songs pertinent to the script. There is no record, however, of its ever being performed.

---

64. Ibid., 296.
65. Ibid., 300.
66. This and the preceding quote come from act 2.3 (*DPW*, 311).
67. *DPW*, 231.

While volume three ended Baillie's *Series of Plays*, she would later publish three additional ones which continued her focus on the human passions: *Romiero: A Tragedy, In Five Acts*; *The Alienated Manor: A Comedy, In Five Acts;* and *Henriquez: A Tragedy, In Five Acts*, all appearing in *Dramas* in 1836. Meanwhile, in this fruitful publication year of 1812, Baillie's social activities also continued. She saw *Julius Caesar* at Covent Garden, "naturally heavy & not very interesting"; she saw Scott's friend Daniel Terry act at the Little Theatre in a new melodrama taken from John Moore's novel *Zeluco*, said to have been an inspiration for Byron's *Childe Harold*; and she continued her social visits.

Baillie proceeded to read critically the works of her colleagues, but one such unsolicited reading seems to have occurred with Scott's *Rokeby* (1813). Apparently, Baillie's friend and neighbor, publisher Thomas Longman, was given the draft by Scott around October 1812. Longman must have passed the first proof copy on to Baillie without telling Scott; and when she wrote to Scott on October 13 about how much she admired the poem, he, much surprised, wrote a letter of disapproval to James Ballantyne.[68] Baillie clearly heard of his annoyance, for in a succeeding letter dated November 7, she apologized for Longman's action, not realizing it was inappropriate, and suggested that Ballantyne was more to blame than Longman, who did not "care a jot for poetry" and only wanted her response. Feelings were mended, and Scott saw that Baillie soon got an early copy of *Rokeby* from the author himself. Meanwhile, Joanna's brother was about to be released from Windsor on the death of George III; Scott, not so positively, anticipated the ascension of the Prince Regent in a note to Baillie in 1813:

> I fear that . . . the fatal termination of the poor old monarchs [sic] illness will soon (if it has not already) restore Dr. Baillie to his family. I would I could augur well of what is to follow but alas! a public defiance of morality is but a bad bottoming for a new reign: it is incalculable the weight which George the 3d derived from his domestic conduct. But we must hope the best & none is more willingly to hope it than I who would do my little best for the Crown of England if it hung upon a hedge stake. When I shall come to rummage your portfolio & eat your pudding at Hampstead is very uncertain.[69]

---

68. See letter in Grierson, 3:175–77.
69. NLS 1750, f. 140.

Scott would not visit London for some time, but Baillie was very much occupied, and her *Family Legend* was playing in Newcastle (1813). Unfortunately, however, after the publication of her volume three in 1812, it seemed that the London theater managers would compound their early rejection of her plays; they had yet another setback in store for her.

Notwithstanding her previous failure at Drury Lane, after reading some of her plays, Lord Byron began an attempt in 1815 to convince the management there of her merit and asked that they support a revival of *De Monfort*. Byron had long been an admirer of Baillie's plays, and his relationship with Anne Isabella Milbanke, Baillie's young friend, secured his support. When the much-edited version of *De Monfort* failed under Kean's representation, however, Byron seems to have lost interest.[70] Meanwhile, Baillie's friend William Sotheby was having similar problems with Drury Lane. In many letters Baillie discusses Sotheby's difficulties in getting his plays represented, often in the context of her own disappointments with the London theaters. While Lord Byron, an active member of the Drury Lane management committee, was supporting Baillie's plays, he may have been obstructing Sotheby's. Byron had written Hobhouse in 1811 that "Sotheby, whom I abused in my last [letter], improves, his face is rather against him, & his manner abrupt & dogmatic, but I believe him to be much more amiable than I thought"; and even though he praised Sotheby in *English Bards and Scotch Reviewers* and generally kept on friendly terms with him, Byron, after his exile, attacked the writer in *Beppo*, in the first canto of *Don Juan*, and in *The Blues: A Literary Eclogue*.[71] In a later letter to John Murray, Byron claimed that he "endeavoured to advance his [Sotheby's] petty attempts at Celebrity;—I moved the Sub Committee & Kinnaird—& Kean & all the Aristocracy of Drury Lane—to bring out his play—whose insufferable Mediocrity gave it a great chance of success—I bore with him—the Bore."[72] Byron justified his attacks on Sotheby by the incident of an anonymous critical letter, but the more likely reason surfaces in a comment to Samuel Rogers about Sotheby's "airs of patronage—which he affects with young

---

70. See the following chapter for a more detailed account of the Byron/Baillie relationship.

71. Reiman, vii.

72. Qtd. in Reiman, viii. Byron refers to his attempt to convince the management to produce Sotheby's *Ivan* in 1816, which was withdrawn after only a few rehearsals.

writers—& affected both to me and *of* me—many a good year."[73] After his later exile, Byron simply had no use for the English aristocracy of which Sotheby was a part. Disappointed at his lack of success in having his drama *Ivan* represented at Drury Lane and distressed by the death of his son William, Sotheby left England in May 1816 to spend a year on the continent but later returned to publish some of his best works.

During these years of active publishing for both Baillie and Scott, they were devoted friends and corresponded steadily about literature and about family matters. Even Agnes Baillie participated in the correspondence, and in May 1816 Charlotte Scott wrote to thank her for sending her own special plants for the landscape at Abbotsford.[74] That same year, Sophia and Matthew Baillie were devastated by their daughter Elizabeth Margaret's desire to marry Capt. Robert Milligan, "a mere soldier," as Joanna Baillie wrote to Scott in July of that year:

> I know you are truly interested in what concerns my happiness, and I am going to tell you of an event in our family which deeply concerns us all and has one way or another agitated our minds very much for these some months past. My Niece is going to be married; and tho' she has chosen a very worthy young man, whose family we have long known & highly respect, yet our anxiety for her happiness has been very great, perhaps unreasonably so, and I would not live the last April & May over again for a great hire. She is a very clever woman, fond of books and with a mind & taste well cultivated; he is a plain honest Soldier, whose education has been quite neglected and who, dogs & horses & military matter excepted, has little information on any subject. This being the case, you may believe we had all of us many discouraging thoughts in regard to her future happiness, and her poor Mother above all has been very anxious; but the young man himself has behaved under some very trying circumstances and throughout the whole of the affair, with so much sense & delicacy & sweetness of temper & forbearance, that we now, thank God! begin to hope with some confidence that she will really be happy. You will wish them all good I know, when I

---

73. Qtd. in Reiman, ix.
74. RCS HB.ix.13.

tell you that he was one of our brave Dragoons at Waterloo, where he was what was called severely wounded. He is to remain in the army, and hopes soon to get into the guards which are never ordered abroad but on actual service. He has a good moderate fortune, and being admirably fitted both in mind & body for a Soldier, it is the best plan. His name is Milligan, and it was a Sister of his, who sat next you when you last dined with us at Hampstead. . . . And a thing is to follow this marriage. . . I am going abroad with the new married pair and my Nephew William to spend some weeks & see part of Switzerland & Geneva.[75]

Baillie did, in fact, accompany the young couple. And while the family's anxiety was reasonable, the couple appear to have been compatible and lived most of their lives with their only daughter, Sophia Milligan (1817–82), near the coast at Ryde where all the Baillies often visited.

Very little is documented about Elizabeth Margaret or her husband Capt. Robert Milligan; he was obviously unwell during the latter part his life and suffered from wounds received as a young soldier in France. Clearly, Baillie, skeptical about marriage at best, wanted Elizabeth to be happy in this union, for she was very close to her niece. Elizabeth Margaret shared Baillie's love of literature and must have been very talented, as some handsome watercolors by her are housed in the Wellcome Institute's Poynter Collection. Baillie often refers to Elizabeth's love of poetry and music. Moreover, Baillie's confiding in Scott about the marriage is typical of her personal relationship with him. In a letter dated February 1816, just before her trip to Switzerland with the young married couple,[76] Baillie praised Scott's recently published *Paul's Letters to his Kinsfolk* but concluded that "it would have been better to have given them not as the letters of a fictitious person, altho' the introductory letter is a very good one of its kind."[77] He, in turn, suggested on her

---

75. See NLS letter 3887 ff.83–85 to Scott dated 2 July 1816; *Letters*, 353–55.

76. Baillie later wrote in her memoirs to William Baillie that the scenes from Mont Blanc and the Alps added "to the indwelling treasurers" of her heart, and she recalls the mountains that she and William watched together through a cloud that "seemed at that moment to have nothing to do with the earth" (WI MS 5613/68/1–6).

77. NLS 866 ff.68–72; *Letters*, 348.

return that certain alterations be made to her *Columbus* in *Metrical Legends*.

During Baillie's intimate friendship with Scott, only one event seems to have strained their relationship—the separation of Lord and Lady Byron. While Byron had befriended Baillie in 1815, or at least endorsed the revival of *De Monfort* at Drury Lane, his ensuing mistreatment of her friend Anne Isabella Milbanke caused Baillie to reprimand even Scott for his favorable October 1816 review of *Childe Harold* (Canto III) in *The Quarterly Review* as follows:

> We have felt ourselves very much affected by the perusal of these poems, nor can we suppose that we are singular in our feelings. . . . The work of the poet is indeed before the public, but the character, the habits of the author, and events of his life and the motives of his writing, are known but to the small circle of literary gossips, for whose curiosity no food is too insipid. . . . The time therefore appeared to be passed when the mere sin of having been dipped in rhyme was supposed to exclude the poet from the usual business and habits of life, and to single him out from the herd as a marked deer expected to make sport by his solitary exertions for escape. . . . The family misfortunes which have for a time lost Lord Byron to his native land have neither chilled his poetical fire, nor deprived England of its benefit. The Third Canto of Childe Harold exhibits, in all its strength and in all its peculiarity, the wild, powerful and original vein of poetry which, in the preceding cantos, first fixed the public attention upon the author.[78]

Baillie's February 1817 response was candid and angry:

> O! why have you endeavoured to reconcile the world in some degree with that unhappy man at the expence of having yourself, perhaps, considered as regarding want of all principle and the vilest corruption with an indulgent eye? indeed my good, my kind, my unwearied friend, this goes to my heart! I truly believe that you have done it to cheer in some degree the despair of a perishing mind and rouse it to make some effort to save itself; but this will not be: you

---

78. "Art. IX.–1. Childe Harold's Pilgrimage, Canto III . . . and other Poems," *The Quarterly Review* 16:31 (1816): 172–208.

cannot save him tho' by that effort you may depress, a most worthy character who has been already so sinned against, and who bears the deepest part of her distress in silence. And now that I am taking the privilege of a Friend I had almost said of a Mother to rate you thus, let me ask why you have reviewed Lord Bs poetry in a strain of praise which in my simple opinion is far beyond its real merit? I may not think you insincere and therefore I must even believe that your wits have been a wool gathering. . . . What I should consider as bad in Wordsworth I can never believe is good in Lord Byron.[79]

Along with Baillie's affront to Wordsworth's poetry, in the same letter she also attacked Byron's integrity and cited his stay in Switzerland with "a married man who has run away from this country and a Girl whom he has seduced." She had not identified the couple, however, as Percy Shelley and Mary Godwin.[80] What prompted Baillie's response was a February 19 letter from Lady Byron asking that she intervene with Scott, to whom Lady Byron had attributed the review. Baillie acted quickly, for she, too, was upset.[81] Nevertheless, this anxious period resolved through Scott's apologies, Baillie and he mended their discord; and she enthusiastically read his subsequent *Guy Mannering*, two of whose chapters he headed with quotations from Baillie, and *Tales of My Landlord*. Meanwhile, Scott asked to see her draft of *Metrical Legends*.

In addition to her continued worries about Lady Byron, 1817 proved to be a stressful year for Baillie's family as well. In November Dr. Matthew Baillie was summoned to Claremont for the confinement of the Prince Regent's only daughter Princess Charlotte Augusta. She had been estranged from her father because of his separation from her mother, and in 1816 she married Prince Leopold of Saxe-Coburg. On November 5, after two days of labor, she gave birth to a still-born son, and she died a few hours afterwards. While Dr. Baillie had been called to attend the birth, he reportedly spent the day in the library while the princess was attended by his

---

79. NLS 3888 ff.37–39; *Letters*, 363–64. See further discussion of Baillie's relationship with Lord and Lady Byron in chapter 4.

80. Though Baillie seldom mentions Shelley or his work, she must have known of him, for Scott surely did. Mary Shelley was writing to Scott as late as 1829.

81. OU Lovelace/Byron 62, ff. 157–58. This article is bound in *The Quarterly Review* volume of October 1816.

brother-in-law, Dr. Sir Richard Croft, the husband of Sophia Baillie's sister Margaret. Dr. Croft committed suicide a few months later, even though the labor had been in accordance with the best contemporary practice. While Croft was blamed by the public for Charlotte Augusta's death, the Prince Regent was gracious to him. Furthermore, Dr. Baillie was clearly distressed but believed that Croft had done all he could.[82] Joanna did not write to Scott again until July 1818 and then stated that next to burdening her brother she most hated to bother Scott with problems. She passed on a friend's questions about Scottish history, however, and complained that their correspondence had been too sparse for a few months. Her subject then turned to her improvements on *Columbus* and to domestic matters.

In 1820 Agnes and Joanna moved from the Hampstead home near Red Lion Hill (today known as Rossylyn Hill) that they had occupied for over twenty years to Holly Bush Hill (the area also called Windmill Hill), where they would remain the rest of their lives.[83] Today this is still a lovely area just off the upper end of High Street, with earlier vintage houses mixed with large Victorian ones lining the narrow, well-kept street. The house the sisters moved into was not pretentious, but neither was it small. At the same time her brother and sister-in-law were moving from their long-time residence on Grosvenor Street to the more fashionable Cavendish Square, and Dr. Baillie insisted on contributing £100 to his sisters' new lease.[84]

---

82. See both Crainz's account (39) and Rose Weigall's 1874 *Brief Memoir* about the princess.

83. It has been recorded incorrectly by historians for years that the Baillies moved to this location in 1806 on the death of their mother and remained there for over fifty years. The *Rate Books* (tax records) for the Hampstead parish of St. John confirm this move in 1820, however, as do the following letters from Baillie to Margaret Holford Hodson: "But it seems to be a season of change–with us, for Agnes & I also are about to quit the house in which we spent 21 years, and my Brother has at last been released from his long attendance at Windsor" (#11, 12 February 1820). The letter following provides a more specific address: "If I were as strong as I have been I would walk to Hendon to see you, for our new house is nearer you than the old one, being on what is called Holly Bush hill & very near the heath, but besides old age a cold & fatigue from moving &c has made me a very poor creature at present" (#12, 29 March 1820) (see *Letters*, 554–57). In addition, her 1850 contract with Longman shows her address as Hollybush Hill, Hampstead; and many of her letters written between 1822 and the 1840s contain the return address as "Holly bush Hill." This final residence is now called Bolton House.

84. Crainz, 142. See note to Joanna Baillie dated 22 November 1819

In the midst of these domestic disruptions, Baillie was putting the finishing touches on her historical verses entitled *Metrical Legends of Exalted Characters* (1821), a work begun much earlier and inspired by her friendship with Scott and her admiration of his historical romances:[85]

> In the great & deserved sensation of admiration excited by the Poems of Walter Scott, a few years later, I had my share, and the generous encouragement I always received from him was certainly of great use in keeping me to my work. The fascination of his heroic Ballads made the drama less interesting for a time and then an idea of Metrical Legends of exalted Characters, in which there should be no mixter [*sic*] of fiction in the events . . . first came into my head. . . . You know that I have been in Switzerland and have seen objects there which you would naturally expect me to notice but during the short time I was in that sublime region, my mind was occupied with anxious thoughts, and . . . I carried nothing home with me to add to the indwelling treasures of my heart. . . . I did not carry home with me what I might have done under different circumstances. The clouds seen in my youthful days floating across Benlomon[d] . . . as seen from the high lands of Longcalderwood, were my chief store of mountain-Ideas and continued so through life.[86]

Infused with illusions of Scotland, *Metrical Legends* was also allied to Scott's historical poetry. It is difficult to know how much or in what way Scott may have reshaped these poems, but Baillie alluded to his revisions to *Columbus* in a letter from June 1819. He would also ask to see her *Legend of Lady Griseld Baillie* a few months later:

---

from Matthew Baillie: "I cannot be satisfied without bearing a share at least in the expence of your new Lease–Agnes and you must allow me to pay one Hundred Pounds towards it, and I can not take a refusal without being hurt" (RCS HB.ii.35c).

85. Baillie writes to William Sotheby as early as August 1814 that she has been "amusing myself in a new path altogether, and have been really & truly writing in rhyme, a kind legend of our great hero Wallace" (HB.ix.23; *Letters*, 197). According to NLS letter 3888 ff.73-75 to Scott (*Letters*, 370-71), *Lady Griseld Baillie* was written around 1817 and *Columbus* a little earlier.

86. WI MS 5613/68/1-6; *Letters*, 13.

I have some time ago corrected & altered & copied out fair all my 3 Metrical Legends viz of William Wallace, Lady G. Baillie & Columbus. To this last in the way of reflection or imagery I have added nearly a third, besides altering all that you directly found fault with; for tho' you did not for fear of discouraging me too much, absolutely tell me that the poem was dry & bare, I had <u>gumption</u> enough to guess at your thoughts, and I hope I have profited by your opinion as much as if you had really set it down in black & white. I want to know from you how I should proceed in offering this small volume of poetry to the Booksellers. Unless I get a thousand guineas for it I will not publish at all. I mean to give Mr Longman the first offer, and should he decline it, as probably he will, I would offer it next to Constable or Murray or any body you would advise me to.[87]

Baillie probably did profit from many of Scott's comments, certainly from his experience with publishers, and their collaboration was typical for many writers as a significant part of the creative process.

Baillie revised *Legends* while her sister Agnes spent three weeks in Paris during 1819. Although Joanna had encouraged her to go, she lamented to Scott that far too many British families went abroad to reside for long periods of time, which seemed unpatriotic and unjust. Meanwhile, she wrote of Susan Ferrier's first work, *Marriage: a Novel*,[88] and of Sarah Siddons's private "performances": "Her manner is too solemn & her voice too deep for familiar society, and having her mind little stored except with what is connected with her profession." But Baillie still saw Siddons on social occasions and respected her as a performer who drew her acting "from a deeper source than actors generally do."[89] In January 1820 she

---

87. NLS 3890 ff.132–35; *Letters*, 389–90.

88. Susan Edmonstone Ferrier (1782–1854), Scottish novelist known for satirical sketches on society, published her first novel *Marriage* in 1818 (anonymously), followed by *The Inheritance* in 1824, and *Destiny*, dedicated to Scott, in 1831 (see *DNB*, VI:1255, and *The Feminist Companion to Literature*, 368).

89. NLS 3890 ff.132–35; *Letters*, 390. Baillie and Siddons were never of the same temperament, but in later years they were on friendlier terms, as she explained to Scott in 1827: "And this naturally leads me to mention a visit which we had last week from Mrs Siddons when she very kindly read to us in the evening a part of Othello with as much power & truth of expression as ever. Her & I take to one another very kindly now (NLS 3905 ff.260-261; *Letters*, 441).

sympathized with Scott's loss of his mother Anne Scott, who had died on Christmas Eve 1819. In answer to her questions about publishing negotiations, Scott soon wrote to assure Baillie that any publisher would make money on her *Legends* by giving her the sum she required and encouraged her to expect more from her bookseller:

> [I have] found great comfort in making my returns from a work contingent by selling only one edition at a time the bookseller paying all expences and ensuring me half of the free profits by granting bills for that amount at publication. . . . But as to your right to ask £1000 if you prefer. . . . A first edition in 4to would clear the booksellers.[90]

Scott's advice was sound, and Longman did, of course, publish *Metrical Legends of exalted Characters* in 1821, followed by a new edition of *A Series of Plays* that same year. As Baillie finalized *Legends*, she also anticipated Scott's upcoming visit in 1820: "I need not tell you how glad I shall be to see you in March. There are many times since I saw you last when I would have been very thankful to be well assured that I should ever see you again."[91] Baillie was passionate in her anticipation of seeing Scott once again, and it is only in correspondence with him that such sincere affection predominates. Coming to London in March to receive his baronetcy, Scott spent a quiet Sunday in Hampstead with Baillie and their mutual friend John Richardson and was then thrown into a flurry of visiting and entertaining. Joanna and Agnes would also visit Scott at Abbotsford that following November, when the two writers surely talked of his work on *Kenilworth* and *The Pirate* (1821) and of her upcoming *Legends*.

Metrical Legends of exalted Characters includes three historical legends, *William Wallace*, *Columbus*, and *Lady Griseld Baillie*, and four shorter pieces entitled "Lord John of the East: A Ballad," "Malcolm's Heir: A Tale of Wonder," "The Elden Tree: An Ancient

---

90. Grierson, 6:96.
91. NLS 3891 ff.3–4; *Letters*, 394.

Ballad," and "The Ghost of Fadon." As Baillie states in the "Preface" to these romances,

> I have ventured upon what may be considered, in some degree, as a new attempt,—to give a short descriptive chronicle of those noble beings, whose existence has honoured human nature and benefited mankind.[92]

Combining fictitious circumstances with both history and biography, Baillie's first memorial would be to William Wallace, the hero "of whose name some sensation of pride and of gratitude passes over every Scottish heart."[93] Her third memorial would be similarly nationalistic in its recognition of Lady Griseld Baillie, a woman virtually unknown to history but exhibiting "a perfection of character which is peculiar to woman."[94] Her remembrance of this heroine clearly furthered her feminist agenda. Baillie admitted that she struggled with the problem of how to write this woman's life, having to rely on domestic details sometimes "considered as vulgar and mean" rather than on documented historical fact. As Catherine Burroughs suggests, Baillie's dramatic theories open "ways of

---

92. *DPW*, 705.
93. Ibid., 707. William Wallace 1272?–1305), Scottish general and patriot famed for his skill and almost superhuman strength, led a successful Scottish uprising against Edward I for which he was executed in 1305. In both English and Scottish records, Wallace stands as the chief champion of the Scottish nation in its struggle for independence and the chief enemy of Edward in his premature attempt to unite Britain under one sceptre. It has been said that Wallace's natural hatred of the English and their king was the measure of the natural affection of his own people (see *DNB*, XX:563–72, and James A. Mackay's *William Wallace: brave heart* [Edinburgh and London: Mainstream, 1995]).
94. Ibid., 709. Lady Grisell Baillie (1665–1746) was the daughter of Sir Patrick Hume of Polworth and Grisell Kerr. She reportedly saved her father's life (under suspicion for participating in the Rye House Plot) by hiding him in the family vault near Redbraes Castle; her father's friend Robert Baillie was hanged, drawn and quartered on the same charge in 1685. The family fled to Utrecht, exiled with other Scottish Presbyterians, and Grisell made a secret voyage back to Scotland to rescue her sister and the family's fortune. At the 1688 revolution she and her mother returned to Britain in the company of the Princess of Orange. She married George Baillie, son of the executed Robert, in 1692, and helped manage his and her father's estates. Her works include *Orpheus Caledonius or a Collection of the Best Scotch Songs set to Music by W. Thomson* (1726) and *The Household Book of Lady Griselle Baillie* (1692-1733) (Janet Todd, ed., *British Women Writers* [New York: Continuum, 1989], 28–29).

appreciating women's contributions to both public and private stages."⁹⁵ The same may be said of *Lady Griseld Baillie*. While *Lady Griseld* is a non-dramatic work, Baillie captures in the legend the spirit and strength of a Scottish heroine. Somewhat different is her memorial to Christopher Columbus, prompted by his "boldness" as a "discoverer" with the "gentleness and humanity of a Christian" and largely inspired by her reading of Herrera's *History of America*.⁹⁶ These traits Baillie likens to those of a clan chieftain like Wallace, thus endowing Columbus with a similar heroic status and allowing him a place with her two Scottish nationalists.

After the emergence of *Metrical Legends*, Baillie wrote to Mary Berry in October of 1821 that "I am told they are pretty well received in Scotland, but I dont think they are much liked in this southern part of the kingdom."⁹⁷ She was to some extent correct, and various reviews followed. But a fragment of a critique by Mrs. Anne Grant (1755–1838) of Laggan, dated by Edinburgh University Special Collections as 1822, alludes to *The Legend of Lady Griseld Baillie* as follows:

> The most illustrious person to whom Miss Baillie has assigned a place in her temple of well earned fame is a female whom we are proud to claim as our countrywoman. . . . In the pleasing task of recording congenial [?] virtues Miss Baillie seems quite at home . . . inspired by her subject.⁹⁸

A critic for the *Monthly Review* of September 1821 also found *Lady Griseld Baillie* the most palatable legend, but his overall review was far from gracious, beginning with *A Metrical Legend of Wallace*:

> Miss Baillie has made a full acknowledgement of minor obligations to Sir Walter Scott in her preface: but too much of thought and feeling, as well as of style and manner, is surely borrowed . . . from 'Lay of the last Minstrel.' . . . It is a higher and nobler instrument of poetical music which Joanna Baillie is qualified to strike. She seems to us

---

95. Burroughs, *Closet*, 115.
96. *DPW*, 708. Antonio de Herrera y Tordesillas's (d. 1625) *History of America* had been translated by John Lloyd Stevens (1805–52). Baillie mentions in her letters that both she and Agnes were reading Herrera along with William Robertson's *History of America* (1777) at this time.
97. RCS HB.ix.17; *Letters*, 170.
98. EU Gen 1995/31.

*con*descending from the due station of her genius, when in company with Sir Walter Scott she walks down into the regions of octosyllabic verse, and quits her early manner of treating heroic subjects in heroic strains.[99]

Postulating that "much indeed remains in 'Wallace' of most unexceptionable merit" and quoting particularly pleasing passages from *The Legend of Christopher Columbus*, the critic finally asserts,

> The most pleasing tale in the book is the legend of 'Lady Griseld Baillie'. . . . Although a domestic subject, in the general character of the story, it is rendered susceptible of the most elegant poetry in many parts of it by the exquisite tact of the writer; and, where she fails in *verse*, she remains an interesting *prose*-narrator of singular events: but, in our panegyric, we here intend to mingle no slight reprehension, when we call the fair author a *prose*-narrator of anything which she intends to be *verse*. . . . Although Mr. Crabbe,[100] and all his degenerate critics, were to vow together on the altar of Nonsense that this is verse, we would not believe them. Mr. Wordsworth's corroborating asseveration would also be cast in without effect.

It seems that while Francis Jeffrey censured Baillie for rejecting his design for drama, this critic censured her as surely for allowing Scott's design to influence her writing. What *was* she to do with so much advice on all fronts?

The critics' barbs may have annoyed Baillie, but she dwelt neither on them nor solely on her compositions in progress. Keeping

---

99. "Art. XII. *Metrical Legends of exalted Characters*," *The Monthly Review* XCVI (1821): 72–81.

100. George Crabbe (1755–1832) was a parish doctor before deciding to travel to London and pursue a career in writing. He took orders, becoming a curate in 1781, and established himself as a poet with *The Village* and its grim picture of rural poverty. Crabbe met and became friends with Sir Walter Scott. Throughout the Romantic movement, Crabbe persisted in presenting a precise, realistic vision of rural life and landscape. Byron called him "Nature's sternest painter yet the best," while Scott referred to him as "the English Juvenal" (*OCEL*, 237).

up with news from Scotland, she wrote to Scott's friend Henry Mackenzie in April 1822, concerned about the news of Sir Alexander Boswell's bizarre and untimely death. Son of biographer James Boswell, Alexander, an antiquary and poet, had established a private press at Auchinleck in 1815 for the production of unique texts. In 1821 Boswell became involved with the Tory paper *The Beacon*, which printed some bitter attacks on James Stuart, a writer to the Signet. When the *Glasgow Sentinel* replaced the earlier paper, it continued the attacks, and on 27 March 1822 Stuart ultimately engaged Alexander Boswell in a duel. Boswell died as a result, and Baillie declared that such a melancholy event should put a stop to personal attacks in periodical publications. "I believe he [Boswell] was in many respects a worthy man," wrote Baillie "and one is inclined to make that lamentation over him that King David did over one of the brave Captains of Israel, 'Did'st thou die as a fool dyeth'."[101] Meanwhile, she thanked Mackenzie for subscribing to her next project, *A Collection of Poems, Chiefly Manuscript*, and asked him to put his name on the subscription list that Scott was keeping for her in Edinburgh.

A Collection of Poems, Chiefly Manuscript, and from Living Authors followed *Metrical Legends* from Longman in 1823, the excitement of its publication dampened by the death of Baillie's brother on September 23 of that year. Joanna's brother Dr. Matthew Baillie, attending George III during many years of illness along with Drs. Heberden and Willis, had been well paid for his services, his accounts showing that from 1813–20 he received £23,327 from the appointment.[102] The Baillies purchased Duntisbourne House in 1806, used first as a country retreat but later as a permanent home, which William Baillie would inherit.[103] Dr. Baillie was at Duntisbourne as Queen Caroline lay dying in 1821 and was implored to go at once to London to attend her. As he had always sympathized with the controversial wife of George IV, he went as asked but later wrote his granddaughter that there was nothing he could do for the poor queen, "who died in poverty and

---

101. See *DNB*, II:890–92 for details of Boswell's duel and death. Baillie's quote comes from 2 Sam. 3.33. See NLS 124 ff.43–44; *Letters*, 1132–33.

102. Crainz, 143 (from Mrs. Baillie's account book 1792–1844, property of P. H. Jobson, Esq.).

103. Anne Carver, *The Story of Duntisbourne Abbots* (Gloucester: Albert E. Smith, 1966), 27.

unbefriended."[104] This series of events is outlined in Joanna's letters to Scott, and her devotion to her brother is uncompromising. She seems never to have recovered fully from his unexpected death on 23 September 1823 and wrote to Scott on 28 September:

> My dear friend,
> I doubt not you are already informed of the heavy affliction it has pleased God to visit us with, tho' in the notices sent to Scotland of the sad event, as is the custom there, your name was, I know not how omitted; and I feel well assured that you symathize [sic] with us truly.[105] I feel as if my Sister & myself stood now alone in the world, belonging to no body, and that what remains of our life which in the course of nature cannot now be very long, can be but a gloomy portion,—No more cheerful sunshine for us! But it is wrong to think of ourselves when there is the poor Widow by our side & those who are nearest of all, to say nothing of the many who will miss a kind & skillful friend, for they are spread broad & wide and are not all clothed in black who will mourn for him whom we have lost.[106]

Baillie's sister-in-law Sophia did struggle with Matthew's death; she became physically ill shortly after and recovered very slowly from her grief. In answer to Scott's concerned letter, Joanna wrote in February 1824 that "our dismal blank cannot be filled up and every

---

104. Carver, 32. George IV's wife Caroline was the daughter of George III's sister, thus George IV's cousin and wife. It was a loveless marriage of convenience, and the couple separated after the birth of their first child, Princess Charlotte. After George IV's accession, Caroline came back from Italy to claim her rights as Queen. A bill to dissolve the marriage based on her alleged adultery was proposed to the House of Lords but never put to vote; she died on 7 August 1821.

105. Dr. Matthew Baillie died 23 September 1823. A few days later his brother-in-law Thomas Denman wrote that

> it is now quite evident that from the time of their leaving London at the end of June there was no reasonable chance of recovery. His dreadful depression of spirits, which they endeavoured to ascribe to some disorder of the nerves, was only one of the symptoms of an exhausted constitution, attending a gradual decay of all vital power. . . . He appears to have gone on rapidly losing strength till a very few days before his death, when he became delirious, but he expired at length with the most perfect tranquillity. (qtd. in Crainz, 56)

106. NLS 3897 ff.84–86; *Letters*, 421.

day some thing reminds us of it painfully. . . . Poor Mrs Baillie is better than when I wrote last, and begins again to speak somewhat in her natural voice."[107] On Dr. Baillie's death, his wife was comforted by many of his personal and professional acquaintances, and her son William profited from his father's wide range of associations.[108] A bust of Dr. Baillie by sculptor Sir Francis Legatt Chantrey was soon placed in Westminster Abbey; further, in an address to colleagues, Sir Henry Halford confirmed that "The same principles which guided Dr. Baillie in his private and domestic life governed his public and professional behaviour. He was kind, generous and sincere."[109] As evidence of his generosity, Matthew remembered his two sisters in his will with an undisclosed amount in trust.[110]

Shortly after Dr. Baillie's death, Scott's daughter Sophia, Baillie's favorite who had married John Gibson Lockhart in 1820, became seriously ill from the delivery of a daughter in January 1824. The daughter lived only two days, and Baillie asked Scott for news of Sophia Lockhart and of her eldest son John Hugh, a sickly child who would die in 1831.[111] While her severe cramps after the birth alarmed the doctors, Sophia recovered, but she always suffered after the births of her children and died in 1837 at a young age of thirty-eight. However, even at these mentally and emotionally trying times, Baillie continued to work and keep abreast of social issues. In this same letter about his daughter, Baillie encouraged Scott to promote Felicia Hemans's drama *The Vespers of Palermo* with the Edinburgh theater managers. Always concerned with social issues, she also apprised him of her recent communication with James Montgomery on suppressing the use of chimney sweeps (climbing boys) in favor of a Scots ways of cleaning chimneys, a method which required using a broom and brush mechanism on long ropes.[112] More creative interests continued.

---

107. NLS 3898 ff.56–57; *Letters*, 423.
108. See NLS letter 10995 ff.38–40 dated 27 April 1824, in which Sophia Baillie thanks Mr. Moore (probably surgeon James Moore) for allowing her son to follow "his honoured Father, and to be associated with such Friends."
109. Qtd. in Rudolf, 10.
110. PRO PROB 11/1676.
111. John Hugh Lockhart became the Hugh Little John of Scott's *Tales of a Grandfather*.
112. See letter to James Montgomery, Sheffield, dated 5 February 1824 (WI MS 5608/41 & 44; *Letters*, 1216–17).

Chapter 3

While Baillie's fascination with Scott's historical romances and with the sublime in nature may have inspired her later dramatic works, much of her subsequent creativity was also directed toward poetry and "charitable" editing. During the difficult period of Matthew's illness the year before, Baillie had been soliciting manuscript poems for a proposed poetry anthology to be sold by subscription. In 1822, requesting unpublished works from her author friends, she intended to edit a volume of poetry for the benefit of a needy friend, Mrs. James Stirling, and to call it *A Collection of Poems, Chiefly Manuscript, and from Living Authors* (London: Longman, Hurst, Rees, Orme, and Brown, 1823).[113] Most of her letters from 1822–23 refer to this edition, which contained poems by Walter Scott, Thomas Campbell, Anne Home Hunter, Robert Southey, William Wordsworth, George Crabbe, Anna Laetitia Barbauld, Samuel Rogers, Felicia Hemans, Anna Maria Porter, Anne Grant of Laggan, Baillie, and many others; and it earned well over £2,000 with its subscription. Baillie's letters throughout this task reveal her good business sense, tenacity, critical perception, and tactful editing. She had no compunction about returning inferior poetry for revision, as indicated in her April 1822 letter to Sir John Herschel:

> Many thanks, my dear Sir, for the verses [you] have sent me. They would have been considered as good, composed under the most favourable circumstances, and in a Stage Coach with all that clatters about—scouring rooms & passages, they are wonderful. My Sister & Mrs Elliot are clear for their being inserted in my Collection, and so should I, but for a hankering after something of your composition written with more deliberation and not in a subject connected with the arts . . . . Writing so well in so short a time and in a Stage Coach, what would you not do in the silence of your own chamber, and reasonable time allowed for it? That savours too much of a learned Wrangler[114] who considers poetry as a mere play thing, undeserving of either time or consideration.

---

113. The Baillie family was a very charitable one. Not only did Joanna donate the proceeds from many of her works to charitable causes, Dr. Matthew Baillie gave an average of £500 per year to charity (Crainz, "Account Book," 141–59).

114. wrangler: debater, disputant; candidate who has been placed in the first class in the mathematical tripos at Cambridge (*OED*).

> Pray think upon this, and let me have something more to my fancy, altho' this is sufficiently so to be considered by me as deserving a place in a better collection of poetry than mine probably will be.[115]

Baillie's playful but candid criticism was well taken, for the famous astronomer must have sat down immediately with pen in hand to appease her and quickly sent her five *revised* poems. Three she included in her collection: "the Lark," the Lament," and "the Sailor's departure." When the collection was completed and copies were ready in 1823, Baillie handled their circulation herself and sent instructions to Longman for the physical distribution to subscribers as follows:[116]

> 128 copies for Mrs Brown of Russel[l] Square. (I dont know the number but I dare say Mr Brown's name is on the door)
> 50 copies to Mrs Baillie, 25 Cavendish Square and she will continue to receive parcels of 50 or 40 copies every other day till she has supplied the west end of London & other places which she or her friends take charge of —
> 40 copies to be sent to Hampstead directed to me. —
> 24 for Manchester, Blackburn & Liverpool to be put up separately & directed as the list points out, but all the copies for the same place put up in one outer cover & directed to any agent you please (carriage paid)
> 30 for Oxford directed for Mr Parker Bookseller and to be sent to Mr Ridington St: Pauls Church Yard & the inclosed letter put into the parcel. Coach Carr. paid[117]

---

115. Sir John Herschel (1792–1871) was a friend of Baillie, though it is unclear when or where Herschel first met her; it is probable they met through her brother Dr. Matthew Baillie. Herschel must have admired her work, for his journal entry for 1 January 1837, states that he has just "Read Miss Baillie's Martyr" (*Herschel at the Cape: Diaries and Correspondence of Sir John Herschel, 1834–1838*, ed. David S. Evans, et al. [Austin: University of Texas Press, 1969], 273). It appears from some of the other letters in the Royal Society collection, however, that Herschel might have had a more familiar relationship with Agnes (*Dictionary of Scientific Biography*, VI:323-28). Also see RS HS3.19; *Letters*, 788.
116. NYPL Berg 2 A.L.S. to Longman; *Letters*, 1160.
117. Because this line has been marked through, it is very difficult to read. The "coach carr. paid" note is in the publisher's hand. The publisher

> 61 for Ayr-shire, directed to Messrs McCormick & Cairnie, Printers in Ayr, (carriage paid) The list inclosed for them to be put into the parcel.—
> 243 for Glasgow, directed for Miss Murdock No. 3 North Wellington Place Glasgow, and the inclosed list to be put into the package. (carriage paid)
> 88 for Edinburgh to be put up separately & directed according to the names in the list &c and sent in charge to any body you please (carriage paid)[118]

The opportunity to engage herself in a work which required only minor creative effort on her part probably gave Baillie the diversion she needed for dealing with Matthew Baillie's death and with the succeeding gloom that invaded the family. At the same time, it both aided her friend and provided the reading public with a sample of some admirable late Romantic poetry, uniting famous poets with unfamiliar ones. This anthology attests to Baillie's lack of literary snobbery, for she consistently read and supported writers in all stations; she gathered the poems for her collection from her friends—from Walter Scott and William Wordsworth to John Richardson and Margaret Holford Hodson. Ultimately, she thanked Scott for his support of the project in July of 1823: "In short I took hold of your strong arm at the very beginning and, leaning upon that, put forth my hand and caught at all the rest of the Poetical Brotherhood likely to do me any good."[119] Her letter continued with praise for individual contributors, including Henry Gally Knight, Catharine Fanshawe, Felicia Hemans, and others. Scott's *Mac Duff's Cross* was chief in the volume. When she wrote to Scott again, it would be to relay the devastating news of her brother's death.

After Matthew's death in 1823, Joanna's nephew William Baillie became the Squire of Duntisbourne Abbots. William had been provided an expensive education at Westminster School and at Oxford and was later called to the Bar. He was clearly attached to his aunts Joanna and Agnes and visited them frequently, almost every day in their last years, and kept his own family close to them. He knew a great many interesting people, many of them friends of

---

has made a check mark beside each of these listed addresses, probably as he has sent them out.

118. Here the publisher has noted "to A. Black." He has also made another entry to the list: "32 for Bath."

119. NLS 3897 ff.3–4; *Letters*, 419.

Joanna, such as Maria Edgeworth and Sarah Siddons. That he was interested in genealogy is indicated in Joanna's letters to him, and he was responsible for having his great-uncle John Hunter's body moved from the vaults of St. Martin's in the Fields to Westminster Abbey. He was present at the trial of Queen Caroline, whom his uncle Thomas Denman defended,[120] and later acted as Judge's Marshal to him. Apparently, though, William Baillie never practiced law but traveled and managed his estates as a gentleman farmer. William married Henrietta Duff, the daughter of a Scottish Minister, in 1835, shortly after being introduced to her at the house of Dr. John Baron in Margaretta Terrace, Cheltenham; Dr. Baron later left his house to the young couple.[121]

On her brother's death, Joanna Baillie seems to have lost much of her early endurance and to have chosen a more private life, probably because Matthew had been one of her earliest champions and the loss was hardly bearable. She had also now reached sixty and, perhaps, in losing Matthew faced her own mortality, realizing that what *she* considered true literary acceptance was not to be hers during her lifetime. Baillie continued to keep up with current events, however, and was deeply sorrowed by Scott's financial ruin in 1825.

Following an economic crash in 1825, Scott and his partners Ballantyne and Constable found themselves facing bankruptcy. Partly through his own mismanagement, but mostly through that of Ballantyne, Scott confronted the possibility of losing his beloved Abbotsford from his personal liability of some £130,000. He attempted to clear the debt by writing more profusely than ever. His efforts were successful, but most Scott biographers believe, as did Baillie, that it shortened his life. During this difficult period Scott failed to write to Baillie for over a year. When she sympathized with his distress but reminded him of his neglect on 3 October 1825, his

---

120. Caroline of Brunswick (1768–1821) remained for most of her married life separated from her husband George IV. When George became king in 1820, Caroline rejected an offer of £50,000/year to stay abroad, returning to England to claim her place as queen. Her cause was embraced by George's many enemies, and a government-sponsored bill to annul the marriage had to be withdrawn. Thomas Denman, one of her counselors, in a theatrical flourish implored the Lords to remember that Christ himself forgave a woman taken in adultery (John Cannon, ed., *The Oxford Companion to British History* [Oxford and New York: Oxford University Press, 1997], 169–70).

121. John Baron, M.D., (1789–1851) was a physician who spent much of his life in Cheltenham and was a friend of Dr. Matthew Baillie (*DNB*, I:1189). Also see both Crainz and Carver, 34–35.

melancholic apology was soon forthcoming: "It did not require your kind token of undeserved remembrance my dear friend to remind me that I was guilty of very criminal negligence in our epistolary correspondence."[122] Further strain came with the death of his wife Charlotte on 14 May 1826 as he was completing *Woodstock*. He followed almost frantically with *Chronicles of the Canongate* and *The Life of Napoleon Buonaparte* in 1827. In October, following Charlotte's death, Baillie lamented the loss of Abbotsford's kind, considerate "Hostess" that God had seen fit to take and remembered a happier time when visiting the estate was "a sunny spot in our existence"—in a Wordsworthian moment recalling "spots of time": "Alas! as we grow old those remembered spots become the brighter from the surrounding gloom that intervenes."[123]

Scott agonized that he was in Edinburgh when Charlotte died in May as daughter Anne nursed her to no avail. But Scott's own health was soon to suffer as well. After publishing *The Fair Maid of Perth* and *Tales of a Grandfather* in 1828 and *Anne of Geierstein* in 1829, he suffered a stroke of apoplexy in 1830. Baillie was forever convinced that the strain placed on Scott from his partners' mismanagement brought on his illness, but she also blamed much of his personal debt on numerous thoughtless travelers who came to Abbotsford to stay with the famous writer for days on end and compared his disadvantage to that of his American contemporary Thomas Jefferson, who had declared a personal debt of $107,000 in 1826 and, similarly, faced losing Monticello and its contents.[124]

---

122. Letter to Baillie dated 12 October 1825, qtd. in Grierson, 9:236.
123. NLS 3903 ff.131–33; *Letters*, 438.
124. All over Virginia, in the aftermath of the panic of 1819, farms of cash-poor, land-rich planters were being auctioned. In January 1826 Jefferson himself was $107,000 in debt and suddenly responsible for two $10,000 loans for which he had co-signed. On January 19 he called for his grandson Jeff to propose a lottery that would sell off his nail-making mills and about 1,000 acres of land to clear the debts, but because lotteries were illegal, he had to obtain approval from the General Assembly. Jefferson's lottery bill passed by only a few votes, but in its final form the bill required that Jefferson sell everything–Monticello, its contents, slaves, horses, land, etc. He could only plead with his creditors to be generous and grant his deathbed request to free five of his closest servants, asking the University of Virginia to employ them. Monticello, like Scott's Abbotsford, had been a constant stop for dignitaries and travelers. Jefferson had no presidential pension and had gone $30,000 deeper in debt while in office. See Willard Sterne Randall, *Thomas Jefferson, A Life* (New York: Henry Holt, 1993), 585–91.

Always defending Scott, in March of 1826 she had cited for him the root of his problems:

> Many years ago in a letter to me, after mentioning gratefully the many happy circumstances that had attended your progress in life you added "I stand in awe of my own good fortune[.]" That awe may now be removed and having felt reverses like other men, you will afterwards be the happier for it. All this is well, and I think of it on your behalf with pleasure and as I said before with pride, but there is another view of the subject or rather <u>part</u> of the subject which gives me no satisfaction but on the contrary makes me whenever I think of it grumble & growl like an evil spirit; and that is the multitude of impudent Travellers with letters of introduction from their as impudent friends who have abused your hospitable nature & made Abbotsford for so many summers an Inn & a Tavern for way faring Idlers of all sexs [sic] & ages. I have no charity for such people. Travellers are the most selfish & the most impudent of human beings; and that you should have been their prey to such a degree provokes me, so that I must per force give some vent to my humour.[125]

Similarly, she complained to several of her friends about visitors who took advantage of Scott. While she came to Scott's defense in particular, she seemed to dwell on financial problems of the time and concerned herself also with the debts of the Milligan family, since Robert Milligan had married her niece Margaret in 1816.[126]

---

125. NLS 3902 ff.157–61; *Letters*, 434–35.
126. Dr. Ruth Paley, formerly at the Public Record Office at Kew, uncovered the following concerning financial difficulties of the mercantile house of Milligan and Robertson (not Robinson as Baillie records). Several bankruptcy cases are recorded under the name of Milligan, but the one most closely matching the time of this letter and the reference to West India Merchants is the 1828 bankruptcy file for Colin Robertson, Duncan Davidson Milligan, and Robert Milligan Dalzell of Milligan Robertson & Co., West India Merchants, 32 Fenchurch Street (PRO ref. B3/4340). Creditors included John Baillie (£2458) and Margaret Baillie (£1079) both of Devonshire Place, the estate of Robert Milligan deceased, late of Hampstead (£2836), Mrs. H. D. Milligan of Hertford Street (£145), J. Hughan and M. Milligan of Cotswold (£1189) and James Baillie, deceased, late of Bedford Square (£4861). The bankrupts' balance sheet indicates debts and liabilities of £337,536, with a plus balance of £119,965; the apparent surplus arises from stating the sums due on mortgage of West

Because of her longevity, Baillie witnessed the deaths of most of her closest friends and many family members, but a major blow came with the death of Sir Walter Scott on 21 September 1832. After one of Scott's last visits to London (1828), he recorded a meeting with his old friend:

> Breakfasted with Joanna Baillie and found that gifted person extremely well and in the display of all her native knowledge of character and benevolence. She looks much more aged however. I would give as much to have a capital picture of her as for any portrait in the world. She gave me a Manuscript play to read upon Witchcraft.[127]

Meanwhile, Baillie wrote to Margaret Holford Hodson in November 1831 that she had seen Scott twice while he was in town and "thought him looking remarkably well & in good spirits."[128] This was to be their last meeting before his death. The poignant loss of her closest friend was clear in Baillie's letter to John Gibson Lockhart, Scott's son-in-law, on 2 October 1832:

> The stroke of death has restored him again to our imagination in all the power & vigour & generous affections of his best days. All the world admired him, and that admiration was accompanied with a love & good will that are rarely joined to such a sentiment. Had not my admiration been so accompanied, I should have been most ungrateful, for a steady friend he was to me on every occasion. Whilst I had some popularity in the world and during the much longer period in which I have had none, he never passed an opportunity of bringing me, by flattering mention or quotation &c. into favourable notice; and when I wanted a literary contribution or service of any kind, who was so ready & so liberal as himself? It was a pleasing & proud observation for me, when one of the proofs given by some of the public

---

India property at the full amount of principal and interest. Though the actual bankruptcy is recorded in 1828, it would not have been unusual to have a space of time between ceasing to trade and formal bankruptcy proceedings.

127. See Scott's 18 April 1828 entry in W. E. K. Anderson, ed., *The Journal of Sir Walter Scott* (Oxford: Clarendon, 1972), 460. *Witchcraft* would appear in *Dramas* in 1836.

128. CLS 51; *Letters*, 631.

critics why he must be the Author of the Waverley Novels, was because there were so many quotations in them from J Baillie. And that critic said well; for who but himself would have honoured me so much. Forgive this talking of myself, for I feel at this moment like the man who on the loss of his Mother called out "who will love me now!"[129]

These last words come from the passionate despair of Joanna Baillie, *not* from one of her characters in a play on the passions.

Finally, in an excerpt from her 1832 *Lines on the Death of Sir Walter Scott*, Baillie commemorated her friend and at the same time set up a rather antagonistic contrast between his poetry and that of her one-time associate Lord Byron:

> Men of all nations, of all creeds, all ranks,
> Will owe to thee an endless meed of thanks,
> Which more than in thy passing, checker'd day
> Of mortal life, they will delight to pay.
> For who shall virtuous sympathies resign,
> Or feed foul fancies from a page of thine?
> No, none! thy writings as they life are pure,
> And their fair fame and influence will endure.
>   Not so with those where perverse skill pourtrays
> Distorted, blighting passions; and displays,
> Wild, manic, selfish fiends to be admired
> As heroes with sublimest ardour fired.[130]

This passing took from Joanna Baillie more than just a friend; aside from her close family ties, it quite possibly ended the most intimate relationship she ever had. She spent much of 1833 soliciting contributions for the Abbotsford subscription that would fund his monument.[131]

---

129. NLS 931 No. 39; *Letters*, 831–32.
130. From *Lines*, in *DPW*, 793. See William Brewer's focus on this in "Joanna Baillie and Lord Byron," *KSJ* XLIV (1995): 165–81.
131. Baillie was impatient that contributions were coming in slowly, and she lamented to Margaret Holford Hodson in January 1833 that "I hope this subscription will at last collect a respectable sum, a very large one I dare no longer expect. So much universal love & admiration of the man and so much tardiness in that which would most usefully testify it, I do not understand" (CLS 55; *Letters*, 637–38).

During these later years, Baillie had become a correspondent and friend of many of the Boston Unitarians, including Harvard professor Dr. Andrews Norton. By the time of Scott's illness and death, she had turned her interest to a complex and arguable subject—religious dogma—and her publication of *A View of the General Tenour of the New Testament Regarding the Nature and Dignity of Jesus Christ* in 1831 incurred the wrath of Thomas Burgess, the patronizing and single-minded Bishop of Salisbury. Others were somewhat startled, too, but according to biographer Lockhart, Scott may have been more concerned with public reaction than with Baillie's unorthodox religious arguments. Scott's 14 May 1831 diary entry related that "Mackay, it being Sunday, favored us with an excellent discourse on the Socinian controversy, which I wish my friend Mr. Laidlaw had heard." Lockhart's note is that on the 17th Scott spoke affectionately of Miss Ferrier, "who showed less affectation than any famous woman—Joanna Baillie hardly excepted." He then alluded, regretfully, to the fact that Baillie had "entered on the Socinian controversy"[132] and that he had sent her *View of the General Tenour* on to Laidlaw, who supported her views.[133] This is Scott's last diary entry about his old friend, because he would become very ill and die the following year. Contrary to Carhart's implication that because Scott did not remember her again in his journal he showed his disappointment in her religious stance, the fact is that Scott later met her in the fall of 1831 while he was in London.[134] It is difficult to believe that Walter Scott, who certainly had political, religious, and literary differences with Baillie before, thought the less of her for her anti-Trinitarian stance.

Whether or not Baillie was aware of the fact or even cared at this point, Scott's passing deprived her of the greatest literary sponsor

---

132. Founded by Lælius and Faustus Socinus, two Italian theologians of the sixteenth century, Socinians denied the divinity of Christ.

133. Lockhart, V:335.

William Laidlaw (1780–1845) became a steward to Scott at Abbotsford in 1817, proving himself an exemplary servant, a worthy counselor, and a devoted friend. When Scott was ill in 1819, Laidlaw and Ballantyne wrote from his dictation most of the *Bride of Lammermoor*, and Scott probably owes credit for several of his novels to Laidlaw's suggestion that he devote some writing to Melrose. When Scott's financial problems occurred, he had to release Laidlaw but retained him as his secretary shortly after; Laidlaw remained at the post until Scott's death in 1832. Laidlaw wrote several lyrics but is remembered mostly for his song "Lucy's Flittin" (*DNB*, XI:397–98).

134. CLS letter to Hodson, 11 November 1831; see note 128 above.

she would ever have. Now seventy, she felt the loss much as she had felt the loss of her brother nine years earlier; each death exhausted her a bit more. It has been noted that Baillie and Scott were captivated by each other and that Scott's relationship with his wife Charlotte was probably strained by her illnesses and possible opium addiction in later years.[135] While it is both unscholarly and unjust to speculate that theirs was more than mutual professional admiration, it is also difficult to ignore the tone of the letters between the two and the unremitting support that they gave each other. Scott's recent biographer John Sutherland writes that Scott developed a "particular skill in charming literary ladies" and that Baillie was a "notable conquest,"[136] placing her in the position of an infatuated rather than respectful woman. But Scott supported the literary efforts of several nineteenth-century women writers, including Anna Seward, whose works he edited in 1810. If there were any infatuation involved in the Scott/Baillie relationship, however, it was clearly mutual. One *would* like to believe, in fact, that a woman with Joanna Baillie's intensity did not go through life without ever having had a lover, of either sex, but there is no concrete evidence of any such relationship—unless it appeared in the Scott letters she so prudently burned after his death:

> We went one morning to see poor Mrs Lockhart, who was kind & confidential, and in a natural state of sorrow, mixed with great thankfulness that her Father was released from much suffering. The very end, however, thank God! was easy. Since we returned home, I have been employed in reading over all his letters to me; and they will all (except about 20 which I have reserved or burnt) be put into Mr Lockhart's hands to use as he thinks fit.[137]

Such was Baillie's affinity for reticence and privacy.

Finally, even though literary collaboration was common among authors, it remains to be argued whether Scott helped or hindered Baillie's literary genius. While his support may have provided the encouragement she needed after 1806, her *Poems* and her two major

---

135. Sutherland, 289.
136. Ibid., 112.
137. See NLS letter Acc 9467/15 to Anne Elliott dated 13 November 1832; *Letters*, 477.

volumes of *A Series of Plays* had been published well before she met him. Ironically, his unconditional praise of her could have actually set critics like Francis Jeffrey against her. While Baillie was constantly learning and adapting new knowledge, her move away from drama to *Metrical Legends* may have been a reflection of Scott's own historical focus, for she shared his loyalty to Scotland. Nevertheless, Baillie was not timid about experimenting with different writing styles. In fact, she seemed to thrive on reinventing her genius.

4

"Not a semblance of display": A Circle of Friends (1808–1830s)

The early nineteenth century brought with it rules for private, professional, and social conduct. In private, erudite but unmarried women like Joanna Baillie were confined to the daily endeavors of visiting and writing family and friends, attending benign social functions, reading, performing minor chores at home, and supporting charitable and religious organizations. According to bank archivists, Joanna and Agnes Baillie opened a joint bank account at Coutts's bank in London in 1806.[1] That they were financially situated to keep at least one maid and a cook is evident in many of Baillie's letters; in confirmation, the 1811 census for the Hampstead parish of St. John records five women living in the Baillie household at that time, three of them servants. Joanna also sometimes alluded to her own baking and making marmalade during the holidays. And she and Agnes regularly owned a cat; Joanna demonstrated her affinity for felines in "The Kitten" before 1809 and even as late as 1840 wrote to Lady Charleville about a litter of black kittens having just been born, one for the Lady's choosing.[2] To Margaret Holford Hodson Baillie would confess in 1820, "as we grow older we become more like the cats who seem to be related to places rather than to people."[3]

The Baillie sisters read voraciously—works from all fields and from men and women writers alike. Agnes was the professed "antiquarian" of the family but, unlike the eccentric figure in Scott's *The Antiquary* (1816), practiced her love of history only as a "polite pursuit." An essential element in Hume's "historical age," explains Rosemary Sweet, antiquarianism "provided the raw material from

---

1. This information comes from Coutts & Co., Archivist's Department, London. Unfortunately, early records were kept in large ledgers, and it is impossible to separate Agnes's transactions from Joanna's. Baillie mentions Coutts in her letters and knew banker Thomas Coutts personally. Coutts bank was established in the late seventeenth century and still stands within sight of its early location in the Strand.

2. Baillie mentions "The Kitten" in two early letters, one to Scott in 1809 (NLS 3878 ff. 180–84) and one to Ballantyne in 1810 (HL/HM 19701). The late letter to Lady Charleville (UN My 815) is dated ~1848 by the library.

3. CLS 11; *Letters*, 555.

which the narratives of history could be fashioned" and "pervaded many facets" of British culture.[4] Surely, Agnes's knowledge of such history and antiquarian scholarship contributed to the details in Joanna's historical dramas and legends. The sisters must have read to each other almost every night when home by the fire, sampling many works—from novels, poetry, and drama to newspapers, travel logs, histories, and scientific compositions. Joanna Baillie's allusions to specific works are too numerous to list here, but they included everything from the publications of Scott and Edgeworth to titles like Stephens's *Incidents of travel in Yucatan* and the *Christian Examiner*. Baillie relished the works of both early and contemporary women writers, some very obscure today. In *Women's Reading in Britain, 1750–1835*, Jacqueline Pearson asserts that in the Romantic period women writers were far more numerous and women readers more influential than they had been in centuries before, and this created some anxiety for their male contemporaries. Pearson cites Anne K. Mellor's argument that despite the "construction of romanticism in the academy through the works of six canonical male writers," women writers produced at least half of the literature published in England between 1780 and 1830:

> Some had high contemporary reputations, like Felicia Hemans and Joanna Baillie, and many were commercially successful. In 1798 William Lane, founder of the Minerva Press, listed ten "particular and favourite authors" on the Minerva list: all were women.[5]

But, as Pearson argues, women in Romanticism "are most visible even today on the margins of male Romanticism," though the first generation of Romantic poets seemed to harbor fewer anxieties about female rivals than did later generations.[6] Still, Wordsworth's preface to *Lyrical Ballads* is considered the manifesto of English Romanticism, even though Baillie put much of the same theory into practice years before it in her *Poems*. By the second generation, however, anxieties about women authors had become entrenched:

---

4. See Rosemary Sweet's discussion of antiquarianism in "Antiquaries and Antiquities in Eighteenth-Century England," *Eighteenth-Century Studies* 34.2 (2001): 181–206.
5. Pearson, 33.
6. Ibid., 34–35.

Scott begins *Waverley* with "an elaborate suppression of prior", mostly female, "narrative models", distancing himself from Radcliffean Gothic or the sentimental fiction of Lady Morgan and associating his work instead with masculine authority-figures imaged as a "knight with his white shield". . . . Of the canonical Romantics, Byron's reading of women writers and views on women readers is most fully documented, obsessively articulated, and ambivalent.[7]

Of course, because Baillie addressed some of the same "masculine" ideals in her plays and later in her *Metrical Legends*, writers like Scott and Byron were less inclined to devalue works from her pen than those from other women writers; but playwriting was still considered by many as a "masculine" endeavor.

In their introduction to *Women and Playwriting in Nineteenth-Century Britain*, Tracy Davis and Ellen Donkin assert that while critics and managers of the nineteenth century questioned the legitimacy of women's playwriting, male playwrights did not prosper either: "The stage was rough enough for gentlemen—Byron, Coleridge, and Tennyson all fare badly in theatrical posterity." But success was almost impossible for women playwrights. In addition, as "long as the criterion for success [was] synonymous with the legitimate theatres," the possibilities narrowed considerably. The two patent houses, Covent Garden and Drury Lane, along with the Haymarket and a handful of other royal theaters throughout England, Scotland, and Ireland, were considered the only "major" theaters, so the odds of achieving success in this elite group were low at best.[8] While the situation "officially loosened" after 1843, it was too late for Baillie to make a comeback. Between 1808 and 1836, however, at least six of Baillie's most popular plays were performed several times in Britain and America.[9]

Beyond the current professional pursuits, Joanna remained involved with her family. She and Agnes regularly wrote and visited Matthew and Sophia Baillie and their two children, Elizabeth Margaret and William, and their children later on. Baillie also spent her time addressing social ills like chimney sweeping and cruelty to

---

7. Ibid., 35–36.
8. Tracy D. Davis and Ellen Donkin, eds., Introduction, *Women and Playwriting in Nineteenth-Century Britain* (Cambridge: Cambridge University Press, 1999), 3–5.
9. See "Chronology" for a list of these performances.

animals[10] and in supporting various charities—from writing letters of recommendation to help worthies gain church positions to soliciting votes to get needy children accepted by orphan asylums and benevolent societies. She was concerned with church and state politics as well as with the temperance movement and mailed tracts to friends such as Anne Elliott in support.[11] But she was not so rigid as to censure a private drink, thanking Scott in November 1813 for the good bottle of old whiskey he had sent: "I reckon I shall drink your health in the first glass thereof about Xmas time with true good will and as much glee as a respectable person of my years can decently indulge."[12]

Baillie's private life was no doubt more dynamic than the lives of many women in her class, and loyalty to her friends and a deep-rooted benevolence earned her the title of "Lady Bountiful."[13] Her keen interest in politics differentiated her from many women of the time, and she never failed, especially with the Tory Sir Walter Scott, to argue her Whig sympathies. She declared her fondness for George III and sympathized with the King's illness during her brother Matthew's attendance on him at Windsor. When George III became incapacitated in 1811, however, she also gave support to Prince Regent, later George IV, and "corrected" Scott's interpretation of Barbauld's "Eighteen Hundred and Eleven, A Poem" (1812):

> I greatly admire & approve your spirit in what you say regarding the struggle for national independence. But I think the meaning of Mrs Barbauld's poem is in some degree mistaken by you as it has been by many people. Tho' she condemns the system that has prevailed for many years of being constantly at war, she looks forward to the unhappy change which she supposes will take place in this country as a thing that must happen in the natural course of events in the course of ages, as we learn from experience learning & arts have travelled over the globe from one country to

---

10. See NLS 3898 ff.56–57 letter to Scott (February 1824) and WI MS 5608/41 and 44 on her suggested "Scotch way of Cleaning Chimneys." Baillie published a pamphlet against the abuse of animals in 1826 entitled "A Lesson Intended for the Use of the Hampstead School" (Camden Town: Miller, 1826).

11. See NLS Acc 9467; *Letters*, 470–71.

12. NLS 3884 ff.189-191; *Letters*, 326.

13. Henderson Waddell and J. J. Waddell, *By Bothwell Banks* (Glasgow: Hobbs, 1904), 89.

another remaining permanently nowhere, and not as a misfortune soon or suddenly to befall us. Her poem has been greatly admired here by people not at all agreeing with her in politics and who have no greater love for GeNLS Hall or the American's [sic] than yourself. Her hopes of the Americans I believe arises from her having had no connection with them and knowing little about them. Have you ever seen her lines on the King's illness?[14] To sweeten your mind in regard to her, I will send them to you some day: they are full of respect & delicate comiseration [sic], and are perhaps the most touching verses ever written by any subject upon any Prince.——It would please me to see you a Whig tho' not such an outré one as would to [sic] for a Westminster election.[15]

Along with the political front at home, Baillie had also been keeping up with the menace of Napoleon Buonapart over the years and wrote happily to Scott on 8 December 1812 about the emperor's recent defeat in Russia.[16]

This early part of the century was a time of economic and social change in Britain. By 1819 industrial depression had set in, and the Peterloo Massacre was the culmination of social unrest.[17] By 1824

---

14. Barbauld's "On the King's Illness" came after George III suffered a relapse of porphyria in July 1811 from which he never recovered. The regency had been declared in February 1811. See *The Poems of Anna Laetitia Barbauld*, ed. William McCarthy and Elizabeth Kraft (Athens: University of Georgia Press, 1994), 307.

15. NLS 3883 ff.118–21 dated 7 November 1812; *Letters*, 314.

16 In September 1812, Napoleon entered Moscow with 95,000 men and found the city almost deserted. Installing himself and his staff in the Kremlin, he awaited czar Alexander's proposal for terms. Winter was too near for a march to the capital at St. Petersburg where the czar resided, and while Alexander waited him out, Napoleon's troops, finding riches of all sorts, were not finding the needed shoes or meat. The French army began to die from exposure, malnutrition, and disease. Finally, opting for a withdrawal to Smolensk and its supplies, Napoleon left Moscow in October. As the French army marched north, Cossacks almost captured Napoleon, but he arrived in Smolensk on November 13, having lost most of his horses and troops. Escaping the Russians again in December, Napoleon turned his *Grande Armée* over to Murat and departed for Paris; by 19 December 1812, he was back in the Tuileries. French records show that 210,000 Frenchmen were killed, captured, or disappeared in Russia (see Owen Connelly, *Blundering to Glory: Napoleon's Military Campaigns* [Wilmington, Delaware: Scholarly Resources, 1984], 157–81).

17. In St. Peter's Fields, Manchester, in 1819, an orderly meeting of about 60,000 citizens gathered to hear a radical speaker. The crowd,

previously enacted laws against trade unions had been repealed, and business began to boom again. But the boom was to be short lived, the economy collapsing in 1825; by 1830 unemployment and starvation lead to riots in the south, and many rioters were hanged or transported to Australia. To make matters worse, England was invaded by a cholera epidemic in 1831, with its traces remaining well into the late 1830s, and 50,000 deaths ensued throughout the British Isles.[18] This was the atmosphere in which Baillie lived and wrote.

In the professional arena, however, most women of Baillie's status could aspire to little, writing being one of the most acceptable accomplishments as long as it was neither competitive nor offensive—both qualities defined by the patriarchy. Against all odds, however, the nineteenth century was replete with accomplished women writers; and Baillie clearly spent many hours devoted to her profession, especially in her early-to-middle years, when she probably spent almost every day writing new poems and plays and revising old ones. In the social sphere, Baillie could be especially independent, partly because of her age. She visited, attended dinner parties, and occasionally went to the playhouse. According to etiquette, visits had to be returned in a fashionable amount of time, which created an endless cycle. Dinner parties, writes Daniel Pool, were a social essentiality that could be an ordeal for a hostess, given their enormous attention in contemporary etiquette books. Because dinner parties were usually organized for improving the acquaintance of those who could be helpful in society and for producing animated conversation, a hostess carefully selected guests who would not be socially or politically uncomfortable together.[19] The fact that Baillie was a customary guest at the homes of hosts such as Samuel Bentham, Thomas Carr, Samuel Hoare, Samuel Rogers, and William Sotheby suggests that her personality and

---

however, was broken up by a "nervous" militia called in by the local authorities, and between ten and fifteen people were killed and hundreds wounded by sabers or trampled by the ensuing panic. "Peterloo Massacre" was a name immediately applied by a local radical paper, and it became the symbol of tyranny for the working classes (Altick, 84).

18. See Sir Macfarlane Burnet's *Natural History of Infectious Disease*, 3rd ed. (Cambridge: Cambridge University Press, 1962), 331-32.

19. Daniel Pool, *What Jane Austen Ate and Charles Dickens Knew: From Fox Hunting to Whist-the Facts of Daily Life in 19th-Century England* (New York: Touchstone, 1993), 72-73.

conversation, enhanced by her broad Scots accent, were sought out routinely.

When Baillie moved to Hampstead in the mid-to-late 1790s with her sister and mother, she had moved into the London suburb long known for its heath and for its healthy air and water. As early as the seventeenth century, the area boasted a spa near Well Walk, with boarding houses and villas available for temporary residents. When the popularity of the wells died near the end of Queen Anne's reign, these buildings were developed into permanent residences. By then, Hampstead had become known as a health resort, and this was responsible for most of the fine new buildings and opulent dwellings constructed in the eighteenth century.[20] By the time Baillie had become a resident, Hampstead also afforded a close-knit circle of writers and humanitarians. Apart from the Hampstead *literati*, Baillie met William Wordsworth in 1808,[21] the Benthams some time before 1810,[22] Lord Byron between 1813 and 1815 after becoming friends with Anne Isabella Milbanke (later Lady Byron) in March 1812, and with Annabella's friend Mary Montgomery some time later. Margaret Holford Hodson cultivated a friendship with Baillie around the same time, their correspondence lasting to Baillie's death in 1851. There is no evidence, however, that Baillie ever knew John Keats or read his poetry, even though he would have been living only a short distance from her before his early demise. In addition, her only comment on Percy Shelley appears in an 1834 letter to Mary Montgomery and alludes to unidentified American poetry which sometimes shows "touches of the too fanciful Shelly [*sic*] school which it would be better without." Old liaisons continued, however, with Mary Berry, William Sotheby, Anne Elliot, Samuel

---

20. Christopher Wade, *The Streets of Hampstead* (London: Camden History Society, 1984), 11–12.

21. Baillie describes meeting Wordsworth and Southey in the Lake District in 1808. Wordsworth provided two sonnets, "Not love nor war" and "A volant tribe of bards," for Baillie's 1823 *Collection of Poems*. Baillie writes to Scott in October 1808 about meeting Wordsworth (and Southey) on her visit to the Lakes (see NLS Scott letter 3877, f. 158–61; *Letters*, 239–43).

22. Baillie mentions Samuel Bentham, younger brother of Jeremy Bentham, often in her letters. Jeremy Bentham writes on 20 November 1810 that he "dined at the Miss. B.'s who had been to see their brother the Dr at Windsor"; Samuel encourages his uncle on 2 January 1813 that "If you will be so good to come you shall lead down the first dance with Miss Joanna Baillie" (see Stephen Conway, ed., *The Correspondence of Jeremy Bentham* [Oxford: Clarendon, 1994], 8:83 and 300).

Rogers, the Lockharts, Maria Edgeworth, and others. While Baillie's relationship with Wordsworth over the years was somewhat detached, her early professional relationship with Byron was quite intense, ended only by his abuse of her friend Annabella. But even after the widely publicized separation, it was primarily Byron's poetry that Baillie read and criticized, especially in her letters to Scott.[23]

Baillie met William Wordsworth on a walk in the Lake District in October 1808.[24] Whether or not she had met him personally at an earlier date is unclear, but the two poets never seem to have been close friends, though she was later quite attached to his daughter Dora. In 1808 she detailed for Scott their early encounter:

> My Sister & I were delighted with the Lakes, tho' the weather was not favourable; and we did see two of the Poets you mention viz. Wordsworth & Southey,[25] who were both very civil & attentive to us. Wordsworth came over to Ambleside which was our head quarters for a little time, and spent a compleat [sic] day with us there at our Inn, and took us to see many of his favourate [sic] spots in the neighbourhood. He is a man with good strong abilities and a great power of words, but I fear there is that soreness in regard to the world & severity in his notions of mankind growing upon him that will prevent him from being so happy as he deserves to be, for he is I understand a very worthy man. We saw his sister too, whom you have probably heard of, and were very much pleased indeed with the sweetness & modesty of her appearance, the shortness of our visit at his house not

---

23. See William D. Brewer's "Joanna Baillie and Lord Byron" for an excellent account of this relationship and its affect on Byron.

24. William Wordsworth (1770–1850) is mentioned by Baillie several times in various letters. Margaret Carhart writes that Baillie probably did not meet him until around 1812 (Carhart, 23). But, in fact, Baillie describes the meeting here in 1808.

25. Robert Southey (1774–1843), a college friend of Coleridge and later with Wordsworth, was Poet Laureate from 1813–43, having accepted a pension five years earlier. Given the pronounced Jacobinism of his youth, several of Southey's contemporaries, especially Byron and Hazlitt, felt he had betrayed the principles of his youth in such acceptance (*OCEL*, 923). Southey moved to Greta Hall, Keswick, in 1803 so that his wife Edith Fricker Southey could be near her sister Sara Fricker Coleridge.

permitting us to become better acquainted with her.²⁶— We drunk tea with Southey & his wife at Keswick in a magnificent library with as many gold-lettered books glancing on us from the shelves as would have honoured the Library of a Peer. He is an animated agreeable man, with a certain degree of the Beau or fine Gentleman in his appearance that amused without displeasing us.²⁷

By the time of this meeting, Wordsworth had published *Lyrical Ballads* and *Poems in Two Volumes* and had completed *The Prelude*. Baillie, of course, read his poetry and sometimes alluded to particular lines in her letters; she even loaned her own personal copy of *Lyrical Ballads* to postal reformer Francis Freeling. In 1812 she empathized that Wordsworth, like herself, had fallen under Edinburgh critic Francis Jeffrey's "condemnation"[28]—and the reviewer would be even more biting in his 1814 review of *The Excursion*, his famous essay beginning with "This will never do!" But Baillie, who attempted realistic descriptions and comparisons in her own poetry, sometimes saw Wordsworth's language as unnatural. When Scott praised Canto III of Byron's *Childe Harold's Pilgrimage* in the *Quarterly Review*, she cited specific personifications to him in February 1817 that gave "meanness instead of sublimity to the discription," concluding that "What I should consider as bad in Wordsworth I can never believe is good in Byron."[29] Nevertheless, Baillie and Wordsworth inadvertently saw each other at the homes of mutual friends like banker Samuel Hoare,[30] and Wordsworth declared her the "model of an English Gentlewoman."[31] In November 1820 Baillie related to Scott that she had recently been seated beside the poet at a dinner at the Hoares':

---

26. Dorothy Wordsworth (1771–1855) spent her life in the Wordsworth household, accompanying the poet on his walks while her health allowed.
27. NLS 3877 ff.158–61; *Letters*, 240.
28. NLS 3882 ff.7–11; *Letters*, 295.
29. NLS 3888 ff.37–39; *Letters*, 364. See a longer excerpt from this letter in chapter 3.
30. Samuel Hoare, who married Louisa Gurney, was Lady Byron's banker, and Baillie was a close friend of his family. He purchased Hampstead Heath House in 1790 near the Baillies. Children Joanna Baillie mentions include Jane, Joseph, and several others.
31. Qtd. in Carhart, 3.

> He is thin but has got rid of a complaint in his eyes which some months ago threatened him with the loss of sight. He is going home with a mind full stored with Lake, clouds, & Mountains for the benefit of the next poem he writes, which from what I learnt afterward from Mrs Hoare, will probably be the continuation of the Wanderer.[32]

And Wordsworth, having just returned from a tour of Switzerland, Italy, and Paris, listened eagerly to her account of her recent visit to Abbotsford.

It is peculiar that two poets, with so much in common stylistically, seem to have had few (at least not documented) discussions about poetry. But Baillie, beneath Wordsworth in recognition, was neither intimidated nor provoked by his success. She linked him with Milton in a letter to Sir Thomas Noon Talfourd in 1836, referred to him as the "Philosophical Wordsworth" in a letter to Margaret Holford Hodson in 1837, and acknowledged (to Hodson) in June 1839 his well-deserved honorary D.C.L. from Oxford:

> I mentioned above how little poetry is regarded at present, but I ought in fairness to have noticed the great applause & honours bestowed on Wordsworth last week at Oxford.[33] A deep admiration of his genius has gained upon the public within these last ten years, particularly the Scholars of Cambridge & Oxford. Yesterday I heard a very vivid account

---

32. 1820 brought a four-volume edition entitled *The Miscellaneous Poems of William Wordsworth* which included bibliographical material and edited poems that Wordsworth then regarded as his canon of miscellaneous work. By 11 July 1820 he was again traveling to Calais with Mary, Dorothy, and Thomas Monkhouse and party. The tour was a "reenactment of formative experience," writes Stephen Gill, but Wordsworth was fifty now (338). Determined to return to the Alps at the end of the journey, he and his party went first to Belgium to the battlefield of Waterloo, moving on to the Cologne Cathedral, the Rhine Gorge, and Falls at Schaffhausen and into the mountains. While Mary and Dorothy wrote accounts of the journey, Wordsworth produced only a series of unimaginative poems, published in 1822 as *Memorials of A Tour on the Continent, 1820*. The tour ended in Paris, where Mary met Annette Vallon for the first time. The Wordsworths returned to England in November 1820 (see Stephen Gill, *William Wordsworth: A Life* [Oxford: Clarendon, 1989], 336–40).

33. William Wordsworth was awarded an honorary D.C.L. from Oxford on 12 June 1839, along with honors to Sir John Herschel (*DNB*, XXI:938, IX:716).

> of it in a letter from Lady Herschel to her Mother Mrs Stewart,³⁴ who said the applauses given to her husband were great, but those to Wordsworth were deafning [sic] & unbounded. I saw him not long ago when staying with Mrs Hoare; his eyes were free from enflamation & his whole face in its very best looks, so he would do some credit to the Muses with his Doctor's scarlet robes upon him.³⁵

In 1842, however, Baillie alluded to Wordsworth's "most unpoetlike" opposition of his daughter Dora's marriage to merchant Edward Quillinan, but their conflict was later resolved. Baillie continued to see Wordsworth on social occasions, introducing her great niece Sophia Milligan to him at the home of the Hoares in 1845 and hearing the Poet Laureate's account of Queen Victoria's ball in May of that same year. At the same time, Baillie wrote to Lady Byron about Wordsworth's distress over the railroad's intrusion into Windermere, the eastern region of the Lake District which had been such an inspiration for his descriptions in *The Prelude*.³⁶

While Baillie and Wordsworth met socially on many occasions, their only professional venture came with her edition of *A Collection of Poems, Chiefly Manuscript, and from Living Authors*, appearing from Longman in 1823 as a subscription for the benefit of her old school friend Mrs. James Stirling. Baillie began soliciting contributions for the collection in 1822, careful to invite unpublished poems from writers whose work she deemed worthy. When she made her request to Robert Southey in July 1822, she also alluded to his neighbor Mr. Wordsworth's two beautiful sonnets, "Not love nor war" and "A volant tribe of bards," sent for her collection at a time when his son William was very ill. To Wordsworth himself, she sent the following thanks from Cavendish Square on 11 July 1822:

> I received your letter with the two beautiful sonnets yesterday, and I feel very sensibly how good you are in attending to my request at a time when your mind is so painfully occupied. I hope you are by this time, in some

---

34. Mrs. Alexander Stewart was Margaret Herschel's (wife of Sir John Herschel) mother.

35. CLS 79; *Letters*, 682.

36. Baillie's niece Elizabeth Margaret Baillie Milligan had one child, Sophia, born in 1817. Wordsworth succeeded Southey as Poet Laureate in 1843. See *Letters*, 778, concerning the railroad.

degree at least, relieved from your anxiety by the medicines having had the desired effect on your Invalid. I heard of the alarming accident that lately befell yourself just the day after my letter to you was sent to post, and I regretted when too late that I should at such a time trouble you about any thing.[37] I hope Mrs Wordsworth & your sister will forgive me for having done so, for I guess that they would be more disturbed about it on your account than you would be yourself.——

I am greatly obliged to you for what you have sent me. The first sonnet is full of pleasing & soothing images and is my greatest favorite; but they are both beautiful and will do great honour to my collection. My packet of contributions is now swelling to a considerable size and I hope to produce an acceptable and rather curious volume.[38]

Though the two poets collaborated on this single collection, there is no evidence that they confided in one another their critical theories of poetry, nor did Wordsworth seem to impress Baillie as Scott and others did. On the other hand, as editor Jonathan Wordsworth suggests, it is quite possible that she influenced Wordsworth more than we know. It cannot be overstated that Baillie had published her first volume of poems and two volumes of plays before she met the most famous writers of her time; and, certainly, *Poems*, and possibly even her first volume of *A Series of Plays*, had been composed before her permanent move to Hampstead in the mid-to-late 1790s.

Probably around 1808 or even earlier, Baillie became intimate with Anne Elliott of Devon, and the two women made regular extended visits to each other's homes for two decades. There is virtually no information available on Elliott, for she never published or married, which makes her life difficult to trace. In the early nineteenth century, Egland House, in the parish of Awliscombe, was apparently the home of Anne's brother, the Rev. Luther Graves Elliott (d. 1846), and his wife, whose eldest son was barrister George Percy Elliott (1800–1874). The family was not originally from Devon,

---

37. Though some Wordsworth sources mention an accident around this time, they are not specific. The tour guide in the Lake District near Dove Cottage, however, points out a bridge in the Lake District where the accident may have occurred. The story is that Wordsworth was walking across when he met a woman in a horse–drawn carriage; the horse reared, and Wordsworth was forced to leap over the railing into the creek below.

38. WLMSA, Wordsworth Trust; *Letters*, 1221–22.

so Elliott's baptismal records are not there today.[39] A collection of papers at the Devon Record Office includes an agreement entered into by Thomasine Elliot [sic] (described as a spinster of Honiton) for the building of Egland House in 1804, and the collection also includes leases of the house after 1835 by George Percy Elliott of the Temple, London.[40] Along with different spellings of Elliott (Elliot), the date of Anne Elliott's death is also unclear. Devon county records show that Thomasine Anne Elliott of Egland House, Awliscombe, age seventy-six, was buried at Dunkswell church on 7 April 1835; and a memorial inscription in the church shows that she died on 1 April 1835, the daughter of Rear Admiral George Elliott, late of Copford, Essex.[41] A letter dated and postmarked December 1835 to Margaret Holford Hodson mentions Elliott's death. But in an earlier letter to Mary Montgomery postmarked 1834, Baillie also wrote of Elliott's death, so there are clearly discrepancies in recorded material.

Baillie was at Anne Elliott's in the late summer of 1809, for she apologized to Scott for being absent as he worked on the production of her *Family Legend*. She was in Devon again in 1813 and in 1818 and recalled when she, Anne, and Maria Edgeworth had taken shelter in Frognal from a rain shower and encouraged Anne in 1819 to visit London soon. Their visits and correspondence continued until close to the time of Elliott's death. Baillie's letters to and about Anne Elliott are warm and informal, and she often recalled fondly her friendly conversations with Elliott—a woman who fell outside her literary circle—along with the Devon cream and the community's ritual production of cider.

Back in the London intellectual and social circle, Baillie became acquainted with Germaine de Staël (1766–1817) and wrote to Scott in November 1813 that she longed to begin reading her newest work.[42] In addition, Sir Samuel and Lady Bentham were also prominent in her life. Sophia Fordyce had married Sir Samuel Bentham in 1796 and survived him many years. Samuel, a naval

---

39. I thank archivists at the Devon County Council, Devon Record Office, for what little biographical information we could find on Anne Elliott. Mrs. Thomasin Anne Elliott, Egland, also appears in the "Index Indicators" of *The Gentleman's Magazine*, 1817 (page 194 of part 2).

40. Devon Records 5333M/E1.

41. See indexes of the Devon County Council, Devon Record Office, Exeter.

42. de Staël's *De l'Allemagne* (*On Germany*) had appeared in 1810. It is possible, however, that Baillie is referring to one of her earlier novels (*Delphine* and *Corinne*).

architect, engineer, and inventor of mechanical contrivances, was knighted in 1831 and died that same year, only months before the demise of his brother, Utilitarian proponent Jeremy Bentham.[43] While Jeremy Bentham's legacy, in addition to rationalizing the spirit of competitive capitalism, was the whole central and local British (and to an extent American) executive government,[44] Samuel's contribution to society was largely scientific. Baillie was writing to her "dear friend" Sophia Bentham as early as 1805 and into the 1830s and was also a friend of the Bentham's youngest daughter, Sarah Le Blanc (d. 1864), who in 1842 engaged Baillie's interest in "striving to vindicate her Father's right to be considered as the inventor of the floating Break-water about to be considered at Plymouth" and for which a patent was to be granted to an undeserving young engineer.[45] Both Joanna and Agnes visited and dined with the Benthams, offered to keep their daughters Clara and Sarah while the parents were in France in 1822, and faithfully passed on to Lady Bentham current stories of their niece and nephew Elizabeth Margaret and William Baillie. Clearly, the Benthams' home was a seat for extensive philosophical and scientific discussion. Baillie would have hardly been uncomfortable in this arena, having long cultivated discussions with people such as economist Thomas Malthus, whose sister he visited in Hampstead;[46] astronomer Sir John Herschel, one of her correspondents; and scientist Sir Humphry Davy. Having grown up in a famous medical family, Baillie was engaged by these philosophic and scientific friends, but the impact on her personal and

---

43. *DNB*, II:281–84.
44. Richard D. Altick, *Victorian People and Ideas* (New York: Norton, 1973), 139–40. The *Westminster Review*, which continued from 1824 to 1914, was for its first twelve years the tool of Jeremy Bentham's radical party and aimed to define the place of literature, education, and religion in their ideal state. The *Review*'s target audience was the middle class, gradually becoming dominant following the Reform Bill of 1832. It persisted as a sound, respectable journal and attained the added distinction of being the first English review to have a woman, Mary Ann Evans (George Eliot), as assistant editor from 1852–54 (see George L. Nesbitt's *Benthamite Reviewing: The First Twelve Years of The Westminster Review, 1824–1836* [New York: Columbia University Press, 1934], v and 172). *Westminster Review* 33 (March 1840): 401–24 contained a review of Baillie's work.
45. ML 215c; *Letters*, 515.
46. HU MS Eng 944, 32; *Letters*, 976.

professional life came more from acquaintances such as Annabella Milbanke and other women.

Joanna Baillie was introduced to Anne Isabella Milbanke in 1813 and, subsequently, to Lord Byron. Anne Isabella, Annabella to friends and family, was an only child born to Sir Ralph Milbanke and Judith Noel Milbanke on 17 May 1792 at Elemore Hall, Seaham, Durham. Encouraged by her educated mother, Annabella learned early to think critically, to read, and to write. And her father taught her works from Shakespeare to Darwin. Additionally, she developed an avid interest in astronomy and mathematics. At the age of seventeen, Annabella spent a season (1810–11) with her mother in London, seeing Kemble in the theatre and attending numerous concerts. On 22 March 1812 Annabella reportedly began reading the much-talked-about *Childe Harold*. On 25 March, according to an account to her mother, she saw Lord Byron for the first time:

> Yesterday I went to a *morning* party at Lady Caroline Lamb's, where my curiosity was much gratified by seeing Lord Byron, the object at present of universal attention. . . . I did not seek an introduction to him, for all the women were absurdly courting him, and trying to *deserve* the lash of his Satire. I thought that *inoffensiveness* was the most secure conduct, as I am not desirous of a place in his lays. Besides I cannot worship talents that are unconnected with the love of man, nor be captivated by that Genius which is barren in blessings. So I made no offering at the shrine of Childe Harold, though I shall not refuse the acquaintance if it comes in my way.[47]

The acquaintance came a few weeks later on 13 April at Lady Gosford's home, and she reported to her mother further:

> I have met with much evidence of his [Byron's] goodness. You know how easily the noblest heart may be perverted by

---

47. For this letter and other general information above see Malcolm Elwin, *Lord Byron's Wife* (London: Macdonald, 1962), 106. Unfortunately, Elwin's biography does not go beyond the end of Lady Byron's marriage to Lord Byron, as if her life held no significance after that; her letters to Baillie and others certainly prove otherwise.

unkindness—perhaps the most easily a *noble* heart, because it is more susceptible to ungenerous indignities.[48]

After a second meeting, Byron approached Annabella's aunt, Lady Melbourne, to write to her on his behalf "about his interest in this 'amiable Mathematician'."[49] Thus was the stage set, amidst warnings from Lady Caroline Lamb and others, for Annabella's greatest infatuation. Rejecting his first marriage proposal in 1812, yet continuing to correspond with him, she married the poet on 2 January 1815 after a four-month engagement. John Cam Hobhouse, Byron's good friend and witness to the ceremony, later wrote:

> Miss M. was firm as a rock, and during the whole ceremony looked steadily at Byron. She repeated the words audibly and well. Byron hitched at first when he said "I, George Gordon" and when he came to the words "With all my worldly goods I thee endow" looked at me with a half smile.[50]

What happiness that came was short-lived, and the one year of marriage to Byron combined passion and torment for both parties. According to Annabella's own accounts, trouble appeared the day after the marriage when Byron became morose and alluded to his family's history of madness. The violence which followed is difficult to assess, for many of Annabella's accounts were written after the separation in order to supply her legal adviser Stephen Lushington with evidence in her favor for child custody.[51] Their only daughter Ada had been conceived in March, about the time that the Byrons were on a visit to the poet's half-sister Augusta Leigh, with whom

---

48. Elwin, 108. The progress of this relationship can be followed in the many letters offered in Elwin's biography, letters from the Lovelace Papers to which Byron's principal biographer, Leslie Marchand, had no access at the time of his research.

49. Betty A. Toole, *Ada, The Enchantress of Numbers* (Mill Valley, CA: Strawberry Press, 1992), 7.

50. Elwin, 249.

51. Stephen Lushington (1782–1873) was one of the attorneys involved in the Byron separation settlement. He was also retained as counsel for Queen Caroline before the House of Lords and made a masterly speech in her defense in October 1820. He was an ardent reformer, supporting the abolition of capital punishment, and an able advocate. He married Sarah Grace Carr (d. 1837), the daughter of Mr. and Mrs. Thomas William Carr of Hampstead, in 1821; the Lushingtons had five sons and five daughters (*DNB*, XII:291–93).

Byron had allegedly been intimate. According to biographer Betty Toole, it was a visit Lady Byron would always remember and replay in her mind:

> During the visit (information derived from statements to her attorney a year later) Lady Byron analyzed every move, watched every interaction of Augusta and Byron, and determined that she would be their guardian and save them from the evil, real or imagined, that was between them. Byron's recollection did not note anything extraordinary happening on the visit.[52]

Augusta Ada Byron was born the following 10 December 1815; by then the marriage was beyond repair. Biographer Ethel Colburn Mayne suggests that Annabella had begun to take refuge in the possibility that her husband *was* mad, even though she did not really believe it, and went so far as to consult Dr. Matthew Baillie concerning Byron's mental state.[53] Finally, after returning to the home of her parents in January 1816, the separation process began. Annabella later wrote of Byron:

> He required of a woman's attachment—to use an expressive Scotch phrase—not *heart to heart*, but *heart at his feet*—and mine was laid before him. But this was not enough. . . . There is *no* vice with which he has not endeavoured to familiarize me.[54]

Though Byron seemed disposed to reconciliation, it did not take place. Annabella never remarried. While she wrote her friend Mary Montgomery in 1853 that "there were pre-existing causes of separation,"[55] it seems that friends of both parties did little to aid the partnership at its inception and plenty to cause grief after its

---

52. Toole, 8.
53. See Elwin's account and Leslie A. Marchand's *Byron, A Biography*, 3 vols. (New York: Knopf, 1957). Dr. Baillie had also been consulted in July 1799 on the best treatment for Byron's deformed foot, and he designed a brace and later a special shoe for the child (Crainz, 60).
54. Ethel Colburn Mayne, *The Life and Letters of Anne Isabella, Lady Noel Byron* (New York: Charles Scribner's Sons, 1929), 166–67.
55. Mayne, 119.

demise.[56] Gossip thrived, some of it fueled by the Byrons themselves.[57]

In the years that followed, Lady Noel Byron had sole custody of her daughter Ada and tried hard to keep her secluded from gossip mongers; but after Lord Byron left England in 1816 for the continent, he kept in contact with Ada through Augusta Leigh.[58] For the first seven years, mother and daughter lived in homes outside London. When Annabella went away for health cures or visits, Ada was kept by her grandparents or by Lady Byron's friends, Louisa Chaloner, Mary Montgomery, or Selina Doyle.[59] Ada had several governesses

---

56. In *Ada, Countess of Lovelace, Byron's Legitimate Daughter* (London: Murray, 1977), Doris Langley Moore reprints a later letter from Lady Byron's friend Mrs. De Morgan:
> After a conversation with Miss M. [Montgomery] on some of Lady B's present difficulties & the trials she had passed through, Miss M. said she believed there was no crime which Lord B had not committed. I could hardly believe this, but she told me the cause of the Separation, *or one cause*, . . . when she narrated the story of Mrs Leigh, *very nearly* as lately given by Mrs Stowe, I was greatly horrified, and *possibly may have taken it for granted* this was the *only* reason of the Separation. (35)

57. See note 56 above. Doris Langley Moore also gives a select list of Lady Byron's confidantes, all of whom she told some part of the story. They included Lady Olivia Acheson, Joanna Baillie, Louisa Mary Barwell, Henry Allen Bathurst, George Anson Byron, Thomas Campbell, Sarah Carr (later Mrs. Lushington), Selina Doyle, Lady Gosford, Lady Grey, Anna Jameson, Medora Leigh, Hugh and Mary Montgomery, Sarah Siddons, Harriet Beecher Stowe, to name a *few* (*Ada*, 370).

58. Thomas Moore later wrote,
> The circumstances under which Lord Byron now took leave of England were such as, in the case of any ordinary person, could not be considered otherwise than disastrous and humiliating. He had, in the course of one short year, gone through every variety of domestic misery;—had seen his hearth ten times profaned by the visitations of the law, and been only saved from a prison by the privileges of his rank. He had alienated (if, indeed, they had ever been his) the affections of his wife; and now, rejected by her, and condemned by the world, was betaking himself to an exile which had not even the dignity of appearing voluntary, as the excommunicating voice of society seemed to leave him no other resource. (Thomas Moore, Esq., *Letters and Journals of Lord Byron: with Notices of His Life*, 2 vols. [New York: J. & J. Harper, 1830], 2:3)

59. Lady Byron wrote to Hugh Montgomery on Ada's second birthday that "Nothing but the danger of my own safety or my child's welfare would induce me to revive accusations of any kind" (Mayne, 275). Meanwhile, Byron wrote, "My child is very well, and flourishing, I hear; but I must see

and was also taught by her mother, a strict disciplinarian. In 1826, two years after the death of Lord Byron, Annabella, Ada, and a group of friends embarked on a tour of the continent; when they returned, Annabella began making serious plans for Ada's education. It was then that Dr. King (head of the Brighton Cooperative Society), Sophia Frend, and Arabella Lawrence, all family friends, began to supervise Ada's studies until they were replaced in 1832 by a series of tutors for chemistry, Latin, shorthand, and music. At this time Annabella and Ada moved to Fordhook, a mansion near London that had been the home of Henry Fielding. It was also at this time that Ada met mathematician Charles Babbage, who would later fire her passion for mathematics and mechanics. In 1835 nineteen-year-old Ada was introduced to William, Lord King, whom she married after a brief courtship and with whom she had three children.[60]

During Annabella's courtship and marriage to Byron, she reportedly met Joanna Baillie for the first time in March 1812, saw a great deal of her afterwards, and said "'farewell' with feelings of reverence and gratitude which will survive the longest separation."[61] In her journal entry after their first encounter, Annabella declared,

> Went to Hampstead & introduced myself to the Miss Baillies. Miss Joanna pleased me very much by the character of simplicity & truth that appeared in her countenance & manner. Not a semblance of *display*—only the modest cheerfulness and unambitious sense of a mind untainted by vanity.[62]

As did other friends and writers, Annabella clearly mistook Baillie's reserved confidence for an "unambitious sense of mind." She wanted Byron to meet Baillie and wrote to him in 1813 that

> The more I see of Authoresses, the more I admire in Joanna Baillie a perfect exception to their *professional* failings. I must

---

also. I feel no disposition to resign it to the <u>contagion of its grandmother's society</u>" (Thomas Moore, 2:814; emphasis in original).

60. Their children were Byron Noel (Lord Ockham, b. 1836), Anne Isabella Noel (Baroness Wentworth, b. 1837), and Ralph Gordon Noel (Baron Wentworth, b. 1839).

61. Qtd. in Mayne, 65.

62. Elwin, 169–70n.

repeat my wish that you knew her, and if yours has not abated, might not the introduction be easily accomplished?[63]

But Byron reportedly put off the meeting and argued that he was shy in introducing himself to new people. He did meet Baillie some time between 1813 and 1815, however, for Baillie discussed such a meeting in a January 1815 letter to Walter Scott:

> Since you left town I have seen your friend & admirer Lord Byron oftener than once: he has very kindly sent me a very handsome copy of all his works, and invites me in the most gratifying way to give some of my plays to Drury Lane as he & his colleagues wish to begin their management by producing something of mine. For this I feel myself mostly indebted to Lady Byron & partly to yourself. You have always been in the way like my good Genius to do me a good turn when it could be done: and I can only say in return that it delights my heart to be obliged to you. I have told Lord B. that I do not intend to offer any new plays to a London Theatre but shall be very proud to have any of those already published produced upon their boards, and shall be at all times ready to alter & arrange any of them for the stage in any way they may desire. Whether this will really come to any good I know not, but it is at least something not disagreeable to think of in the mean time. Ld B. has his eye upon De Monfort which he thinks will suit Kean. He thinks [that] to please the generality of the audience I must give some stronger reason for De Monforts [sic] hatred and I think to please all ~~parts~~ classes of the audience I must alter the ending of the piece which does not produce good stage effect in its present state.[64]

Byron's 1815 promotion as a member of the Drury Lane Theatre management sub-committee was short lived, however, even with Baillie's eagerness to edit the play to "fit" the general audience. In "Joanna Baillie and Lord Byron," William Brewer argues that Byron's response to Baillie as an innovator "helps us understand his attitudes towards the roles of gender and power in female literary production, and Baillie's plays on the passions had a profound

---

63. Mayne, 74.
64. See NLS letter 3886 ff.39 (1815) to Scott; *Letters*, 338.

influence on Byron's dramas."[65] After the Kean production of *De Monfort* foundered, however, Byron seems to have lost interest in its revival, "even though he continued to believe that 'there are fine things in all the Plays on the Passions'."[66] Seeing Baillie as a sort of "literary aggressor," Byron, who claimed he "fear[ed] nobody but Miss Edgeworth," may have been both intrigued and intimidated by her ability to portray what some considered masculine passions.[67] In 1798 critics and readers alike had, after all, assumed that the anonymously published *Series of Plays* had been written by a man.

Exactly what happened at Drury Lane in 1815 is not totally clear, but Ellen Donkin, like Baillie herself, attributes her lack of success there to possible animosity from manager Richard Brinsley Sheridan, who may have become "unfriendly" to her as early as 1801 because she had spoken critically of contemporary drama, *his* domain, in her "Introductory Discourse."[68] Aloma Noble also blames the cultural climate, because the "first half of the nineteenth-century was a period entirely unfavorable for legitimate drama on the London stage," the keynote of the time "discontent—general, constant, and indefinite."[69] In addition, argues Noble, the royalty and aristocracy were indifferent to the stage, and prostitutes still plied their trade there as they had in the old days and made the theater atmosphere repulsive to many middle-class citizens. There could be other explanations as well; it is even possible that support from Byron may not have been considered in certain circles as an entirely positive recommendation for a woman playwright's career. Oddly enough, in a letter from Lady Byron to Baillie dated October 1817, she relayed a message from Byron, who had simply written her

---

65. See similar discussion in chapter 2, and see Brewer's "Joanna Baillie and Lord Byron." Donald Reiman also outlines Byron's debt to Baillie in his Introduction to the 1977 Garland reprint of her works: As in Byron's plays, "The important dramatic action really takes place within the mind of the protagonist, and its external manifestations are primarily debates between the protagonist and a series of supporting characters representing aspects of his divided self" (qtd. in Brewer, 174).

66. Brewer, 168.

67. Ibid., 171.

68. Donkin, 168. Also see Baillie's 1801 letter to her friend Miss Millar, NLS 9236 ff.307 (*Letters*, 1106–7), in which she states that "I have for a long time heard from so many different quarters that Mr Sheridan (for you guess very right) is unfriendly to me, that I cant help giving credit to it, but in the present case it does not appear that he has had any thing to do with it."

69. Noble, 116–17.

about their daughter Ada, that "If you see Joanna Baillie—tell her that Kean is going at last to act De Monfort—which I urged him to a hundred times in 1815"; Byron regretted that he would never see the performance.[70] Although no such performance occurred, Baillie felt indebted to Byron for his support and had been, with reservation, pleased with Annabella's marriage. Her earlier letter of January 1815 had congratulated the pair as follows:

> My dear Lady Byron,
> I have been enquiring eagerly of the newspapers which do not come to us every day, when I might address you by this name, and it is only within these two days that I have learnt the happy event has taken place.[71] I send you my most hearty congratulations. Be but as happy as I wish you, and you & your Lord will be enviable creatures indeed. That you are so, it is impossible to doubt; and that you may long very long continue to be so I sincerely & ardently wish. I believe few young pairs have ever been matched together possessing so many qualities for producing happiness of the highest kind; and I am sure no Poet I ever know or heard of, ever matched himself so poetically, so wisely & so well. May a blessing be upon all this that will go with you thro' life![72]

If Baillie anticipated in any way the miserable failure of this marriage, she concealed it in her optimistic wish.

Unfortunately, Baillie's letters to Lady Byron during the ensuing separation and legal battle with her husband are missing after August 1817, with sustained correspondence beginning again in 1829. But her letters to Scott during 1816 and 1817 provide an entertaining perspective on the Byrons' separation, for Baillie seemed initially caught between her strong friendship with Lady Byron and

---

70. OU Lovelace/Byron 62, ff.159–60. This letter was written after the Byrons' separation, and parts of it have been cut out. In addition, Baillie's letters to Lady Byron between mid-1817 and 1829 are missing, but some of Lady Byron's letters to Baillie during these years exist in this collection. I find no such record of a performance of *De Monfort* at Drury Lane until 1821, though *The Family Legend* was performed there in May 1815.

71. Anne Isabella Milbanke married Byron on 2 January 1815. I find no correspondence between her and Baillie during the marriage, possibly due to Baillie's propensity to burn letters she considered too personal.

72. *Letters*, 734.

her regard for Lord Byron as a fellow poet.[73] On 26 February 1816, however, she apprised Scott of the current rumors and became more and more agitated in the course of her writing:

> You must have heard a good while ago reports of Lord & Lady Byron's separation, and it was generally said that this was occasioned by his improper connection with a beautiful Actress of Drury Lane.[74] It is not however believed, by those who have the best opportunity of knowing, that gallantries as they are called of any kind had any thing to do with it. Your kind & manly heart will be grieved when I tell you, from authority that cannot be doubted, that he has used her brutally, and that no excuse can be pleaded in his behalf but <u>insanity</u>. For the credit of human nature, proofs of this are so strong that in any court of justice they would procure a separation, and I believe a legal separation will soon be settled.[75] When I say <u>brutally</u> I use the word that was made use of to me, not knowing any particulars as to the manner of it, tho' I fear it has been very bad. Symptoms of this mental disorder began to shew itself the first week after their marriage. His nearest relations declare that Lady Byron behaved throughout in this most trying situation like an Angel; and from what I know myself of the sweetness & kindness of her nature, & the good sense calmness & self-possession of her character, I can easily believe that every thing was done on her part to conciliate—not irritate him. I had good cause to know that her motives for marrying him were of a very generous nature bordering on romantic, and there is scarcely a man in England who would not have

---

73. NLS letter 3888 ff.37–39 to Scott particularly displays this conflict (*Letters*, 362–63).

74. Lady Byron returned home to her parents in January 1816 after only a year with Lord Byron. Marchand writes that Lady Byron had not been happy with Byron's "absorption in Drury Lane affairs . . . and his familiarity with actors and actresses in the greenroom" (Marchand, 2:539). Apparently, a climax occurred on January 3 "when Byron came to [Lady Byron's] room and talked with 'considerable violence' on the subject of his affairs with women of the theater" (Marchand, *Byron*, 2:557).

75. Byron later stated that "Wherever the wrong lies, it does not lie in her: she is perfect in thought, word, & deed" (qtd. in Johnson, 515). Byron agreed to the terms of the separation on 17 March 1816 and left England forever; Dr. Matthew Baillie had been consulted on Byron's sanity earlier (see Marchand).

thought himself blessed & honoured in being the husband of such a woman. Her happiness now, at the age of 24 is wrecked for life.[76]

In the midst of composing this letter, Baillie was interrupted by an unidentified friend who informed her that according to the marriage settlement "the whole of Lady Byron's large fortune will go to him after her Mother's death, except three hundred a year which is her pin money." When Baillie sat down to finish the letter, she implored Scott to write to Byron and "stir up his pride by telling him that the only way he can justify his character from the suspected meaness [sic] of having married from sordid motives will be by settling of his own free accord a liberal income on his wife." But Baillie also naively suggested this might be a means of Lady Byron's returning to him. This seems to be the only favor Scott ever refused Baillie, and in her reply of 17 March, she conceded that it had been too much to ask, thinking him on a better "footing" with Byron than he actually was.

Interesting here is how intimate this circle of writers was, how fast scandal traveled without the aid of modern communication devices, and how Baillie finally seemed to "dismiss" Byron from her circle soon after his infamous break with Annabella. While Baillie often gossiped about political matters in her correspondence, she was mostly reticent about the intimate lives of her friends, almost to the point of disinterest; so her attention to the Byrons' struggles and her later complete and obvious rejection of the poet seems almost out of character for her. Brewer points out, however, that probably the most significant difference between Lord Byron and Baillie from the beginning had to do with their moral principles, for Byron, often a nihilist, clearly clashed with Baillie's devout and conservative Christianity. Ultimately, Byron became to her a sort of "domestic monster who broke the heart of [her] dear friend."[77] What details Baillie really knew about the couple's domestic affairs is uncertain, but she was certainly acquainted with the settlement details and with the later custody battle for Ada. Apparently, the knowledge was sufficient to make her turn away from Lord Byron.

Baillie was constantly concerned about Annabella's health, and she wrote to Scott in July of 1817 that Lady Byron was temporarily staying at her mother's house and "in bad health, very much

---

76. NLS 866 ff.68–72; *Letters*, 346.
77. Brewer, 165.

occasioned I believe by the state of her mind."[78] Annabella lived, of course, another forty-three years, but she was adept at soliciting sympathy. When Lady Byron traveled to Scotland in 1817 to see Scott after her separation, Baillie was concerned that she was traveling alone. Instead, Annabella apparently traveled with friend Frances Carr, also a companion of Baillie. When Scott saw Annabella, his "heart ached for her all the time [they] were together; there was so much patience and decent resignation" in her countenance.[79] From the 1820s Baillie continued as Annabella's friend, but their correspondence turned from poetry and public performance to mutual acquaintances, personal health, raising Ada, and Annabella's work with schools and "co-operative" plans of education. There was some correspondence between Lady Byron and Agnes Baillie as well. When Thomas Moore's *Life of Lord Byron* appeared in 1830, discussions between Lady Byron and Joanna returned to the original scandal and concern that Moore had mislead his readers about the Milbankes' part in the separation. In letters from that year, Baillie also reported that she had informed Miss Edgeworth that Lady Byron was preparing an "answer" to Moore. She even saw that Felicia Hemans, Rose Lawrence, John Gibson Lockhart, many of her neighbors, and American Unitarian minister William Ellery Channing received copies of this rebuttal, in addition to Maria Edgeworth—thus crossing continents with information (clearly, the nineteenth-century version of "networking").[80] Lady Byron had apparently been to visit Joanna's sister-in-law Sophia Baillie as well, who wrote to Annabella in February 1830 in support of her "decision upon this occasion" and confirmed that her statement was "particularly clear and simple"—Sophia also hoped that the strain of all this would not encroach upon her "little remaining stock of health."[81]

After this hectic year of the 1830 *Life*, Baillie and Lady Byron settled back into discussions about family, literature, associates, health, and charities. In August 1835 Annabella sent Baillie lines from elegies she had composed for a friend and asked about the advertisement for Baillie's forthcoming *Dramas*. During the 1840s

---

78. NLS 3888 ff.108–9; *Letters*, 372.
79. Mayne, 274.
80. Edgeworth quickly thanked Baillie for the pamphlet that was "dignified and simple–and clearly effects its purpose," clearing her parents of the rumors that they urged Annabella to separate from Byron (OU Lovelace/Byron 62, ff.72).
81. OU Lovelace/Byron 62, ff.226–27.

Baillie also corresponded with Annabella's daughter Ada, Lady King, mostly about her mother and her children; but as early as October 1826, Ada was sending Baillie news of her trip to Switzerland and to Heidelberg, the beauty of its scenery pleasing her more than any place.[82] Ultimately, Baillie's tribute to Lady Byron appeared as part of "Miscellaneous Poetry" in *Fugitive Verses* and was entitled "Recollections Of A Dear And Steady Friend," excerpted as follows:

> To early friends her love was firm and fast;
> Beneath her roof they gather'd oft and cast
> A faint reflected gleam of days gone by,
> And kindly smiled on them her soft blue eye.
> Mary Montgomery! nobly sounding name,
> And worthy she to bear it. Oft would come
> Their youthful kindred; to an easy home.[83]

It was through Lady Byron that Baillie met Mary Millicent Montgomery, Annabella's closest friend from girlhood to Annabella's death in 1860. It is almost impossible to demonstrate Mary Montgomery's significance in this circle without the aid of Lady Byron's, Baillie's, and her own letters because there is little biographical evidence available on her. Mary, suffering from spinal afflictions, was a semi-invalid to whom Annabella constantly referred as "doomed to an early grave," though she outlived Annabella.[84] In 1812 Annabella wrote that she arrived in London at the Gosfords' home in Cumberland Place to "Such a welcome—and M.M. looking better for a moment, but soon pale and weak again" and in an 1813 letter told Byron of her valued friend Montgomery going abroad for medical advice.[85] Almost every letter associated with Mary Montgomery, Baillie's included, contains some reference to Montgomery's health and often to Lady Byron's as well. In 1813 Lady Byron revealed to Lady Gosford that

> Every one of my friends has a different influence on my humour. MM makes me romantic; you make me thoughtful; HM light-hearted (with a few exceptions); Joanna humble;

---

82. OU Lovelace/Byron 168, f.85.
83. *DPW*, 809.
84. Catherine Turney, *Byron's Daughter, A Biography of Elizabeth Medora Leigh* (New York: Charles Scribner's Sons, 1972), 157.
85. Mayne, 23, 67.

By___ religious; Miss Raine reasonable; Miss Doyle sanguine; Dr. Fenwick diffident, &c. &c.[86]

Mary Montgomery's brother Captain Hugh Montgomery, the "HM" mentioned above, was a casual friend with whom Annabella corresponded for many years and was considered by some to be a suitor. But biographer Mayne calls Hugh Montgomery Lady Byron's "man of straw."[87] Lady Byron wrote to both Mary and Hugh before her marriage to Byron, during the separation, and for many years after the break up of her marriage—while others often wrote to the Montgomerys *about* Lady Byron, Joanna Baillie included. Lord Byron's definitive biographer, Leslie Marchand, and others believe that Lady Byron's distress from her failed marriage was increased in 1818 by letters from the Montgomerys, who, after seeing Byron in Venice, maliciously reported him "Extremely fat . . . bloated and heavy."[88] After their separation, however, Colonel Montgomery informed Annabella that Byron talked "kindly and nobly of her."[89] But Mayne argues that the Montgomerys were too prone to "inflict wounds which might well have been spared for her [Annabella] through their malicious stories of Lord Byron."[90] Lady Byron ultimately wrote Hugh Montgomery that she resented "the unkin-like action of all the Lambs, except William, being mourners at Lord Byron's funeral," the misery of which, says Mayne, broke her down and made her ill for many weeks.[91] Mrs. Augustus De Morgan, another companion of Lady Byron, revealed that the Montgomerys

> had been the harbingers of everything unpleasant they could convey about Byron while he was still alive—not that they had known him but they were resolved to fortify his wife against reconciliation—and they never tired of speaking ill against him after his death.[92]

---

86. Ibid., 73.
87. Ibid., 62–63.
88. Marchand, *Byron*, 2:478; Doris Langley Moore, *The Late Lord Byron: Posthumous Dramas* (Philadelphia and New York: J. B. Lippincott, 1961), 485–86.
89. Mayne, 258.
90. Ibid., 295.
91. Ibid., 301.
92. D. Moore, *Ada*, 34–35. Mrs. De Morgan also revealed that,
   from 1832 to 1837, I stayed frequently either at Fordhook or at Col. Montgomery's, Acton Lodge, Acton: Col. M's sister, Miss Montgomery . . . had been as a sister to Lady Byron from their

Montgomery's animosity, however, may have been due to an early satirical attack to which Annabella alluded in an early journal:

> In the journal Miss Milbanke kept when she was first greatly taken with Byron but not yet in love with him, she wrote that he had spoken "satirically of one of my best *friends* whom he did not know except by sight & report." The only intimate friends of hers whom he could know even by sight were Lady Gosford (M.G.) and Miss Montgomery (M.M.). A few weeks later she noted that "he seemed to have an unpleasant impression of M.M.'s countenance though he spoke of the cleverness which it indicated."[93]

Because Baillie's relationship with Mary Montgomery was born of her friendship with Lady Byron, her correspondence with Montgomery concerned itself mostly with matters of family, health, and their mutual confidante Lady Byron. Montgomery wrote from the position of a younger friend sending news of the same and often giving the Baillie sisters thoughtful small gifts. Never, however, do Baillie's letters to Montgomery reveal the close relationship that appears in her letters to Scott, for instance, or even to Lady Byron for that matter. In October 1826, for example, Baillie thanked Mary Montgomery for her gift of a "Market purse," sympathized with her "Tic douloureux," discussed the recent travels of Lady Byron and Ada, and speculated on the health of Annabella's father Ralph Milbanke.[94] Baillie's letters most often turn to the topic of Lady Byron and just as often to the subject of illness. On 1 January 1827,

---

> childhood. She was the confidante of all her troubles and knew *all* those things of which other friends were only partially informed. . . . After a conversation with Miss M. on some of Lady B's present difficulties & the trials she had passed through, Miss M. said she believed there was no crime which Lord B had not committed.(35; emphasis in original)

This is also quoted in note 56 above. Mary Montgomery was remembered in the will of Lady Byron's daughter, Ada Byron King (Lady Lovelace).

93. D. Moore, *Ada*, 35n.

94. OU 93, ff.159–160; *Letters*, 848–49. *Tic douloureux* means, literally, a painful twitching or habitual pain.

however, Baillie wrote of their new year's party, what the Scotch call Hogmanae, at John Richardson's, where they feasted on "Grouse—& Black lock & short-bread and all kinds of Northern dainties," and of the upcoming dinner at the Carrs'.[95] By 1830 Baillie was discussing with Montgomery Annabella's "Remarks" to be added at the end of Moore's biography on Lord Byron as a means of "vindicating" her parents and about the gossip which had ensued. Further, around 1833 she thanked Montgomery for sending a recent review of her *Lights and Shadows of German Life* (1833). In December of 1833 Baillie again worried about Lady Byron's health and told Montgomery about attending a "curious" lecture on phrenology, given for the men and women of the Scientific Institution at the Hollybush Tavern, and speculated humorously about the heads of various statesmen.[96] Her letters to Montgomery during the 1820s and 1830s are casual and chatty and focused on upcoming marriages, dinners, and mutual friends. The two corresponded well into the 1840s. In January 1841 Baillie discussed a more serious topic—conditions in Ireland and the new Pope (Gregory XVI),[97] about whose character all Protestants were speculating:

> His character & probable course of action is a most interesting subject of speculation to all reasonable protestants at present. He seems to be sent into the world to promote peace & liberality in the midst of all these religious bickerings about things of no importance. It would be well if some of our Bishops & Dignitaries here had a little of his good sense, and above all if the Irish Catholic Clergy had a

---

95. OU 93, ff.163–164; *Letters*, 851–53.

96 Phrenology was a theory developed by Gall and Spurzheim that an individual's mental powers consisted of separate faculties, each of which had its organ and location in a definite region of the surface of the brain, the size and development of which was commensurate with the development of the particular faculty; hence, the study of the external conformation of the cranium as an index to the development and position of these organs, and thus of the degree of development of the various faculties (*OED*). Many nineteenth-century writers were interested in or mentioned phrenology in their works, including Charlotte Brontë and Joseph Conrad.

97. OU Lovelace/Byron 93, ff.219–220; *Letters*, 883. Pope Gregory XVI (d. 1846) and his successor, Pius IX (d. 1878), both set themselves solidly against change and modernity, and Catholic theology at this time aimed at being restorative rather than progressive (*The Encyclopedia of Religion* [New York: Macmillan, 1987], 12:434).

similar spirit to their excellent Pontiff—I am sure your heart must bleed for the state of your poor Country at present. It is said that the priests forbid the poor starving people to receive <u>protestant</u> bread! But hunger will overcome bigotry if any thing can. These are dismal times, yet no doubt it is good both for countries & individuals to suffer such trials; we know that every thing is wisely & well ordered to bring about ultimate good. Our Queen met her Parliament yesterday but I have heard nothing of it yet; she & her Counsellors have a tangled web to unravel and must be strongly supported to do much good.[98]

Baillie, a nonconformist herself, maintained throughout her life an interest in almost all religious orders.

A little before Baillie met Annabella Milbanke and Mary Montgomery, she began to promote a writer by the name of Margaret Holford Hodson (1778–1852), to whom she was introduced some time between 1810 and 1813, the date of Baillie's first letter to Hodson. Margaret Holford Hodson was the eldest daughter of Allen Holford, esq., of Davenham and Margaret Wrench Holford, author of plays (the first, *Neither's the Man*, published in 1799), several poems, and a four-volume novel published in 1801 (*First Impressions, or the Portrait*). Margaret followed her mother's example and developed an early interest in literature, her first work, an 1809 metrical romance entitled *Wallace, or the Fight of Falkirk*, mentioned in the *Quarterly Review*. She followed with a collection entitled *Poems* in 1811 (which includes an ode to Anna Seward), *Margaret of Anjou* in 1816, and a collection of poems entitled *The Past* in 1819. In 1820 came her *Warbeck of Wolfstein*, dedicated to Joanna Baillie, with its protagonist clearly an unfavorable representation of Byron. A translation entitled *Italian Stories* followed in 1823 and, published after her marriage to the Rev. Septimus Hodson, *The Lives of Vasco Nuñez de Balboa and Francisco Pizarro*, dedicated to Robert Southey

---

98. In 1839 Queen Victoria had lost the services of her "dear and excellent Lord Melbourne" and was faced with a Tory Prime minister. Sir Robert Peel gained the post in 1841, immediately demanding a change in the ladies of the bedchamber. Showing a new-found self reliance, Victoria refused. On 3 September 1841 she held a council at Claremont at which the former Ministers surrendered their seals and her new Ministers took them (Giles St. Aubyn, *Queen Victoria, A Portrait* [New York: Atheneum, 1992], 35, 122–57).

in 1832.[99] Holford contributed two poems to Baillie's *A Collection of Poems, Chiefly Manuscript, and from Living Authors* in 1823: "On Memory—written at Aix-la-Chapelle" and "Lines suggested by a Portrait of the Queen of France."

In an animated letter to Scott dated 4 February 1810, before she had actually met the author, Baillie first mentioned Holford's work:

> Have you yet seen a Poem called Wallace or the Fight of Falkirk? It is written in imitation of you, and seem'd to my Sister & I as we read it the other day a work of great merit. It is written, as I am told, by a Lady. She can set her lance at rest, hang her battle axe to her saddle bow, clasp her haberk [sic] & her habergeon, raise her battle cry & ring her slogan with the best military antiquarian of you all; and she abounds in striking thoughts & spirited lines of your irregular measure, that carry one on eagerly; but her powers of discription, and of touching the heart are not equal to her other merits, and the character of Wallace is not the Wallace Wight that one would wish it to be. However, of all the Imitators & followers you are likely to have, and they will probably be a long train, you are not, I think, likely to meet with one that will do you more credit. It is but fair to confess, however, that I have read the Poem only once, and am giving my opinion of it rather rashly. Did you receive verses some years ago from a Lady of the name of Holford? This, I believe, is the writer of Falkirk Fight; and I am told she was very much hurt that you never took any notice of those verses. If this be so, it is a hole in your manners that will not easily be bouched up; and I see she does not mention you in the Preface nor make any allusion to you in the course of the Poem.[100]

Baillie's reprimand was obviously well taken, for Scott immediately responded, as Baillie confirmed on 13 March 1810:

---

99. Because there is little information available on Margaret Holford Hodson, the biographical information here comes from very short entries in the *DNB*, IX:968, and in *The Feminist Companion to Literature in English*, 531-32.

100. NLS 3879 ff.13-15; *Letters*, 252-53.

> I will now say a word or two upon your business of Miss Holford, for those, who have got above ordinances, generally I believe, attend, as I have done, to their own business in the first place. I wrote without losing time after I got your letter, to my Friend Mrs Elliott, who is acquainted with a friend of Miss Holford, who is one of the learned Ladies of Bath, desiring her to convey your message to the said Friend for Miss H. and I daresay it has been, or will be done very handsomely. Your excuse for not writing to her formerly, is a very pretty excuse, but dont suppose it will pass with me: you had a better reason for not writing than not liking to write <u>one</u> letter about yourself & your poetry; you were afraid of having an unknown sentimental correspondent saddled upon your back, no very desirable thing I readily admit, and so on this score you will stand fully excused in my mind, whatever you may do in Miss Holford's. I dont think her character of Wallace will be popular; but not exactly for the reasons you give for it, and therefore I hope they will not prevent that Poet from undertaking a picture of our favourite Hero, to whom it of right belongs.[101]

By January 1815 Baillie was thanking Scott for the handsome compliment he had paid to Miss Holford, namely, his noting her *Wallace* in Canto 5 of his *Lord of the Isles*. So from her initial reproach just a few years before, Baillie ultimately elicited for Holford a compliment in print from the most popular writer of the nineteenth century—just one example of her commitment to her female contemporaries.

Baillie's correspondence with Margaret Holford Hodson continued until at least the 1840s (a few letters are undated), and she also wrote about her to associates less famous than Scott. By the 1820s the two were visiting often, for Joanna and Agnes had just moved from the Hampstead house they had lived in since 1799 to Holly Bush Hill (the general area also called Windmill Hill because of the two windmills constructed near its summit) and were closer both to the Heath and to Holford's house. The Baillie sisters' house was apparently the lovely, three-story red brick house called Bolton House today. The historical register states mistakenly that the two sisters lived there for over fifty years, but the *Rate Books* (tax records) for the Hampstead parish of St. John confirm their address

---

101. NLS 3879 ff.33–35; *Letters*, 257.

change around 1820, as do Baillie's letters.[102] Baillie and her neighbor Miss Holford also corresponded about reading works from Hannah More to Walter Scott and about their neighbor and friend, the writer Catharine Maria Fanshawe, with whom Baillie often dined.[103] In addition, Baillie and Holford wrote of politics and of their afflictions and those of their friends. Margaret, like Lady Byron and Mary Montgomery, suffered through various periods of illness, one during 1825 which Baillie thought would prove fatal. Additionally, in 1838 Baillie lamented Hodson's being subjected to "blistering" as a remedy for her hearing loss, and she warned her friend February 1839 about her use of Morison's pills.[104]

---

102. As also noted in chapter 3, CLS letters to Margaret Holford state: "But it seems to be a season of change–with us, for Agnes & I also are about to quit the house in which we spent 21 years, and my Brother has at last been released from his long attendance at Windsor" (#11, 12 February 1820). The letter following provides a more specific address: "If I were as strong as I have been I would walk to Hendon to see you, for our new house is nearer you than the old one, being on what is called Holly Bush hill & very near the heath, but besides old age a cold & fatigue from moving &c has made me a very poor creature at present" (#12, 29 March 1820) (see *Letters*, 554–57).

103. Catharine Maria Fanshawe (1765–1834), the second of three daughters of John Fanshawe, Esq., Clerk of the Board of green cloth in the household of George III, suffered from ill health, lived with her sisters in Berkeley Square for many years, and contributed "Epistle to the Earl of Harcourt" and others (anonymously) to Baillie's *Collection of Poems, Chiefly Manuscript, and from Living Authors* in 1823. See Reading University Library's Longman Collection for Baillie's epitaph, excerpted in note to Montgomery letter 93, ff.187-189 (*Letters*, 864–65):

> A ready sparkling wit & playful imagination, made her company delightful; and from her talents for conversation, she would long have been remembered by her contemporaries, had she possessed no other. She was also distinguished by a genius for Poetry, peculiar to herself, in which flushing thoughts, sportive fancy & whimsical, grotesque conceptions, chastened & corrected by her high sense of religion & very refined taste, mingled most harmoniously. Few of her poems have been printed.

104. Blistering through the use of a vesicatory was administered during the eighteenth and nineteenth centuries much like bloodletting, but I have found little information to explain the theory behind the practice.

James Morison was attacked for "quackery" in 1836 when a coroner discovered that the deceased had been taking Morison's pills. The Morison cure was based on a theory that bad blood was the cause for all diseases and that heavy and frequent purgation, using vegetable laxatives, was the cure. Morison produced the purge in his Vegetable Universal pills, available in two strengths and containing aloes, jalap, colocynth, gamboge, cream of tartar, rhubarb, and myrrh and prescribed as many as thirty

Margaret Holford Hodson was for many years a close friend of the poet Robert Southey, who stayed with her and her husband in December 1829. In fact, most of Baillie's references to Southey appear in her letters to Hodson, and in February 1837 she sympathized with the poet's unhappy marriage to Edith Fricker Southey, who suffered from mental illness and would, consequently, die insane in November of that same year.[105] Baillie also discussed with Hodson Wordsworth's opposition to his daughter Dora's marriage to merchant Edward Quillinan in May of 1841 and called the Poet Laureate's conduct "most unpoetlike because the Lover was not rich."[106] Although Southey remained Hodson's closest literary associate, it is likely she met Wordsworth through him at some time. Hodson also knew Henrietta Bowdler well and probably forged the connection between Baillie and Bowdler, whom Baillie saw on occasion.[107] One such encounter came in September 1826, when Baillie visited Bowdler at Lady Mordant's. Baillie was impressed with Bowdler's clear intellect, as she discussed some of the improvements Napoleon had introduced to France, namely, the use of balloons in military field operations.[108] A few months earlier, Baillie had reflected

---

pills a day (Roy Porter, *Health for Sale: Quackery in England, 1660–1850* [Manchester: Manchester University Press, 1989], 228–30).

105. Shortly after Edith Southey's death, Baillie confided to Hodson: "Poor man the loss of his Wife must be a very great relief to him! as a husband his conduct has been most exemplary, and I hope he will enjoy his old age in Peace" (CLS 73 to Hodson, dated 18 January 1838; *Letters*, 671). Poet Laureate Robert Southey would die in 1843.

106. CLS 88, dated 1 January 1842; *Letters*, 698. See Stephen Gill's *William Wordsworth: A Life* for details on the poet's opposition.

107. Henrietta Maria Bowdler (1754–1830) was author of *Poems and Essays* (1786), *Sermons on the Doctrines and Duties of Christianity*, which appeared anonymously, and *Pen Tamar, or the History of an Old Maid* (posthumously, 1830) (see Chester Lee Lambertson, "The Letters of Joanna Baillie [1801–1832]" [Ph.D. diss., Harvard University, 1956], cxxv–cc).

108. Lady Mordant could either be Lady Elizabeth (Prowse) Mordaunt (d. October 1826), wife of Sir John Mordaunt, or, more likely, Lady Marianne (Holbech) Mordaunt (d. June 1842), wife of Sir Charles Mordaunt (see *Burke's Peerage and Baronetage*, 2 vols. [London: Burke's Peerage Ltd., 1975], 1882–83).

After balloons were conceived in 1782 by Montgolfier, the possibility for their use in military field operations was obvious. Aerostatic institutes were started in Paris to build airships for surveillance, and these captive balloons were actually used in the early Revolutionary wars. At the battle of Fleurus in 1794, Captain Coutelle remained above Austrian lines and telegraphed the movements of the enemy to the French army. A fully

on the death of Russian Emperor Alexander I.[109] These historical references exemplify Baillie's keen interest in current events and the variety of subjects she introduced in her letters to Hodson. Of all her women friends, however, Baillie seemed to hold her highest personal and professional esteem for Irish writer Maria Edgeworth.

Maria Edgeworth (1767–1849), probably Baillie's closest "literary friend" after Scott, first focused her writing on educational topics but became best known for her novels. Baillie and Edgeworth met in 1813 and formed a close friendship thereafter.[110] Because Edgeworth was also a friend of Scott, Baillie's allusions to her in letters to him are too numerous to mention in full, but shortly after meeting Edgeworth for the first time, she responded to Scott's notion that he would like to see the two friends together,

> If you would give a silver sixpence as you say, to see us together, each of us would I am sure have given a silver crown . . . to have seen you a third in our party. I have found her a frank, animated, sensible & amusing woman, entirely free from affectation of any kind; and of a confiding & affectionate & friendly disposition that has really gained upon my heart. We met a good many times in large parties, & thrice in a more familiar way; and when we parted she was in leave like one who takes leave of an old friend. She has been received by every body—the first in literature & the first in rank, with the most gratifying eagerness & respect, and has pleased—I should rather say delighted them all. She is cheerful, & talks easily & fluently; seems interested in every

---

equipped balloon accompanied Napoleon Bonaparte to Egypt but there is no record of its being used in military maneuvers (Theodore Ayrault Dodge, *Napoleon, A History of the Art of War, From the Beginning of the French Revolution to the End of the Eighteenth Century, With a Detailed Account of the Wars of the French Revolution*, 4 vols. [1904–7; New York: AMS, 1970], 1:40).

109. Russian Emperor Alexander I (1777–1825) died in the remote area of Taganrog on 30 November 1825, making correspondence and burial arrangements difficult; Prince Volkonsky alone had the presence of mind to dispatch couriers with letters to the Dowager Empress, Grand Duke Constantine and the Senate (see E. M. Almedingen's *The Emperor Alexander I* [New York: Vanguard, 1964], 218 and 223).

110. See Scott letter NLS 3884 ff.184–187.

subject that comes into play, and tells her little anecdote or story (when her Father does not take it out of her mouth) very pleasantly.[111]

By 1813 Scott was also writing to Edgeworth, as was Agnes Baillie, so Maria was often a subject between the two Scots.[112] Edgeworth wrote to Baillie after her visit to France and Switzerland in 1821, promising that "you shall not be plagued with my attempts to describe what you have seen & felt & what you must know to be beyond all description" and declaring her admiration of Baillie's *Griseld Baillie*.[113]

During their long relationship, Edgeworth related a humorous anecdote about the Baillies to her sister Lucy (January 1822): "I have been four days resolving to get up half an hour earlier that I might have time to tell you, my dear Lucy, the history of a cat of Joanna and Agnes Baillie's." The story goes that a Mr. Brodie of the Royal Society had come into some Woorara poison (used by certain native cultures for poisoning arrows) with which to experiment on a cat. When the cat was given the poison, it fell over and appeared to be dead. After an hour or so of rest, the cat got up, apparently, perfectly fine. Brodie repeated the experiment with the same result. While the scientist was thoroughly engaged with this experiment, the cat clearly was not. Somehow Dr. Baillie's young son William took compassion on the feline and asked Mr. Brodie to let him carry her away. With or without consent, it appears that he did just that—and brought the cat to his aunts Joanna and Agnes. "Then the puss's prosperous days began," wrote Edgeworth. "Agnes made a soft bed for her in her own room, and by night and day she was the happiest of cats; she was called Woorara, which in time shortened to Woory." Sadly, however, after a few weeks the ungrateful cat marched off and was never heard of again, and, Edgeworth concluded, "It is supposed that she took to evil courses."[114]

More serious subjects were frequently topics of Edgeworth's letters to and about Baillie. In March 1824 it was the pressing Irish

---

111. NLS 3884 ff.184–187; *Letters*, 322–23.
112. Unfortunately, Edgeworth's letters are scattered through various repositories; a few are owned by the Royal College of Surgeons of England (see HB.ix.36a–b). Many are included in Hare's *The Life and Letters of Maria Edgeworth.*
113. RCS HB.v.83.
114. Augustus J. C. Hare, ed., *The Life and Letters of Maria Edgeworth*, 2 vols. (London: Edward Arnold, 1894), 2:51–52.

question of Catholic emancipation: "if the chance or power of obtaining the goods of this life were equalized . . . between Catholics & Protestants," wrote Edgeworth, "I am convinced you would hear no more of Catholicism in Ireland in 20 years."[115] The following year she wrote of her trip with Sir Walter Scott to Killarney and described some of the settings that Baillie would read about in Edgeworth's lately published *Irish Tales*.[116] Meanwhile, Baillie continued to praise Edgeworth's work to readers and writers like Anne Elliott, Lady Davy, Margaret Holford Hodson, Lady Byron, John and Sophia Lockhart, and, especially, to Harvard divinity professor Dr. Andrews Norton, to whom she confessed in April 1829: "Mrs Hemans & Miss Edgeworth you cannot well prize more highly than I do."[117] Meanwhile, Edgeworth renewed her personal acquaintance with Baillie in 1830 and informed her aunt Mrs. Ruxton in December that "I have seen dear good Joanna Baillie several times, and the Carrs. It has been a great pleasure to me to feel myself so kindly received by those I liked best in London years ago."[118] Later in April 1834 Baillie apprised Norton,

> We have all been delighted with Miss Edgeworth's new work—Helen which must by this time have reached you. Her characters are admirably drawn and her story interesting & powerfully worked up for its moral purpose. Her powers have not been weakened by age, and this all her friends rejoice to see. I think you & Mrs Norton know her personally. Her Brother Sneyd Edgeworth was with us yesterday, and gave a very good report of her health.[119]

In January 1840, Baillie wrote about Edgeworth to yet another American, philanthropist George Ticknor:

> I believe you are personally acquainted with Miss Edgeworth, who is estimated as she ought to be in your Country: I had a letter from her last night with a good account of herself every way. Still writing but very doubtful

---

115. RCS HB.v.86.
116. RCS HB.v.87.
117. HU MS Eng 944, 4; *Letters*, 912.
118. Hare, 2:170.
119. HU MS Eng 944, 4; *Letters*, 912.

as to publishing any thing more in her life time. However this may be, her bright mind is still in healthy conditions.[120]

Affectionate letters continued between the two women into the late 1840s. In August 1844 Edgeworth declared, "I do not believe that two authoresses, blue or green or whatever colour ever loved one another more heartily than we two do—Scotch and Irish as we are!"[121] In short, Edgeworth and Baillie were enduring colleagues and intimate friends.

Another correspondent between the 1820s and 1830s was Baillie's younger contemporary Felicia Hemans. Hemans (1793–1835), poet, hymn writer, and essayist, published multiple works, among them *Poems* (1808), *The Restoration of Works of Art to Italy* (1816), *Modern Greece* (1817), *Hymns for Childhood* (1827), *Records of Woman* (1828), and *National Lyrics and Songs for Music* (1834). Educated by her mother and tutored by friends, Hemans published her first book of poetry when she was only fifteen. She married Captain Alfred Hemans, an Irishman serving in the Royal Welsh Fusiliers with her brother, and bore five sons; but her marriage ended after the birth of her fifth son (~1818), and her husband then departed for Rome. Hemans continued to publish and tried playwriting in 1823 with *Vespers of Palermo*, performed briefly in London; her other dramatic poems such as *The Siege of Valencia* and *Samson Agonistes* were not intended for performance. After the death of her mother in 1827, Hemans moved near Liverpool and then to Dublin in 1831, where she published four more books. She had met Sir Walter Scott in 1829, as did most of the women closely associated with Baillie, and she contributed "Belshazzar's Feast" to Baillie's 1823 *A Collection of Poems*. Hemans often contributed to the *Edinburgh Monthly Magazine* and to *Blackwood's*. While she is said to owe much to the eighteenth century for her style, she also clearly owes much to the Romantic writers of her day.[122]

Although Baillie wrote to and about Felicia Hemans, the two writers apparently never met, for Baillie mourned in a letter to Dr. Andews Norton on Hemans's death in 1835 that

---

120. Dartmouth MS. Ticknor 840116; *Letters*, 1081–82.
121. RCS HB.v.90.
122. Todd, 327–28. Some errors appear in Todd's biographical sketch and are corrected in Wolfson's review of Baillie's *Collected Letters*.

> The melancholy expectation expressed in your letter regarding Mrs Hemans was very soon fulfilled. She is now gone to the many great poets who have charmed the world in different countries & different ages and there is not one of them all whose Lyre emitted sweeter or more touching sounds than her own.[123] I hope she will receive the honours due to her in her own country and in yours there can be no doubt that she will, for I rather think you took precedence of us in appreciating her as she deserves. I never had the good fortune to become personally acquainted with her, though letters & sometimes little friendly offices past between us, but I always hoped to become so, my own advanced age appearing to me the most probable obstacle to this gratification. Who would have thought of her going first![124]

It is unfortunate that Baillie and Hemans did not meet and that there are very few extant letters between the two, but Baillie read her works and recommended them to her other literary friends. She wrote William Sotheby in 1824, for example, about Hemans's *The Siege of Valencia; A Dramatic Poem and The Last Constantine: with Other Poems* (1823):

> Had it been in a dramatic form, she would as you said, have run me very hard and perhaps more than that. But fortunately for me she has shaped it into a poem in the Spencerian [sic] measure, and now it belongs to Lord Byron to be jealous of her not me.[125]

Certainly, while Baillie promoted her contemporaries, she also kept an eye on her competition and often measured her own work against theirs. But in May of 1824 she thanked Scott for his "friendly exertions" in favor of Felicia Hemans's tragedy, probably *Vespers of Palermo*, which had been performed at Covent Garden and Edinburgh.[126] Earlier, Hemans opened her *Captive Knight* with dedicatory lines from Scott's *Lady of the Lake,* and in 1828 she dedicated *Records of Woman* to Baillie. Baillie had sent Hemans a copy of her "little school lesson" on cruelty to animals ("A Lesson

---

123. Felicia Hemans died in Dublin on 16 May 1835.
124. HU 12; *Letters*, 932–34.
125. RCS HB.ix.31; *Letters*, 227.
126. NLS 3898 ff.163–166; *Letters*, 426–27.

Intended for the Use of the Hampstead School," 1826) in 1827 and complimented Hemans's "friend Mr. Channing" on his *Remarks on the Character and Writings of John Milton*.[127] Additionally, in a hastily written letter to Baillie postmarked 1828, Hemans remarked on the whereabouts of her own recent portrait by West, asked about gothic Romanticist Lady Dacre, thanked her for her last letter, and confessed that from childhood her thoughts had often turned to Baillie with a mingling of affection and awe.[128] This connection was completed with the addition of Dr. Andrews Norton, who had edited *Poems by Mrs. Hemans* in 1826-28 and was also an associate of both Baillie and Channing. In April 1829 Baillie's feminist position was clear as she assured Norton that his praise of her, Hemans, and Edgeworth was well justified: "while you do us honour you do us justice, and it is from men like yourself that we receive it and prize it: the half-learned & weaker part of your sex have always set their faces against us."[129] Both Norton and Baillie lamented the early demise of Hemans in 1835.

One woman writer that Baillie seems to have met only once was Susan Edmonstone Ferrier (1782-1854). Ferrier, a Scottish novelist known for satirical sketches on society, published her first novel *Marriage* in 1818 (anonymously), followed by *The Inheritance* in 1824 and *Destiny*, dedicated to Scott, in 1831. Baillie wrote Margaret Holford Hodson in May 1830 that Ferrier, visiting a London physician for her cataracts, had lately come to see her "with a note of introduction from a mutual friend in Edin^r." But Baillie, who was often very candid, was apparently not impressed: "I found her a very diffident, retiring, simple minded & mannered person, at least so she appeared to me."[130] Her comment to Scott much earlier in June 1819 that the author of *Marriage* had pursued "with some success the peculiar manners of the Scotch Highlanders" implies that Baillie was not particularly fond of her novels either.[131] Baillie was, however,

---

127. HM 31515; *Letters*, 1093-94. William Ellery Channing's work on Milton appeared in 1826.
128. WI MS 5615/109/1-2.
129. HU MS Eng 944, 4; *Letters*, 912.
130. CLS 45; *Letters*, 619. Interestingly, Scott wrote in his journal that Ferrier had "less affec[ta]tion than any female I have known [who] has stood so high, even Joanna Baillie hardly excepted" (qtd. in Anderson, 655).
131. NLS 3890 ff.132-135; *Letters*, 389.

supportive of American novelist Catharine Maria Sedgwick,[132] whom she met at least twice in England in 1839, and she wrote Margaret Holford Hodson on August 19 that "A more simple (the best sense of the word) unpretending person I never met with. She is a woman of very good sense and no over strained sentiment, and that with her excellent talents enables her to be a very useful author to the middling & lower classes of her own country folks."[133] This party meeting at the home of William Harness also included Jane Porter and Thomas Campbell.[134]

While creative women were an integral part of Baillie's circle, she could claim just as fair a number of famous men. Writer Thomas Campbell had long been part of Baillie's assembly, probably meeting her after she moved to Hampstead in the later 1790s rather than earlier in Scotland. Thomas Campbell (1777–1844), born in Glasgow and educated at Glasgow University, was a friend of Byron and editor of the *New Monthly Magazine*. He contributed "To the Rainbow" to Baillie's *A Collection of Poems* in 1823. And in later years he helped found London University, which he called, "the only important event in his life."[135] As late as January 1830 Campbell

---

132. Catharine Maria Sedgwick (1789–1867) was one of the first authors to draw from American life for material for fiction. Many of her works possessed a strong moral purpose, endeavoring to render wholesome living and unaffected goodness attractive. *Redwood* (1824), while conventionally romantic in plot, relied on a simple home life for backdrop. She was among the most popular writers of her time, and Hawthorne called her "our most truthful novelist" (*DAB*, VIII:547–48).

133. CLS 80; *Letters*, 685.

134. William Harness (1790–1869), writer and Anglican minister, is best known for his eight volumes *The Dramatic Works of William Shakespeare* (1825), followed by *Literary Remains of Catharine Maria Fanshawe, Life of Mary Russell Mitford*, etc. Intimate friends included Baillie, Lord Byron, Crabbe, Southey, Wordsworth and others of the same circle (*DNB*, VIII:1300).

Jane Porter (1776–1850) was a childhood friend of Walter Scott in Edinburgh but moved to London in 1803 where she met Hannah More and Laetitia Barbauld. Her works include romance *Thaddeus of Warsaw* (4 vols., 1803), the successful novel *The Scottish Chiefs* (5 vols., 1810), drama *Switzerland*, acted at Drury Lane in 1819, *Sir Edward Seaward's Narrative of his Shipwreck and consequent Discovery of certain Islands in the Caribbean Sea* (3 vols., 1831), etc. Baillie acknowledged her indebtedness to Porter's *Scottish Chiefs* when writing her *Wallace* for *Metrical Legends*, and Scott, given credit for developing the historical novel, might surely be indebted to Porter as well (*DNB*, XVI:182–84).

135. *DNB*, III:844–48.

wrote to remind Baillie, who was then visiting her sister-in-law at 33 Cavendish Square, not to forget an upcoming evening diversion:

> I beg you not to forget the kind promise you made me to honour my evening party of Monday next, the eleventh, with your presence—If you are prevented from coming I shall be liable to . . . many of my visitants with a "take in" as I held out the prospect of seeing you for one of the chief inducements to their visit—[136]

Still sought out for social occasions, Baillie, then almost seventy, was especially a part of Samuel Rogers's social life,[137] contacting him whenever she was in town at Cavendish Square. She solicited his "good office" and influence in the Literary Fund in October 1830 for a Miss Hedge of Colchester, probably author Mary Anne Hedge, who was in need of financial aid.[138] Their friendship was clearly informal and caring. Back in town a few months later, Baillie wrote,

> If you are in Town, this is to give you notice that I am in Town, and very willing to breakfast with you and to bring my Sister in my hand any morning you choose to name after Wednesday. We shall remain here till towards the end of next week. I was very much obliged by your last friendly note, promising your support to the Colchester authoress Miss Hedge, regarding the Literary fund; it would be a very

---

136. NLS 2257 ff.180.

137. Letters from Rogers to various recipients are scattered throughout UK archives. An RSC letter dated 20 July 1829 is one of many invitations to his famous breakfasts (HB.ii.85).

138. The Royal Literary Fund was started in the late eighteenth century and still exists. Created to offer temporary relief to "persons of genius and learning, or their families, who shall be in want," its assistance was confidential. Those in need could apply for assistance and support their case through members' testimonials as well as with samples of their published work (see R. H. Super, "Trollope at the Royal Literary Fund," *Nineteenth Century Literature* 37.3 [1982]: 316).

Mary Ann Hedge has twelve volumes listed in the *British Museum General Catalogue of Printed Books* (Vol. 100), including several children's books published in Colchester between 1819 and 1824: *Samboe: or the African boy* (1823), *Juvenile Poems* (1823), and *The Orphan Sailor-Boy; or Young Arctic voyager* (1824).

desirable thing to procure some relief for one who so well deserves it.[139]

Two years later the good-humored Baillie thanked Rogers for some editing assistance:

> You once called me, and not very long ago, an ungrateful hussey and I remember it the better because I really thought I deserved it. But whether I did or not, when I tell you now that I have read Sir John Herschell's book twice or rather three times over,[140] have been the better for it both in understanding & heart, and mean to read parts of it again ere long, you will not repent having bestowed it upon me. And now I mean to thank you for another obligation that you are not so well aware of. Do you remember when I told you, a good while since, of my intention of looking over all my works to correct them for an Edition to be published after my decease,[141] should it be called for, and your giving me a hint never to let a <u>which</u> stand where a <u>that</u> might serve the purpose, to prefer the words while to whilst, among to amongst &c? I acquiesced in all this most readily, throwing as much scorn upon the rejected expressions as any body would do, and with all the ease of one who from natural taste had always avoided them. If you do, you will guess what has been my surprise and mortification to find through the whole pages of even my last Dramas <u>whiches</u> whilsts & <u>amongst</u>, &c where they need not have been, in abundance. Well; I have profited by your hint though I was not aware that I needed it at the time when it was given, and now I thank you for it very sincerely.[142]

---

139. UCL 14/33; *Letters*, 806.
140. Rogers called astronomer Sir John Herschel's *Discourse on the Study of Natural Philosophy* (1831) the finest work of its kind since the publication of Bacon's *Novum Organum* (see *Recollections of the Table–Talk of Samuel Rogers*, ed. Alexander Dyce [London: Moxon, 1856], 196.
141. This, of course, would turn out to be *The Dramatic and Poetical Works of Joanna Baillie* (London: Longman, Brown, Green, and Longmans, 1851).
142. UCL 14/35; *Letters*, 806–7.

As do many of her letters, this one confirms Baillie's concern with improving her works throughout her life, and she was never afraid of advice from those she respected.

Rogers had been one of Baillie's early acquaintances in London. He reviewed the first volume of *A Series of Plays* for the *Monthly Review* in September 1798, and he was the first person her nephew William Baillie notified upon her death. Although more famous Romantic poets than Rogers took the spotlight during his lifetime, he remained a central figure in the literary scene of the time. Rogers became an active member of popular society and accumulated a vast art collection in his lifetime. He counted among his friends almost everyone of literary and political significance, including Baillie, Byron, Wordsworth, Tennyson, Barbauld, Scott, Moore, Sheridan, Tooke, Dickens, and prominent Americans like Emerson, Bryant, Irving, Longfellow, and Melville. Almost everyone of importance was invited to breakfast or dinner conversations at his home, as evidenced by the numerous allusions to him in virtually every journal, memoir, and collection of letters from the first half of the nineteenth century, as well as in his own letters and journals.[143] Rogers recognized the superiority of other poets of his time, but he never relinquished his ambition to write. He was a member of the Royal Society, the Literary Club, and was offered the laureateship in 1850 at Wordsworth's death but deferred the position to Tennyson. Rogers's publications included *The Voyage of Columbus* (1810), *Poems* (1813), *Jacqueline, A Tale* (1814, published with Byron's *Lara, A Tale*), *Human Life, A Poem* (1819), and *Italy, A Poem* (1822, revised and illustrated in 1828). Throughout his life he was known for his sharp, though not always witty, tongue, his charitable work, his extensive art collection, and his intellectual conversations. Having outlived most of his friends, he died quietly in 1855.

During this very active part of her later life, Joanna Baillie was entertaining and being entertained, not sitting perpetually home by the fire. In addition, performances of her plays included *The Separation* at Covent Garden in February 1836 and *Henriquez* at Drury Lane in March. Baillie wrote of these performances and of visits from Sarah Siddons and her daughter Cecilia and of continual soirees with the Thomas Carr family and with writer and Anglican minister William Harness. She solicited aid from the London Orphan

---

143. See *Recollections of the Table–Talk of Samuel Rogers*, ed. Alexander Dyce, and P. W. Clayden, *Rogers and His Contemporaries*, 2 vols. (London: Smith, Elder, 1889).

Asylum for a child deprived of both parents and supported struggling writers like Mary Anne Hedge and the Corbett sisters.[144] She received visits from American physicians Dr. Jacob Bigelow (1787–1879) and Dr. Francis Boott (1762–1863), and she kept up with Jeffersonian politics through William Ellery Channing. Always interested in government, Baillie read Frances Burney D'Arblay's *Diary and Letters 1778–1840* in 1842 and lamented to Dr. Andrews Norton that she had only met the writer once. But she ended her critique of D'Arblay's diary on a political note:

> I agree with you very much in what you say of Mad^{me} D'Arblay's book and her own character, excepting your belief that the "groundwork" of it was originally simplicity & irresolution. From what one reads in the book one might very well be lead to suppose so; but it does not very well agree with <u>traits</u> I have heard of her in former days, for I never met her in my life but once, in an evening assembly at Lady Herres's where she came with Mrs Montague [sic].[145] This was soon after my Sister & I first came to London. I believe the account she has given of her early days and the society she met in her Father's house is very true. We knew very well the clever & eccentric Lady Strange whom she mentions so often, and some others of that <u>coterie</u>. The book in question has been read here in every house; for young & old, rich & poor like to know the private history & habits of a Court. The stiff ceremony of George the III^d was soon broken through by

---

144. The Corbett sisters first published *The Odd Volume* in 1826, following with the novel *The Busy–bodies* in 1827. In 1831 they edited a two-volume collection entitled *The Sisters' Budget* with works by various authors, including Margaret Holford Hodson's "The Conspirator." The Corbetts' other works included *Tales and Legends* (1828), *Elucidations of Interesting Passages in the Sacred Volume* (1835), and *The Oriental Key to the Sacred Scriptures* (1837). Their first names are never mentioned (see *National Union Catalog Pre 1956 Imprints*, 122:429, and *British Museum General Catalogue of Printed Books to 1955*, 6:268).

145. Joanna, Agnes, and their mother moved to London after Dr. William Hunter died in 1783, so this would have been Mrs. Elizabeth Montagu (1720–1800), author and society leader, whose home in Hill Street, Mayfair, was a central point for intellect and fashion. The "founder" of the bluestockings, she was a friend of Frances Burney, Hannah More, Hester Piozzi, and other intellectuals. William Beattie dedicated his first collection of poems to Mrs. Montagu (*DNB*, XIII:687–91). I have not identified Lady Herres and Lady Strange.

his successors; and had he been an absolute king like Louis 14, he would have been less stiff. If you should ever in the changes of time have a king set over you, the more you limit his power, the more ceremonious he will be.[146]

In the meantime, Baillie had been reading Rose Lawrence's *The Last Autumn at a Favourite Residence and other Poems: and recollections of Mrs Hemans* (1836) and *Memoirs of Hannah More* (edited by William Roberts in 1834) in the midst of her own writing and socializing.

Much like her comfortable friendship with Samuel Rogers was Baillie's relationship with her neighbor John Richardson. Richardson (1780–1864) was a parliamentary solicitor who for thirty years discharged the duties of crown agent for Scotland and is reputed to have been the most learned peerage lawyer of his time. He had refined literary tastes and in 1821 was introduced to George Crabbe at Joanna Baillie's house. He corresponded regularly with Walter Scott, whose deathbed he attended shortly before Scott's demise. Richardson married Elizabeth Hill, a close friend of Thomas Campbell, in 1811, and they had several children,[147] one of whom Baillie would remember in her will. John Richardson submitted "Song—Her features speak the warmest heart" for Baillie's 1823 *Collection*; and in a letter dated 18 January 1842, he confessed to Baillie, "It is, as it has long been, a great pride and gratification to me to have enjoyed your friendship; a few circumstances of my life have afforded me more real pleasure."[148] It was John Richardson who exerted a great deal of effort to help Baillie trace the family ancestry for her nephew William.

Parish doctor and writer George Crabbe (1754–1832) also claimed Joanna Baillie as an associate. Crabbe had taken orders and become a curate in 1781 but soon established himself as a poet in 1783 with *The Village* and its grim picture of rural poverty. Crabbe became friends with Sir Walter Scott and throughout the Romantic movement persisted in presenting a precise, realistic vision of rural life and landscape. Byron called him "Nature's sternest painter yet the best," while Scott referred to him as "the English Juvenal."[149] Crabbe submitted "Hope and Memory" to Baillie's *Collection of Poems*

---

146. HU MS Engl 944, 25; *Letters*, 961–62.
147. *DNB*, XVI:1118–19.
148. NLS 3990, f.41.
149. This brief biographical information comes from the *OCEL*, 237.

in 1822, which she returned for revision.[150] And in 1823, around the time of Matthew Baillie's brief but fatal illness, Joanna was concerned with Crabbe's health, too, because he had been visiting Dr. Baillie for a pain in his face, a sort of *tic douloureux* as she called it. Crabbe had just visited Scott in Edinburgh, and Joanna sent news to Scott of the irritating habitual pain Crabbe was experiencing and noted Crabbe's visit and the eccentricity of his personality: "what he thought of your Highlandmen &c lies in his own breast along with many other odd enough matters I daresay, but may, hereafter, perhaps, see the light."[151] Correspondence about Crabbe's facial pain continued, along with Baillie's comments about a remedy of bark mixed with snuff. Baillie must have been in company with Crabbe often, for her close friends the Hoares were part of their common interest.

As well as being well known in literary circles, Baillie claimed many artists and scientists as associates. She may have met painter Sir Thomas Lawrence (1769–1830) through her sister Agnes or her brother Matthew, for the correspondence housed in London's Royal Academy of Art includes letters to Lawrence from both Agnes and Dr. Matthew Baillie. Joanna appears to have corresponded sporadically with the painter between 1812 and 1829, her last letter posted just a month before his death in January 1830. Thomas Lawrence was a child prodigy, having drawn ovals of Mrs. Siddons, Admiral Barrington, and others before he was seventeen, when he began to paint in oils. In September 1787 Lawrence entered the schools of the Royal Academy and began a long friendship with Sir Joshua Reynolds. By 1792 Lawrence was living in Old Bond Street, and his portrait of George III at that time marked his progress in royal favor as Painter in Ordinary to the King. Dozens of paintings followed, and after the death of portrait painter John Hoppner in 1810, Lawrence had no rival. His love of art was genuine and strong, but while shining in society, he was not a particularly sociable man. He reserved his friendships with women mostly to those who were married, but he fancied himself in love with several different women, one of them Fanny Kemble.[152] Baillie often invited Lawrence to her house for dinner, and he sketched her niece Elizabeth Margaret

---

150. Leeds University Crabbe Vol. IV, 122; *Letters*, 1070.

151. See NLS 3898 ff.81–83 and other letters to Scott (*Letters*, 426).

152. This general biographical information comes from Douglas Goldring's *Regency Portrait Painter: The Life of Sir Thomas Lawrence, P.R.A.* (London: Macdonald, 1951) and notes from the Royal Academy's archives.

Baillie in 1812. In 1816 he was reading Baillie's *Henriquez* in manuscript and offering comments on the inability of present-day actors to portray such a character. He subscribed to her *A Collection of Poems* in 1823 and may very well have submitted a poem of his own, though it appeared anonymously if he did. Baillie's last letter to Lawrence in December 1829 thanked him for reserving a box for her at Covent Garden, where she saw the young Fanny Kemble in her debut as Juliet in *Romeo and Juliet*.

Around 1820 Joanna Baillie had became allied with astronomer Sir John Herschel (1792–1871), the only child of Sir William Herschel and Mary Baldwin Pitt. John's father William was himself a pioneer in astronomy, coming from Germany to England as a poor scientist and ultimately being called the father of stellar astronomy.[153] John followed his father's example but chose to work in more varied scientific fields, becoming as celebrated in his time as Einstein was to be in the next century. Having made many discoveries herself, John's aunt Caroline Lucretia Herschel, both an astronomer and a trained musician, took special interest in his career and encouraged his interests in astronomy and in photography. John and his wife Margaret Brodie Stewart traveled to the wilds of Africa where he drew pictures of flowers, many of which Margaret colored, and contributed enough scientific discovery to botany to gain recognition in that field as well. Of their twelve children, several were well known, including Caroline (Hamilton-Gordon), woman of the bedchamber to Queen Victoria; William James, initiator of the use of fingerprints for the purpose of identification; Alexander Stewart, physicist and astronomer; and Constance (Lubbock), author of *The Herschel Chronicle*.

It is uncertain when and where Baillie met Sir John Herschel, but it is probable they knew each other through Herschel's father William, for she usually sent her regards to him and Lady Herschel as if she had been long acquainted with both. John Herschel admired Baillie's work and submitted several poems for her 1823 *Collection of Poems*, and in his journal entry for 1 January 1837 he recorded that he had just read "Miss Baillie's Martyr."[154] The two corresponded almost to the end of Baillie's life and often discussed the works of the German poet Schiller, whose works Herschel

---

153. This general biographical information comes from both the *Dictionary of Scientific Biography* and from David Evans, *Herschel at the Cape: Diaries and Correspondence of Sir John Herschel, 1834–1838*.

154. Evans, 273.

translated. Baillie's last letter of September 1850 thanked him for his kind words about her *Ahalyla Baee* and *Rayner*.

Because of her close connection with Sir Walter Scott, it was inevitable that Baillie would be close to John Gibson Lockhart (1794–1854), for Lockhart married Scott's oldest daughter Sophia (1799–1837), Baillie's favorite, in April 1820. Lockhart's and Scott's mutual interest in Goethe brought them together in 1818, and it was not long until John Gibson had fallen in love with the young Sophia Scott. On their marriage, the couple settled in a cottage on her father's estate, keeping the intimate family circle intact. After a visit to Abbotsford, Maria Edgeworth described John Lockhart as handsome, reserved, silent, and sensitive, while she defined Sophia as small, elegant, and graceful, her father always doting on her.[155] The couple moved to London's Pall Mall in 1825 when John Murray offered Lockhart the editorship of the *Quarterly Review*, and Lockhart produced admirable biographies on Robert Burns, Napoleon, and, most importantly, *The Life of Scott* in seven volumes (1837–38) after the author's death in 1832.

Baillie probably did not meet Lockhart before his marriage to Sophia Scott, for she appears not to have made any visits to Scotland between 1818 and 1820; but she became well acquainted with him after the couple's move to London because she loved Sophia dearly and saw her as often as she could. In an undated fragment of a letter, Maria Edgeworth implied that Baillie was not "particularly partial to Lockhart," but there is no such evidence of this in her correspondence. In fact, Baillie often invited him to her home. In April 1838 American philanthropist George Ticknor recorded a visit to Baillie during which she spoke of Lockhart "with a kindness that is uncommon when coupled with his name, and which seemed only characteristic of her benevolence."[156] Baillie corresponded with both John Gibson and Sophia Lockhart, especially about Scott and about the Lockharts' children, but she also discussed literary works and professional concerns with John Gibson, seeking his support of James Hyslop for the Vinerian

---

155. See *Miss Edgeworth's Life and Letters* qtd. in Lockhart's *Memoirs of the Life of Sir Walter Scott*, 4:128. Biographical information on Lockhart herein comes from the *DNB*, XII:47–49.

156. See *Life, Letters and Journals of George Ticknor*, 2 vols. 5th ed. (Boston: James R. Osgood, 1876; Johnson Reprint Corporation, 1968), 2:153.

Scholarship in 1826 and asking his opinion of her "Lines on the Death of Sir Walter Scott" in 1832 before she made them public.[157]

When the first volumes of Lockhart's *Life of Scott* appeared in 1837, however, Baillie did not hesitate to voice her concerns. She had given Lockhart, at his request, her own letters from Scott (with the exception of about twenty very personal ones) to use for the biography. Her feminist sensibilities rising, she objected to at least two quotations from Scott's letters to other correspondents which Lockhart had included, one in which the author had referred to Lydia White as a "blue stocking" and another in which he described Anne Grant of Laggan as "cerulean" and surrounded by "fetch-and-carry mistresses and misses," her "tongue and pen . . . rather overpowering."[158] Sophia Scott Lockhart had endured several illnesses associated with childbirth, and after she died in 1837 at the young age of thirty-eight, Baillie seems not to have kept very close contact with John Gibson.

Baillie's friendship continued through these first three decades of the nineteenth century, of course, with playwright Mary Berry, who noted in one of her early journals on 10 June 1808 a visit with Baillie; and in August of that same year Berry lamented their lack of time together:

> You and I have crossed over and figured in, in an odd way this last year. I wish there had been any *setting and footing together*, in the course of our jigging about.—I now in Scotland, and you in England—I yesterday at Millheugh, and you perhaps at Little Strawberry Hill. What a pretty place Millheugh is! . . . We saw not a human creature either to welcome or forbid us their premises, which being all open, we committed no trespass. I tried the echoes with some lines of Basil; but they were dumb, and only muttered in return for your name something about muslin at Glasgow, a pattern of a handkerchief, and some stories of the poor in the village. Your heroic muse should have taught them better in such a romantic spot.[159]

---

157. Lockhart had actually asked Baillie to write this elegy, to which she agreed only out of her "debt of gratitude" to Sir Walter and to Lockhart (NLS 931 No.45; *Letters*, 828).
158. See Lockhart, ii:65 and iv:165.
159. Lewis, 2:367.

Communication between the two writers proceeded, but Baillie's life was hectic during the next year with revisions to her *Family Legend* for Scott's 1810 production in Edinburgh. During the decade of 1810–1820, as she completed volume three of *A Series of Plays*, Baillie appeared to be relatively happy in her family life and in her professional life. She wrote to Berry about both in August of 1817:

> To speak still of my own things I do not disdain to inform you that my Constantine, was produced as a Melo Drama at the Surrey Theatre this summer, and had a run to good houses of 34 nights. I went to see it the last night but one. The Manager had presented the greater part of the dialogue unaltered and tho' it was viley [sic] recited and badly acted, yet by dint of shew & magnificence and the story being clearly made out, it had a very good effect. Perhaps Mrs Damer has told you that Mr Arnold at the Lyceum Theatre brought out a good while ago my comedy of the Election changed into an Opera.[160] He altered it, I think, with considerable skill, and it was admirably acted and very well received, yet it did not bring good houses. The Winter Theatres were open at the time; Kemble was acting all his characters over for the last time; Miss O'Neal was acting under an impression that she might not be spared another year; and Talma, during part of the time, was reciting in the Opera house.[161] I believe it has been acted about 12 times

---

160. Dramatist and theater manager Samuel James Arnold (1774–1852) had several plays represented at Drury Lane and in 1809 obtained a license to open the Lyceum in the Strand as an English opera house, remodeled and enlarged by architect Samuel Beazley in 1816 (*DNB*, I:584–85). *The Election* had appeared in volume 2 of *A Series of Plays: in which it is attempted to delineate the stronger passions*, etc.

161. Baillie's reference is probably to actress Elizabeth O'Neill (1791–1872), later Lady Elizabeth Becher, who played Ellen in a Dublin version of *Lady of the Lake* and debuted as Shakespeare's Juliet in Covent Garden in 1814; though she took some comic roles, she excelled at tragedy but left the stage in 1819 when she married an Irish MP (*DNB*, II:74–75).

François Joseph Talma (1763–1826) was a French tragic actor educated in England. A friend of Napoleon, he made his debut in Paris in 1787 in Voltaire's *Brutus* and first introduced on the French stage the custom of wearing costumes of the period represented in the play. His dramatic roles were numerous (*The New Century Cyclopedia of Names*, ed. Clarence L. Barnhart, 3 vols. [New York: Appleton–Century–Crofts, 1954], 3:3788).

and I dont know whether they have done with it yet or not. M<u>rs</u> Damer was kind enough at my desire to patronize it one night by her presence.— Along with these high honours I have become, since I wrote you last, a Great Aunt. My Niece brought a little Girl into the land of the living better than a month ago.[162] She has recovered well, and the child tho' small is thriving. She & it are gone for a few weeks to her Father's near Windsor, for the benefit to themselves of the country air & for the pleasure & amusement of the new-made Grand Father & Mother.[163]

While Baillie would later rejoice also in the arrival of her nephew William's children, this first grand-niece Sophy remained her favorite.[164]

At the same time, Baillie continued her work with George Thomson and composed lines for "A Scotch Song," "Song, Written for an Irish Air," "Song for an Irish Melody," "Song, for a Scotch Air," and others, presenting twelve songs to him as his "sole property for ever"[165] as she worked on her own *Metrical Legends of Exalted Characters* for publication later in 1821. Meanwhile, she was rewriting the conclusion to *De Monfort* for Kean's November 1821 production at Drury Lane.[166] Others, too, solicited her for material, for in a letter from Allan Cunningham to David Laing[167] dated 29

---

162. Elizabeth Margaret, the only daughter of Matthew and Sophia Denman Baillie, married Capt. Robert Milligan on 11 July 1816, and the couple, with only daughter Sophia, lived at Ryde for most of Joanna's life. The Baillie family had not been particularly happy about Elizabeth marrying a soldier (see letters to Scott dated 1817).

163. RCS HB.ix.34; *Letters*, 168–69.

164. William and Henrietta Baillie's first child would also be named Sophia after William's mother, but her full name would be Sophia Joanna Baillie (1836–82).

165. BL Add. Ms. 35,265, f.79; *Letters*, 130.

166. See CLS 1 to Kean stating, "If I should have anything further to say regarding De Monfort, I will write it down and leave it at your house, when I pay my respects to Mrs Kean which I hope to do before long" (*Letters*, 1076).

167. Allan Cunningham (1784–1842), born in Dumfriesshire and married to Jean Walker, was a miscellaneous writer and friend of Scott, producing several works, including *Remains of Nithsdale and Galloway Songs* (1810), *Traditional Tales of the English and Scottish Peasantry* (1822), and four volumes entitled *The Songs of Scotland, Ancient and Modern* (1825), and an edition of *The Works of Robert Burns* (1834) (*DNB*, V:308–10).

November 1822, Cunningham must have answered Laing's request to ask Baillie for lyrics:

> I have not formed an acquaintance with Joanna Bailie [sic]—if I should meet her which is more than probable, I shall introduce your name and mention your wish—she has knowledge . . . and enthusiasm enough to know that to comply with such a request is in itself honourable. I shall give you a copy of any song or ballad of mine.[168]

Baillie was clearly pressed by many for literary contributions of all sorts, and at one point she started to refuse. A request she probably felt she could not deny, however, came from Dr. Baird, Principal of the University of Edinburgh, in January 1824:[169]

> The Church of Scotland has for many years adopted some Poetical "Translations & Paraphrases" into the Psalmody of its congregation in addition to the "Psalms of David." A general wish is felt here to . . . obtain a new Collection. . . . My object Madam, in now addressing you is to take the liberty of requesting to know from you whether you would be

---

Scottish antiquary David Laing (1793-1878) was at the time of this letter editing a collection called *Fugitive Scottish Poetry* (1823-25), principally of the seventeenth century. When Scott founded the Bannatyne Club in 1823, which was to consist of thirty-one members, for the printing of unedited materials or rare tracts relating to the history and literature of Scotland, his friend Laing as made secretary and chief organizer. Laing left a valuable collection of manuscripts to Edinburgh University (*DNB*, XI:401-2).

168. EU La.IV.6.

169. See NLS 3435 ff.127-28 and Baillie's reply ff.129-30 (*Letters*, 1135). Baird was also soliciting the help of Thomas Campbell and William Sotheby.

George Husband Baird, D.D., (1761-1840) was principal of the university of Edinburgh and considered an evangelical rather than a moderate. Family ties put him often into cultivated circles. In 1799 Principal Baird was translated to the new North parish church and in 1801, on the death of Dr. Blair, was appointed his successor in the high parish church where he remained until his death. He was married to the eldest daughter of Thomas Elder, lord provost of Edinburgh. Towards the close of his life, Baird, supported by the General Assembly, gave all his efforts to a project to educate the poor in the highlands and islands of Scotland (*DNB*, I:917-18).

disposed to honour & benefit such an Association by giving it the aid of your very popular & powerful talents.

Busy with her own work and recovering from the death of her brother Matthew, Baillie graciously agreed and responded that she would be honored to be a part of the psalmody of her native country because she seldom sat "in an English church without regretting that taught & hired singers should ever have had any thing to do with public worship."[170] Her early interest in the church service would in the next few years mature into a complex theory of Christian doctrine and emerge in *A View of the General Tenour of the New Testament Regarding the Nature and Dignity of Jesus Christ* in 1831.

This period of Baillie's life, culminating with the death of Scott in 1832, may have been her most public, but her activity did not end here. She wrote and revised, continued her charitable endeavors, and kept abreast of current events. When cholera invaded England in 1831, she mused to Anne Elliott on December 19:

> But who does not at present think of the great uncertainty of human life, particularly the old who cannot strive with any severe disease? But we are not alarmed as some of our neighbours are about the Cholera, who are securing to themselves a present illness from fretting at the prospect of it.

Baillie was clearly concerned about the epidemic but not distressed—nor did she appear to consider herself, now seventy, one of the "old." In fact, as she further related to Elliott, her social life was continuing as usual:

> We had a little party last night in honour of Young Sam! Hoare & his bride to which your Nephew kindly promised to come, but was prevented by a very stormy evening. The Richardsons & some other neighbours were with us, and they chatted & the wind roared, and there was no want of sound, I assure you.[171]

Baillie's coping ability manifested itself in her letters and in her ability to turn from any crisis, even the loss of her brother Matthew

---

170. NLS 3435 f. 139; *Letters*, 1137.
171. NLS Acc 9467; *Letters*, 474.

and Walter Scott, to focus on work and friends. Much of her persistency and strength, however, evolved from the religious convictions that would pervade her later life.

5

"The stamp of her strong mind": Critical Reading and Religious Philosophy (1831–1850)

During the last two decades of Joanna Baillie's life, England faced massive unemployment and government attacks on trade unions. In 1833 the Factory Act declared that children between nine and thirteen could work no longer than twelve hours a day or forty-eight hours a week, and by 1839 leaders of the Chartist movement planned a general rebellion of the working class, beginning with the Newport Rising in which four thousand armed men marched on Newport and were met by soldiers who opened fire and killed twenty-four of them. By 1841 one in eleven Englishmen was on poor relief, and infectious disease was rife in the slum areas of industrial towns. In 1842 the Mines Act stipulated that women and children could no longer work underground, and by 1846 the Corn Laws had been repealed, just as the potato famine caused hundreds of thousands of deaths in Ireland. In an attempt to curb cholera, laws were enacted in 1847 to stop the dumping of sewage into the Thames; and the Public Health Act of the following year improved sanitation, water supply, and drainage. By 1851, the year of Baillie's death, the population of London had reached over two million.

While such social and economic explosion engulfed her country, Joanna Baillie focused on literary enterprises and religious dogma. Besides an American edition of her *Complete Poetical Works* (1832), British editions of *Dramas* appeared in 1836, *Fugitive Verses* in 1840, *Ahalya Baee: A Poem* in 1849, and *The Dramatic and Poetical Works of Joanna Baillie* in 1851, the last volume (composed specifically for her heirs) over which she exacted control. Her most controversial publication, however, appeared in 1831 entitled *A View of the General Tenour of the New Testament Regarding the Nature and Dignity of Jesus Christ*.

The parish church of St. John was the "established" Anglican church of Hampstead, and its cemetery was where all parish members, including Baillie, were buried until later in the nineteenth century. Early on, however, the village was a site for several nonconformist groups; thus the area proved suitable for Baillie's unconventional religious views. William Howitt explains in his *Northern Heights of London* that the "Old Presbyterian Chapel," where Rochemont Barbauld was minister from 1789 to 1802, had allegedly been established in the reign of Charles II by one of the ejected ministers. Barbauld followed a Mr. Fuller but left for the chapel at Newington in 1802 and was succeeded by Mr. Methuen, who retained the position until he died in 1815. Mr. Joyce (author of *Scientific Dialogues*) took the position for about a year, replaced by Mr. Shields (a Scot), who returned to his own country in 1819 and was followed by Mr. Catlow, who died in 1820. Apparently, the Presbyterian Chapel was for a time without a full-time minister, and Howitt believes that services were sometimes conducted by students from the General Baptist Academy at Newington Green and for a short time afterwards by William Wilson from Crewkerne. Finally, the church found a full-time minister in the Rev. G. Kenrick, who remained there for about sixteen years, succeeded by Dr. Thomas Sadler. The Presbyterian Chapel was remodeled around 1828, but in 1862 it was abandoned for a new one, the inauguration services conducted by Dr. Sadler and the Rev. James Martineau. By then, a little above the site of the old Presbyterian Chapel and at the bottom of High Street stood the new church of the Trinitarian Presbyterians; the old Presbyterians had earlier become Unitarian at a time when religious change carried many into that sect.[1] Meanwhile, Protestant and Catholic nonconformists flourished there too, with the Roman Catholics in Holly Place early in the century and the Baptists on Heath Street by mid-century.

Baillie, who was raised by Church of Scotland parents, eventually, through her early association with the Barbaulds and others in that circle, moved from Presbyterian to Unitarian doctrine at a time when many writers and artists were doing so. There is no record, however, of her ever having been a member of the established Unitarian church in Hampstead; in the mid-1820s she still professed herself a Church of Scotland member and helped the Rev. Baird of Edinburgh revise the church psalmody in 1824:

> I received your very obliging & flattering letter two days ago, and beg of you to believe that I shall think myself very highly honoured in being in the slightest degree useful to the psalmody of my native country & that church to which I belong & for which I feel the most perfect & grateful respect.—I shall do my best, guided by your directions, and if

---

1. See William Howitt's *The Northern Heights of London, or Historical Associations of Hampstead, Highgate, Museum Hill, Hornsey, and Islington* (London: Longmans, Green, and Co., 1869), 164–65.

> I fail, it will not be from having spured [sic] to set the whole bent of my mind & affections to the work. I feel however great misgivings as to the success that may attend it. . . . Before I do any thing, I should like to see the book of additional Psalmody which you so obligingly propose to send me, lest I should versify passages which have been better done already and so have labour in vain.[2]

If the Rev. James Baillie was indeed a Moderate, a more liberal attitude toward church procedure probably influenced his children. So while Baillie may have declared herself a Church of Scotland affiliate, her later theological arguments were closer to Unitarianism.

At the time, Unitarianism consisted of three centers of development. First was the Socinian movement in Poland (now almost defunct); second, the English anti-Trinitarianism of the seventeenth century and onward, arising through rationalist Calvinism and Enlightenment religion; and, third, the breakup of New England Calvinist covenant theology. The Unitarian church was not formally recognized in England until the latter part of the eighteenth century, the first in London being called the Essex Street Chapel (1774). Unitarianism developed in America independently of the European movement, and the more liberal branch there insisted that Jesus was a man who taught that all men are divine and are sons of God and denied that Jesus claimed to be part of the Deity. A break between the liberal and conservative factions in the Congregational Church occurred in Baltimore around 1819 when William Ellery Channing defended his Unitarian views by appealing to the scriptures for support and argued that the doctrine of three persons in the Godhead was not a fundamental doctrine of Christianity. Baillie read and praised Channing's discourses and declared to Mary Berry in July 1833 that

> His views of our Saviour's character as the strongest proof of the faithfulness of his revelation and the History of him contained in the Gospels, is beautiful, noble, and powerful in moving the heart and convincing the understanding; and few unprejudiced minds, I should think could withstand it. His discourses too on self-denyal, so powerfully supporting the rights of natural reason as that thing belonging to us, God's best gift, which is <u>not</u> to be denied; and the excellent

---

2. NLS 3435 ff.129–30; *Letters*, 1135–37.

purposes stated by him, for which those that ought to be denied are brought into the world, evil passions, bodily pain &c; are most ably & eloquently shewn. And can there be any thing more persuasive & powerfully applied to our feelings & conduct than the two last discourses on that verse from St: Paul. "Grace be with all them that love our Lord Jesus Christ in Sincerity."?[3] The 8th discourse on "Fools make a mock at sin,"[4] makes one tremble like Felix before the Apostle. In short I have found it to be a book that deals more powerfully with head & heart than any book I ever read.[5]

It was head and heart that led Baillie to Unitarian principles, not enthusiasm devoid of reason.

Unitarianism was, and is, a religious movement emphasizing the unipersonality of God in opposition to Trinitarianism; more important is its focus on the goodness of mankind and on respect for human achievements. Included in this sect were many of Baillie's friends and correspondents, including Lucy Aikin, Lady Byron, Fanny Kemble, Henry Wadsworth Longfellow, John Merivale, Jane Porter, Samuel Rogers, Catharine Sedgwick, the Rev. Andrews Norton, George Ticknor, and many others in England and America.

In his article "The 'Joineriana': Anna Barbauld, the Aikin Family Circle, and the Dissenting Public Sphere," Daniel White investigates the Aikin family circle, of which Baillie was a part, to "define the pressure exerted by nonconformists" and to

> argue that the mode of collaborative production signified by Barbauld's metaphor associated this alliance of middle-class civil and nonconformist religious values with sensibility and the plenitude of the intimate sphere—the Aikin family circle and the Warrington community—thus domesticating these progressive values and authorizing Barbauld to disseminate them . . . to the nation.[6]

---

3. See Eph. 6.24.
4. See Prov. 14.9.
5. RCS HB.ix.59; *Letters*, 172.
6. Daniel E. White, "The 'Joineriana': Anna Barbauld, the Aikin Family Circle, and the Dissenting Public Sphere," *Eighteenth-Century Studies* 32.4 (1999): 511–33.

Lucy Aikin, Laetitia Barbauld's niece, was one of Baillie's first friends in London; and through both aunt and niece, Baillie was surely attracted to Barbauld's sensibility inherent in *Miscellaneous Pieces in Prose* (1773) and in *Poems* (1773). These volumes present what White defines as a "Joineriana" of "modern Dissenting political, religious, economic, and intellectual values,"[7] values which Baillie adopted in her Whig and Dissenting ideologies as a sort of contemporary Presbyterian. These ideologies were most likely the basis for her friendship with Harvard divinity professor Dr. Andrews Norton and her eventual link to other Boston intellectuals. Furthermore, Scottish educational principles had long been admired in America, especially at Harvard with its nonconformist roots, and that may have accounted for Dr. Norton's interest in nationalist writers like Baillie.

    The impact of the Scottish rhetorical tradition and Scottish moral philosophy on the history of English literary studies in North America, explains Franklin Court, extended from the early eighteenth century well into the nineteenth. Scots-Irish immigration into America was significant during that time, and the immigrants brought with them a fervent desire for independence, especially in government, and a concern for community education, most often supported by their Presbyterian ministers who had been educated in Edinburgh and Glasgow. In 1742, for example, the Rev. Francis Alison, a Scots-Irish Presbyterian minister who had been influenced by Francis Hutcheson in his youth, began to combine the teaching of English grammar, composition, and literature in his Maryland academy. Alison designed a curriculum that went far beyond the school's concentration on divinity studies, as he taught composition and examined his students' compositions critically. His students then began to analyze literature in much the same way, concentrating heavily on "modern" texts by Addison and Steele, Johnson, Dryden, and other secular writers. By the end of the eighteenth century, the University of Pennsylvania had adopted Alison's critical-analysis focus and offered the study of ethics, economics, politics, logic, and rhetoric through its Moral Philosophy Department. Yale soon followed this revision in education and combined oratory and the critical study of English literature. In 1819 Edward Tyrell Channing assumed Harvard's Boylston Chair of Rhetoric and Oratory and supported his lectures and articles on literary criticism with the philosophies of Scots like Thomas Reid; at

---

    7. Ibid., 521.

this same time Dr. Andrews Norton was just beginning to modernize the Harvard Divinity School.[8]

Andrews Norton (1786–1853) was a literary and biblical scholar born in Hingham, Massachusetts, the last child of Samuel and Jane (Andrews) Norton. He graduated from Harvard in 1804, attended graduate school, preached for a period in Maine, taught a year at Bowdoin College, and was appointed tutor at Cambridge in 1811. He then became librarian of Harvard College and lecturer on the Bible in 1813. By 1819 he had been appointed Dexter Professor of Sacred Literature in the Harvard Divinity School, but he resigned his post in 1830 to continue literary and theological work in Cambridge. Norton contributed essays to several journals, but his most important published work, one often referenced in Baillie's correspondence, is his treatise on *The Evidences of the Genuineness of the Gospels*; the first volume appeared in 1837 and the second and third followed in 1844. In 1852 he published a volume of essays entitled *Tracts on Christianity*, and *Internal Evidences of the Genuineness of the Gospels* appeared posthumously in 1855. Norton was consistently involved in theological controversies. But, occupying the position of conservative Unitarianism and accepting liberal Christianity, he was disinclined to associate himself with denominational lines. In 1833 he printed *A Statement of Reasons for not Believing the Doctrines of Trinitarians*, and his address in 1839 *On the Latest form of Infidelity* was interpreted by many, and possibly misinterpreted, as a reply to Emerson's *Divinity School Address* from the preceding year. Norton played an important part in editing general literature and in 1826–28 produced *Poems by Mrs. Hemans*; in 1833–34 he edited *The Select Journal of Foreign Periodical Literature* in four volumes with Charles Folsom. In addition, many of his own verses can be found in modern hymnals.

In 1821 Norton married Catharine Eliot of Boston, daughter of Samuel Eliot, and the couple had six children, four of whom survived infancy. One of these, Charles Eliot Norton, the only surviving son, became a distinguished scholar, graduated from Harvard in 1846, and later received honorary degrees from Cambridge, Oxford, Harvard, Yale, and Columbia for literary and biblical studies; his sister Grace Norton became well known for her

---

8. This is a much simplified summary of Franklin E. Court's "The early impact of Scottish literary teaching in North America," in *The Scottish Invention of English Literature*, ed. Robert Crawford (Cambridge: Cambridge University Press, 1998), 134–63.

work on Montaigne. The Nortons lived most of their married life in Cambridge, Massachusetts, at "Shady Hill," a mansion which Andrews built at the time of his marriage and which eventually became a center of influence in literature and art.⁹

Baillie began writing both Dr. and Mrs. Norton around 1827; the first letter in the Houghton Library collection is dated November 6 of that year and replies to Dr. Norton's letters and "packet" which had enclosed a letter from Felicia Hemans and, probably, Norton's edition of *Poems by Mrs. Hemans* (1826–28) as well. Baillie had just read his "Inaugural Discourse" delivered at Harvard in August 1819 and his "Thoughts on True and False Religion," published in the September/October 1820 edition of *The Christian Disciple*. She praised his eloquence as she thanked him for his desire to publish all of her works in America. Although editions of single plays by Baillie had been published there previously, it was not until 1832 that *The Complete Poetical Works of Joanna Baillie* appeared in Philadelphia from Carey and Lea. Dr. Norton and other Cambridge intellectuals became her strongest supporters, and even Edgar Allan Poe considered her the foremost literary woman in England.

Through Norton, Baillie acquired yet a new circle of nonconformist friends. She became acquainted with his brother-in-law and philanthropist George Ticknor (1791–1871), with theologian and surgeon John Ranicar Park (1778–1847), with biographer and historian Jared Sparks, and with others in the Boston area, most of them attached to the Unitarian circle. She corresponded with Norton about literature, her own and others', and about matters of church and state in both countries. Prompted by a petition being circulated by writer Harriet Martineau in 1836, Baillie wrote to Norton about Bulwer Lytton's plan to petition the American Congress for copyright protection because foreign writers were handicapped there by Congress's refusal (until 1891) to protect their copyrights.[10] Baillie signed the petition herself, explaining to Norton that what persuaded her was that the reform would be "greatly for the advantage of the American Authors, and therefore there is more chance of our being successful with your Government."[11] When Norton's *Evidences of the Genuineness of the Gospels* appeared a

---

9. *DAB*, XII:568–69.

10. American publishers did not have to pay royalty fees on English books, so they often preferred to reprint them instead of supporting their own American writers (Henry Bamford Parkes, *The United States of America: A History*, 3d ed. [New York: Knopf, 1968], 275).

11. HU MS Eng 944 (15); *Letters*, 940.

short time later in 1837, Baillie focused on the work's "common-sense" arguments, which came at a time when the Oxford Movement with its "zealous Divines" threatened "to establish the authority of tradition as equal to scripture," likely, in her opinion, to do more harm than all the German philosophers combined.[12] Her letters notified Norton of the onset of cholera in Italy and of famine in Ireland, discussed young Victoria's ascent to the throne, defended the economic theories of her friend Thomas Malthus, and turned at one point to the question of women's suffrage:

> I have not seen Miss Martineau since her return to England [sic] and it is but lately that we have read her book.[13] The discriptive part of it is beautiful & I think decidedly marked with genius & often with good feeling. Her political discussion, always referring to abstract principles, puts me in mind of the old diversion of steeple hunting where one was obliged to go in a direct line to a certain object, over walk & house-tops or whatever else might intervene. Nor do I think her own sex would be benefitted [by] the labor she would have to be made in their favour; quite the contrary. The Matrons of London would have a bad time of it if they could divorce their husbands as easily as they can in Edin^r for every depraved man who wanted a new wife would torment the old one till he obliged her to divorce him, and as long as a woman's property cannot be taxed in any way different from a man's she would get nothing but trouble by having equal suffrage with him; <u>and</u> if our law as it stands makes the property of a wife (when not settled other wise) belong to the husband, it obliges him to pay her debts or go to prison in her stead if he refuses to do so.[14]

---

12. See HU MS Eng 944 (17); *Letters*, 943–44. The Oxford Movement, or Tractarian Movement, aimed to defend the Church of England as a divine institution while reviving the High Church traditions of the 1600s. Such figures as John Henry Newman, R. H. Froude, and Edward Pusey were prominent in the movement (Altick, 208–19).

13. This is most likely a reference to *Society in America*, 3 vols. (London: Saunders and Otley, 1837).

14. HL MS Eng 944 (17); *Letters*, 945. Divorce and property laws were in sharp contrast in England and Scotland, which presented a problem by the eighteenth century when people crossed borders frequently. In England, for example, the sole ground for full divorce was by Act of Parliament only for a wife's adultery; but after 1573 Scotland's Commissary Court could grant divorce for adultery by husband or wife, as

While Baillie's comments to Norton seem to ring of anti-feminism, she was, rather, ruled by reason and saw no benefit in equal suffrage without legal protection for women with degenerate husbands. Despite the fact that she does not discuss specific cases of abuse in her correspondence, Baillie was keenly aware of the pitfalls of marriage and of the wife's lack of legal rights. Her plays are beset with unhappy relationships.

Meanwhile, Baillie critically examined the works of American writers that Norton sent to her, including Louisa Jane Park Hall's *Miriam* (1837) and *Joanna of Naples* (1838), James Abraham Hillhouse's blank-verse dramas (*Percy's Masque, Hadad,* and *Demetria,* 1819–1839), Caroline Kirkland's *A New Home–Who'll Follow?* (1839), and Hannah Farnham Lee's *The Log-cabin, or, The World Before You* (1844). Further, she regretted that she had missed a visit from American poet Henry Wadsworth Longfellow in 1842 while she was away from home. She discussed with Norton the works of William Ellery Channing and often mentioned receiving and answering letters from Channing, and she grieved over Channing's death in 1842.[15] Baillie maintained great respect for Norton's theological views, and the works she read by him and by Dr. Channing may have prompted her own analysis of the Trinity in *A View of the General Tenour of the New Testament*. She continued her friendship with the Nortons until her death, and letters to them brimmed with literary, political, and religious theories.

When Baillie's *A View of the General Tenour of the New Testament Regarding the Nature and Dignity of Jesus Christ* appeared in 1831, just a year before Scott's death, it worried her old friend Scott, always on the opposite political and religious side from her. And he recorded in his journal on 17 May 1831 that Baillie had entered into the Socinian controversy and that he believed "this gifted woman" was "hardly doing herself justice" and doing something "not required at her hands." Scott admitted, however, that his old friend William Laidlaw thought it the "finest thing in the world."[16] Nevertheless, Baillie's essay immediately incurred the wrath of Thomas Burgess,

---

well as for desertion for four or more years. A prolonged Anglo-Scottish battle over law and jurisdiction prompted English lawyers to support the passage of the Divorce Act in 1857 (Lawrence Stone, *Road to Divorce: England 1530–1987* [Oxford: Oxford University Press, 1990], 357–59).

15. Baillie often mentions her letters to and from Dr. Channing, but I have been unable to locate any of these manuscripts.

16. Qtd. in Anderson, 655.

the Bishop of Salisbury. Thomas Burgess, D.D. (1756–1837) became a scholar of Corpus Christi College, Oxford, in 1775. While Burgess was an undergraduate, he re-edited Burton's *Pentalogia*, took his BA in 1778, received his MA in 1782, and was elected a fellow in 1783. After his ordination as deacon and priest in 1784, his first church appointment was examining chaplain to Bishop Shute Barrington of Salisbury (1785), where he remained as prebendary of Salisbury from 1787 to 1803. In the meantime, Burgess published various classical works and gradually turned his attention to sacred studies. He learned Hebrew, promoted Sunday schools in the diocese of Salisbury, wrote a pamphlet against the slave trade, and became a friend of Hannah More and other evangelicals. In September 1791 Burgess was appointed to one of the valuable prebends of Durham Cathedral and in 1798 held the prebend of Islington at St. Paul's. He continued to take an interest in religious and educational movements and in 1803 was appointed bishop of St. David's, where he devoted himself to the reformation of his diocese, thereby making his mark on the Welsh church. In 1804 he established the "Society for Promoting Christian Knowledge and Church Union in the Diocese of St. David's" to raise the standards of classical education and to provide Sunday schools for the poor. In 1825 he was promoted to the bishopric at Salisbury, where he established a church union society much like that of St. David's, and was energetic in visiting, educating, and ordaining. In 1836 he stood firmly against Lord Melbourne's Irish church policy and denounced both Catholics and Unitarians in a series of tracts.[17]

Burgess was an indefatigable laborer, and for years he exhausted the patience of the Royal Society of Literature with his argument that the treatise *De Doctrina Christiana* could not have been written by Milton because of its doubtful orthodoxy regarding the Trinity.[18] In most of what he wrote, he defended a cherished principle or

---

17. This general information about Burgess's life comes from the *DNB*, III:313–14.

18. While not a biblical term, "trinity" implies the coexistence of Father, Son, and Holy Spirit in the unity of the Godhead, representing the crystallization of the New Testament. Thus in I Cor. 12.4–6, Paul correlates "Spirit," "Lord," and "God"; a similar correlation appears in the benediction of II Cor. 13.14. The Old Testament concepts of Wisdom and Spirit of God (especially Prov. 8.22) have influenced many New Testament passages used as foundations for the later formulation of Trinitarian doctrine (George Arthur Buttrick, ed., *The Interpreter's Dictionary of the Bible: An Illustrated Encyclopedia*, 4 vols. and Supplement [New York: Abingdon Press, 1962], 711).

opinion and often threw away discretion and impartiality, characteristics which would certainly explain his extended, if not overbearing, argument with Baillie about the Trinity and his *Remarks on the general tenour of the New Testament, regarding the nature and dignity of Jesus Christ* (Salisbury: Brodie, 1831) in response to her *A View of the General Tenour of the New Testament*.

The controversy between Burgess and Baillie was rooted in their Anglican and Unitarian doctrinal positions respectively and was instigated by the Bishop after her publication in 1831. At first Baillie was patient with his argument for the Trinity and attempted to explain her own stance that "without previous instruction in the doctrine of the Trinity, a person of plain sense might read the whole of the New Testament without being aware of such a doctrine being contained in it" and to convey that she certainly did not mean to imply disrespect for him or for the established church.[19] However, as the Bishop became more and more aggressive in his attempt to prove her wrong, her patience clearly dwindled. In October 1831 she eventually began to attack flaws in his argument, citing her own list of biblical references in her support:[20]

> Permit me to mention two of the texts that you seem to think most convincing on your side of the argument. (Phil. II–6th) "He thought it not robbery to be equal with God."[21] Our unlearned man on reading this, would certainly, if he stopped there, consider it as a very bold expression, but if he continued to read the whole passage throughout, ending in these words—"Wherefore God hath highly exalted him, and given him a name which is above every name, that at the name of Jesus every knee should bow of things in heaven and things on earth and things under the earth, and that every tongue should confess that Jesus Christ is Lord to the

---

19. This 5 October 1831 letter to Burgess can be found in the 2d edition (1838) of *A View of the General Tenour* and in *Letters*, 992.

20. See OU Miss Engl. Letters, c. 133, ff.18–33; *Letters*, 994–95.

21. Phil. 2.5–8: "Let this mind be in you, which was also in Christ Jesus: Who, being in the form of God, thought it not robbery to be equal with God: but made himself of no reputation, and took upon him the form of a servant, and was made in the likeness of men: And being found in fashion as a man, he humbled himself, and became obedient unto death, even the death of the cross."

glory of God the Father"[22]—he (our unlearned man) would, I think, very naturally conclude that the word <u>robbery</u> must be an improper translation, because inconsistent with what follows it.—The other passage is from St: John's Gospel. "I and my Father are one."[23]—Were he again to stop short here, he would think it a very strange expression, but were he to read the whole chap. (and I think that which follows) he would find these words also—"Neither pray I for these alone (his Disciples) but for them also which shall believe on me through their word; that they all may be <u>one</u> as thou Father art in me and I in thee, that they also may be <u>one</u> in us, that the world may believe that thou hast sent me, and the glory which thou gavest me, I have given them; that they may be one, even as we are one; I in them and thou in me, that they may be made perfect in one, and that the world may know that thou hast sent me and hast loved them as thou hast loved me"[24]—Were he, I think, to read all this, he would certainly suppose that the word <u>one</u> was only intended to express a union of affection & concord, not of identity, which would not at all lead him to the discovery of the Trinitarian doctrine.

I now come to that which is argued at the end of your letter regarding the man of Etheopia [sic] & the Apostle Philip. Doubtless it is desirable to receive instruction on obscure subjects; the Etheopian was reading a sacred prophesy and could not possibly understand it; had an account of our

---

22. Phil. 2.9–11: "Wherefore God also hath highly exalted him, and given him a name which is above every name: That at the name of Jesus every knee should bow, of *things* in heaven, and *things* in earth, and *things* under the earth: And *that* every tongue should confess that Jesus Christ *is* Lord, to the glory of God the Father."

23. John 10.29–30: "My Father, which gave *them* me, is greater than all; and no *man* is able to pluck *them* out of my Father's hand. I and *my* Father are one."

24. John 17.19–23: "And for their sakes I sanctify myself, that they also might be sanctified through the truth. Neither pray I for these alone, but for them also which shall believe on me through their word; That they all may be one; as thou, Father, *art* in me, and I in thee, that they also may be one in us: that the world may believe that thou hast sent me. And the glory which thou gavest me I have given them; that they may be one, even as we are one: I in them, and thou in me, that they may be made perfect in one; and that the world may know that thou hast sent me, and hast loved them, as thou hast loved me."

Saviour's life & precepts been put into his hands to read, he would not have returned, after doing so, such an answer as that which is recorded in the Acts, but would have judged of it as his own reason directed; and would not, I conceive, by Philip or any of the Apostles have been reproved for doing so.[25]

Not only was Baillie unintimidated by the Bishop's persistent effort to prove her wrong, but she was also quite clear in her own argument, never bending to his self-conceived superiority. By December 1831, however, in an attempt to support his case further the Bishop had sent her an "appendix" on Sir Isaac Newton's suppressed theological arguments and stressed that Newton was, in fact, a Trinitarian.[26] But as biographer Richard Westfall contends, Newton's manuscripts elucidated the distinction between God the Father and God the Son, and the "first fruit of Newton's theological study was doubt about the status of Christ and the doctrine of the Trinity."[27] Baillie cleverly dodged the Bishop's red herring that Newton was not a true Unitarian and declared that whatever Newton's beliefs, they did not settle the point as to the doctrine itself.

This argumentative correspondence between Baillie and the Bishop continued for two years and formed the basis for her second edition of *A View of the General Tenour* in 1838, in which she incorporated both parties' letters with her discourse. Certainly, some people agreed with Baillie's theological argument, for an anonymous review in 1831 evaluated the work as follows:

> This is a singularly modest, interesting, and useful publication. It has only recently come under our notice, and we regard it as calculated to be very serviceable with present times, when discussions are maintained with so much animation regarding every question connected with the church. The authoress is the celebrated Miss Joanna Baillie, and it affords a pleasing evidence that time has not subdued

---

25. See Acts 8.26–39. An Ethiopian, having heard Philip preach "unto him Jesus," asks what would hinder his being baptized. Philip replies, "If thou believest with all thine heart, thou mayest. And he answered and said, I believe that Jesus Christ is the Son of God. . . . and they went down both into the water, both Philip and the eunuch; and he baptized him."

26. OU C.133 ff.24–25; *Letters*, 1000–1001.

27. Richard Westfall, *The Life of Isaac Newton* (Cambridge: Cambridge University Press, 1993), 121.

the high tone of moral and religious feeling, and vigor of intellect by which she has so long been distinguished. . . . In this course there is more worldly wisdom than downrightness of purpose.[28]

In a lengthy argument, the reviewer summarizes Baillie's main points and emphasizes her clarity and rational focus. And in a February 1834 letter to Baillie, Lady Byron also pointed out the strengths of her argument.[29]

Notably, at this time Baillie was not only scrutinizing philosophical theories, but scientific theories as well. When her friend astronomer Sir John Herschel published a work which, in Baillie's eyes, supported the doctrine of the Trinity, she wrote to him in June 1847 that his views had given her "some pain."[30] His following reply was written immediately on the back of her letter:

> My dear Madam
> I cannot conceive how it can have been possible to make out any connection between any astronomical observations of mine and any doctrine High or low about the Trinity. The only doctrine the contemplation of the Stars has ever impressed on my mind is that of the Power Wisdom and Goodness of God manifested on a scale of stupendous grandeur, and the insignificance of Man in every respect except in those moral & intellectual attributes which render him capable of contemplating these manifestations and worthy to do so which he is not to himself alone, and only by God's grace and favour. I am really almost curious to know what can have been the observations you allude to & what expressions of mine verbal or printed can have given rise to such an idea.
> But I remember at the Cape hearing from a friend up the country that a report had got about among the Dutch farmers nay had been preached from the pulpit that "the very place where naughty people go" was assuming a reality—for that I had seen it in my telescope—a thing evth surprised me not a little at the time but w^h afterwards I thought I could trace to the fact that I had seen a star (which any body may

---

28. NLS 7439, ff.86–93.
29. OU Lovelace/Byron 62, ff.170–71.
30. RS HS3.22 and HS22.321; *Letters*, 792–93.

see if they turn a long telescope on B Crucis—it being in the field of view with that Star) as red as blood—or as red as fire—which you will.

So pray do not let anything you hear of me in the least disturb you on the score you speak of. I am content to receive matters of faith above my comprehension with a quiet mind being well convinced that the best escercise [sic] of faith lies in reposing with confidence on what we do understand—on the goodness and promises of God revealed to us in language which there is no mistaking both in Scripture and in Nature. All here are well. Believe me &c
yours very faithfully
(Sd) J. F. W. H.

Satisfied with his contrite reply, Baillie thanked him for his gracious letter, her mind no longer troubled. While her concern with the doctrinal argument about the Trinity at this time may sound like an obsession, it was clearly not her only focus, for she was still scrutinizing important works in all genres just as she always had.

In her seventies, Baillie read the works of newly acclaimed writers such as Charles Dickens and worked steadily on her *Dramas* to be published in three volumes by Longman in 1836.[31] In 1839 she wrote to Margaret Holford Hodson about Charles Dickens, "whose works of humour & crimes have been so much read & admired."[32] She apparently did not meet him, but she remarked that she had been told the author was a handsome man, whose bust had just been completed by sculptor Angus Fletcher, the son of her friend Elizabeth Fletcher. Baillie was busy cleaning out drawers and clearing away letters, and at the same time an American edition of *The Complete Poetical Works of Joanna Baillie* was appearing (1832), along with a second edition of *A Collection of Poems, Chiefly Manuscript* in London that same year.

In 1835 Baillie's only nephew William Hunter Baillie married Henrietta Duff. William's own note of 15 February 1866 states that Henrietta was the daughter of the Rev. D. Duff, a well-respected clergyman of the Church of Scotland and former minister in

---

31. Baillie wrote to Lady Bunbury some time after 1834 about reading "loads of periodicals, from Dicken's [sic] things downward (NLS 10279 ff.69–70; *Letters*, 1152), but I find no evidence that she ever met the author.

32. CLS 78; *Letters*, 680–81.

Perthshire; her mother was the daughter of Professor Baron of St. Andrews.[33] Joanna took William's quiet wife into her heart immediately, probably glad that her thirty-eight year old nephew had finally settled down. William, Dr. Matthew Baillie's only son, had inherited a significant amount of money and property on his father's death; and, though he matriculated Oxford in 1815, receiving a B.A. in 1819 and an M.A. in 1823, and was called to the Bar, he apparently never practiced law. Instead, he lived as a squire of the manor of Duntisbourne Abbots and gentleman farmer all his life. At some point in 1838 William inherited physician John Hunter's property in Scotland after Hunter's only surviving son, Major John Hunter, died with no heirs. A letter from Joanna Baillie to William's wife Henrietta concerning this recent inheritance alluded to Major Hunter as "our very eccentric cousin" and stated that she knew William would "not be much puffed up in becoming by this means a Scotch Laird":

> We are thankful that he had a friend that comforted him in his last days, and he did well to leave this friend his moveable property, yet we wish that some part of it had been given to his Brother in law Col. Charliwood [sic] who has so well deserved it.[34] But perhaps he was not quite aware how much his Sister owed to her good husband.[35]

---

33. WI MS 5613/38.

34. Lady Campbell, Agnes Margaretta Hunter (1776–1838), surviving daughter of John Hunter and Anne Home Hunter and cousin to Baillie, married Sir James Campbell first; after his death she married Col. Benjamin Charlewood, retaining her title. She had no children. (Baillie often misspells Charlewood as Charliwood.) John and Anne Home Hunter had only one other son who survived them, the Major Hunter mentioned above. Apparently, there is some mystery about Major Hunter, who left the army after short service and passed the rest of his life an exile in Toulouse.

35. See WI MS 5617/89. Unfortunately, this letter was inadvertently left out of my recent *Collected Letters* chapter of family correspondence. Interesting excerpts from it are as follows:
> My Dear Henrietta
>> I am somewhat of the latest in thanking you for the abundant supply of Poultry for our Christmas feasting, but writing has not been my vocation for some time past and I am in that respect faulty with all my friends. We have enjoyed the luxury of dining on one of the fowls, the very finest I ever saw upon a table, the other we have for a nursery feast to the children of our next door Neighbour, who smacked their little lips at it, I doubt not, and the

This succession to the estate of Long Calderwood in Scotland, however, prompted William's interest in the family pedigree which he asked Joanna and John Richardson to confirm.[36] Richardson wrote in January 1839, "I had not before read of Williams [sic] becoming a Scottish Laird & it was a very great gratification to me to know that he had succeeded to an inheritance in the land of his forefathers"; Richardson confirmed that he would determine the value of the property for William and continue his genealogical search of the Baillie family in Scotland.[37] William seemed devoted to his old aunts, but his "profession" as a gentleman may have carried with it a certain amount of pretense which was partly revealed in his need to establish a pedigree. A biting but amusing letter from cousin Janet Hunter to William Clift,[38] dated 14 August 1831, reveals that William

---

>Grand Turkey still hangs by the heels. . . . You may be sure we enjoyed the few days that Grandmama spent with us (for she was then truly the Grandmama) and you & William & the dear Children made a great party & a very pleasant part of our daily conversation. The baby she boasts of us the perfection of early babyhood, Matthew she is very well pleased with, but Sophy, dear little Sophy with all her mimickry [sic] & fancy & gentleness, is the very light of her eyes and the joy of her heart. . . . Your Xmas however would be somewhat gloom with the death of your good Grandmother; I hope your own Mother has recovered from the shock and will look forward to the comfort of being with you. . . . William too would, though in a much small degree feel some gloom from the death of poor Major Hunter, our very eccentric cousin. . . . You will be pleased to hear that your Aunt Agnes is now quite recovered. She has been down stairs to day to Breakfast and seem[s] quite disposed to resume her usual active habits. [A short paragraph then follows from Agnes Baillie.]

36. This is the autobiographical document quoted in chapter 1 herein.

37. WI MS 5613/20. There are several pages included in MS 5613 from Richardson's tracing the Baillie line.

38. William Clift was born in Cornwall in 1775 and came to live with John Hunter in London when he was seventeen, only twenty months before Hunter's death. His task was to write, make drawings, dissect, and take charge of the museum. Clift found himself a member of a very large household which stretched from Leicester Square eastward to Castle Street with a further property at Earl's Court. Clift copied volumes of Hunter's manuscripts and thus saved nearly half of his work, the rest being lost when Everard Home burnt manuscripts in 1823 "because they were unfit to meet the public eye." The Royal College of Surgeons took care of the museum in 1800, appointing Clift as conservator, and he became Fellow of the Royal Society in 1823 (RCPSG 30).

Baillie may have sometimes appeared a bit pompous even to his aunt Joanna:

> I delivered Miss Clift's message to Mrs Joanna Baillie when she said she thought she had already written something in her Album, but if not she would be most happy to do so now—who do you think dined with us but William Baillie!, his aunts told me, they had asked him to meet with my cousin Jane, and us: so, we thought <u>this</u> would be sufficient to prevent him, but no in he walked at five oclock to the astonishment of I am sure every one present and really behaved better than I ever saw him: to be sure it <u>was</u> all acting, but then, it was well done and he deserves credit even for that. When he was going away he said in the most falsette [sic] voice ever heard assumed "is there anything I can do for you dear Aunt Agnes"—no my love said the blinded aunt. Pray Aunt Joanna let me do some commission for you, it will give me such pleasure—I have nothing for you to do said Joanna in a sharper tone than I had ever heard her assume which showed that she at least was not duped by appearances; several times during dinner he had caught Hannah and I smiling at what we thought uncommon delicacy of sentiment for him to assume: his mother and sister are going to reside at <u>Dunce</u>boure for a short time.[39]

Joanna Baillie clearly did not suffer fools, but William and Henrietta remained close to her and Agnes, and the two sisters were particularly fond of Henrietta. The couple had eight children, and when Henrietta died in 1857 at only forty-nine, William never remarried. In fact, only two of their eight children ever married.[40] Like Joanna and Agnes, several generations of Baillies women seem not to have been preoccupied with the necessity of marrying.

---

39. RCPSG 30/14.
40. Their children were Sophia Joanna (1836–1882), Matthew John (1837–1866), William Hunter (1838–1895), John Baron (1841–1868), Helen Mary Henrietta (1843–1929), Agnes Elizabeth (1846–1925), Robert Denman (1850–1870), and Henrietta Clara Marion (1853–78). Agnes Elizabeth married Robert B. Oliver in 1875, and Henrietta Clara Marion married James Maconechy in 1871. The Baillie line survives today only through the union of Henrietta Clara Marion Maconechy's daughter Muriel Catherine Dorothea Maconechy and Thomas B. Jobson, whose son Patrick Hunter Jobson is Dr. Matthew Baillie's great-great grandson.

Nonetheless, William Baillie's family was well respected by the Duntisbourne community. As proof of that, on 11 July 1893, just a year before his death, the Constitutional Club there presented William with an engraved ebony walking stick for the kindness and generosity of his family.[41]

Beyond her family, Baillie also maintained contact with Dr. William Beattie and with Anna Jameson in her later years. William Beattie, M.D. (1793–1875) was born at Dalton, Annandale, the son of architect and surveyor James Beattie. His mother was said to have had "poetical tendencies," which William learned from her. The Beatties later settled in Dumfriesshire, and at fourteen William went to school at Clarencefield Academy under the rectorship of Mr. Thomas Fergusson who taught him Latin, Greek, and French. In 1812 Beattie became a medical student at Edinburgh University, took his medical degree in 1818, and remained there another two years, "teaching, lecturing, translating, and conducting a small private practice."[42] He later practiced medicine in Cumberland and in 1822 was preparing to settle in Russia when he became engaged to Miss Elizabeth Limmer, a wealthy lady whom he married in 1822. He was introduced by her family friend Admiral Child to the duke of Clarence (later William IV) and attended the duke's family on a visit to the courts of Germany. After traveling extensively in France, Italy, Switzerland, and Germany, he entered a medical practice at Worthing but left again in the following March to accompany the duke and duchess of Clarence to Germany. In 1827 Beattie became a licentiate of the Royal College of Physicians in London and established himself at *Rose Villa* in Hampstead, where he met Joanna Baillie and practiced medicine for the next eighteen years. When his wife died in 1845, he gave up regular practice as a physician but continued to give medical advice to clergymen, writers, and friends without accepting fees. During his lifetime he was foreign secretary to the British Archæological Society, fellow of the Ethnological Society, member of the Historical Institute, and member of the *Institut d'afrique* in Paris.

William Beattie was a frequent contributor to periodicals and between 1835–36 published two poems, *John Huss* and *Polynesia*, along with an historical work entitled *Ports and Harbours of the*

---

41. WI MS 5616/1, newspaper clipping.
42. General biographical information comes from the *DNB*, II:25–27. Some of the following footnoted information on editions comes from listings in *The National Union Catalogue*.

Danube. Later came his works *Switzerland, Scotland, The Waldenses, Castles and Abbeys of England*, and *The Danube*. Beattie also edited the *Scenic Annual* (for which Thomas Campbell was supposed to be responsible), *Beckett's Dramatic Works*, and *Lives of Eminent Conservative Statesmen*. He was a friend of Samuel Rogers and a long-time friend of Thomas Campbell, who selected Beattie as his biographer; Beattie ultimately produced *The Life and Letters of Thomas Campbell* in three volumes in 1849. Campbell probably would never have been buried in Westminster Abbey nor had his statue placed in "Poet's Corner" but for William Beattie. Beattie died childless on 17 March 1875 at Portman Square at the age of eighty-two, and it is reported that he left an autobiography, which has never been found.

Correspondence between Beattie and Baillie was sparse and lasted mostly through the 1830s, but Beattie was considerably younger than she, and their relationship seems to be based on her mentoring of him. Both were friends of John Richardson, and Baillie invited both to dinner at her house on various occasions. Beattie sent many of his works to Baillie for her editorial suggestions, and she was straightforward with criticism or praise. He, in turn, praised her *Dramas* in February 1836 as follows:

> I w'd add that while I have uniformly admired the truly [sic] originality of . . . I have been often startled by their genuine touches & Picture[s] which qui[c]ken the pulse—make the voice faulter in the middle of the sentence and carry their appeal direct to the heart.—knowing that I am addressing the author I would not have said so much were I not fully aware that this much & much more than this you must hear from authorities against whom it is impossible to shut the Ear.—There is indeed so far as my heavy . . . go—but <u>one</u> opinion of the Dramas.[43]

When *Dramas* appeared in 1836, Joanna Baillie was seventy-four, but her mind was as keen as ever. She complained only of occasional colds and minor aches. Incidentally, while health was a common topic of her letters, Baillie seems to have escaped serious illnesses of all sorts, even with influenza and cholera raging through

---

43. CLS 8; *Letters*, 1014. Ellipses indicate holes in the ms. letter.

London several times during her life.[44] Nevertheless, many of the plays appearing in *Dramas* had been written much earlier, and Baillie categorizes all but three of them as *Miscellaneous Plays* in the 1851 complete edition. When the three-volume *Dramas* appeared in 1836, several reviews were forthcoming. An early one from *The Athenæum* appeared in January 1836 and praised Baillie as follows:

> The coming of a new comet which no one had foreseen, or an eclipse of the sun which no one had predicted, would not puzzle astronomers more than the appearance of these Dramas by Joanna Baillie has amazed critics. Of the remaining books of Wordsworth's 'Excursion' we have heard, and of a domestic epic by Southey, and other works of inspiration, frost bound in manuscript by these cold and ungenial times; but of twelve new dramas by the authoress of 'Plays on the Passions' we had not heard a whisper, and their coming has pleased and surprised us.[45]

Shortly afterwards, Dr. John Wilson acknowledged in *Blackwood's* that "on laying down Volume First, which we read through . . . we felt that Scott was justified in linking her name with that of Shakespeare."[46] George Moir also proved to be a kinder critic than Jeffrey had been of the last volume of *A Series of Plays* in 1812, and in his *Edinburgh Review* article from April of that year concluded that while the many plays were unequal in merit, "Their contents will not, on the whole, disappoint expectation." On a more personal note, alluding to the power of Baillie's mind, he added,

> Miss Baillie, it is true, never writes anything on which the stamp of her strong mind is not here and there impressed; and there are none of the dramas contained in these volumes which do not, to some extent, awaken curiosity and interest. . . . This great work then is completed—and in a manner

---

44. The first world-wide epidemic of cholera, attacking the intestines through contaminated food or water, began in 1817 in India and spread to Russia and western Europe. England was invaded in 1831 with approximately 50,000 deaths resulting throughout the British Isles. Four other pandemics during the nineteenth century showed similar characteristics (see Sir Macfarlane Burnet's *Natural History of Infectious Disease*, 331–32).
45. *The Athenæum* (January 1836): 4.
46. *Blackwood's Edinburgh Magazine* 39 (1836): 265–80.

worthy of its commencement: a noble monument of the powerful mind and the pure and elevated imagination of its author. Looking on it, as it now stands before us,—a finished whole, we owe it to Miss Baillie and to ourselves to say, that we regard it with pride and admiration.[47]

However, in a note from 1836 in Lady Byron's hand (simply entitled "Notes of Mrs. J. Baillie's Conversation"), Annabella discussed points of Baillie's argument in the *General Tenour* and noted that Baillie had talked about the recent article in the *Edinburgh Review* which compared her to the writers of the Elizabethan Age and spoke of her great inferiority.[48] Baillie had also noted both *The Athenæum*'s and *Blackwood's* reviews in letters to Margaret Holford Hodson as they appeared in 1836. Clearly, Baillie was interested in the reception of her work, and she seems to have read almost every review which involved her and may have indeed taken them more personally than she should have.

Baillie's final multi-volume work, *Dramas* (1836), includes the following plays in its three books:

> *Romiero: A Tragedy, In Five Acts*
> *The Alienated Manor: A Comedy, In Five Acts*
> *Henriquez: A Tragedy, In Five Acts*
> *The Martyr: A Drama, In Three Acts*
> *The Separation: A Tragedy, In Five Acts*
> *The Stripling: A Tragedy, In Five Acts*
> *The Phantom: A Musical Drama, In Two Acts*
> *Enthusiasm: A Comedy, In Three Acts*
> *Witchcraft: A Tragedy In Prose, In Five Acts*
> *The Homicide: A Tragedy in Prose, With Occasional Passages In Verse, In Three Acts*
> *The Bride: A Drama, In Three Acts*
> *The Match: A Comedy, In Three Acts*

In the "Preface" to *Dramas* the author explains that while most of these plays had been written at a much earlier time, all but the previously published *The Martyr* and *The Bride* were new to the public. She had never intended to publish any of them in her

---

47. "Miss Baillie's *Dramas*," *The Edinburgh Review* 63 (1836): 73–101.

48. OU Lovelace/Byron 62, ff.176–77.

lifetime and hoped that on her death they would be offered to some of the smaller theaters in London:

> But the present circumstances connected with our English Theatres are not encouraging for such an attempt; any promise of their soon becoming so is very doubtful; and I am induced to relinquish what was at one time my earnest wish. This being the case, to keep them longer unpublished would serve no good purpose, and might afterwards give trouble to friends whom I would willingly spare. They are, therefore, now offered to the Public, with a diffident hope that they may be found deserving of some portion of its favour and indulgence.[49]

The circumstances were that very few new plays were being released in London and "revivals" were standard; in addition, the complexion of the audience had changed since the early Romantic period, as fewer and fewer "respectable families" went to the theater because of the rude audiences and immodest prostitutes.[50] Realizing that she would have no more success in getting representation for these plays than she had received for most of her earlier ones, Baillie released her last reserve.

Volume one of *Dramas* opens with *Romiero: A Tragedy, In Five Acts*, another play on the passions which focuses, along with *The Alienated Manor*, on jealousy. The setting is Romiero's castle on the shore of the Mediterranean, the time the fourteenth century. When Zorada, Romiero's wife, finds her father Don Sebastian shipwrecked on their shore, she hides him and plans his escape; for he is a political fugitive, and Romiero has sworn to return him to the king of Castile. Like Othello, Romiero is a jealous husband, but his suspicions need no fuelling from an Iago; he is sufficiently paranoid on his own. When he finds Zorada missing from their bedchamber, he immediately suspects an intrigue with young Maurice, who is actually in love with Zorada's friend Beatrice. While Zorada is

---

49. *DPW*, 312.
50. See discussion of this decline of the nineteenth-century theater in Nagler, 476.

wounded but passive in the face of Romiero's verbal attacks, Beatrice actively defends her sex to him:

> *Bea.* Are you not well, my lord?
> *Rom.* No damsel; *well* was banish'd from the world,
> When woman came to it.
> *Bea.* Fy! say not so.
> For if deprived of women, what were men?
> Like leafless elms stripp'd of the clasping vine;
> Like unrigg'd barks, of sail and pennant bare;
> Like unstring'd viols, which yield no melody.
> Banish us all, and lay my life upon it,
> You will right quickly send for us again.[51]

Romiero treats women like trivialities, and Baillie suggests that he has married too young a wife for his own insecure nature. His possessive and unhealthy love for Zorada is contrasted against Maurice's healthy love for Beatrice. Zorada is simply trying to save her father, but in one of several volatile scenes, Romiero rants at her:

> Thou'st played me false; thou art a worthless woman;
> So base, so sunk, that those whose appellation
> Brings blushes to the cheeks of honest women
> Compared to thee are pure.—Off! do not speak![52]

Ultimately, Romiero accidentally murders his wife in an attempt to kill her father. While he is tragic, Romiero fails to elicit the reader's sympathy, a fact of which Baillie was well aware.

Shortly after the appearance of *Dramas*, Baillie felt it necessary to defend her flawed hero in an essay entitled "On the Character of Romiero" for *Fraser's Magazine* (vol. 14). She recommended the essay to both Margaret Holford Hodson and Dr. Andrews Norton in November and to George Thomson in December of 1836, stating that those who disliked and condemned the character of her jealous man ought to read her defense of him. She explained to Hodson:

---

51. *DPW*, 331–32.
52. Ibid., 331.

> I am not presumptuous enough to suppose that I can altogether vindicate Romiero; but in simply laying before the reader my own intentions in delineating this character, something very near a vindication may, perhaps, be found. I have endeavoured to represent him as a man fastidiously delicate in everything connected with the affections of the heart. This is shown by his former concealed attachment to a Lady which was only discovered after her death—by his being so distressed at the idea of Zorada's love having passed from him to another, that he at first thinks the further personal criminality scarcely worth considering—by his not enduring when that criminality is from circumstances made to appear probable or presumptive, even in his aggravated agony, to have her name coupled with any gross epithet. This, it appears to me, is a jealousy dealing particularly with the affections of the heart, not being afraid or suspicious of more ignoble wrongs; and therefore jealousy that (as its frailty indeed) might belong to a noble nature.[53]

"We sympathize with suspicion, as with all other emotions," continued Baillie, "according to its object." Her response was the direct result of a *Quarterly Review* article by her "very friendly critic" (Jeffrey), whose censure she also reiterated to Margaret Hodson as she defended her character Romiero:

> The passion of jealousy may co-exist with the noblest qualities of our nature; but a jealous disposition—and such seems that of Romiero,—is something mean & degrading; it is almost impossible to make it assume that dignity which is necessary to great tragic interest.

Any reader who has concluded that Baillie was disinterested in the acceptance of her work need only examine her defense of and series of letters about *Romiero* to understand how seriously she took its critical reception.

Following the tragedy *Romiero* is *The Alienated Manor; A Comedy, In Five Acts*, set in the English countryside. Its focus is on jealousy and on women's boredom in marriage. In fact, Mrs. Charville, married only a few months to a jealous husband, laments to her sister-in-

---

53. CLS fragment, undated; *Letters*, 719.

law Mary that "Matrimony is a duller thing than I took it to be."[54] Her only amusement is in matchmaking, and because she acts as a liaison between Mary and Freemantle, her husband suspects her of an intrigue herself. Though not as disturbed and dangerous as Romiero, Mr. Charville is rude, peevish, and possessive. As Anne Mellor argues, Mr. Charville, like protagonists Basil and De Monfort, wreaks havoc on himself and his family as a result of his obsessive passions.[55] When he opens and reads a letter posted by his wife to one of her childhood girlfriends, it is easy to lose all compassion for him. In an argument with Mr. Charville about her alleged "affair," she declares to her husband that she is a dutiful wife, and he retorts, "You are dutiful, and that makes you grave."[56] Indeed, her situation is grave and one wonders how she can come to a reconciliation with her husband in the end, even though he admits that he has been "a very selfish fellow."

In addition to portraying the darker side of marriage, Baillie introduces three comical, if not problematic, characters in *The Alienated Manor*. She unites an estate improver named Sir Level Clump, a German philosopher named Smitchenstault, and a black servant named Sancho to voice her opinions about the environment and about German philosophers, and she presents in Sancho a problematic minority character much like Ohio in *Rayner*. Neither Sancho nor Ohio are sympathetic characters, even though Baillie deplored the racial prejudices present in her country and in America. Her stand on protecting the environment was also clear, and she always preferred untamed landscapes to manicured ones. The absurdity of Clump's planning is apparent when he advises Freemantle about improving his land: "The readier and more common method, now-a-days, is to cut down the wood on one part of the ground, to pay for beautifying the other." To which Freemantle responds, "A good device, Sir Level; but my worthy mother likes the old woods as they are; and you might as well bring her own grey head to the block, as lift an axe against any veteran oak on the estate." Baillie had said as much to Scott about the clearing away he would have to do for building Abbotsford, and she fought throughout her residence in Hampstead to save the Heath from developers. Meanwhile, German philosopher Smitchenstault gives the author a chance to ridicule his kind, for she was none too

---

54. *DPW*, 342.
55. Mellor, *Mothers*, 93.
56. *DPW*, 345.

fond of German philosophers and complained to Dr. Andrews Norton in 1837 that they and the "zealous Divines at Oxford" were detrimental to the church.[57] The problematic character, however, is the black servant Sancho, who appears in only a few scenes. His dialect is exaggerated, like Ohio's, but he is not malicious like the character in *Rayner*. He is, however, somewhat dangerous; in defending his master, he threatens to shoot Mr. Charville, who has brought about his master's bankruptcy. Probably, Baillie, who seemed to be trying to embrace minorities as much as any white English gentlewoman could in the early nineteenth century, knew very little of other races. But this play, which would have been well suited to the stage, manages to combine Baillie's feminist, environmental, and philosophical comments and even alludes to sentimental novels and to the ills of physical abuse and self love.

After *Manor* comes Baillie's final play on passions. *Henriquez: A Tragedy, In Five Acts*, on remorse is set in the thirteenth-century town of Zamora. *Henriquez* is one of the plays that Victorian critic Fred Rowton estimates in *The Female Poets of Great Britain* as well designed for the stage (along with *The Separation*) and which he argues "clearly shows that with performers sedulously bent on carrying out the author's design, and willing to sacrifice momentary applause for ultimate appreciation, Mrs. Baillie's Plays would be as forcible in action as they are striking on perusal."[58] This play about remorse is just as clearly about jealousy, since the protagonist Henriquez murders his friend Don Juan de Torva because he believes his wife Leonora is in a love relationship with Juan. Basing his rash suspicions on a private letter from Leonora, which he has no business reading in the first place, Henriquez never even questions his wife but believes the worst of her and seeks out Juan to murder him outside the castle. Baillie's discovery scene comes in Act 2, where we learn that Don Juan was on his way to beg for the hand of Mencia, Leonora's sister, and Leonora was simply meeting Juan to let him in the gates and to help plead his case. Henriquez does not immediately admit to the murder, and young Antonio, who is also in love with Mencia, is imprisoned as the only suspect. When it is clear that his friend Don Juan has left all his property to

---

57. HU MS Eng 944 (17); *Letters*, 943–44. Baillie complained both of German philosophers and of The Oxford Movement to Norton and to others.

58. Qtd. in Burroughs, *Closet*, 200.

Henriquez, the general cannot cope with his guilt and remorse, and in the end he saves Antonio through his confession to the king.

Like *Othello*'s Desdemona, Leonora is never given a chance in this drama to plead her innocence. In fact, her husband does not even give her the right to know that he considers her inconstant. Henriquez acts on insinuations made by his young servant Blas, reads his wife's mail in her private quarters, kills his best friend, and alienates his wife. While his later remorse is convincing, it does not seem to come until the reading of Juan's will, after which is revealed the "dark mysteries of human nature"[59] which occupy his mind. Oddly, Henriquez does not spend the night before his execution with his wife Leonora. So even though he is somewhat exonerated as a person, he is never convincingly exonerated as a husband.

Baillie had written at least the first two acts of *Henriquez* as early as 1812, for she promised Scott in April that she would send him a copy of this tragedy, "The story of which I have scetched [*sic*] out in the form of an anecdote taken from an old chronicle."[60] After reading the draft, Scott asked Baillie how she presumed to prevent the audience from anticipating the conclusion and suggested that she read the notes to Southey's *Cid*. By 1815 Sir Thomas Lawrence was also reading her draft, and she valued his opinion of it as an "acting play" in particular. When the play finally came out in *Dramas* in 1836, Baillie happily notified Margaret Holford Hodson on March 19 that *Henriquez* was being performed that very evening at Drury Lane. According to the author, actors George and Sarah Bartley had been reading scenes from the play aloud at social gatherings,[61] but

---

59. *DPW*, 375.
60. NLS 3882 ff.128–131; *Letters*, 301.
61. George Bartley (1782?–1858) was a comedian born in Bath whose father was box-keeper at the Bath theatre. George acquired stage experience as a youth, appearing at Cheltenham in 1800 as Orlando in *As You Like It*. His London debut was in 1802, though for some time he was apparently employed as an understudy. In 1809–11 he unsuccessfully managed the Glasgow theatre, subsequently acting with increasing reputation as a comedian in Manchester, Liverpool, and other locations. In 1814 he married his second wife, Sarah Smith, a successful tragic actress who appeared that same year as Ophelia at Drury Lane while George appeared as Falstaff, thereafter his favorite character. In 1818 the Bartleys made a successful trip to America, and on their return Bartley accepted a winter engagement at Covent Garden. In 1829 when Covent Garden's management collapsed, Bartley headed the actors who came forward with a proposal to furnish funds and recommence performances. The loss of his son at Oxford led to Bartley's retirement from the stage. His only remaining child, a daughter, died shortly afterwards and Mrs. Bartley in

Vandenhoff performed the title role at Drury Lane instead of Bartley. This play ends Baillie's theme of human passions.

Although the next play in the volume, *The Martyr: A Drama, In Three Acts,* moves away from her focus on the passions, it was ultimately bound with the last three plays of that nature in volume one of *Dramas.* It appeared originally, however, as a single edition from Longman in 1826, and Baillie had written it several years earlier than that.[62] Her detailed "Preface" to this play focuses on her period of religious and philosophical inquiry and examines both an earthly paradise and Christianity in its purer state:

> The Martyr whom I have endeavoured to portray, is of a class which I believe to have been very rare, except in the first ages of Christianity. . . . but, from the pure devoted love of God, as the great Creator and benevolent Parent of men, few have suffered but when Christianity was in its simplest and most perfect state, and more immediately contrasted with the mean, cheerless conceptions and popular fables of Paganism.[63]

This tragedy, set in Rome at the time of Nero, takes much of its particular details about Christian martyrs from John Fox's *History of the Martyrs* and tells the story of Roman soldier Cordenius Maro who, after witnessing Nero's persecution of Nazarenes, is himself converted to Christianity by Sylvius, a centurion. Baillie chooses a Roman soldier as her hero to portray "one whose mind is filled with adoring awe and admiration of the sublime but parental character of the Deity, which is for the first time unfolded to him by the early teachers of Christianity."[64] Cordenius Maro is to have the hand of Portia, the daughter of Roman senator Sulpicius, but Cordenius relinquishes both Portia's love and Nero's promised promotions in

---

1850. Bartley then appeared as Falstaff at Windsor Castle in a performance arranged by Charles Kean, taking his farewell performance on 18 December 1852 after a fifty-year career (*DNB,* I:1255–56). The Bartleys were instrumental in getting Baillie's plays performed in America.

62. See CLS 30 (*Letters,* 585) to Hodson: "I have just made up my mind to send my Drama called the Martyr which you read & approved of years ago, to the press, and shall send a note to Longman this evening to tell him so" (2 March 1826).

63. *DPW,* 509.

64. Ibid., 511.

affirmation of his new faith. When Cordenius is sentenced to the arena to face a ravenous lion, his pagan friend Orceres, awed by this soldier's faith and courage, mercifully shoots him through the heart with an arrow.

This brief plot summary is certainly a simplification of Baillie's *Martyr*, for the drama is filled with Christian philosophy and with Baillie's own stance that Christ on earth was a man sent by the Father to teach us how to live. The play was clearly a complement to her detailed anti-Trinitarian argument in *A View of the General Tenour of the New Testament Regarding the Nature and Dignity of Jesus Christ* in 1831. Like *The Bride*, this moral play was translated into the Cingalese (Sinhalese) language at the request of Sir Alexander Johnston.[65] And Baillie seemed to have a special fondness for it, writing to Margaret Holford Hodson on 2 March 1826 that she had just decided to send it to Longman as she desired it to be published in her lifetime. From its inception, however, Baillie did not intend *The Martyr* for representation, its subject too sacred for the stage. But she handled the subject matter adroitly. Even though the play is didactic, it stirs emotion and is sincere in its presentation of Christian faith. Similar in its didacticism, *The Bride* is more "preachy" and less emotionally charged. *The Martyr* is the only such religiously dogmatic play in Baillie's collection, as her following play, *The Separation*, moves to yet another focus.

Beginning with *The Separation: A Tragedy, In Five Acts*, Volume Two of *Dramas* allegedly moves away from plays on passions. But it is difficult, if not impossible, to create tragedy without the impetus of some sort of passion. In fact, the protagonist Garcio summarizes his own predicament in one line, "the fierce turmoil of contending passions."[66] Set in a small province of Italy, this play opens with the deathbed confession of servant Baldwin that Ulrico, the brother of Garcio's wife Margaret, was in fact murdered many years ago. When Baldwin reveals that Garcio murdered Ulrico because he could not get his approval to marry Margaret, the confession finally makes its way to Margaret, who then begins to harbor doubts about her

---

65. Sinhalese was the language of Sri Lanka. Sir Alexander Johnston (1775–1849), reorganizer of the government of Ceylon, led a reform movement there which modernized the educational system, established religious freedom, and fostered emancipation of slaves. When Johnston returned to England in 1819, Lord Grey declared in the House of Lords that his conduct in Ceylon had "immortalized his name." In 1823 Johnston founded the Royal Asiatic Society in England (*DNB*, X:940–41).

66. *DPW*, 543.

husband. Desperate, yet strong enough to confront Garcio, Margaret elicits his confession and mandates that they must separate. In an impressively emotional scene, Garcio pleads his love for her:

> Heav'n bids us part! Then let it send its lightning
> To strike me from thy side. Let yawning earth,
> Op'ning beneath my feet, divide us. Then,
> And not till then, will I from thee be sever'd.[67]

Garcio blames his former youth and military background for his capacity to murder at will; then he departs with a hermit, his confessor, never more to live with his wife and young son. In order to see Margaret, however, he returns at intervals as a hooded hermit begging alms. In the end Garcio dies in this disguise as he defends his former castle from the Marquis of Tortona, a military bully who has tried in vain to force his affections on Margaret in her husband's absence.

The Separation, argues Burroughs, offers one of Baillie's several plots involving a heroine "who exerts her values in the face of challenges to her sense of rectitude" and is countered by combative men who sermonize on women's weaknesses.[68] Actually, three men in this play are in love with Margaret, or at least they want to possess her: Garcio, Tortona, and Garcio's friend Rovani. Rovani's affections are the most complex; he constantly implies that because Margaret acts strangely upon Garcio's return from war, she must be guilty of an affair. But Rovani, too, is aroused by her and is pleased when Tortona thinks that Margaret may be in love with him. This play about guilt, doubt, and jealousy is also essentially about men who misinterpret women's actions and emotions. Margaret, after all, prevails as the strongest and most rational of the cast and even stands in battle to defend her castle in the end.

In 1808 Baillie was visiting Edinburgh and reading, at Scott's request, the manuscript of his Gothic melodrama *The House of Aspen*, a work he said that Baillie's plays had put him "entirely out of conceit with."[69] In *Aspen* she found similarities to her *Separation*, and she urged Scott not to think that she had borrowed the idea from him when he read her play in a forthcoming volume. When her play actually did appear almost thirty years later, it was presented at

---

67. Ibid., 541.
68. Burroughs, *Closet*, 141.
69. Qtd. in Johnson, 186.

Covent Garden and, "acted to very good houses for 8 nights and then stopped."[70]

The next play in volume two, *The Stripling: A Tragedy, In Five Acts*, is a prose tragedy set in London and its environs and written, she explains in a note to the text, when

> Master Betty, known by the name of the Young Roscius, was in the highest favour with the public, and before I had seen him perform; but, upon after consideration, was not offered to the theatre. It appears to me, in reading it again, after a long lapse of years, to be a play not ill suited to a very young actor, at the beginning of his career; being in prose, and having, I hope, no false, overstrained passion in it, to mislead him into ranting or exaggerated expression, either as to gesture, voice, or face.[71]

While she had seen Betty perform, there is no evidence that Baillie had met the young actor personally, but surely she had discussed him with actor friends. According to Baillie, *The Stripling*'s plot was based on a melancholic event which had occurred many years before in Glasgow, wherein a son was convicted of murdering the only witness who could convict his father of a capital offence. In her play, however, the crime is forgery, its necessity brought on by gambling debts. Mr. Arden's false friend Robinair, who has been in love with Mrs. Arden, is the witness who can convict Arden, for he is the one who introduced Arden to gambling and encouraged his crime in the first place. When Mrs. Arden comes to Robinair for help, it becomes clear that he is driven by jealousy and the desire for revenge, and his price for saving Arden is Letitia Arden herself. Letitia finds herself in the unfortunate position of being married to an irresponsible gambler, and her only means of aid is a licentious villain. Robinair, "mad with prosperity," makes her position clear to her:[72]

> Now will the days of thy scorn be remembered with bitterness, when, wife to a degraded husband, thou lookest timidly up to the eyes of a protector—even him whom thou

---

70. CLS 68 to Margaret Holford Hodson (15 June 1836); *Letters*, 658.
71. *DPW*, 551. Around 1805, as England's classical repertoire was being eclipsed by melodrama, a child actor by the name of William Henry West Betty was stealing the spotlight from the Kembles (Nagler, 419).
72. *DPW*, 558–59.

has rejected with disdain—Let this once be, and I shall feel it worth all the—No; I will not call it villany—my provocations would justify any thing—all the artful management it has cost me.

Letitia Arden is yet another of Baillie's female casualties, because being married to either of the two men proves equally oppressive in the end.

Young Edmond Arden, who is only fifteen years old at the time of the tragedy, is the central character and would have provided, as Baillie surmised, a noteworthy role for a young actor. Her ability to write such a part with a particular actor in mind demonstrates that she was not as lacking in knowledge of acting as critics have often concluded, for young William Betty was in the early part of the nineteenth century upstaging even the Kembles. Young Arden's is a believable and passionate role, and his confession and accidental death in the final scene would have provided an exceptional arena for the dramatic talents of a young melodramatic actor. Baillie clearly knew what she was about in developing this part for a young actor like Betty, and it is unfortunate that he was never given the opportunity to perform it. Her next play moves from this melodrama in prose to a libretto of the Highlands.

Recalling the location of *The Family Legend* but departing from Baillie's other comedies and tragedies, *The Phantom: A Musical Drama, In Two Acts*, set in the "*Western Highlands of* Scotland, *and afterwards in the city of* Glasgow," opens on a lush scene of mountains, greenery, rocks, and Highland revelers complete with bagpipe.[73] Apparently, music historian George Thomson had a professional interest in this short musical, for in 1838 he asked Baillie if he could include songs from both *The Phantom* and *The Bride* in his collection of Scottish tunes.[74] A country wedding is the occasion for the music in the drama, but it is only a subplot to a more complex account of love relationships. Highland chief Dunarden promotes a match between his son Malcolm and Alice, daughter of the prosperous Provost of Glasgow. Instead of desiring the admirable Alice, however, Malcolm is in love with her friend Emma Graham—and so is Alice's brother Claude. Emma, however,

---

73. Ibid., 570.
74. Baillie gives her consent to Thomson on 11 January 1838 but does not identify the songs; there are many in *The Phantom* but only two in *The Bride* (BL Add. Ms. 35,265 f.261; *Letters*, 145).

succumbs to a plague in Glasgow, appears as a phantom to Alice while she is a guest in the Dunarden household, and appeals to her as follows:

> The room in which I died, hath a recess
> Conceal'd behind the arras, long disused
> And now forgotten; in it stands a casket,
> The clam shell of our house is traced upon it;
> Open, and read the paper therein lodged.
> When my poor body is to earth committed,
> Do this without delay.[75]

To the dismay of Malcolm and Claude, the mysterious paper proves to be Emma's formal contract of betrothal to Basil Gordon—who, to the aversion of Emma's father, is both "a Gordon and a papist."

As the gothic *Phantom* unfolds, so do contrasts between the highlands and lowlands, between the upper and lower classes, and between lust and love. Included in the play are also anti-papist sympathies embraced by the lower classes, comments on the psychology of weeping, sublime descriptions of the Scottish landscape—and Baillie's usual cynicism about marriage contracts. When Malcolm describes his idyllic highland home to Alice, Claude fears that he will indulge his sister's "fancy with romantic visions." But Marian is quick to point out the reality of highland life:

> One thing, you would observe, he has omitted
> In the description of his bonnie glen,—
> The cottage matron, with her cumbrous spade,
> Digging the stubborn soil; and lazy husband
> Stretch'd on the ground, or seated by the door,
> Or on his bagpipe droning some full dirge.[76]

Malcolm is then forced to admit that "our mountain matrons / In useful virtues do excel their mates," and asks, "in what earthly region is it otherwise?" These young people are passionate, and the men are somewhat impulsive; but while this play is quite melodramatic, it provides a forum for the playwright's consistent opinion that the only true marriage is one based on mutual love and

---

75. *DPW*, 579.
76. Ibid., 575.

agreement, not one contracted for the improvement of social status or wealth.

Last in volume two of *Dramas* comes *Enthusiasm: A Comedy, In Three Acts*, in which Baillie's Lady Worrymore appears as "an ardent admirer of the Muses, but no critic."[77] This kind of denial, argues Burroughs, is typical of the Romantic woman writer who feared taking too critical a stance and thus being considered too "masculine" in her intellectual grasp.[78] But Lady Worrymore is, in fact, pretentious and given to praising poetry and prose whose quality she is incapable of judging. This is another of Baillie's plays about male/female relationships. Lady Worrymore believes that her husband's taste is far beneath that of the *literati* with whom she associates. When Lady Worrymore discovers that a nationalistic speech she has praised on the Corn Bill has actually been written by her husband Lord Worrymore, she must be reconciled to his expertise; Lady Shrewdly closes the play by asserting that "A wife who has taste and capacity enough to admire the talents and genius of her own husband, is most happily endowed."[79] Ultimately, this play is about pretense, poetry, and politics. Lord Worrymore's speech on the Corn Bill reflects Baillie's ever-present political concerns. Her friend Alexander Dirom (d. 1830) of Dumfriesshire had authored *An Inquiry into the Corn Laws and Corn Trade of Great Britain* in 1796, and she would later write Dr. Andrews Norton in November of 1845 that "Sir R. Peel has had the courage to open the Ports here for the free reception of corn from all parts of the world."[80] Ever abreast of current events and political situations, Baillie manages to incorporate in *Enthusiasm* current political concerns with her consistent focus on the difficulty of relationships. The play that follows, however, takes on a much different tone.

Witchcraft: A Tragedy In Prose, In Five Acts, opens volume three of *Dramas*. It differs from most of Baillie's other plays in tone and

---

77. Ibid., 594.
78. Burroughs, *Closet*, 29-30.
79. *DPW*, 613.
80. See eleven letters from Baillie to General Alexander Dirom edited by W. H. O'Reilly in "Unpublished Letters of Joanna Baillie to a Dumfriesshire Laird," *Dumfriesshire and Galloway Natural History and Antiquarian Society: Transactions and Journal of Proceedings* 18 (1934): 10-27.

Statesman Sir Robert Peel (1788-1850) supported free trade, and his ministry eventually pushed through the repeal of the Corn Law on 26 June 1846. He resigned on June 29 (*DNB*, XV:655-68).

type but is set in Scotland like her successful *Family Legend*. Adrienne Scullion contends that

> The play is one of Baillie's most unusual, notable for a distinctive and sustained attempt at linguistic realism . . . something of a psychological thriller set against a backdrop of religious intolerance and the fear of hellish witchcraft. The play offers a remarkably bleak vision of character and community.[81]

Bleak it is, as innocent women are almost burned at the stake by a frenzied mob. Baillie understands the "psychology that motivates and performs," argues Susan Bennett, in a world of superstition and despair.[82] As in *Witchcraft*, Baillie's plays "do not merely offer alternative images of women," writes Jeffrey Cox, "they offer a critique of various conventional modes of dramatizing women."[83] Baillie thanked Margaret Hodson in September 1826 for suggesting that John Stow's chronicles on witchcraft might be of interest to her, but she replied that her drama already contained "as good an appointment of Witches as I can afford to maintain."[84] She also wrote to Scott about *Witchcraft* in 1827, amused that her Renfrew witches might eventually be endorsed upon "the polite stage":

> I have nothing left to say but that I finished my prose Tragedy on Witchcraft which I mentioned to you a great while ago, and after having let it lye by & reading it again at a considerable distance of time, I am inclined [to] think favourably of it.[85]

---

81. Scullion, 164.

82. See Susan Bennett's "Genre trouble: Joanna Baillie, Elizabeth Polack—tragic subjects, melodramatic subjects," *Women and Playwriting in Nineteenth-Century Britain* (Cambridge: Cambridge University Press, 1999), 227.

83. Qtd. in Bennett, 230.

84. CLS 33; *Letters*, 596. John Stow[e]'s (1525?–1605) work appears in *Three fifteenth-century chronicles, with historical memoranda by John Stowe, the antiquary, and contemporary notes of occurances written by him in the reign of Queen Elizabeth.*

85. NLS 3905 ff.260–261; *Letters*, 440.

Witchcraft was not introduced on the stage, however, though it is one of Baillie's most chilling gothic dramas. She was motivated to write a play on witchcraft, she explained, by reading that very curious and original scene in Scott's *Bride of Lammermuir* in which "the old women, after the division of largess given at a funeral, are so dissatisfied with their share of it, and wonder that the devil, who helps other wicked people willing to serve him, has never bestowed any power or benefits upon them." It was the design of Baillie's play, however, "to illustrate this curious condition of nature" in which women might actually believe themselves to have had intercourse with the "Evil One, consequently to be witches."[86] In a journal entry dated 22 July 1827, Scott recorded,

> Rose a little later than usual and wrote a letter to Mrs. Joanna Baillie. She is writing a tragedy on witch craft. I shall be curious to see it—Will it be real Witch craft—the *Ipsissimus Diabolus* [the very devil himself]—or an impostor—or the half crazed being who believes herself an ally of condemnd [sic] spirits and desires to be so? That last is a sublime subject.[87]

Scott's hopes for that last sublime subject were satisfied, for *Witchcraft* is complete with a distracted woman, a thwarted burning at the stake, and Baillie's themes of intolerance, suspicion, and "the tyranny of uncontrolled passions."[88] The text offers an aesthetic experience easily transferred to formidable images in the mind.

Following *Witchcraft* is *The Homicide: a Tragedy in Prose, with occasional Passages in Verse, in Three Acts*, set in the *"free imperial city of* Lubeck, *and at sea."*[89] Like many of Baillie's plays, this one, argues Burroughs, was designed for actors who could perform in a style that would be later considered "romantic," making use of "muttered, imperfect articulation," suppressed voices, and rapid bursts of sounds appearing to proceed from distress. In addition, for this play Baillie suggested lighting effects to solve the problem of dealing with untalented actors and helping to hide their "countenances" when necessary,[90] further indication that she

---

86. *DPW*, 613.
87. Anderson, 331.
88. *DPW*, 643.
89. Ibid.
90. Burroughs, *Closet*, 112.

understood both staging and delivery. When Van Maurice is sentenced to die for the murder of Baron Hartman, a murder of which he is innocent, his friend Claudien confesses that he killed Hartman in self defense; and the play ends happily as Claudien is reunited with Van Maurice's sister Rosella. Rosella complicates a feminist reading of this play, for she has flirted with Hartman in order to hide her secret engagement to Claudien, thus fueling the jealousy that results in Hartman's physical attack on Claudien. Hartman is, however, overbearing and suspicious and respects neither Rosella's privacy nor her refusals. However, unless Claudien secures the approval of the court, he cannot marry Rosella, and she may be forced into an odious union with Hartman—again Baillie's focus is on unempowered women.

In an interesting endnote to *The Homicide*, Baillie explains that because "a gentleman professionally conversant on these subjects" opposed Claudien's confession on board a ship caught in a storm, she wrote two alternate scenes that might prove less melodramatic and more practical to stage.[91] Further, the spatial sweep of the storm scene in general would have been almost impossible to stage.[92] Two alternate scenes follow her note. And though she preferred her original scene, her willingness to try alternatives proves that she still focused on performance and audience, not just on readers.

For her next play, *The Bride: A Drama, in Three Acts,* set in Ceylon, Baillie provides a separate "Preface" and explains that the play was solicited by her friend Sir Alexander Johnston, whose travel tales also gave her the inspiration for *Ahalya Baee*. After *The Martyr* was translated into the Cingalese (Sinhalese) language, Johnston apparently suggested that Baillie write a play "more peculiarly appropriate to the circumstances of that island, which would naturally have a stronger moral effect on the minds of its inhabitants."[93] She readily complied, producing a moral play about Christian forgiveness and advocating monogamy in the bargain. This is a play of cinematic proportions like parts of *The Homicide* and would have been very difficult to stage if a director had tried to remain true to Baillie's stage and set directions. But because her

---

91. *DPW*, 664–65.
92. Dr. Paula Backscheider notes that a spatial sweep is generally characteristic of Scottish art. Baillie would have most certainly been influenced by that genre.
93. *DPW*, 665.

purpose was to translate this into another language, in this case it seems that her target audience was her foreign readers.

The Bride is a play about man's desire to possess women, casting aside the old for the new; it is also about masculine control and about woman's inability to reject that control in many societies. When in his polygamous society Chief Rasinga sets his sights on a young mountain bride, his only wife Artina is devastated. To arrest her grief, Artina's brother Samarkoon kidnaps the new bride; however, Samarkoon is then captured by Rasinga and sentenced to death as a traitor. After Artina attempts to free her brother from his cell, the Chief declares her fate to be the same—death. But Rasinga knows that he is morally wrong and even asserts in his early passion for this young woman that "there's ecstacy in those bright gleams; / Ay, and though cross'd with darkness black as midnight, / I will enjoy this momentary radiance."[94] But the bride is only a pawn, and when Samarkoon asks her to decide between Rasinga or him, she laments, "My choice! a modest virgin hath no choice."[95] Rasinga appears in his most despicable state when he angrily justifies his rejection of Artina and protests,

> That I—that I alone must be restrain'd!
> The very meanest chief who holds a mansion
> May therein take his pleasure with a second,
> When that his earlier wife begins to fade,
> Or that his wearied heart longs for another.
> Ay, this may be; but I am deem'd a slave,
> A tamed—a woman bound—a simple fool.[96]

Meanwhile Juan de Creda, a Christian in this non-Christian society, tries to move Rasinga with the story of Jesus forgiving the two thieves on the cross. It is Rasinga and Artina's son, though, who finally moves his father to mercy, as he determines to die with his mother rather than live with this father who has condemned her. In an emotional scene, Rasinga experiences a spiritual conversion, pardons both Samarkoon and Artina, and presents the young bride to Samarkoon. Although the ending is happy enough for most of the characters, the bride clearly has gained nothing but a younger, single man in this bargain—no power of refusal, no equality. Plus,

---

94. Ibid., 671.
95. Ibid., 673.
96. Ibid., 679.

Artina's forgiveness of her husband's cruelty in the heat of passion requires a great leap of faith from the reader.

Baillie was just beginning *The Bride* in 1827, but she acknowledged to Margaret Holford Hodson in August that Sir Alexander Johnston had not yet provided much help with her story. In September she relayed to Hodson that

> Since I wrote last I have been carefully looking over Dr Dray's account of Ceylon for something to work upon for the purpose I formerly mentioned, but I can find nothing at all in the form of a story or event to do me any good; I have only gleaned two [or] three peculiarities of atmosphere & customs which must (for want of better) do me hard service in the way of metaphor & illustration, that I may write as like a Cingaleese as I can.[97] Did you ever hear of the Boodhoo rais which shine & move about in Mid-day, as our Northern lights do at night? They are ominous too and foretell evil every month of the year, may excepted.
>
> You may guess I have not much to say when I am troubling you with Boodhoo small as my paper is, and you will guess right.—[98]

Nevertheless, by January 1828 she confirmed to Hodson that her "Cingaleese Drama" was well under way, sent her a draft of it the following month that she might "peruse it in that spirit of friendly partiality which has so long acted in my favour," and requested that it be read only by Hodson and her husband.[99] *The Bride* was complete and in the publisher's hands (H. Colburn of London) by July 1828; it appeared in Philadelphia from C. Neal that same year. When Baillie wrote to Dr. Andrews Norton in April of 1829, it was to discuss the recent production of Mary Russell Mitford's *Rienzi* (1828) and to forward a copy of *The Bride*.[100] This drama seems to have

---

97. I have not identified this Dr. Dray or his work, but the Drays of London are mentioned in *Blackwood's Index* (XIII:708), with no more specific information. The British East India Company had seized control of Ceylon in 1796 during the French Revolution, making it a British Crown Colony in 1802.

98. CLS 37; *Letters*, 603.

99. CLS 39; *Letters*, 605.

100. Mary Russell Mitford (1787-1855), essayist, playwright, novelist, and poet, is best remembered for *Our Village* (1824-32). Her easy conversational style won her the praise of Charles Lamb; and her most

represented a Christian mission for Baillie, and she took its demands seriously. It is also one of the few plays in which she outlines in her correspondence much of her writing process and the play's subsequent development.

Like so many of Baillie's plays, *The Match: A Comedy, In Three Acts*, the final comedy in volume three of *Dramas*, again deals with issues of marriage and freedom. Burroughs believes the play mocks "The bluestockings' salon-like gatherings and the alarmed responses to their intellectualism," as the lady-in-waiting worries that her mistress Latitia Vane might take it into her head to give up gay dressing for learning and books and become "a blue-stocking virtuoso."[101] *The Match*, however, does not condemn intellectual women, for its leading female character, Latitia Vane, is rational and concerned that marriage insures a loss of freedom. At thirty-two, she speculates about Sir Cameron Kunliffe's second proposal of marriage: "What shall I do! Suffer him to think meanly of my motives; and give up all my plans too of living a distinguished single woman, in a house of my own,—the patroness of arts, the encourager of genius, the loadstar in society!"[102] Plays from the Restoration and eighteenth century had long satirized learned women, but Baillie's comedy only suggests that Latitia should be more selective in putting her faith in certain intellectuals. When phrenologist Dr. Crany reads Kunliffe's head as revealing evil and destructive inclinations, we learn that he has done so only because he wants Latitia for himself; and Baillie's inclusion of phrenology in this play adds to its significance as a piece of popular culture. A final discovery scene discloses that Kunliffe has been worrying unnecessarily about a mistake in a testamentary deed and that his estate is secure, so he becomes a less suspicious and more pleasant character at the end. In a humorous scene Latitia accepts a "match" with him and declares that they both have room for personality reform.

The Match would have been an easily-staged situation comedy, and even today its issues are relevant and its scenes witty, complete with cross–dressing. Baillie's phrenologist Dr. Crany is reminiscent of Thomas Shadwell's Sir Nicholas Gimcrack of *The Virtuoso*; indeed,

---

successful play, *Rienzi* (1828), was presented at Drury Lane to considerable public acclaim. Her later years were spent nursing an aged father (Todd, 470-71).
101. Burroughs, *Closet*, 163.
102. *DPW*, 687.

much of this play has Restoration comedy characteristics. Baillie, ever intrigued by science, was interested in the public's curiosity about phrenology, and she wrote to Mary Montgomery around 1833 about a lecture on the subject:

> I wish you had been here the other evening to have attended a very curious lecture on Phrenology which was delivered to our Ladies & Gentlemen of the Scientific Institution at the Hollybush Tavern. They would have admitted you as a stranger, though we of the place, not being subscribers could not be admitted. Besides chusing Nurses & Nursery Maids by the examination of their sculls, according to the rules of his art, he advised the chusing of statesmen too by a similar examination. Unfortunately for us, there is but one of our present Administration who has a head[;] that is Lord Grey who has one that is magnificent.[103] Mr Pitt,[104] he proceeded to say would have been a good statesman if he had had a head, but Nature not having given him one, he did as well as he could without it.[105]

By April 1845, however, Baillie was more skeptical and reviewed, for Lady Byron, Robert Chambers's *Vestiges of the natural history of Creation*, attributing the book's popularity to "its kindredship to Phrenology, and the machinery-dispositions of the present times."[106] *The Match*, a jovial and clever comedy, ends *Dramas*.

Dramas, Baillie's last collection of plays, was received with mixed criticism, and in 1836 Samuel Coleridge's daughter Sara wrote her own critical estimation of the three volumes to her friend Miss Trevenen:

> Have you seen Mrs. J. Baillie's twelve new dramas? One critique says they have the same vigor of thought and felicity of language as her earlier productions, but that they are not so sustained nor so well united, nor have the same propriety of action or character. The passion of hatred is powerfully exhibited in the comedy of "The Election." Successful and

---

103. This is probably a reference to Whig statesman second Earl Charles Grey (1764–1845).
104. William Pitt (1759–1806) the younger was prime minister and advisor to George III.
105. OU Lovelace/Byron 93, ff.198–199; *Letters*, 859–60.
106. OU Lovelace/Byron 62, ff.129–130; *Letters*, 776.

admirable as Mrs. Baillie's dramas are, I can not think it a good plan to announce one particular passion in the title-page of a play; it leads you to expect to find the laboring author, rather than a picture of life itself transmitted through the author's mind and hand in the following pages.[107]

While Sara Coleridge's criticism calls to mind Jeffrey's early complaints about Baillie's experiment with singular passions, *Dramas* actually moves away from such a singular focus to include works ranging from situation comedy to religious drama.

Dramas completed Baillie's last grand publication of original plays. While they were not received with as much enthusiasm as her early *Series of Plays*, they were still much in the same style and also in the style of plays by contemporaries like Wordsworth and Coleridge. All chose Shakespeare as their model and created tragedies that were fundamentally moralizing and didactic, but Baillie's subtext usually dealt with the hazards of marriage. Her exotic settings, too, were common, for readers and audiences of the early nineteenth century were interested in travel books, in the medieval, and in foreign cultures—as was Baillie. Unfortunately, because she read more than she went to the theater at this point in her life, Baillie may have been more in tune with readers than she was with the contemporary theater audiences who were becoming less and less serious about seeing profound drama. By now she had little to do with theater managers, and many of her earlier acting friends were either retried or, as in the case of Mrs. Siddons, dead.

On the emergence of *Dramas* in the late 1830s, Joanna and Agnes were probably spending most of their evenings at home, for a letter from Sophia Denman Baillie to her daughter-in-law Henrietta on 27 January 1838 related her intention of visiting Hampstead, "as your Aunts are not at present disposed to leave their own fireside. Indeed who is!"[108] In 1837 Lockhart's first volume of Scott's *Life* appeared, and Lady Byron suggested to Baillie that she must certainly be proud that her friend had found such a competent and

---

107. See *Memoir and Letters of Sara Coleridge Edited by Her Daughter* [Edith Coleridge] (New York: Harper and Brothers, 1874), 121.
108. WI MS 5616/50.

judicious biographer. But Baillie, who had not given Lockhart her most personal letters from Scott, was not pleased with all of the biographer's entries.[109]

Well into her seventies, Baillie continued to stay abreast of politics and the activities of the newly crowned "young Queen," and she wrote to her nephew's wife Henrietta in June 1837 that she had just come from church where she heard prayers offered up for the first time in behalf of Victoria, "prayers which I hope will be heard. But our Clergyman, who is a very high Church Tory, made no allusion at all to the good king we have lost, only exhorting us under every calamity to put our trust in God."[110] Further, Baillie lamented that the bountiful harvest enjoyed by Hampstead contrasted with the distress of the Irish women and children begging in the lanes. Around 1838–39 Lady Byron wrote to Baillie about the playwright's recently implied interest in writing on "Juvenile Reformation" and suggested to her some reading, though there seems to be no evidence that Baillie carried through with the project.[111] In the letter that follows, Lady Byron related to Baillie her recent acquaintance with two Unitarians, one of them Mr. Johns, a minister for the poor. Her topic then turned to religious philosophy, as it often did. Lady Byron also regularly provided Baillie with news of her travels, of whom she had met, and what she had read. Lady Byron knew Joanna's sister-in-law Sophia and called on her often when in London; it was in Sophia Baillie's drawing room that historical painter Charles Landseer hung his *De Monfort* in 1841, a painting which had been commissioned by Lady Byron.

In 1842 Baillie was celebrated in verse by her younger friend Hartley Coleridge, the eldest son of Samuel Taylor Coleridge, for which she sent her thanks on 28 April of that year:

To Joanna Baillie

Long ere my pulse with nascent life had beat,
The ripe spring of thy early Paradise
    With many a flower, and fruit, and hallow'd spice,
    Was fair to fancy and to feeling sweet.

---

109. Baillie was unhappy with at least two comments about "bluestockings." See chapter 4.

110. WI MS 5616/48; *Letters*, 64.

111. OU Lovelace/Byron 62, ff.191–92. Letter is not postmarked but seems to follow those from late 1838.

> Time, that is aye reproach'd to be so fleet,
> Because dear follies vanish in a trice,
> Shall now be clean absolved by judgment nice,
> Since his good speed made thee so soon complete.
> But less I praise the bounty of old Time,
> Lady revered, our Island's Tragic Queen,
> For all achievements of thy hope and prime,
> Than for the beauty of thine age serene,
> That yet delights to weave the moral rhyme,
> Nor fears what is, should dim what thou hast been.[112]

While there is no evidence that Baillie was ever a friend of Hartley's famous father, she maintained a correspondence with both Hartley (1796–1849) and his sister Sara (1802–52), who had married her cousin Henry Nelson Coleridge in 1829. Baillie's interest in the Coleridge children was enhanced by her interest in their uncle Robert Southey, and Baillie's letters to Sara Coleridge often referred to Southey and problems related to his family. Both Hartley and Sara were talented writers but were ultimately cast in the shadow of their more famous father. Sara invented children's games and wrote tales, including *Phantasmion* (1837). Hartley taught school for a time, published a series of biographies entitled *Biographia Borealis* (1833) and *Worthies of Yorkshire and Lancashire* (1836), and a collection of sonnets in 1833. His most worthy literary effort, however, was an edition of Massinger and Ford in 1840. His brother Derwent published Hartley's biography in 1849 and edited his poetical and prose works in 1851. Hartley's "To Joanna Baillie" made the author, as she assured him, "vainer than a Lady of my age ought to be, or is consistent with what you have expressed regarding me in the last line of your elegant verses."[113]

By this time, Baillie and writer Anna Jameson, also a friend of Lady Byron, had formed a close friendship. Exactly when Jameson met Baillie is unclear, but their mutual literary circle made their friendship inevitable. Jameson was a feminist long before the movement emerged as a social and political force and advocated equality for women both in marriage and in education. In *The Contours of Masculine Desire: Romanticism and the Rise of Women's*

---

112. See *Poems by Hartley Coleridge, With A Memoir Of His Life By His Brother* [Derwent Coleridge], *in Two Volumes* (London: Edward Moxon, 1851), II:25.
113. HRH ALS to Coleridge, Hartley; *Letters*, 1176.

Poetry (1989), Marlon Ross determines that "in reconstructing women's experience 'out of men's fictions' Jameson parallels poets like Hemans, Lucy Aikin, Laetitia Landon and Joanna Baillie."[114] Baillie, Jameson's senior by some thirty years, had from her very first plays attempted to reconstruct the *reality* of women's experience—women who were often the object of men's passions—and her directive to her juniors to demonstrate these realities was significant.

Anna Murphy Jameson (1794–1860) was an essayist, travel writer, and art historian born in Dublin on 17 May 1794, the oldest of five daughters of Denis Brownell Murphy, an Irish miniature painter of considerable ability. The family moved to England in 1798 and finally settled at Hanwell. Anna was talented and at the age of sixteen became a governess to the family of the Marquis of Winchester. Around 1821 she was introduced to Robert Jameson, a young artistic lawyer, and their engagement ensued. It was, however, broken off; and Anna Murphy accepted another position as governess, accompanying her pupil to France and Italy for about a year. The diary she kept there was later published by a speculative bookseller named Thomas as *A Lady's Diary* and again taken up by publisher Colburn and sold as *The Diary of an Ennuyée* (1826). Having spent four years as governess to several families, Anna was reconciled with Robert Jameson, and they married in 1825 and moved to Tottenham Court Road in London. The couple appear never to have been suited for each other. Anna described him as cold and reserved; he probably found her too gregarious and intellectual. After just four years of marriage, Robert moved, without Anna's objection, to Dominica to be a judge; she became an active writer, seldom living with her husband, though she came, at his request, to meet him in Canada for a short time from 1836–38. On her return to England, the separation seems to have been fairly complete. Meanwhile, Anna accompanied her father and friends on many tours through Canada, the Low Countries, and Germany. Her circle of friends included Joanna Baillie, Lady Byron (with whom she later quarreled), Fanny Kemble, Elizabeth Gaskell, Jane Welsh Carlyle, and the Brownings; and her many publications comprise *Loves of the Poets* (1829), *Celebrated Female Sovereigns*, 2 volumes (1831), *Memoirs of the Beauties of the Court of Charles II* (1831), *Characteristics of Women*, 2 volumes (1832, dedicated to Fanny

---

114. Qtd. in Judith Johnston's biography *Anna Jameson: Victorian, Feminist, Woman of Letters* (Hants, England: Scolar Press, 1997), 199.

Kemble), *Winter Studies and Summer Rambles* (1838), and the voluminous *Sacred and Legendary Art* (1848–52).

Extant correspondence at the National Library of Scotland between Baillie and Jameson begins around 1839, late in Baillie's life, but the two clearly knew each other well before because those late letters are unassuming and casual. While Baillie writes about reading Jameson's work, including her translation of Amelia of Saxony's plays, she does not comment on Jameson's personal life, especially on her estrangement from her husband. One can only assume that in the early nineteenth century, marital discord was not a proper subject for letters and was better left to the privacy of the parlor. Even though at least two of Baillie's closest friends, Anna Jameson and Lady Byron, suffered unhappy marriages and separations, Baillie discussed the topic rarely and prudently. Through Jameson, Baillie met Catharine Maria Sedgwick, often kept up with Jameson's activities through Lady Byron, and usually asked in her letters about Jameson's two sisters, Eliza and Charlotte Murphy, for whom Anna was the major supporter. All of this circle were friends of the William Harness family and of writer and activist Harriet Martineau. Jameson solicited Baillie as a critical reader and sent the translation of Princess Amelia of Saxony's dramas (*Social Life in Germany*, 1840) to her in 1839; she also notified Baillie of a review in the *Westminster Review* of the latter's work.[115] Baillie had sent Jameson a copy of her newly edited *View of the General Tenour of the New Testament Regarding the Nature and Dignity of Jesus Christ* when the second edition appeared in 1838, and in the early 1840s she lamented the fact that Jameson had just returned from travels to see the church in distress:

> I feel mournfully what you say of the moral state of my country, contrasted with its beauty & grandeur. You have

---

115. The *Westminster Review*, which continued from 1824 to 1914, was for its first twelve years the tool of Jeremy Bentham's radical party and aimed to define the place of literature, education, and religion in their ideal state. The *Review*'s target audience was the middle class, gradually becoming dominant following the Reform Bill of 1832. It persisted as a sound, respectable journal and attained the added distinction of being the first English review to have a woman, Mary Anne Evans (George Eliot), as assistant editor from 1852–54 (see George L. Nesbitt's *Benthamite Reviewing: The First Twelve Years of The Westminster Review, 1824–1836*, v, 172). *Westminster Review* 33 (March 1840): 401–24, contained a review of Baillie's work.

come to it at an unhappy time, when people are all quarrelling about religion, and every one thinks himself or <u>her</u>self wiser than their neighbours, and the Lay Patrons of the various Parishes are replacing the Clergy who have seceded with others as wrong headed & bigoted to please the people.[116] So I hear from an intelligent friend who generally views those subjects with great calmness. I remember well in old times the stilness [sic] of a fast day, but it was a stilness of solemnity not of form; and the sacrement [sic] being given in most parishes as a yearly commemoration of the greatest event that ever took place upon earth, the people received from it a deeper impression than we may suppose they do in this country where it is administered every month.—[117]

Baillie's religious conservatism and her criticism of the Oxford Movement did not, however, indicate total intolerance for religious beliefs not conforming to hers. A dissenter herself, she celebrated, for example, that Roman Catholics were eventually restored the right to vote; but her observation to Jameson elucidates her disdain for ritual void of emotion.

Jameson's circumstances were altered in 1854 by the death of her husband who had made no provision for her in his will, but her friends rallied to her support and raised an annuity of £100 by subscription. She spent her later years working on her *Sacred and Legendary Art* volumes and died at Ealing, Middlesex, on 17 March 1860 from the effects of a severe cold contracted on a wintry day's walk home from the British Museum, where she had been working on

---

116. Though the Oxford Movement began in 1833, leaders of the group were publishing their *Tracts for the Times* into the 1840s. This could be the struggle to which Baillie alludes, but it is more likely about the break in the Church of Scotland which occurred in 1843, when the Free Church of Scotland was formed under the leadership of Thomas Chalmers. In 1847 the secessionists of the eighteenth century united to form the United Presbyterian Church of Scotland, and in 1900 this body merged with the Free Church to form the United Free Church of Scotland, which in 1929 was rejoined with the Church of Scotland. Milestones in the separation of the church from the state were the transfer of church schools to civil authorities and the abolition of ecclesiastical patronage (see C. S. Black's *The Scottish Church* [1952] and J. H. S. Burleigh's *A Church History of Scotland* [1960]).

117. NLS Acc 8663 (17); *Letters*, 1037.

her *History of our Lord*. A marble bust of Anna Jameson now stands in the National Portrait Gallery in London.[118]

Like many of these women friends, Baillie retained a lively spirit well into old age. She turned away from drama to publish *Fugitive Verses* in 1840, with a second edition appearing in 1842. Account ledgers from publisher Edward Moxon's business with Baillie indicate that the first edition run of five hundred copies had realized a profit of £137 by November 10 to be divided between author and publisher, so sales were successful though the run was small.[119] *Fugitive Verses* is a beautifully bound volume, small in width but thick in pages, incorporating the early verses from her 1790 *Poems* along with "Miscellaneous Poetry" and "Verses on Sacred Subjects." Her "Preface" to the volume explains its purpose as follows:

> I believe myself warranted in calling the contents of the following pages "Fugitive Verses," for by far the greatest portion has been in some way or other already before the public, though so scattered among various publications and collections, that it would be very difficult now for any one but myself to bring them together. . . . This book then, does not hold out the allurement of novelty. . . . The occasional pieces for the first time offered to the public, have another disadvantage to contend with. Modern Poetry, within these last thirty years, has become so imaginative, impassioned, and sentimental, that more homely subjects, in simple diction, are held in comparatively small estimation. This, however, is a natural progress of art, and the obstacles it may cast in the way of a less gifted, or less aspiring genius, must be submitted to with good grace. . . . Some Scotch expressions, as might naturally be expected, interfered with clearness of meaning and harmony of sound to an English reader, and some of those I have changed; but I have not been willing, unless when it appeared necessary, entirely to remove this national mark.[120]

---

118. See Todd, 351–53, and *DNB*, X:667–69, for general biographical information herein.

119. By November, 447 of the 500 copies had been sold. See RCS HB.ix.66–67.

120. Preface to *Fugitive Verses* (London: Moxon, 1840).

Baillie knew her readers, and she knew that the Romantic innovations of the early nineteenth century were giving way to Victorian ideals of the age of chivalry. In some respects, the Romantic sublime was being displaced by morality and realism and culminating in social movements like Benjamin Disraeli's "Young England." Baillie welcomed such transition. Visiting her at this time was her old nemesis critic Francis Jeffrey, who wrote, "I found her as fresh, natural, and amiable as ever, and as little like a tragic muse." Two years later he described her as "marvellous in health and spirits, and youthful freshness and simplicity of feeling, and not a bit deaf, blind, or torpid. . . the prettiest, best-dressed, kindest, happiest beauty of fourscore that has been seen since the flood."[121] After his harsh review of Baillie's plays in 1812, it seems that Jeffrey tried to reclaim her trust; it is not apparent that he ever did.

In the 1840s Baillie was also still providing literary advice to American writers such as Lydia Howard Huntley Sigourney, who thanked her in March 1842 for her "items of literary intelligence" and told her about her visit to Abbotsford and how "desolate it appeared without the master-spirit."[122] And Baillie was continuing her long-time correspondence with Lady Davy.

Lady Jane Davy (1780–1855) was the only daughter and heiress of Charles Kerr of Kelso and Jane Tweedie. She was married in October 1799 to Shuckburgh Ashby Apreece, baronet of Washingley, Huntingdonshire, but he died in 1807 without children. Jane then retired to Edinburgh and opened her doors to the intellectuals of the city. She was a continental traveler and reportedly a remarkable beauty with grace and manners, and in April 1812 she married the esteemed chemist Sir Humphry Davy (1778–1829), a close friend of

---

121. Qtd. in Lockhart, V:336n.

122. A former school teacher, American writer Lydia Howard Huntley Sigourney (1791–1865), born in Norwich, Connecticut, was best known for *Traits of the Aborigines of America* (1822), *Biography of Pious Persons* (1832), *Letters to Young Ladies* (1833), and *Select Poems* (1838). Between 1840 and 1850 she published fourteen additional volumes, mostly revisions of her earlier works, including *Pocahontas, and Other Poems* (1841), Spenserian stanzas modeled on Felicia Hemans's *The Forest Sanctuary*, and *Illustrated Poems* (1849). Perhaps in search of new subjects, Sigourney went abroad in 1840, visiting literary figures such as Joanna Baillie, Anna Jameson, Maria Edgeworth, Samuel Rogers, and William Wordsworth (see Edward T. James, ed., *Notable American Women 1607–1950: A Biographical Dictionary*, 4 vols. [Cambridge: Harvard University Press, 1971], III:288–90). See RCS HB.ix.40 and L. H. Sigourney's *Pleasant Memories of Pleasant Lands* (Boston: Munroe, 1842).

Samuel Taylor Coleridge. Two months later he dedicated to her his *Elements of Chemical Philosophy*, and in 1813 the couple went on a lengthy foreign tour, accompanied by Sir Humphry's friend the scientist Faraday. Apparently, the trip was not free from strain, for Jane Davy was sometimes demanding and not particularly comfortable around "simple students of science." Humphry was brilliant and a bit of a loner, so the couple were probably poorly matched from the beginning. Jane did not join her husband on his last journey to the continent, and he died there from a series of strokes in May 1829.

Baillie knew Lady Davy as early as 1813 and wrote to her as late as 1850. Both the Davys and Matthew Baillie's family lived at Grosvenor Square for several years, so Joanna Baillie probably met Lady and Sir Humphry as neighbors or through the scientific community attached to Dr. Baillie. Humphry Davy and Matthew Baillie were close professional acquaintances, but Davy must have also held great personal appeal for other members of the Baillie family. Mrs. Matthew Baillie wrote that there was a shyness about him, even though an expert chemist by his early twenties; and she remarked that his eyes

> were most remarkable, radiant with genius, and the most bright and beaming expression of intellect that can possibly be conceived. They were of a clear and brilliant blue, with a very sweet as well as powerful expression, and when he became warmed and animated in conversation . . . it was impossible to have seen him and have supposed him any ordinary person.[123]

Joanna Baillie sometimes corresponded with Sir Humphry, but most often with Lady Davy, about their mutual friends the Carrs, about their families, and about the Davys' friends in Geneva, some of whom Baillie met during her travels there in 1816. In 1829 Baillie apologized that she had mistakenly attributed an "offensive" review of Barbauld's *Eighteen Hundred and Eleven* to Lady Davy's friend Lord Dudley and wrote of her intention to read the current review of Horne Tooke in the *Quarterly*.[124] Many of Baillie's later letters reply

---

123. Qtd. in June Z. Fullmer's *Young Humphry Davy* (Philadelphia: American Philosophical Society, 2000), 344.

124. John Horne Tooke (1736–1812), radical politician and philologist, established his literary reputation with *Epea Ptepoenta: or, the*

to Lady Davy's correspondence from Italy and apprise her friend of visits from Maria Edgeworth and of current art exhibitions and social gatherings. In May 1841 she notified Davy that Charles Landseer had just exhibited his painting of De Monfort. In 1842 she wrote Davy about the wide acclaim of Frances Burney D'Arblay's *Diary and Letters*, and Baillie always kept her well informed about both the Baillie and Scott families. As late as 1849 Baillie sent thanks to Lady Davy for her gift of a brace of grouse. And in a final brief note, probably from 1850, Baillie replied to Davy's last letter and apologized that her own mind and pen had now become slow and confused.

By 1849 Baillie's health was beginning to wane. In 1845 she had lost her closest family friend, her sister-in-law Sophia Denman Baillie, who died at the age of seventy-four on August 5. Two years after her husband Matthew's death in 1823, Sophia had written her last wishes and testament, requesting a simple funeral and disposing of the "principal part of that property" over which she had control as appeared to "be the intention of their Father [Matthew Baillie]."[125] That intention was, of course, primarily for son William Baillie. Even with this loss of her friend Sophia, Baillie's work ethic did not diminish significantly. She completed *Ahalya Baee: A Poem* in 1849 as she worked on her "monster book," the complete collection of her works.

Baillie began *Ahalya Baee: A Poem*, published by Spottiswoods and Shaw for private circulation, at least ten years before its appearance. She mentioned the poem to Mary Montgomery in March 1840 as a "Metrical Legend to keep company, after I am gone, with the Legends I have already publish'd":

Diversions of Purley (1786–1805), an extensive grammar. A second edition was published by Richard Taylor in 1829 (2 volumes) with revisions from the author's copy; it was both attacked and acclaimed. Tooke was among the first to see languages as historical developments rather than fixed structures, stressing the importance of Gothic and Anglo-Saxon. The work was praised by exponents of Utilitarianism, and Tooke's friends included Mill, Bentham, Coleridge, Godwin, and Paine (*DNB*, XIX:967–74).

125. WI MS 5616/9.

> How far it may be deemed worthy to do so I know not, for I have not yet shewn it to any body, but I am inclined to think favorably of it my own self. How far my own self is a good critic in this case I may not venture to say. The subject of it is an Eastern Ranie or Queen, the celebrated Ahalya Baee (celebrated in India I mean).[126]

As the inspiration for this new legend, Baillie credited Sir John Malcolm, who had been "powerfully charmed by the character of Ahalya Baee" in his travels to India.[127] Like her other legends, Baillie explains in the "Introduction," this poem adds "no fictitious circumstances to the story or characters" and is embellished only by "supposed feeling and description."[128] This the last of Baillie's heroines is the epitome of strength and compassion. Both a judicious ruler and a devoted mother, Ahalya Baee watches one son die and an adopted son go to war, to return only for the "bier of death." Exhausted by care and fatigue, the "regent Mother" dies at the age of sixty and is praised as follows:

> For thirty years—her reign of peace—
> The land in blessings did increase
> And she was bless'd by every tongue
> By stern and gentle, old and young.
> . . . .
> Yea, even children at their mothers' feet,
> Are taught such homely rhyming to repeat:—
> "In better days, from Brahma came,
> To rule our land, a noble Dame;
> Kind was her heart, and bright her fame,
> And Ahalya was her honour'd name!"[129]

Like her Lady Griseld Baillie, Baillie's Ahalya Baee is a combination of authority and domesticity far superior to the warring rulers around her. She represents what may be assessed as the epitome of

---

126. OU Lovelace/Byron 93, ff.215–16; *Letters*, 879.
127. Sir John Malcolm (1769–1833), Indian administrator and diplomat, was appointed at age thirteen to a British regiment at Madras. He was in Bombay in 1802 when the Mahratta war broke out, remained there for several years, and there began his *History of Persia* (*DNB*, XII:848–56).
128. *DPW*, 839.
129. Ibid., 847.

womanhood for Baillie, but she is ultimately a victim in the patriarchal arena of war and confirms that women's commitment to sustaining life directly contrasts with men's engagement in war and violence. In Baillie's conflict of genders, man prevails in the physical world, but woman prevails in the spiritual—according to this feminist octogenarian, the sublime state.

In these last years, Baillie labored zealously at compiling one last collection of her complete works, *The Dramatic and Poetical Works of Joanna Baillie*, published in 1851 shortly before her death. This "monster" book, as she called it, was edited mostly for her heirs, but it was also one final move to leave her mark as a woman writer. In her final contract with Longman dated 13 April 1850, the publisher agreed that "Messrs. Longman and Co. shall publish at their own expense and risk The works of Joanna Baillie in one volume,"[130] so they were hardly afraid of failure at this point in their long years of dealing with the author. After the 1851 first edition, *The Dramatic and Poetical Works* appeared in two subsequent editions from Longman, Brown, Green, and Longmans, one later in 1851 and another in 1853.

Up to her death, Joanna Baillie remained concerned about friends and about the community she had inhabited for fifty years, and she wrote happily to her neighbor Lady Charleville when the "dreaded Heath-bill" had been withdrawn.[131] The controversy began in 1829 when Sir Thomas Wilson, Lord of the Manor, petitioned to build houses *on* the heath; the argument raged for forty years, when at his death in 1869 the conservationists finally won. Baillie analyzed the argument over the years, and she never lost her interest in politics in general. A declared Whig, she often argued with Scott over his Tory sympathies and kept up regularly with Poor Law

---

130. RCS HB.ix.63.

131. UN My 821; *Letters*, 1044. Catherine Maria, first Countess of Charleville, married James Tisdall who died in 1797, leaving a son and daughter. In June 1798 she married Charles William, 1st Earl of Charleville, with whom she had a son, later Lord Tullamoore. She lived in the leading literary society of George IV and the early Victorian era, and friends included Baillie, Byron, Edgeworth, Sarah Siddons, and others; she died on 24 February 1851—the day after Baillie (See R. Warwick Bond, ed., Introduction to *The Marlay Letters, 1778–1820* [London: Constable, 1937]).

Test and Corporation Acts, and problems in Ireland, for she and Agnes read daily newspapers right along with the more erudite material she discussed with her colleagues. In February 1845, for example, Baillie lamented to Mrs. Leckie, Edinburgh author of *The dream of the Western Shepherd*, that England's "bloody victory" in India had "occupied the thoughts of many of us very painfully; I hope there are none in whom you are particularly concerned among the slain. Our poor neighbour Mrs Haines has lost a son."[132] Because she had many friends with sons in the military, as her niece's husband had been, Baillie kept abreast of British military engagements throughout the world as a supplement to her penchant for politics.

Still, in these last years Baillie was plagued by visitors. While she was gracious, she sometimes balked at seeing so many strangers. Many of the requested visits came from Americans. One such visitor was writer Margaret Fuller, who visited Hampstead in 1846 and "marveled at the octogenarian's Roman strength and praised her 'singleness of mind'."[133] Two years later a letter to Baillie from Lydia Howard Huntley Sigourney, dated March 21, provided an introduction for the Rev. Mr. Bellows and his wife from the city of New York; they simply wanted to meet the author of the *Plays on the Passions*.[134] A similar letter followed from Orville Dewey on 23 March 1848 who argued a case for a group of "sensible people," one of whom was writer Caroline Kirkland.[135] Whether or not these visits

---

132. England's retaining British India as a "profitable colony" gave rise to countless military engagements on the borders of British territory with Indian potentates who threatened security of trade. These motives led to the conquest of Sind (1841-63) and the Sikh wars of 1846-47 and 1848-49. While the conquest of the Sikh state resulted in England's annexation of the Punjab, it also led to eventual Indian mutiny (Sally Mitchell, ed., *Victorian Britain: An Encyclopedia* [New York and London: Garland, 1988], 844).

133. Arthur W. Brown, *Margaret Fuller* (New York: Twayne, 1964), 94. My thanks to graduate research assistant Staci Lewis, East Tennessee State University, for adding this reference from her own research on Fuller.

134. WI MS 5615/33.

135. See WI MS 5615/32. Orville Dewey (1794-1882) was a Unitarian clergyman, author, associate of Dr. Channing at the Federal Street Church in Boston from 1821-23, and later pastor at several other Boston churches. He received the degree of D.D. from Harvard in 1839 and became the fourth president of the American Unitarian Association from 1845-47. Publications include *Discourses on Various Subjects* (1835), *The Old World and the New* (1836), *The Works of Orville Dewey* (1844), and numerous sermons and addresses. He opposed both slavery

took place is not altogether clear, but Baillie wrote about the visitors who did come from all places and professions until her death in 1851.

Joanna Baillie was almost eighty-nine years old when she died in the winter of 1851. She was tired and ready for the end when she wrote to her American friend Dr. Norton in January 1850 about their current winter:

> My Sister & I have suffered considerably; she more than myself. Memory is failing with both to a distressing degree. We will enquire after friends whom we have loved and have been in their Graves twenty years and the next day, perhaps, Enquire for them again. Need I say more than this?

But she was still sound enough to continue her reading and discussions of literature with him:

> Miss Aikin was in good health when I saw her not long since and will be pleased to know that you have enquired after her. She has had enjoyment with the younger Xmas folks lately and has been a cheerful comforter to those more advanced[.]
>
> I may now say how much we are pleased with your friend Mr Ticknor's work on Spanish Literature;[136] it is a treasure for any Library and he has been very bountiful in bestowing it upon me. My love for Chivalry & ballads will follow me to the grave.
>
> Remember me affectionately to my friends of Dr Channing's family, to Mrs George Lee, and to Miss Sedgwick. I owe much to the kind partiality of my American friends: that

---

and abolitionism, subjecting himself to attack from North and South; but he reportedly had a natural eloquence and preached with insight and ability (*DAB*, V:272).

Caroline Kirkland published *A New Home—Who'll Follow?* in 1839. Kirkland moved to southern Michigan in 1830 and wrote with an eye for wit and detail about the old Northwest and small-town society (Robert E. Spiller, *et al.*, *Literary History of the United States*, 4th ed. [New York: Macmillan, 1974], 763).

136. George Ticknor's *History of Spanish Literature* was published in three volumes in 1849.

I have been so much regarded by them, will raise me in the estimation of my own country.[137]

Still anxious about her "estimation," that was one of the last long letters Baillie wrote. Only a few shorter letters were sent at later dates to her niece Elizabeth Margaret Milligan, Lady Byron, Sir John Herschel, Lady Charleville, Mrs. Richard Owen, Sir Charles Pasley, and Lady Bentham.

Joanna Baillie lived a long, full life, but she was only one of many women writers who shared such longevity. Like Baillie, most of these contemporaries were born before 1770 and were publishing prodigiously at age fifty and above. The players included Laetitia Barbauld, Mary Berry, Frances Burney, Elizabeth Carter, Maria Edgeworth, Mary Hays, Mary Lamb, Harriet Lee, Sophia Lee, Charlotte Lennox, Hannah More, Amelia Opie, Hester Lynch Piozzi, Jane Porter, Clara Reeve, Regina Maria Roche, Sarah Trimmer, Priscilla Wakefield, and Jane West.[138] Like many of these women writers, Joanna Baillie was a nationalist, a conservative, and a feminist. While the combination of these ideologies might seem incompatible today, they did not pose a conflict for Baillie, for her astute understanding of human nature reconciled her to her own medley of opinions and passions.

---

137. HU 39; *Letters*, 987–88 (12 January 1850).
138. See Devoney Looser's *British Women Writers and the Writing of History, 1670–1820* (Baltimore: Johns Hopkins University Press, 2000).

6

"The majesty of a genius": Epilogue for a Poet (1851)

Joanna Baillie died in Hampstead on 23 February 1851 at the age of eighty-eight, having just edited her final "monster work"—*The Dramatic and Poetical Works of Joanna Baillie*—for Longman, Brown, Green, and Longmans. As part of this final chapter to her *Life*, the following letter from Joanna's nephew William Baillie to her old friend Samuel Rogers attests to the playwright's peace of mind and constitution at her passing:[1]

>Tuesday Feby 23 [1851]
>4 Upper Harley Street
>
>My dear Sir
>   I cannot bear that you so old a friend of our family & so much attached to my dear Aunts, should hear an event from the newspapers which I am sure will afflict you very much—My dear Aunt Joanna drew her last breath this day. She was much the same yesterday as she has been for sometime, but after being in bed complained of a pain in her back & chest, & sank till this afternoon about four o'clock when all was over. The pain & weariness she suffered were slight & a more placid termination of life could not be. She only ceased to breathe.
>   My Aunt Agnes behaved with the utmost firmness & seemed afterwards pretty well. She was in some degree confused, but I trust this was only the consequence of agitation, & a perfectly sleepless night. She took some dinner, & afterwards slept, & I left her sleeping. She was to be conveyed to bed as soon as possible, & Dr Evans was to see her the first thing in the morning.
>   I am sure you will be interested in all these particulars & remain
>   Dear Sir
>   yrs very truly
>   WHBaillie

---

1. UCL 14/55 (Sharpe Collection); *Letters*, 18–19.

William Baillie also personally notified many of his aunt's other friends about her death; Lady Noel Byron immediately sent him a note of thanks from Brighton, happy that Baillie's end was a peaceful one.[2] As Mary McKerrow writes, "Joanna declared that she was tired of life, went to bed and died; so managing her own death as completely as she had her family's livelihood—no mean achievement in an age which disapproved of women earning their living."[3]

Paula Backscheider concludes in *Reflections on Biography* that the subject's "dying well" gives us "both a satisfying sense of closure . . . and a narrative of courage in the face of the unknown."[4] Baillie's dignified passing does, in fact, provide a satisfactory ending to a long, productive life. That the playwright worked almost to her death on her final "monster" edition (1851) is clear; that her courage in the face of old age and death never wavered is apparent in one of her last statements to Dr. Andrews Norton:

> Your letter dated Cambridge 11 Dec^r [1849] came to me yesterday and it soothed [and] gratified me. Yes, my excellent friend, we are both I trust travellers on the same varied road & conducted by the same Benevolent & Unerring Guide and conducted to that house in which are many mansions. We both meet again as Kinsfolk; To be near the end of our journey is solemn but not depressing.[5]

That she suffered some in the end is confirmed by her nephew William. But her dying seems much as was her living: calm and unobtrusive. Baillie was buried on 1 March 1851 in the St. John parish cemetery, the ceremony performed by the Rev. Thomas Ainger, whom she had once labeled "Our excellent Pastor here."[6]

---

2. OU Lovelace/Byron 62, ff.39–40.

3. Mary McKerrow, "Joanna Baillie and Mary Brunton: Women of the Manse," in *Living by the Pen: Early British Women Writers*, ed. Dale Spender (New York and London: Teachers College Press, 1992), 164.

4. Backscheider, 91.

5. HU 39; *Letters*, 987.

6. This is extracted from the parish register cited in F. E. Baines's *Records of the Manor, Parish, and Borough of Hampstead in the County of London, to December 31st, 1889* (London: Whittaker and Co., 1890), 366. Thomas Ainger (1799–1863) became curate of St. Giles Reading in 1822 and in 1841 was presented by Sir Thomas Wilson perpetual curacy of Hampstead, which he held until his death (*DNB*, I:188). See NLS Acc 8663; *Letters*, 1027 (to Anna Jameson).

Various obituaries followed Baillie's death. But the note below was excerpted from an earlier Hampstead publication of *The Living and the Dead* (this copy owned by Dr. Williams's Library in London) and released on Joanna Baillie's death:

> There is something exceedingly striking in the appearance of Joanna Baillie. Though she is no longer young, and her features have lost the glow and freshness of youth, the rays of beauty still linger about her countenance, and over its expression the tyrant has had no power. Her face is decidedly tragic, not altogether unlike that of Mrs. Siddons—and capable of pourtraying the strongest and deepest emotion. Her air is lofty and reserved; and if there be a dash of hauteur in her manner, amounting, at times, almost to sternness, there is, on the other hand, something delightfully winning in the tone of her deep fine voice. Her eye—I hesitated long before I could decide its hue, and, after all, I am not quite certain whether it be dark blue or hazel—has a most melancholy expression; though time has not quenched its fire, or bent, in the slightest, her erect but attenuated form. She appeared about 50; thin, pale, and dressed with a Quakerlike simplicity; and though some might be inclined to say she is too conscious of her powers, and to quarrel with the precision of her manner, there is much of the majesty of a genius about her, and, in person altogether, she is one, who once seen, is not easily to be forgotten.[7]

That Baillie was majestic and "conscious of her powers" at the pinnacle of her career proves her no less an actor than the great Mrs. Siddons.

The following obituary is also filed with an early note from Baillie to Sir John Sinclair in the University of Edinburgh Special Collections:

> DEATH OF JOANNA BAILLIE.—We have to announce the decease of Joanna Baillie. She was born in 1762, in the manse of Bothwell, near Glasgow, of which place her father was minister. The works of Joanna Baillie, which appeared anonymously at the end of the last century, when a brilliant phalanx of names had begun to excite general attention,

---

7. Dr. Williams's Library 8.27; *Letters*, 19–20.

created as great a sensation as any production of the period, and the impression which was the result of their first appearance was much heightened when, contrary to all expectation, they were found to be the writings of a woman. This impression was still further increased when it was discovered that the authoress was still young, and always led a secluded life. Several of her dramas have been acted. John Kemble and his sister sustained the chief characters of "de Montfort" [sic] upon several occasions, and the elder Kean selected the same tragedy for one of his benefit nights. The "Family Legend" obtained a considerable run in Edinburgh, where Sir Walter Scott, the warm friend and great admirer of Joanna Baillie, wrote a prologue to this tragedy, while the author of the "Man of Feeling" contributed the epilogue. The "Separation" and "Henriquez" have in more modern times been acted, but the writings of Joanna Baillie are rather adapted for reading than the stage. Though her fame tended greatly to draw her into society, her life was passed in retirement. It was pure and moral in the highest degree, and was characterised by the most consummate integrity, kindness, and active benevolence. Gentle and unassuming to all, with an unchangeable simplicity of manner and of character, she counted many of the men most celebrated for talent and genius among her friends, nor were those who resorted to her modest home confined to the natives of this country, but many from various parts of Europe, and especially from America, sought introductions to her.[8]

Also from the University of Edinburgh Special Collections are excerpts from the 1 March 1851 account of her death in the *London News*:

JOANNA BAILLIE, one of the most eminent female writers and poets that these countries have produced, was a native of Scotland. Her father was the Rev. James Baillie, a clergyman of the Kirk, and, at the time of Joanna's birth, minister of Bothwell parish, near Glasgow; his wife, Joanna's mother, was Dorothea Hunter, sister of the celebrated anatomists William and John Hunter. Joanna Baillie was born in

---

8. EU Dc.4.101-3.

Bothwell Manse, in 1762. Her brother was George the Third's favourite medical adviser, Matthew Baillie, a physician whose name ranks high among those of the distinguished men that have adorned the British annals of medicine: he died in 1823, and his monument is in Westminster Abbey.

Miss Baillie commenced early in life that literary career which was to extend over more than half a century. The first production that stamped her fame was her "Plays on the Passions," one volume of which appeared in 1798; the second volume was published in 1802. Sir Walter Scott was among the ardent admirers of this work. Mentioning in a letter at that time his own "House of Aspen," he says, "the 'Plays of the Passions' have put me entirely out of conceit with my Germanized brat." His esteem of the talents of the author led, in Miss Baillie's case, as in that of Miss Edgeworth and others, to Scott's acquaintance and friendship with the woman. The cordial and agreeable intimacy between Miss Baillie and Scott, which ceased but with the life of the latter, dates from his introduction to her at Hampstead, in 1806, by the translator and poet, Sotheby. Joanna Baillie herself, many years afterwards, described the interview to a friend as one of the most remarkable events of her life....

To the inexpressible grief of all who knew her, this great poet and excellent woman departed this life on the 23rd, at Hampstead, being at the time close on her ninetieth year. In her death passed away, we believe, the last of those maiden authors whose brilliant list includes the names of Edgeworth, Porter, and Moore, and who rendered the literature of this country, a few years ago, illustrious by their original genius, exquisite fancy, and admirable morality.

Notable in this homage is the mention of Dr. Matthew Baillie's monument in Westminster Abbey, which only serves to make the exclusion of his famous sister more biting. Finally, in a newspaper account in the Wellcome Institute archives, Lydia Sigourney recounted a visit to the writer in Baillie's seventy-sixth year,

> It was a brighter vernal day than often occurs under English skies, when I drove thither from London to see Joanna Baillie. I found her seated on the sofa, in her pleasant parlour, surrounded by many pictures, herself, to me, the most pleasant picture of dignified and healthful age.

On her cheek was somewhat more of colour than usual, for she had just returned from a long walk among her poor pensioners. . . . On the same sofa was her sister Agnes, whom she so intensely loved. . . . Between them was seated Rogers, the banker-poet, with locks like the driven snow. . . . I felt that the world could not furnish another such trio, and was grateful for the privilege of beholding it.[9]

A letter written to her long-time friend Miss Anne Millar from a niece, however, provides a more personal perspective regarding the effects of Baillie's passing:

[1851]

My dear Aunt Millar

I went over yesterday to enquire after Mrs Agnes. M^{r} & Mrs W. Baillie were with her & they were engaged in reading Mrs Joanna's will written by herself on a folio sheet. M^{rs} WB is anxious to write herself to tell you in what way you are remembered therefore I will not say more than that with the exception of several legacies, chiefly books, & small articles of jewelry, gifts from distinguished people, she leaves <u>every thing</u> to Mrs Agnes.

M^{r} & Mrs W.B think it best to make no change in her existence or mode of living, but to leave her at Hampstead with her 3 maids, one of them, they say a superior woman, who manages her mistress judiciously—Her temper, they say, would not allow of her having a lady companion, & they intend to watch over her themselves, & pay her bills once every fortnight or 3 weeks—

I found Mrs Agnes in bed, where they say, she is now most comfortable, & where she misses her Sister less than when down in the Drawing Room—She is quite lively & merry occasionally—then sometimes her mind wanders very much & she asks where her Sister is, & why she does not come to look at her the first thing in a morning—& she cries & is very low—Indeed the changes in her spirits, indicate her extreme feebleness & the slenderness of the thread that still holds her life—I cannot believe any one so aged & so worn

---

9. WI MS 5615/47/3.

can live long[10] —She requires either whiskey or brandy & water in small quantities to be administered at short intervals, but suffers very little, or not at all, from any sort of bodily pain—

When I was with her she talked much of Milheugh, & its beauty & dwelt upon the garden, & she took both my hands & said most earnestly "do tell dear Ann Millar that when I can hold my pen steady I shall write her a few lines"—She had been reading the newspaper herself—& all the reading she does, she manages for herself, as she says she does not like to be read to.

Mr W. B is intending to write a short life of his Aunt, & keeps himself the key of the cabinet that contains her papers & correspondence—Mrs Agnes has a will of her own, but Mr W. B is too delicate to speak to her about it, tho' both Mrs W. B & I think that considering Mrs Agnes present condition, & the servants by whom she is constantly surrounded, it ought to be placed at Coutts'—& not left exposed, or liable to be tampered with—When James comes home I will ask him to advise about it for Mr W. B seems to be almost morbidly afraid of the slightest interference, even as to its safe custody—[11]

I hope my dear Aunt Millar these particulars for which you asked will not tend to make you less cheerful—for my part I cannot look upon Mrs Joanna's death with any pain—she suffered so little at the last & was spared all the fretfulness & irritation that are frequently the accompaniments of advanced age, that I look upon her departure as a calm & dignified withdrawal from the world which she had enjoyed so much & when the full time was come for her to complete the absolute condition upon which we all hold life. James is not likely to be home for a week but writes word he keeps free from cold—The children are well, & I have reason to be thankful—With best wishes for your ancle [sic] & hoping to hear soon, I remain

    yr affec   J __ [12]

---

10. Agnes, in fact, lived much longer, dying 27 April 1861 at the age of 101.

11. There are brief manuscript notes at the Wellcome Institute about Joanna Baillie's life (incorporated herein), but I have not located any "short life" written by her nephew William Baillie.

12. NLS 9235 ff.154-55; *Letters*, 21-23. Signature is unreadable but

Accordingly, Joanna's will, now housed in the London Public Record Office, specified that her body "be laid in the vault in the [Hampstead] Churchyard" near her mother and included some of the following specific personal gifts:

> To Agnes Baillie, "All the money and Property I possess"
>
> To William Baillie, "the copy of Byron's poems in four volumes . . . received so bound from the Author many years ago"
>
> To Henrietta Baillie, "fifty pounds sterling" and various books
>
> To Elizabeth Baillie Milligan, "fifty pounds sterling" and various Scott works
>
> To Robert Milligan, "my Copy of the poem of [Rokeby] received by me from the Author"
>
> To Sophia Milligan, "fifty pounds sterling also a book of Scotch proverbs [?]"
>
> To Mary Milligan, "a collection of Songs in three volumes"
>
> To John Richardson's daughter Joanna, "one hundred pounds sterling"[13]

Appointed as a co-executor with nephew William Baillie, Agnes would pass most of Joanna's personal property on to him almost ten years later. Thus William Baillie is responsible not only for preserving many of her manuscripts, but also for safeguarding Dr. Matthew Baillie's and some of the Hunters' private papers; these would eventually be donated by his heirs to the medical institutions that still maintain them. One interesting point about Joanna Baillie's will is that her charity, both gifts and money, was focused

---

probably Janet Millar.
13. PRO PROB II.2128.

primarily on the women who remained a part of her life. William certainly did not need her capital at this point, so she did not mishandle it.

Inside the Hampstead parish church of St. John, where her mother Dorothea had been laid to rest in 1806 and where her sister Agnes would follow in 1861, a memorial stone near the entrance is inscribed as follows:

SACRED

TO THE MEMORY OF

DOROTHEA BAILLIE

SISTER OF THE CELEBRATED BROTHERS

WILLIAM AND JOHN HUNTER

RELICT OF THE REV^D JAMES BAILLIE, D.D.,

PROFESSOR OF DIVINITY

IN THE UNIVERSITY OF GLASGOW

MOTHER OF THE EMINENT PHYSICIAN

MATTHEW BAILLIE

AND OF TWO DAUGHTERS, AGNES AND JOANNA,

THE LATTER BEING THE DISTINGUISHED AUTHORESS

ALL HERE NAMED WERE THROUGH LIFE HIGHLY RESPECTED

DOROTHEA BAILLIE WAS BORN IN LANARKSHIRE IN 1721

AND DIED AT HAMPSTEAD, SEPTEMBER 30TH 1806.

ALSO TO THE MEMORY OF

AGNES BAILLIE

ELDEST DAUGHTER OF JAMES AND DOROTHEA BAILLIE

SHE WAS BORN IN LANARKSHIRE, SEPTEMBER 24TH 1760

AND DIED AT HAMPSTEAD, APRIL 27TH 1861.

ALSO TO THE MEMORY OF

JOANNA BAILLIE

YOUNGEST DAUGHTER OF JAMES AND DOROTHEA BAILLIE

SHE WAS BORN IN LANARKSHIRE, SEPTEMBER 11^(TH) 1762

AND DIED AT HAMPSTEAD, FEBRUARY 23^(RD) 1851.[14]

This would not, however, be the end of Baillie's commemoration, for in 1899 James Donald erected a monument in her honor at St. Bride's Church, Bothwell, in connection with the restoration of the old parish church in the town of her birth. The terra cotta monument's beautiful mosaic panels, with their inscription of the introduction from *Marmion*'s third canto, were hand made in Venice and are intact today. Inside the church remains a lovely, small portrait of a young Joanna Baillie.[15] A special dedication service also ensued on 12 January 1899, and the *Hamilton Advisor* noted that

> In the centre of the ground which has been acquired, an exceedingly interesting monument has been erected to the memory of Joanna Baillie, who was born in the manse of Bothwell. The monument is 16 ft. in height. . . . On the side fronting the street there is a portrait of Joanna Baillie; on another side there is a reproduction of Horatio M'Culloch's painting of Bothwell Castle; on the third there is a representation of the children of Bothwell in the early days of the poetess; and on the fourth the apple and plum trees of the valley of the Clyde.[16]

Fittingly, these beautiful mosaic representations surrounded the poet's likeness with some of the memories she had held dearest.

Thus Baillie prevailed until the end of the nineteenth century, and then she was obscured for most of the twentieth. In short, Joanna Baillie grew up in rural Scotland, the daughter of a Church of Scotland minister. She played outdoors with parish children, and she nurtured a fertile imagination. She was a performer, and she hated the confinement of school and reading—for even as a child she understood that the key to drama was in performance. These early beginnings assured that she would not be snobbish about

---

14. Camden Historical Society Gravestone Survey by C & D Wade, December 1981 (from Hamilton Central Library files), and marker photographed by this biographer in June 2000.

15. Unfortunately, its companion, a matching portrait of Dr. Matthew Baillie, was stolen some years ago.

16. WI MS 5616/15.

relationships or about literature, and she would later manifest her populist ideals in her works and deeds. Her religious education made her charitable, but her critical mind made her later approach to religion both tolerant and unconventional. She was all her life surrounded by intelligent and powerful men, but she did not see herself as subordinate. For whatever reason, she shunned marriage and used her female dramatic characters to speak about its confinement; many of her closest female friends also remained unmarried. She loved her brother Matthew dearly, and she loved Walter Scott in much the same way. Finally, though she was a popular poet and playwright during her lifetime, she was never satisfied with her success, for she knew that successful drama resulted in representation. Baillie had the same ambition as did the famous men around her, but as a woman she had to accept the level of success *afforded* to women like her, Maria Edgeworth, Felicia Hemans, and others—and, clearly, that was not the same level of success enjoyed by Scott and her other male peers. Baillie was also far ahead of her time in strength and ambition, and her intimacy with the scientific community instilled in her a penchant for experiment—in her case directed at new ways of writing poems and plays. Finally, it is impossible that a woman who dramatized the passions as Baillie did could have been as cool and detached as she appeared to some who knew her. Like the actors in many of her plays, Baillie played the role of a dispassionate gentlewoman. If she had a feminist agenda, however, it was to expose through those plays the inequalities between the sexes, especially in personal and professional relationships.

Playwright and theater theorist Joanna Baillie was a vibrant, intelligent woman confined to a patriarchal world; her life spanned the second half of the eighteenth century and the first half of the nineteenth. Aside from her twenty-seven plays, eight metrical legends, and dozens of poems, her great legacy lies in her eloquent letters from which historians and literary scholars can formulate a sense of the intellectual society emerging with early Romanticism. Hers was a time of social, political, and intellectual change, prompted not only by two major revolutions, but also by major shifts in literary style and focus of the imagination. Baillie was a participant in her era and commented on the salient issues of her time. She was never simply a spectator. As Anne Mellor concludes, through the historical, cultural, and political philosophies implicit in her critical introductions and dramas, Scottish nationalist Joanna Baillie often "positions herself as the unacknowledged legislator of the British Nation."[17] To conclude, as some writers have done, that she was unaware of the world outside Hampstead or that her life was uneventful and her later years pitiable is both uninformed and critically naive, for even Baillie's later letters reveal a tenacious and ambitious woman who was receiving visits from friends and family, publishing *Ahalya Baee: a poem* in 1849, and editing her complete works nearly to the time of her death in 1851 at the age of eighty-eight.[18] What is pitiable, however, is Baillie's lack of genuine acceptance in a male-dominated literary society which, while it may have accepted her as an accomplished "gentlewoman," marginalized her critical intelligence and afforded her visibility mostly through her relationships with famous men, from her uncles and brother to Sir Walter Scott and onward. But Joanna Baillie somehow prevailed as a student of human nature and as a strong, creative feminist.

---

17. Mellor, *Mothers*, 42.
18. For whatever reason, Carhart states that Baillie's closing years were "pathetic" (66).

Bibliography

Primary Sources

The primary sources listed below are identified by repository and manuscript collection number.

Bodleian Library, Oxford University. Ms. Autogr. c. 24, ff.183–184; Ms. Eng. Lett. c. 742, ff.229–232; Ms. Eng. Lett. c. 133, ff.18–33; Ms. Talbot c. 19, ff.7–8, ff.17–18 and ff.33–34; Ms. Montagu d. 6, f.73; Dept. Lovelace Byron 62, ff.47–212; Dept. Lovelace Byron 77, ff.65–6; Dept. Lovelace Byron 168, ff.85–97; Dept. Lovelace Byron 93, ff.158–244.

British Library. Add. Ms. 18,204: f. 47, f. 49; Add. Ms. 20,081: f. 12; Add. Ms. 33,544: f. 159; Add. Ms. 33,545: f. 603; Add. Ms. 33,546: f. 24, f. 175, f. 187, f. 315, f. 518, f. 526, f. 534, f. 538–540, f. 542, f. 544–545; Add. Ms. 35,263: f. 217, f. 219, ff. 221–24, f. 227, ff. 229–31, f. 239, f. 247, f. 257, f. 299, f. 304, f. 306, f. 312, f. 318; Add. Ms. 35,264: f. 3, f. 58, f. 80, f. 98, f. 102, f. 219, f. 305, f. 308; Add. Ms. 35,265: f. 69, f. 79, f. 81, f. 106, f. 108, f. 110, f. 173, f. 180, f. 249, f. 261, f. 284, f. 286, f. 290, f. 320; Add. Ms. 37,949: f. 337; Add. Ms. 38,794: f. 1; Add. Ms. 39,316: f. 63; Add. Ms. 40, 856: f. 90; Add. Ms. 41,964: f. 296; Add. Ms. 42,575: f. 28, f. 30; Add. Ms. 46,138: f. 213.

Brotherton Library, Leeds University. Autogr. Let.: Vol. 1, 19; Vol. 1, 20; Vol. 1, 30; Album: (1 letter); Crabbe: Vol. IV, 121, Vol. IV, 122.

Cambridge University Library. Add.8546/I/13; Add.8546/I/14.

Camden Local Studies and Archives Centre and Swiss Cottage Library, London. Letters to Dr. William Beattie (1–15), Letter to Mr. Haines (1), Letters to Margaret Holford Hodson (1–102) and Fragment, Letters to Mrs. Walker (1–2), Unidentified Recipient (1).

Courtney Library, Royal Institution of Cornwall. Enys Autograph Collection No. 66.

Dartmouth College, Baker Library. Mss. Ticknor 840116, 001473, 839229/1.

Devon Record Office. Record 5333M/E1.

Edinburgh University. Gen. 199/31; Gen. 1730 (B24); Gen. 1730 (B23); Gen. 1730 (B27); Gen. 1730 (B34); Dc.4.101–3; La.II.585; La.II.585/1; La.III.584/28; La.IV.6; 23 April 1854 (Corson Collection, letter to Lady Smith); 13 May 1838 (Corson

Collection, letter to Mr. Cunningham); 13 May 1988 (Corson Collection, letter to Anne Elliott).
Fitzwilliam Museum, Cambridge. Holland, ALS, 29/2; MS.3-1966: 104r/v; Henderson. Vol. 1:27/1-4.
Folger Shakespeare Library. To Miss Berry, 1814.
Harrowby Mss Trust. To Sarah [Bentham].
Harry Ransom Humanities Research Center, University of Texas. ALS to Unidentified Recipient; ALS to Bartley; ALS to Gamble; ALS to Hemans; ALS to Mrs. Hoare; ALS to Hartley Coleridge; ALS to Jones, Mrs.- Misc. Sara Coleridge; Ms. Coleridge, Sara (Coleridge) Recip.-3 ALS to Sara Coleridge.
Hornby Library, Liverpool City Libraries. Boaden Vol. 2:254; Kemble Vol. 1:255; Vol. 2:255; Picton Autograph Letters.
Houghton Library, Harvard University. MS Eng 944 (Nos. 1–39).
Huntington Library. KAL44–48; HM1505; HM11404; HM19701-03; HM26145–47; HM31515; HM41082; Sy1; TA191; Rare Book 109990.
Keele University Library. John Anderson Scrapbook, f.61.
Lilly Library, Indiana University. Eng. Lit. MS. (Baillie—No address or postmark).
Mitchell Library, Glasgow City Libraries. Cowie Collection 204c–232c.
National Library of Scotland. 124 ff.18-24; 124 ff.41-44; 581 ff.430.11-12; 581 ff.553.236; 740 ff.29-30; 786 ff.41-48; 851 ff.1-46; 866 ff.68-72; 866 ff.81-82; 867 ff.80-82; 934 No.9; 931 Nos.38-54; 1002 ff.8-14; 1551 ff.229-230; 1553 ff.181-182; 1554 ff.13-14; 1554 f.67; 1558 ff.1-8; 2255 ff.4-5; 1750 ff.109, 118, 140; 2522 ff.1-2; 2524 ff.34-35; 2524 ff.46-48; 2524 ff.74-75; 3278 ff.181-82; 3435 ff.127-30; 3435 f.139; 3435 ff.144-45; 3436 ff.144-45; 3436 ff.168-69; 3436 ff.222-23; 3519 ff.53-54 ; 3519 ff.67-68; 3653 ff.26-27; 3876 ff.48-49; 3876 ff.239-40; 3877 ff.3-7; 3877 ff.39-40; 3877 ff.59-60; 3877 ff.97-98; 3877 ff.158-61; 3878 ff.78-79; 3878 ff.180-84; 3878 ff.189-90; 3879 ff.13-15; 3879 ff.17-18; 3879 ff.33-35; 3879 ff.38-39; 3879 ff.40-41; 3879 ff.47-49; 3879 ff.67-68; 3879 ff.88-90a; 3879 ff.126-128; 3879 ff.156-58; 3879 ff.236-39; 3879 ff.266-69; 3880 ff.25-29; 3880 ff.172-76; 3881 ff.15-19; 3881 ff.122-26; 3882 ff.7-11; 3882 ff.99-103; 3882 ff.128-31; 3882 ff.169-72; 3883 ff.73-76; 3883 ff.105-06; 3883 ff.118-21; 3883 ff.152-53; 3884 ff.26-29; 3884 ff.75-76; 3884 ff.184-191; 3885 ff.31-32; 3885 ff.37-39; 3886 ff.22-25; 3886 f.39; 3886 ff.162-165; 3886 ff.188-90; 3886 ff.208-88 ff.235-37; 3889 ff.135-36; 3889 ff.182-84; 3889 ff.279-80; 3890 ff.3-5; 3890 ff.132-35; 3890

ff.216–17; 3891 ff.3–4; 3891 ff.136–37; 3893 ff.21–24; 3894
ff.37–39; 3894 ff.83–84; 3894 ff.195–96; 3894 ff.226–27; 3895
ff.57–58; 3895 ff.207–08; 3895 ff.241–42; 3896 ff.9–10; 3896
ff.104–05; 3897 ff.3–4; 3897 ff.84–86; 3898 ff.56–57; 3898
ff.81–83; 3898 ff.163–66; 3899 ff.298; 3900 ff.93–95; 3901
ff.113–14; 3902 ff.157–61; 3903 ff.131–33; 3905 ff.260–61; 3908
ff.78–79; 3910 ff.7–9; 6294 ff.51–52; 7439 f.86–93; 9236 ff.1–7;
9236 ff.84–85; 9819 ff.11–12; 10279 ff.65–70; 10995 ff.37–40;
11000 ff.5–10; 15975 f.84; 20437 ff.101–15; 20768 f.115–16; Acc
8663 (19 letters); Acc 9026; Acc 9467 (17 letters); Acc 10479.
New York Public Library. Berg Collection: A.L.S. (m.b.) Baillie to
Henrietta Baillie 1l; Baillie to Dorothea Primrose Campbell 1l;
Baillie to Mrs Farrer 1l; Baillie to William Harness 3 p; Baillie to
Felicia Dorothea Hemans 2l; Baillie to Longman [?] 1l, 2l; Baillie
to Sophy Milligan, Scott letter books, 1:49; Baillie to John
Murray 1l; Baillie to Samuel Rogers 1l; Baillie to Robert Southey
3 p.
——. Pforzheimer Collection: Misc. 3170, Misc. 876, Misc. 3171, Misc.
1343, Misc. 3200, Misc. 3169, Misc. 3383.
Pierpont Morgan Library. Coleorton MA 1581/1–3; MA 2922; Misc.
English Autographs R–V (2 letters).
Public Record Office, London. PRO ref. B3/4340; PRO PROB
11/1676; PRO PROB II.2128.
Robinson Library, University of Newcastle. Trevelyan: GOT 163;
GOT 183:185.
Royal Academy of Art. LAW/2/5, LAW/2/95, LAW/2/122,
LAW/2/124–125, LAW/2/179, LAW/4/95, LAW/5/38,
LAW/5/409.
Royal College of Physicians and Surgeons of Glasgow. RCPSG 30.
Royal College of Surgeons of England. HB.i. 4; HB.ii.19–20, HB.ii.39,
HB.ii.44–45, HB.ii.56c, HB.ii.70, HB.ii.85; HB.v.83, HB.v.86–87,
HB.v.86, HB.v.90; HB.ix.1, HB.ix.8–9, HB.ix.11–36b, HB.ix.39–40,
HB.ix.42, HB.ix.44–45, HB.ix.49–54, HB.ix.56, HB.ix.58–60,
HB.ix.62–67.
Royal Society. HS3.17–26.
John Rylands Research Institute, University of Manchester. English
Ms 351/9; English Ms 372/89; English Ms 732/7 (fragment).
Scottish Record Office. GD88/1/16.
Trinity College, Cambridge. Cullum Q111.
University of Birmingham. H. M. Philip Autograph Album, 55a;
Geo. Gregory, L. Add. 1900 and 1902.
University College London. Sharpe Collection 14/26, 14/28–29,

14/31, 14/33, 14/35, 14/37, 14/39–40, 14/42, 14/44–47, 14/49, 14/51–53, 14/55, 208/19.
University of Glasgow. MS Gen 519/3–7, MS Gen 519/10–12, MS Gen 542/1–14, MS Gen 542/16–17, MS Gen 542/19–21, MS Gen 1515/8, MS Gen 1587:5, MS Gen 1587:51, MS Gen 1587:67, MS Gen 1587:69, MS Gen 1587:77, MS Gen 1587:79.
University of Nottingham, Hallward Library. My 815–824, My 937.
University of Reading. Longman Collection: To Mrs. Smith; To Thomas Longman; To Unknown Recipient; To Louisa [Longman]; Epithet for Maria Fanshawe.
Victoria and Albert Museum. D.26.E3, 1:6; D.26.E3, 1:7.
Wellcome Institute for the History of Medicine. MSS. 5608/36–42, 5608/44; 5613/13–14, 5613/16, 5613/19–20, 5613/38, 5613/55, 5613/58, 5613/60, 5613/68/1–6; 5614/38; 5615/32–33, 5615/37, 5615/47/3, 5615/84, 5615/96, 5615/104, 5615/109/1–2, 5615/128; 5616/1, 5616/9, 5616/15, 5616/46, 5616/48, 5616/50, 5616/62, 5616/64–70, 5616/72; 5617/85, 5617/87, 5617/89.
Dr. Williams's Library, London. Henry Crabbe Robinson Collection: Autographs, Bundle 8.27 II–IV.
Wisbech and Fenland Museum. Ms. to William Smyth.
Wordsworth Trust, Dove Cottage. Letter to William Wordsworth; Letter to Mrs. Henry Coleridge; Letter to Dr. Bell.

Secondary Sources

Aleksuik, Natasha. "Joanna Baillie's 'Thunder' in 1790 and 1840." *Notes and Queries* 48.2: 132–36.
Almedingen, E. M. *The Emperor Alexander I*. New York: Vanguard, 1964.
Altick, Richard D. *Victorian People and Ideas*. New York: Norton, 1973.
Anderson, W. E. K., ed. *The Journal of Sir Walter Scott*. Oxford: Clarendon, 1972.
"Art. IX.–1. Childe Harold's Pilgrimage, Canto III . . . and other Poems." *The Quarterly Review* XVI:XXXI (1816): 172–208.
"Art. XII. Metrical Legends of exalted Characters." *The Monthly Review* XCVI (1821): 72–81.
Ashton, Rosemary. *The Life of Samuel Taylor Coleridge*. Oxford: Blackwell, 1996.
Ayling, Stanley. *George the Third*. New York: Knopf, 1972.
Backscheider, Paula R. *Reflections on Biography*. Oxford and New

York: Oxford University Press, 1999.
Baillie, James William. *Lives of the Baillies*. Edinburgh: Edmonston and Douglas, 1872.
Baillie, Joanna. *The Dramatic and Poetical Works of Joanna Baillie*. London: Longman, Brown, Green, and Longmans, 1851.
——. *Fugitive Verses*. London: Moxon, 1840.
——. "A Lesson Intended for the Use of the Hampstead School." Camden Town: Miller, 1826.
——. *Plays on the Passions*. Ed. Peter Duthie. Ontario: Broadview, 2001.
——. *Poems, 1790*. Ed. Jonathan Wordsworth. Oxford and New York: Woodstock, 1994.
——. *The Selected Poems of Joanna Baillie, 1762–1851*. Ed. Jennifer Breen. Manchester, England: Manchester University Press, 1999.
——. *A Series of Plays: in which it is attempted to delineate the stronger passions of the mind*. Ed. Donald H. Reiman. 3 vols. 1798–1812. New York and London: Garland, 1977.
——. *A View of the General Tenour of the New Testament Regarding the Nature and Dignity of Jesus Christ*. 2d ed. London: n.p., 1838.
Baillie, Joanna, ed. *A Collection of Poems, Chiefly Manuscript, and from Living Authors*. London: Longman, Hurst, Rees, Orme, and Brown, 1823.
Baines, F. E., ed. *Records of the Manor, Parish, and Borough of Hampstead in the County of London, to December 31st, 1889*. London: Whittaker and Co., 1890.
Bell, John, ed. *Bell's Edition of Shakespeare's Plays, As they are now performed at the Theatres Royal in London*. London: John Bell, 1774.
Bennett, Susan. "Genre trouble: Joanna Baillie, Elizabeth Polack—tragic subjects, melodramatic subjects." *Women and Playwriting in Nineteenth-Century Britain*. Cambridge: Cambridge University Press, 1999.
Blain, Virginia, Patricia Clements, and Isobel Grundy, eds. *The Feminist Companion to Literature in English: Women Writers from the Middle Ages to the Present*. New Haven: Yale University Press, 1990.
Bloom, Edward A., and Lillian D. Bloom, eds. *The Piozzi Letters: Correspondence of Hester Lynch Piozzi, 1784–1821*. 3 vols. Newark: University of Delaware Press, 1991.
Bolton, H. Philip. *Scott Dramatized*. London: Mansell, 1992.
Bond, R. Warwick, ed. *The Marlay Letters, 1778–1820*. London: Constable, 1937.

Booth, Michael R. "Nineteenth-Century Theatre." *The Oxford Illustrated History of the Theatre*. Ed. John Russell Brown. Oxford and New York: Oxford University Press, 2001.
Borer, Mary Cathcart, *Willingly to School: A History of Women's Education*. London: Lutterworth Press, 1975.
Brewer, William D. "Joanna Baillie and Lord Byron." *KSJ* 44 (1995): 165-81.
——. "The Prefaces of Joanna Baillie and William Wordsworth." *Friend: Comment on Romanticism* 1.2-3 (1991-92): 34-47.
British Museum General Catalogue of Printed Books to 1955. 253 vols. London: Trustees of the British Museum, 1965.
Broadie, Alexander, ed. *The Scottish Enlightenment: An Anthology*. Edinburgh: Canongate, 1997.
Brown, Arthur W. *Margaret Fuller*. New York: Twayne, 1964.
Bugajski, Ken A. "Joanna Baillie: An Annotated Bibliography." *Romanticism on the Net* 12 (Nov. 1998).
Burnet, Sir Macfarlane. *Natural History of Infectious Disease*. 3d ed. Cambridge: Cambridge University Press, 1962.
Burns, Robert. *The Poems and Songs of Robert Burns*. Ed. James Kinsley. 2 vols. Oxford: Clarendon, 1968.
Burroughs, Catherine B. *Closet Stages: Joanna Baillie and the Theater Theory of British Romantic Women Writers*. Philadelphia: University of Pennsylvania Press, 1997.
——. "English Romantic Women Writers and Theatre Theory: Joanna Baillie's Prefaces to the *Plays on the Passions*." *Re-Visioning Romanticism: British Women Writers, 1776-1837*. Ed. Carol Shiner Wilson and Joel Haefner. Philadelphia: University of Pennsylvania Press, 1994.
——. "Out of the Pale of Social Kindred Cast." *Romantic Women Writers: Voices and Countervoices*. Ed. Paula R. Feldman and Theresa M. Kelley. Hanover and London: University Press of New England, 1995.
Butler, Marilyn. *Maria Edgeworth: A Literary Biography*. Oxford: Clarendon, 1972.
Buttrick, George Arthur, ed. *The Interpreter's Dictionary of the Bible: An Illustrated Encyclopedia*. 4 vols. and Supplement. New York: Abingdon Press, 1962.
Cannon, John, ed. *The Oxford Companion to British History*. Oxford and New York: Oxford University Press, 1997.
Carhart, Margaret S. *The Life and Work of Joanna Baillie*. Vol. 64 of *Yale Studies in English*. New Haven: Yale University Press, 1923.
Carswell, Donald. *Sir Walter: A Four-Part Study in Biography (Scott,*

Hogg, Lockhart, Joanna Baillie). London: Murray, 1930.
Carver, Anne. *The Story of Duntisbourne Abbots*. Gloucester: Albert E. Smith, 1966.
Clarke, Edwin, M.D., F.R.C.P., ed. "James Douglas of the Pouch." *Medical History: A Quarterly Journal Devoted to the History of Medicine and Related Sciences* 18 (1974): 162–71 and 379–402.
Clayden, P. W. *Rogers and His Contemporaries*. 2 vols. London: Smith, Elder, 1889.
Coleridge, Edith, ed. *Memoir and Letters of Sara Coleridge Edited by Her Daughter*. New York: Harper and Brothers, 1874.
Coleridge, Hartley. *Poems by Hartley Coleridge, With A Memoir Of His Life By His Brother, in Two Volumes*. London: Edward Moxon, 1851.
Connelly, Owen. *Blundering to Glory: Napoleon's Military Campaigns*. Wilmington, DE: Scholarly Resources, 1984.
Conway, Stephen, ed. *The Correspondence of Jeremy Bentham*. Oxford: Clarendon, 1994.
Court, Franklin E. "The early impact of Scottish literary teaching in North America." *The Scottish Invention of English Literature*. Ed. Robert Crawford. Cambridge: Cambridge University Press, 1998.
Cox, Jeffrey N. *Seven Gothic Dramas, 1789–1825*. Athens: Ohio University Press, 1992.
Crainz, Franco. *The Life and Works of Matthew Baillie, MD, FRS, L&E, FRCP, etc. (1761–1823)*. Santa Palomba, Italy: PelitiAssociati, 1995.
Crawford, Thomas. *Burns: A Study of the Poems and Songs*. Stanford: Stanford University Press, 1960.
Davis, Tracy D., and Ellen Donkin, eds. Introduction to *Women and Playwriting in Nineteenth-Century Britain*. Cambridge: Cambridge University Press, 1999.
Dictionary of American Biography. Ed. Allen Johnson. 20 vols. New York: Charles Scribner's Sons, 1929.
Dictionary of National Biography. Ed. Sir Leslie Stephen and Sir Sidney Lee. 22 vols. London: Oxford University Press, 1938–.
Dictionary of Scientific Biography. Ed. Charles Coulston Gillispie. New York: Charles Scribner's Sons, 1972.
Dictionary of Scottish History. Ed. Gordon Donaldson and Robert Morpeth. Edinburgh: John Donald, 1977.
Dobson, Jessie. *John Hunter*. Edinburgh and London: Livingstone, 1969.
Dodge, Theodore Ayrault. *Napoleon, A History of the Art of War, From*

the Beginning of the French Revolution to the End of the Eighteenth Century, With a Detailed Account of the Wars of the French Revolution. 4 vols. 1904–7. New York: AMS, 1970.
Donkin, Ellen. "Joanna Baillie vs. The Termites Bellicosus." *Getting into the Act: Women Playwrights in London, 1776–1829*. London and New York: Routledge, 1994.
Donoghue, Emma. *Passions Between Women: British Lesbian Culture 1668–1801*. New York: Harper Collins, 1995.
Dowd, Maureen A. "'By the Delicate Hand of a Female': Melodramatic Mania and Joanna Baillie's Spectacular Tragedies." *European Romantic Review* 9.4 (1998): 469–500.
Duthie, Peter, ed. *Plays on the Passions*. Ontario: Broadview, 2001.
Dwyer, David. "Introduction—A 'Peculiar Blessing': Social Converse in Scotland from Hutcheson to Burns." *Sociability and Society in Eighteenth-Century Scotland*. Ed. John Dwyer and Richard B. Sher. Edinburgh: Mercat Press, 1993.
Dyce, Alexander, ed. *Recollections of the Table-Talk of Samuel Rogers*. London: Moxon, 1856.
Edgell, David P. *William Ellery Channing, An Intellectual Portrait*. Boston: Beacon Press, 1955.
Ellis, Grace A. *A Memoir of Mrs. Anna Laetitia Barbauld, with Many of Her Letters*. Boston: James R. Osgood, 1874.
Elwin, Malcolm. *Lord Byron's Wife*. London: Macdonald, 1962.
The Encyclopedia of Religion. New York: Macmillan, 1987.
Evans, David S., et al., eds. *Herschel at the Cape: Diaries and Correspondence of Sir John Herschel, 1834–1838*. Austin: University of Texas Press, 1969.
Evans, G. Blakemore, ed. *The Riverside Shakespeare*. Boston: Houghton Mifflin, 1974.
Eyre-Todd, George. *History of Glasgow*. 3 vols. Glasgow: Jackson, Wylie and Company, 1934.
Ferguson, William. *Scotland 1689 to Present*. 4 vols. Edinburgh: Oliver and Boyd, 1968.
Flynn, Philip. *Francis Jeffrey*. Newark: University of Delaware Press, 1978.
Friedman-Romell, Beth H. "Staging the state: Joanna Baillie's 'Constantine Paleologus'." *Woman and Playwriting in Nineteenth-Century Britain*. Ed. Tracy C. Davis and Ellen Donkin. Cambridge: Cambridge University Press, 1999.
Fullmer, June A. *Young Humphry Davy: The Making of an Experimental Chemist*. Philadelphia: American Philosophical Society, 2000.

Gamer, Michael. "National Supernaturalism: Joanna Baillie, Germany, and the Gothic Drama." *Theatre Survey* 38.2 (1997): 49–88.

Gilbert, Deirdre. "Joanna Baillie, Passionate Anatomist: From Masquerade to Gothic." Ph.D. diss., University of Denver, 2002.

Gill, Stephen. *William Wordsworth: A Life*. Oxford: Clarendon Press, 1989.

Goldring, Douglas. *Regency Portrait Painter: The Life of Sir Thomas Lawrence, P.R.A.* London: Macdonald, 1951.

Gordon, George, Lord Byron. *The Complete Poetical and Dramatic Works of Lord Byron with a Comprehensive Outline of the Life of the Poet*. Ed. John Nichols and J. C. Jeaffreson. Philadelphia: David McKay, 1883.

Greig, J. Y. T., ed. *The Letters of David Hume*. 2 vols. Oxford: Clarendon, 1932.

Greig, James A. *Francis Jeffrey of The Edinburgh Review*. Edinburgh: Oliver and Boyd, 1948.

Grierson, H. J. C., ed. *The Letters of Sir Walter Scott*. 12 vols. London: Constable, 1932–37.

Guildhall Pamphlet FO 2218. "Joanna Baillie and Her Circle, 1790–1850." London: National Trust, Hampstead Center and Camden History Society, 1973.

Guildhall Pamphlet FO 3155. "The Literary Associations of Hampstead." *The Bookman* 5 (1893): 14–15.

Hadden, J. Cuthbert. *George Thomson, The Friend of Burns: His Life & Correspondence*. London: John C. Nimmo, 1898.

Hare, Augustus J. C., ed. *The Life and Letters of Maria Edgeworth*. 2 vols. London: Edward Arnold, 1894.

Hartnoll, Phyllis, ed. *The Oxford Companion to the Theatre*. 4th ed. Oxford: Oxford University Press, 1983.

Hazlitt, William. *Lectures on the English Poets*. London: Taylor and Hessey, 1818.

Heilburn, Carolyn G. *Writing a Woman's Life*. New York: Ballantine Books, 1988.

Hemans, Felicia. *Records of Woman*. 1828. Ed. Donald H. Reiman. New York: Garland, 1978.

Henderson, Andrea. "Passion and Fashion in Joanna Baillie's 'Introductory Discourse'." *PMLA* (March 1997): 198–213.

Hibbert, Christopher. *George IV, Regent and King, 1811–1830*. New York: Harper and Row, 1973.

Hodson, Margaret Holford. *Warbeck of Wolfstein*. By Miss Holford, Author of *Wallace*. 3 vols. London: Rodwell and Martin, 1820.

Hoskin, Michael A. *William Herschel and the Construction of the Heavens*. New York: W. W. Norton, 1963.
Howitt, William. *The Northern Heights of London, or Historical Associations of Hampstead, Highgate, Museum Hill, Hornsey, and Islington*. London: Longmans, Green, and Company, 1869.
"Index Indicators." *The Gentleman's Magazine* 2 (1817): 194.
Index to Monuments. Camden: Camden Local Studies and Archives Centre, 1986.
James, Edward T., ed. *Notable American Women 1607–1950: A Biographical Dictionary*. 4 vols. Cambridge: Harvard University Press, 1971.
Jeffrey, Francis. [Rev.] "Miss Baillie's *Dramas*." *The Edinburgh Review* 63 (1836): 73–101.
———. [Rev.] "Miss Baillie's *Miscellaneous Plays*." *The Edinburgh Review* 5 (1804–5): 405–21.
———. [Rev.] "*A Series of Plays*, etc., Vol. 3." *The Edinburgh Review* 19 (1811–12): 261–90.
"Joanna Bailey [sic]." *The Dramatic Censor; or, Weekly Theatrical Report. Comprising, in the Form of a Journal, A Complete History of the Stage* XVIII (April 1800).
Johnson, Edgar. *Sir Walter Scott: The Great Unknown*. 2 vols. New York: Macmillan, 1970.
Johnston, Judith. *Anna Jameson: Victorian, Feminist, Woman of Letters*. Hants, England: Scolar Press, 1997.
Kates, Gary. *Monsieur d'Eon Is a Woman: A Tale of Political Intrigue and Sexual Masquerade*. Baltimore: Johns Hopkine University Press, 2001.
Kobler, J. *The Reluctant Surgeon: A Biography of John Hunter*. Edinburgh and London: Livingstone, 1969.
Lambertson, Chester Lee. "The Letters of Joanna Baillie (1801–1832)." Ph.D. diss., Harvard University, 1956.
Landsman, Ned C. "Presbyterians and Provincial Society: The Evangelical Enlightenment in the West of Scotland, 1740–1775." *Sociability and Society in Eighteenth-Century Scotland*. Ed. John Dwyer and Richard B. Sher. Edinburgh: Mercat Press, 1993.
Le Breton, Philip Hemery, ed. *Memoirs, Miscellanies and Letters of the Late Lucy Aikin*. London: Longman, Green, Longman, Roberts, and Green, 1864.
Lewis, Lady Theresa, ed. *Extracts of the Journals and Correspondence of Miss Berry from the Year 1783 to 1852*. 3 vols. London: Longmans, Green, and Co., 1865.
Lewis, Tess. "Madame de Staël: The Inveterate Idealist." *The Hudson*

Review LIV:3 (2001): 416-26.

Lochhead, Marion. *John Gibson Lockhart*. London: John Murray, 1954.

Lockhart, John Gibson. *Memoirs of the Life of Sir Walter Scott*. 5 vols. Boston and New York: Houghton Mifflin, 1901.

Looser, Devoney. *British Women Writers and the Writing of History, 1670–1820*. Baltimore: Johns Hopkins University Press, 2000.

Mackay, James A. *William Wallace: brave heart*. Edinburgh and London: Mainstream, 1995.

MacLaren, I. F. "Quality Control in Surgical Training." *Journal of the Royal College of Surgeons, Edinburgh* 33 (1988): 98–102.

Marchand, Leslie A. *Byron, A Biography*. 3 vols. New York: Knopf, 1957.

——. ed. *Byron's Letters and Journals*. 12 vols. Cambridge: Harvard University Press, 1973–82.

Mather, G. R. *Two Great Scotsmen, The Brothers William and John Hunter*. Glasgow: James Maclehose, 1894.

Martineau, Harriet. *Harriet Martineau's Autobiography*. Ed. Maria Weston Chapman. 6th ed. 2 vols. Boston: Osgood, 1877.

Mayne, Ethyl Colburn. *The Life and Letters of Anne Isabella, Lady Noel Byron*. New York: Charles Scribner's Sons, 1929.

McCarthy, William, and Elizabeth Kraft, eds. *The Poems of Anna Laetitia Barbauld*. Athens: University of Georgia Press, 1994.

McGann, Jerome J. *Lord Byron: The Complete Poetical Works*. Oxford: Clarendon, 1980.

McKerrow, Mary. "Joanna Baillie and Mary Brunton: Women of the Manse." *Living by the Pen: Early British Women Writers*. Ed. Dale Spender. New York and London: Teachers College Press, 1992.

Mellor, Anne K. "A Criticism of Their Own: Romantic Women Literary Critics." *Questioning Romanticism*. Ed. John Beer. Baltimore: Johns Hopkins University Press, 1995.

——. *Mothers of the Nation: Women's Political Writing in England, 1780–1830*. Bloomington and Indianapolis: University of Indiana Press, 2000.

Melville, Lewis. *The Berry Papers: Being the Correspondence Hitherto Unpublished of Mary and Agnes Berry (1763–1852)*. London: John Lane, 1914.

Miller, Mary Ruth. *Thomas Campbell*. Boston: Twayne, 1978.

"Miss Baillie's *Miscellaneous Plays*." *The Edinburgh Review* 5 (1804–5): 405–21.

Mitchell, Sally, ed. *Victorian Britain: An Encyclopedia*. New York and London: Garland, 1988.

Moir, George. "Miss Baillie's *Dramas.*" *The Edinburgh Review* 63 (1836): 73–101.
Moore, Doris Langley. *Ada, Countess of Lovelace, Byron's Legitimate Daughter.* London: Murray, 1977.
———. *The Late Lord Byron: Posthumous Dramas.* Philadelphia and New York: J. B. Lippincott, 1961.
Moore, Thomas, Esq. *Letters and Journals of Lord Byron: with Notices of His Life.* 2 vols. New York: J. and J. Harper, 1830.
Nagler, A. M. *A Source Book in Theatrical History.* New York: Dover, 1952.
National Union Catalog Pre 1956 Imprints. 754 vols. London: Mansell, 1974.
Nesbitt, George L. *Benthamite Reviewing: The First Twelve Years of The Westminster Review, 1824–1836.* New York: Columbia University Press, 1934.
New Century Cyclopedia of Names. Ed. Clarence L. Barnhart. 3 vols. New York: Appleton-Century-Crofts, 1954.
Nicoll, Allardyce. *A History of Early Nineteenth-Century Drama.* 2 vols. Cambridge: Cambridge University Press, 1930.
Noble, Aloma E. "Joanna Baillie as a Dramatic Artist." Ph.D. diss., University of Iowa, 1983.
Noyes, Russell, ed. Introduction to "Sir Walter Scott" in *English Romantic Poetry and Prose.* New York: Oxford University Press, 1956.
Onuf, Peter F., ed. *Jeffersonian Legacies.* Charlottesville: University Press of Virginia, 1993.
O'Reilly, W. H. "Unpublished Letters of Joanna Baillie to a Dumfriesshire Laird." *Dumfriesshire and Galloway Natural History and Antiquarian Society: Transactions and Journal of Proceedings* 18 (1934): 10–27.
Ousby, Ian, ed. *The Cambridge Guide to Literature in English.* Cambridge and New York: Cambridge University Press, 1993.
Oxford Companion to English Literature. Ed. Margaret Drabble. London: Oxford University Press, 1995.
Parkes, Henry Bamford. *The United States of America: A History.* 3d ed. New York: Knopf, 1968.
Peachy, G. C. *A Memoir of William and John Hunter.* Plymouth: William Brendon, 1924.
Pearson, Jacqueline. *Women's Reading in Britain 1750–1835: A Dangerous Recreation.* Cambridge: Cambridge University Press, 1999.
Poe, Edgar Allan. "Critical Notices." *Southern Literary Messenger*

(August 1835): 714–16.

Pool, Daniel. *What Jane Austen Ate and Charles Dickens Knew: From Fox Hunting to Whist—the Facts of Daily Life in 19th-Century England*. New York: Touchstone, 1993.

Porter, Roy. *Health for Sale: Quackery in England, 1660–1850*. Manchester: Manchester University Press, 1989.

Purinton, Marjean D. *Romantic Ideology Unmasked: The Mentally Constructed Tyrannies in Dramas of William Wordsworth, Lord Byron, Percy Shelley, and Joanna Baillie*. Newark: University of Delaware Press, 1994.

——. "The Sexual Politics of *The Election*: French Feminism and the Scottish Playwright Joanna Baillie." *Intertexts* 2.2 (1998): 119–30.

Quayle, Eric. *The Ruin of Sir Walter Scott*. London: Rupert Hart Davis, 1968.

Radley, Virginia L. *Samuel Taylor Coleridge*. New York: Twayne, 1966.

Randall, Willard Sterne. *Thomas Jefferson, A Life*. New York: Henry Holt, 1993.

Reid, H. M. B. *The Divinity Professors in the University of Glasgow*. 2 vols. Glasgow: Maclehose, Jackson and Company, 1923.

Reiman, Donald H., ed. Introduction to *A Series of Plays: in which it is attempted to delineate the stronger passions of the mind*. 3 vols. 1798–1812. New York and London: Garland, 1977.

——. ed. Introduction to *William Sotheby. Saul and Constance de Castille. Romantic Context: Poetry*. New York and London: Garland, 1978.

[Rev. of Baillie's *Dramas*.] *The Athenæum* January 1836: 4.

Robinson, Henry Crabbe. *Diary, Reminiscences, and Correspondence*. Ed. Thomas Sadler. Boston: Houghton, 1876.

Rogers, R. E. *Samuel Rogers and His Circle*. London: Methuen, 1910.

Rosenthal, Laura J. *Playwrights and Plagiarists in Early Modern England: Gender, Authorship, Literary Property*. Ithaca and London: Cornell University Press, 1996.

——. "The Sublime, the Beautiful, 'The Siddons'." *The Clothes That Wear Us: Essays on Dressing and Transgressing in Eighteenth-Century Culture*. Ed. Jessica Munns and Penny Richards. Newark: University of Delaware Press, 1999.

Rosslyn Hill Chapel: A Short History, 1692–1973. Hampstead: Rosslyn Hill Chapel, 1974.

Rudolph, C. Robert. "Annual General Meeting Address." Hunterian Society, 139th Session 1964–65. London: Metropolis Press, 1965.

Schlueter, Paul, and June Schlueter, eds. *An Encyclopedia of British*

Women Writers. New York and London: Garland, 1988.
Scott, Sir Walter. *The Miscellaneous Prose Works of Sir Walter Scott, Bart.* 3 vols. Edinburgh: Cadell, 1847.
—. *The Poetical Works of Sir Walter Scott.* 3 vols. Edinburgh: James Nichol, 1858.
Scottish National Dictionary. Ed. William Grant. Edinburgh: Riverside Press, 1941.
Scullion, Adrienne. "Some Women of the Nineteenth-century Scottish Theatre: Joanna Baillie, Frances Wright and Helen Macgregor." *A History of Scottish Women's Writing.* Ed. Douglas Gifford and Dorothy McMillan. Edinburgh: Edinburgh University Press, 1997.
"*A Series of Plays*, etc." *The Critical Review* 24 (1798): 13–22.
"*A Series of Plays*, etc." *The Critical Review* 37 (1803): 200–212.
Shattock, Joanne, ed. *The Oxford Guide to British Women Writers.* Oxford: Oxford University Press, 1993.
Sigourney, Lydia. *Pleasant Memories of Pleasant Lands.* Boston: Munroe, 1842.
Sinclair, Sir John. *The Correspondence of the Right Honourable Sir John Sinclair, Bart.* 2 vols. London: Henry Colburn and Richard Bentley, 1831.
Slagle, Judith Bailey, ed. *The Collected Letters of Joanna Baillie.* 2 vols. Madison: Fairleigh Dickinson University Press, 1999.
Spender, Dale. *All Sides of the Subject.* Ed. Teresa Iles. New York: Teachers College Press, 1992.
Spiller, Robert E., et al. *Literary History of the United States.* 4th ed. New York: Macmillan, 1974.
Stafford, Fiona. "Blair's Ossian, Romanticism and the teaching of Literature." *The Scottish Invention of English Literature.* Ed. Robert Crawford. Cambridge: Cambridge University Press, 1998.
Stanton, Donna, ed. *The Female Autograph.* Chicago: University of Chicago Press, 1987.
St. Aubyn, Giles. *Queen Victoria, A Portrait.* New York: Atheneum, 1992.
Stone, Lawrence. *Road to Divorce: England 1530–1987.* Oxford: Oxford University Press, 1990.
Strickland, Margot. *The Byron Women.* New York: St. Martin's, 1974.
Super, R. H. "Trollope at the Royal Literary Fund." *Nineteenth-Century Literature* 37.3 (1982): 316.
Sutherland, John. *The Life of Walter Scott.* Oxford: Blackwell, 1995.
Sweet, Rosemary. "Antiquaries and Antiquities in Eighteenth-

Century England." *Eighteenth-Century Studies* 34.2 (2001): 181–206.
Ticknor, George. *Life, Letters and Journals of George Ticknor*. 5th ed. 2 vols. Boston: James R. Osgood, 1876; Johnson Reprint Corp., 1968.
Todd, Janet, ed. *British Women Writers*. New York: Continuum, 1989.
Toole, Betty A. *Ada, The Enchantress of Numbers*. Mill Valley, CA: Strawberry Press, 1992.
Trumbach, Randolph. "London's Sapphists: From Three Sexes to Four Genders in the Making of Modern Culture." *Body Guards: The Cultural Politics of Gender Ambiguity*. Ed. Julia Epstein and Kristina Straub. New York and London: Routledge, 1991.
Turney, Catherine. *Byron's Daughter, A Biography of Elizabeth Medora Leigh*. New York: Charles Scribner's Sons, 1972.
Waddell, Henderson, and J. J. Waddell. *By Bothwell Banks*. Glasgow: Hobbs, 1904.
Wade, Christopher. *The Streets of Hampstead*. London: Camden History Society, 1984.
Westfall, Richard S. *The Life of Isaac Newton*. Cambridge: Cambridge University Press, 1993.
White, Daniel E. "The 'Joineriana': Anna Barbauld, the Aikin Family Circle, and the Dissenting Public Sphere." *Eighteenth-Century Studies* 32.4 (1999): 511–33.
White, Guy Wallace. "Correcting a Cursory Glance: Joanna Baillie's Literary Contribution." http://www3.ns.sympatico.ca/guy.white/subpag22.htm/ 10 August 1998.
Wilson, John. [Rev. of Baillie's *Dramas*.] *Blackwood's Edinburgh Magazine* 39 (1836): 265–80.
Wordsworth, Jonathan, ed. Introduction to *Poems, 1790*. Oxford and New York: Woodstock, 1994.
Young-Bruehl, Elizabeth. *Subject to Biography: Psychoanalysis, Feminism, and Writing Women's Lives*. Cambridge: Harvard University Press, 1998.
Yudin, Mary. "Joanna Baillie's Introductory Discourse as a Precursor to Wordsworth's Preface to Lyrical Ballads." *Compar(a)ison: An International Journal of Comparative Literature* 1 (1994): 101–12.
Zall, P. M. "The Cool World of Samuel Taylor Coleridge: The Question of Joanna Baillie." *The Wordsworth Circle* 13:1 (1982): 17–20.

Index

Aikin, Lucy, 40, 42, 46–47, 50–51, 64, 77, 79–80, 234–35, 276, 286
Ainger, Thomas, 289
Alexander I, Russian Emperor, 210
Alison, Rev. Archibald, 71
Alison, Rev. Francis, 235
Anatomy of the Human Gravid Uterus, 46
d'Arblay, Frances Burney, 94, 220, 282, 287
Arnold, Samuel James, 98–99, 226
Athenæum, 251–52

Babbage, Charles, 194
Backscheider, Paula, 9, 11, 13, 20–21, 125, 268, 289
Bacon, Francis, 84
Baillie, Agnes (sister), 23, 25–26, 32, 35, 40, 46, 49–51, 53–54, 56, 58–60, 80, 85–86, 114–17, 123, 128–29, 136, 138, 144, 151, 155, 157–58, 164–65, 167, 176–78, 182–83, 189, 207, 211, 220, 222, 248, 273, 285–86, 288, 293–96
Baillie, Agnes Elizabeth (Mrs. Robert B. Oliver), 32, 248
Baillie, Andrew (uncle), 37–38
Baillie, Anna (aunt), 38
Baillie, Anne Kirkwood (grandmother), 38
Baillie, Dorothea Hunter, (Mrs. James Baillie) (mother), 22, 25–26, 28, 35, 38, 41–47, 49, 53–55, 57, 59–60, 64, 115–16, 182, 291, 296
Baillie, Elizabeth Margaret (niece). *See* Milligan.
Baillie, George, 38
Baillie, Grisell Lady, 156–61
Baillie, Helen Mary Henrietta, 32, 248
Baillie, Henrietta Clara Marion (Mrs. James Maconechy), 32, 248
Baillie, Henrietta Duff (Mrs. William Baillie), 31–32, 245–48, 273–74, 295
Baillie, Rev. James, D.D., (father), 25, 35–36, 38–43, 46–47, 49–50, 54, 56, 233, 291, 296–97
Baillie, James (nephew), 26, 38–39, 59, 123
Baillie, Jean (aunt), 38

Baillie, Joanna,
An Address to the Muses, 61;
An Address to the Night, 62;
Ahalya Baee, 19, 32, 224, 231, 268, 282–84, 299; *The Alienated Manor*, 252, 255–57; *Arnold*, 72; *Basil*, 28, 66, 68, 71, 77, 83–86, 225; *The Beacon*, 29, 144, 148; "The Black Cock, Written for a Welsh Air," 113–14; *The Bride*, 31, 252, 263, 268–71; "A Cheerful Tempered Lover's Farewell to His Mistress," 62; "A Child to His Sick Grandfather," 62; *A Collection of Poems, Chiefly Manuscript, and from Living Authors*, 30–31, 122, 137, 139, 162, 165–67, 186, 206, 213, 216, 221–23, 245; *Columbus*, 153–54, 156–58, 160–61; *The Complete Poetical Works of Joanna Baillie*, 31, 231, 237, 245; *Constantine Paleologus*, 28, 30, 92–93, 105, 108–110, 226; *The Country Inn*, 105, 107–108; *De Monfort*, 23, 27–31, 63, 66, 68, 74, 77, 83, 85–86, 88–92, 94, 97–98, 103, 108, 133, 136, 138, 141, 150, 153, 195–97, 227, 274, 282, 291; "Devotional Song for a

Negro Child," 106; "A Disappointment," 61, 63; *Dramas*, 31, 142, 149, 171, 200, 218, 231, 245, 250–73; *The Dramatic and Poetical Works of Joanna Baillie*, 32, 61, 114, 218, 231, 282, 284, 288–89, 299; *The Dream*, 29, 140, 144, 146–47; "The Elden Tree: An Ancient Ballad," 158–59; *The Election*, 29–30, 95, 97–101, 226, 272; *Enthusiasm*, 252, 265; "Epilogue to the Theatrical Representation at Strawberry Hill," 27; "Epistles to Literati," 31; *Ethwald*, 28, 51, 95, 97, 100–103; *The Family Legend*, 28–29, 86, 88, 105, 111, 119, 127, 130–38, 140–41, 143–44, 150, 188, 226, 263, 291; *Fugitive Verses*, 32, 60, 201, 231, 279; "The Ghost of Fadon," 159; *Henriquez*, 31, 86, 144, 149, 219, 223, 252, 257–59, 291; *The Homicide*, 252, 267–68; "Hooly and fairly," 114; "The Horse and His Rider," 62; "The Kitten," 176; "A Lamentation," 61, 63; *Legend of Lady Griseld* [Grisell] *Baillie*, 156–61, 211, 283; "A Lesson Intended for the Use of the Hampstead School," 30, 106, 178–79, 214–15; "Lines on the Death of Sir Walter Scott," 31, 172, 225; "Lines on the Death of William Sotheby," 121; "Lines to Agnes Baillie on her birth day," 86; "Lord John of the East: A Ballad," 158; "Malcolm's Heir: A Tale of Wonder," 158; *The Martyr*, 31, 223, 252, 259–60, 268; *The Match*, 252, 271–72; "A Melancholy Lover's Farewell to His Mistress," 61; *Metrical Legends of Exalted Characters*, 30, 153–54, 156–62, 175, 178, 227, 282; *Miscellaneous Plays*, 105–112, 121, 131, 251; "A Mother to Her Waking Infant," 62; *Night Scenes of Other Times*, 61; "On the Character of Romiero," 254–55; *Orra*, 29, 144, 146; *The Phantom*, 252, 263–65; *Plays*, 28; *Poems; wherein it is attempted to describe* Certain Views of Nature and of Rustic Manners; *and also, to point out, in some instances, the different influence which the same circumstances produce on different characters*, 20, 26, 60–66, 77, 94, 127, 174, 177, 187, 279; "A Poet, or, Sound-hearted Lover's Farewell to His Mistress," 62; "Prologue and Epilogue to the Theatrical Representation at Strawberry Hill" (*Fashionable Friends*), 116–17; "A Proud Lover's Farewell to His Mistress," 62; *Rayner*, 60, 72, 105–108, 224, 256; "A Reverie," 61; *Romiero*, 86, 149, 252–55; "Recollections of a Dear & Steady Friend," 201; "School Rhymes for Negro Children," 106; "A Scotch Song," 227; *The Second Marriage*, 95, 102–103; *The Separation*, 31, 129, 219, 252, 257, 260–62, 291; *A Series of Plays: in which it is attempted to delineate the stronger passions of the mind, each passion being the subject of a tragedy and a comedy* (3 vols.), 20, 22, 26–30, 46, 63, 69, 72–74, 77–78, 80–105, 112, 116–17, 124, 127, 140, 142, 144–49, 158, 175, 187, 196, 219, 226, 251, 273, 285, 292; *The Siege*, 29, 144, 147–48; "Song, For a Scotch Air," 227; "Song, Woo'd and Married and A'," 114; "Song, Written for an Irish Air," 227; "A Song, Written for an Irish Melody," 114; "Song, Written for a Welsh Air, Called 'The New

Year's Gift," 113–14; "Song, Written for a Welsh Air, Called 'The Pursuit of Love'," 114; "Song, Written for a Welsh Melody" ("The Maid of Llanwellyn"), 113–14; "The Storm–Beat Maid," 62; *A Story of Other Times*, 63; *The Stripling*, 252, 262–63; *A Summer Day*, 61; "Thunder," 62; "To Fear," 62; *A Story of Other Times*, 62; "To James B. Baillie, an Infant," 38–39; *The Trial [Tryal]*, 29, 77, 86–88; *A View of the General Tenour of the New Testament Regarding the Nature and Dignity of Jesus Christ*, 31–32, 173, 229, 231, 239, 241–44, 252, 260, 277; *Wallace*, 156–61; "Wind," 62; *A Winter's Day*, 56, 61–62; *Witchcraft*, 171, 252, 265–67

Baillie, John Baron, 32, 248
Baillie, Margaret (aunt), 38
Baillie, Matthew (grandfather), 38
Baillie, Dr. Matthew (brother), 10, 22, 25–26, 30, 35, 38–39, 43, 46, 49, 52–56, 58–60, 66, 71–72, 77, 80–81, 85, 97, 115, 123, 129, 137–40, 143, 149, 151, 154–55, 162–65, 167–68, 178–79, 192, 211, 222, 227, 229, 246, 281–82, 292, 295–96, 298–99
Baillie, Matthew John, 31, 37, 248
Baillie monument (Bothwell), 125, 297
Baillie, Principal Robert, D.D., 36–38
Baillie, Robert Denman, 32, 248
Baillie, Sophia Denman (Mrs. Matthew Baillie), 10, 25–26, 32, 58–60, 68, 85, 124, 129, 138–39, 151, 155, 163–64, 166, 178, 200, 217, 227, 273–74, 281–82

Baillie, Sophia Joanna, 31, 248
Baillie, William Hunter (nephew), 25–26, 31, 33, 36, 47, 51, 57, 59–60, 64, 67, 71, 73, 123, 129, 152, 162, 164, 167–68, 178, 189, 211, 221, 227, 245–49, 274, 282, 288–89, 293–96
Baillie, Jr., William Hunter, 31, 248
Baillie, William [James] (brother), 25, 35
Baird, George Husband, D.D., 228–29, 232
Baliol, kings of Scotland, 37
Ballantyne, James, 126–27, 136–37, 149, 168
Baptists, 232
Barbauld, Anna Laetitia (and Rochemont), 24, 63–64, 77–78, 80, 165, 179–80, 219, 231–32, 234–35, 281, 287
Baron, Dr. John, 168
Bartley, George, and Sarah, 100, 258–59
Beacon, The, 162
Beattie, Dr. William, 249–50
Beaumont and Fletcher, 67
Beaumont, George, 120
de Beauvoir, Simone, 22
Bell, John (*Bell's Edition of Shakespeare's Plays, As they are now performed at the Theatres Royal in London*), 57
Bennett, Susan, 15, 266
Bentham, Jeremy, 189
Bentham, Lady (Sophia Fordyce), 67–68, 182, 188–89, 287
Bentham, Sir Samuel, 181–82, 188–89
Bentham, Sarah (Mrs. Le Blanc), 189
Berry, Agnes, 117
Berry, Mary, 47, 49, 52, 56, 71, 73, 93, 100, 115–20, 139, 160, 182, 225–27, 233, 287
Betty, William Henry West, 262–63
Bigelow, Dr. Jacob, 220

Blackwood's Magazine, 213, 251–52
Blair, Hugh, 34
bluestocking, 23, 220, 225, 271, 274
boarding school(s) (Miss MacDonald's), 50–53
Bolton House, 10, 155, 207–208
Boott, Dr. Francis, 220
Boswell, Sir Alexander, 162
Bowdler, Henrietta Maria, 209
Brand, Barbarina (Wilmot). *See* Dacre, Lady.
Brecht, Bertolt (*Mother Courage*), 102
Breen, Jennifer, 15
Brewer, William, 15, 95, 172, 195–96, 199
British Critic, 95
Browning, Robert and Elizabeth Barrett, 276
Brunton, Mary Balfour, 289
Bryant, William Cullen, 219
Bugajski, Ken, 15, 25
Bulwer, Edward, Lord Lytton, 237
Buonapart, Napoleon (and Napoleonic Wars), 109, 143, 180, 209–210, 224
Burgess, Thomas, Bishop of Salisbury, 173, 239–44
Burney, Frances. *See* d'Arblay.
Burns, Robert, 34, 62, 65, 112, 224
Burroughs, Catherine B., 13, 15, 22–23, 76, 84, 86–87, 91–92, 102–103, 142, 159–60, 261, 267, 271
Byron, Ada. *See* Lovelace.
Byron, Lady, Anne Isabella Milbanke, 29, 150, 154, 182–83, 190–205, 212, 234, 244, 252, 272–77, 287, 289
Byron, Lord, George Noel Gordon, 29, 34, 103, 112, 118, 121, 123–24, 143, 147, 150–51, 153–54, 172, 178, 182–83, 190–205, 219, 221
    Beppo, 150; *The Blues: A Literary Eclogue*, 150; *Childe Harold*, 149, 153–54, 184, 190; *Don Juan*, 150; *English Bards and Scotch Reviewers*, 150

Cadell and Davies, Booksellers, 80–81, 104
Campbell, Lady Agnes Hunter (Mrs. Charlewood), 55, 246
Campbell, Thomas, 112, 143, 165, 216–17, 221, 250
Catholic/Catholicism, 204–205, 212, 232, 240, 278
Constable, Archibald, 126–27
Carhart, Margaret, 10, 19, 23, 173
Carlson, Julie, 15
Carlyle, Jane Welsh, 276
Carr, Mr. and Mrs. Thomas William (and family), 181, 200, 204, 212, 219, 281
Carter, Elizabeth, 76–77, 287
Chaloner, Louisa, 193
Chambers, Robert (*Vestiges of the natural history of Creation*), 272
Channing, William Ellery, 200, 215, 220, 233–34, 239, 286
Chantrey, Sir Francis Legatt, 164
Charleville, Catherine Maria, Countess of, 176, 284, 287
Charlewood, Col. Benjamin, 246
Charlotte Augusta, Princess, 154–55
chimney sweeping, 164, 178
cholera, 181, 229, 231, 238, 250–51
Christian Examiner, 177
Clift, William, 247–48
closet drama, 57, 82, 86–87, 121–22, 141–42
Coleridge, Hartley, 274–75
Coleridge, Henry Nelson, and Sara Coleridge, 273, 275
Coleridge, Samuel Taylor, 61, 63, 95, 103, 120–21, 139, 144, 178, 272–75, 281
Consalvi, Cardinal, 123

Constable, Archibald, 126–28, 168
copyright, 34, 237
Corbett, Sisters, 220
Corn Bill, 265
Coutts, Thomas (Coutts and Company), 176
Covent Garden Theatre, 124, 141, 149, 178, 219, 223, 262
Cowley, Hannah, 142
Cox, Jeffrey N., 15, 19, 91, 266
Coxe, Edward, 139
Crabbe, George, 143, 161, 165, 221–22
Crainz, Franco, 15, 25, 38
Critical Review, 81–82, 96–97
Crochunis, Tomas, 15
Croft, Lady Margaret Denman (Mrs. Richard Croft), 25–26, 58–59, 155
Croft, Sir Richard, 26, 155
Cullen, William, 34, 43
Cunningham, Allan, 227–28

Dacre, Lady (Barbarina Brand Wilmot), 99, 124, 215
Damer, Anne Seymour, 117–19, 131–32, 226–27
Davis, Tracy, 178
Davy, Sir Humphry, 189, 281
Davy, Lady Jane (Mrs. Humphry Davy), 212, 280–82
De Morgan, Augustus, and Sophia Elizabeth, 193, 202
Denman, Sophia. *See* Baillie, Sophia Denman.
Denman, Dr. Thomas, and Elizabeth Brodie, 58
Denman, Lord Chief Justice Thomas, 163
Dewey, Orville, 285–86
Dickens, Charles, 118, 219, 245
Dirom, Alexander, 265
Disraeli, Benjamin, 280
divorce, 238–39
Donkin, Ellen, 15, 75, 92, 94, 141, 178, 196
Douglas, James, 44
Douglas, Martha Jane, 44
Dowd, Maureen, 15

Doyle, Selina, 193, 202
Dramatic Censor, 88–89
Drury Lane Theatre, 47, 74, 88–90, 92–94, 109, 121, 124, 136, 141, 150–51, 178, 195–96, 198, 219, 227, 258–59
Dryden, John, 126, 235
Duff, Henrietta. *See* Baillie, Henrietta (Mrs. William).
Duthie, Peter, 15, 89

Edgeworth, Maria, 29, 35, 168, 177, 183, 188, 196, 210–13, 215, 224, 282, 287, 292, 298
Edinburgh Monthly Magazine, 213
Edinburgh Review, 110, 145, 251–52
Elliott, Anne, 98, 132, 139, 165, 174, 179, 182, 187–88, 207, 212, 229
Emerson, Ralph Waldo, 219, 236
Enlightenment, 34, 54, 70, 233
d'Eon de Beaumont, Chevalier Charles, 140
Erskine, John, 34
Erskine, William, Lord Kinneder, 131–32, 135
experiment(s)/experimentation, 45–46, 68, 72–73, 82, 105, 175, 211, 273, 298

Fanshawe, Catharine Maria, 118, 167, 208
feminist/feminism, 19, 21, 35, 72–74, 78, 146, 159, 215, 225, 238–39, 257, 268, 275, 284, 287, 298–99
Ferguson, Adam, 34
Ferguson, Alexander, 41
Ferrier, Susan Edmonstone, 157, 215
Fielding, Henry, 194
Fletcher, Angus, 245
Fletcher, Elizabeth, 245
Fox, Charles James, 94
Fraser's Magazine, 31, 254
Freeling, Sir Francis, 184
Frend, Sophia, 194
Friedman-Romell, Beth, 15, 109–110

Froissart, 136
Fuller, Margaret, 285

Garner, Michael, 15
Garrick, David, 90
Gaskel, Elizabeth, 276
Gentleman's Magazine, 64
George III (George William Frederick), 123, 129, 139–40, 149, 162–63, 179–80, 220–22
George IV (George Augustus Frederick), and Caroline of Brunswick, 140, 154–55, 162–63, 168, 179
German philosophers, 238, 256–57
Gibbon, Edward, 123
Gilbert, Deirdre, 15, 84, 87–88, 95, 103
Gilroy, Amanda, 15
Glasgow Sentinel, 162
Godwin, Mary. See Shelley.
Goethe, Johann Wolfgang von, 224
Gosford, Lady Mary, Countess of, 190, 201, 203
Gothic, 19, 82, 91, 129, 178, 261, 264, 267
Grahame, James, 129–30
Grant, Anne (Mrs. Grant of Laggan), 112, 160, 165, 225
Gray, Rev. Robert, 98
Gregory XVI, Pope, 204–205
Grey, Charles, 272

Halford, Sir Henry, M.D., 164
Hall, Louisa Jane Park, 239
Harness, William, 219, 277
Hayley, William, 65
Hays, Mary, 287
Hazlitt, William, 103
Head, Fanny, 75
Hedge, Mary Ann, 217, 220
Hemans, Felicia, 164–65, 167, 177, 200, 212–15, 221, 236–37, 276, 298
Henderson, Andrea, 15, 73
Henderson, Mr. [?], 136–37
Herrera y Tordesillas, Antonio de, 160

Herschel, Caroline Lucretia, 223
Herschel, Sir John, and Lady Margaret, 107, 165–66, 185–86, 189, 218, 223–24, 244–45, 287
Herschel, Sir William, and Lady Mary, 223
Hillhouse, James Abraham, 239
Hoare, Samuel, and Louisa Gurney (and family), 181, 184–86, 222, 229
Hobhouse, John Cam, Baron Broughton, 150, 191
Hodson, Margaret Holford, 28, 40, 85, 167, 172–73, 176, 182, 185, 188, 205–210, 212, 215–16, 245, 252, 254–55, 258, 260, 266, 270
Hodson, Rev. Septimus, 205
Hogg, James, the Ettrick Shepherd, 112
Holford, Margaret. See Hodson, Margaret Holford.
Holford, Margaret Wrench, 205
Home, Robert Boyne, 55
Hoppner, John, 222
Hume, David, 34, 70, 176
Hunter, Agnes (aunt), 43
Hunter, Agnes Paul (Mrs. John Hunter and JB's grandmother), 43–44
Hunter, Andrew (uncle), 43
Hunter, Anne Home (Mrs. John Hunter), 55–56, 63, 68, 74–75, 77, 85, 89, 112
Hunter, Dorothea. See Baillie, Dorothea Hunter.
Hunter, Elizabeth (aunt), 43
Hunter House Museum, 45–46
Hunter, Isobel (aunt), 43
Hunter, James (uncle), 43
Hunter, Janet (aunt), 43, 247
Hunter, John, Sr. (grandfather), 43–44
Hunter, John (uncle and surgeon), 26, 35, 38, 42, 43–47, 54–56, 89, 168, 246, 291, 295–96, 299
Hunter, Major John, 246

Hunter, Dr. William (uncle), 26, 35, 38, 43–47, 54, 56, 72, 247, 291, 295–96, 299
Hutcheson, Francis, 70, 72, 235
Hyslop, James, 224

imagination, 19, 49–50, 52, 54, 67, 69, 70, 128–29, 142, 171, 252, 297–98
Imperial Review, 95–96
Inchbald, Elizabeth, 23, 142
India, 283, 285
Ireland/Irish, 112, 114, 204–205, 210–13, 227, 235, 240, 274, 285
Irving, Washington, 219

Jacobite, 34, 44
Jameson, Anna, 249, 275–79
Jefferson, Thomas, 169, 220
Jeffrey, Francis, 110, 118, 120, 144–45, 161, 175, 184, 255, 280
Jobson, Thomas, 248
Johnson, Dr. Samuel, 44, 235
Johnston, Sir Alexander, 260, 268, 270

Kean, Edmund, 150, 195–97, 227
Keats, John, 182
Kemble, Frances Anne (Mrs. Butler), 118, 222–23, 234, 276–77
Kemble, John Philip, 27, 88–94, 121, 190, 226, 263, 291
King, Lord William and Lady. *See* Lovelace.
Kirkland, Caroline, 239, 285–86
Kirkwood, Anne. *See* Baillie, Anne Kirkwood.
Klopstock, Friedrich Gottlieb (*Messiah*). *See* Head, Fanny.
Knight, Henry Gally, 167
Kucich, Greg, 15

Laidlaw, William, 173, 239
Laing, David, 227–28
Lamb, Lady Caroline, 190–91, 202
Lamb, Mary, 287

Lamb, Hon. William, Lord Melbourne, 202
Lambertson, Chester Lee, 15
Landon, Laetitia, 276
Landseer, Charles, 274, 282
Lawrence, Arabella, 194
Lawrence, Rose, 200, 221
Lawrence, Sir Thomas, 121, 123–24, 258
Lee, Hannah Farnam, 239
Lee, Harriet, 287
Lee, Sophia, 142, 287
Leigh, Augusta, 191–92
Lennox, Charlotte, 287
Locke, John, 70
Lockhart, John Gibson, 30, 164, 171–74, 183, 200, 212, 224–25, 273
Lockhart, John Hugh, 164
Lockhart, Sophia Scott (Mrs. John Gibson Lockhart), 90, 123, 126, 164, 174, 183, 212, 224–25
Longfellow, Henry Wadsworth, 219, 234, 239
Longman, Thomas Norton, 81, 149, 245, 260, 284
Louis XIV, 221
Lovelace, Ada Byron King (Lord King and family), 191–94, 197, 199, 201
Lushington, Stephen, 191
Lyrical Ballads, 61, 63, 70, 95, 177, 184

Macdonald, Laird Ranald, 137
Mackenzie, Henry, 131–32, 135, 162
Macpherson, James, 34
Malcolm, Sir John, 283
Malthus, Thomas Robert, 118, 189, 238
marriage, 85, 87–88, 102–103, 113, 116, 146–47, 152, 238–39, 255–56, 264, 271, 273, 275, 277, 298
Martineau, Harriet, 118, 237–38, 277
Martineau, Rev. James, 232

masculine/masculinity, 22–23, 74, 91, 95, 109, 178, 196, 265, 275
masquerade, 87–88, 95
Masquerier, John James, 29, 79, 144
McKerrow, Mary, 15, 289
McMillan, Dorothy, 15
Melbourne, Lord. See Lamb.
Mellor, Anne K., 15, 106, 177, 256, 298–99
Melville, Herman, 219
Mercier, Louis-Sebastien, 83
Merivale, John Herman, and Louisa Drury, 234
Meyers, Victoria, 15
Milbanke, Sir Ralph, and Judith Noel Milbanke, 190, 199–200, 203
Millar, Anne, 52–53, 92, 98, 108–109, 293
Millar, Helen. See Thomson, John.
Millar, John, 34, 52, 83
Milligan, Elizabeth Margaret Baillie (Mrs. Robert Milligan) (niece), 26, 29, 33, 59, 68, 123, 129, 151–52, 170, 178, 189, 227, 287, 295
Milligan, Mary, 295
Milligan, Capt. Robert, 26, 29, 32, 123, 151–52, 170
Milligan, Sophia, 30, 33, 152, 227, 295
Milton, John (and works), 54, 57, 185, 240
Mitford, Mary Russell, 270–71
Molière, Jean Baptist, 67
Mont Blanc, 152
Montagu, Elizabeth, 220
Montgomery, Capt. Hugh, 202
Montgomery, James, 164
Montgomery, Mary Millicent, 182, 188, 192–93, 201–205, 208, 272, 282
Monthly Review, 160–61, 219
Moore, John (*Zeluco*), 149
Moore, Thomas, 112, 193, 200, 219

The Morbid Anatomy of some of the most important Parts of the human Body, 26, 66
More, Hannah, 208, 221, 287
Morgan, Lady, (Sydney Owenson), 178
Morison, James (Morison's Pills), 208–209
Murray, John, 150, 224
Mylne, James, 52

New Monthly Magazine, 216
Newton, Sir Isaac, 243
Nicoll, Allardyce, 108
Noble, Aloma, 15, 27, 91, 196
Norton, Dr. Andrews, 45, 107, 212–15, 220, 234–39, 254, 257, 265, 270, 286–87, 289

O'Neill (Becher), Elizabeth, 226
Opie, Amelia, 287
orphan asylums and benevolent societies, 179, 219–20
Ossian, 51, 133
Oxford Movement, 238, 257, 278

Park, John Ranicar, 237
passion(s), 34, 51, 58, 67, 71, 73–74, 79–80, 83–85, 87, 89, 91, 95–96, 98, 101–103, 105, 116, 124, 148–49, 172, 194–96, 234, 255–56, 259–60, 262, 267, 269–70, 272–73, 276, 287, 298
Patton, Janice, 15
Paul, Agnes. See Hunter, Agnes Paul.
Pearson, Jacqueline, 76–77, 177–78
Peterloo Massacre, 180–81
phrenology, 204, 271–72
Piozzi, Hester Thrale, 74–75, 98, 220, 287
Pitt, William (the younger), 123, 272
Poe, Edgar Allan, 35, 237
Pope, Alexander, 143
Porter, Anna Maria, 165
Porter, Jane, 216, 234, 287

Presbyterian (Church of Scotland), 40–42, 47, 228, 232–33, 235, 245
Purinton, Marjean D., 15, 96

Quarterly Review, 126, 153, 184, 205, 224, 255, 281
Quillinen, Edward, and Dora Wordsworth Quillinen, 186, 209

Racine, 67
Radcliffe, Ann, 74
Reeve, Clara, 287
Reiman, Donald, 15, 103–104, 120, 196
Reynolds, Sir Joshua, 222
Richardson, John, 36, 38, 158, 167, 204, 221, 229, 247, 250, 295
Robertson, William, 34
Roche, Regina Maria, 287
Rogers, Samuel, 63–64, 81, 118, 121, 139, 150, 165, 181–83, 217–19, 221, 234, 250, 288
Romantic/Romanticism, 19, 34, 69, 78, 82, 91, 95, 103, 120, 133, 167, 177–78, 198, 201, 213, 221, 225, 253, 264–65, 267, 280, 298
Rosenthal, Laura, 78, 91
Ross, Marlon, 15
Royal Humane Society, 55
Royal Literary Fund, 217
Royal Society, 120, 211, 219
Royal Veterinary College, 55

Sadler, Dr. Thomas, 232
Schiller, Johann Christoph Friedrich von, 224
Schnorrenberg, Barbara, 15
Scotland/Scots/Scottish, 19, 34, 36–37, 44, 53–58, 60, 62, 67–68, 70, 79–80, 112, 122, 133, 137–39, 144, 156, 160, 162–63, 175, 178, 182, 200, 204, 215–16, 220, 222, 224–25, 228, 235, 247, 235, 247, 263–64, 297–98
Scott, Anne, 126, 169
Scott, Mrs. Anne, 158

Scott, Charles, 126
Scott, Charlotte Carpenter (Lady Scott), 125–26, 129, 133, 137, 151, 169, 174
Scott memorial, 127, 172
Scott, Sophia. *See* Lockhart, Sophia.
Scott, Sir Walter, 9, 11–12, 27, 35, 75, 81, 102–103, 107, 111–112, 120, 122–24, 125–77, 179–80, 183–85, 195, 197–200, 203, 206–08, 210–11, 213–15, 219, 221–25, 228, 230, 239, 251, 256, 258, 261, 266–67, 274, 282, 284, 291–92, 295, 298–99
  Anne of Geierstein, 169; *Antiquary*, 176; *Ballads and Lyrical Pieces*, 126; *Bridal of Triermain*, 143–44; *Bride of Lammermuir*, 267; *The Chase*, 125; *Chronicles of the Canongate*, 169; *Fair Maid of Perth*, 169; *Guy Mannering*, 154; *House of Aspen*, 129, 261, 292; *Kenilworth*, 158; *Lady of the Lake*, 123–24, 138, 141, 214; *Lay of the Last Minstrel*, 126–27, 139, 160; *Life of Napoleon Buonaparte*, 169; *Lord of the Isles*, 207; *Marmion*, 125–27, 139, 297; *Mac Duff's Cross*, 167; *Minstrelsy of the Scottish Border*, 126; *Paul's Letters to his Kinsfolk*, 152; *The Pirate*, 158; *Rob Roy*, 130; *Rokeby*, 143–44, 149; *Tales of a Grandfather*, 164, 169; *Tales of My Landlord*, 154; *Vision of Don Roderick*, 141; *Waverley*, 126, 178; *William and Helen*, 125; *Woodstock*, 169; *Works of Dryden*, 126
Scott, Walter, 126
Scullion, Adrienne, 15, 19, 132–33
Sedgwick, Catharine Maria, 35, 216, 234, 277, 286

Seward, Anna, 65, 174
Shadwell, Thomas, 271
Shakespeare, William (and works), 53, 57, 71, 74, 82, 84, 91, 95, 97, 101–102, 149, 223, 251, 253, 258, 273
Sharpe, Charles Kirkpatrick, 128
Shelley, Mary Godwin, 154
Shelley, Percy Bysshe, 154, 182
Sher, Richard, 15, 34, 42
Sheridan, Richard Brinsley, 89–90, 92–94, 123, 136, 141, 196, 219
Siddons, Cecilia, 219
Siddons, Harriet Murray (Mrs. Henry Siddons), 130, 132
Siddons, Henry, 130, 132, 135
Siddons, Mrs. Sarah, 27, 52–53, 66, 79, 88, 90–93, 121, 127, 130, 136, 157, 168, 219, 222, 262, 273, 290–91
Sigourney, Lydia Howard Huntley, 280, 285, 292–93
Sinclair, Sir John, 34, 130, 290
Smellie, William, 44
Smith, Adam, 34, 70
Socinian, 233, 239
Sotheby, William (and family), 63, 118, 120–23, 125, 127, 139, 144, 150–51, 181–82, 214, 292
Southey, Edith Fricker (Mrs. Robert Southey), 184, 209
Southey, Robert, 129, 144, 165, 183–84, 186, 205, 209, 251, 258, 275
Sparks, Jared, 237
Spender, Dale, 20
de Staël, Mme. (Anne Louise Germaine Necker), 118, 188
Stanton, Donna, 20
Stephens, John Lloyd (*Incidents of travel in Yucatan*), 177
Stirling, Mrs. James, 137, 165, 186
Stowe, Harriet Beecher, 193
Struthers, John, 128
Stuart, James, 162
Stuart, Lady Louisa, 131, 133–34
sublime, 19, 137, 156, 165, 172, 259, 264, 267, 280, 284

suffrage, 238

Talfourd, Sir Thomas Noon, 185
Talma, François Joseph, 226
Temperance Movement, 179
Tennyson, Alfred, Lord, 178, 219
Terry, Daniel, 136, 149
Thomson, George, 27, 112–115, 127, 129, 227, 254
Thomson, John, and Helen (?) Millar, 52
Ticknor, George, 212–13, 224, 234, 237, 286
Todd, Janet, 15
Tooke, John Horne, 219, 281–82
Tory, 97, 126, 162, 179, 274, 284
trade unions, 180–81, 231
Trimmer, Sarah, 287
Trinitarian/Trinity, 232–34, 241–45, 260

Unitarian/Unitarianism, 42, 232–35, 237, 240–41, 243, 274

Victoria, Queen, 85, 186, 205, 223, 238, 274
Voltaire, 67

Wakefield, Priscilla, 287
Wallace, William, 158–59, 206
Walpole, Horace, 117–18
Watkins, Daniel, 15
Wellesley, Arthur, 1st Duke of Wellington, 99
West, Jane, 287
Westminster Review, 189, 277
Whig, 94, 97, 179–80, 235, 284
White, Guy Wallace, 15
White, Lydia, 225
Wilmot, Barbarina Brand. *See* Dacre, Lady.
Wilson, Dr. John, 251
Woolf, Virginia, 20–21,
Wordsworth, Dora. *See* Quillinen.
Wordsworth, Dorothy, 183–84, 187
Wordsworth, Jonathan, 15, 51, 61–63, 94–95, 187
Wordsworth, Mary Hutchinson (Mrs. William Wordsworth), 187

Wordsworth, William, 9, 61–63, 95, 121, 124, 144, 154, 161, 165, 167, 177, 182–87, 209, 219, 251, 273
Wrangham, Arch Deacon Francis, 85

Young-Bruehl, Elizabeth 21–22
Yudin, Mary, 15, 83

Zall, P. M., 15, 77

OHIO UNIVERSITY LIBRARY

Please return this book as soon as you have finished with it. In order to avoid a fine it must be returned by the latest date stamped below. All books are subject to recall after two weeks or immediately if needed for reserve.

CF